Communications
in Computer and Information Science 1432

Maria Shehade · Theopisti Stylianou-Lambert (Eds.)

Emerging Technologies and the Digital Transformation of Museums and Heritage Sites

First International Conference, RISE IMET 2021
Nicosia, Cyprus, June 2–4, 2021
Proceedings

 Springer

Editors
Maria Shehade
CYENS Centre of Excellence
Nicosia, Cyprus

Theopisti Stylianou-Lambert
Cyprus University of Technology
Limassol, Cyprus

CYENS Centre of Excellence
Nicosia, Cyprus

ISSN 1865-0929   ISSN 1865-0937 (electronic)
Communications in Computer and Information Science
ISBN 978-3-030-83646-7   ISBN 978-3-030-83647-4 (eBook)
https://doi.org/10.1007/978-3-030-83647-4

This Springer imprint is published by the registered company Springer Nature Switzerland AG
The registered company address is: Gewerbestrasse 11, 6330 Cham, Switzerland

Preface

The RISE IMET International Conference on Emerging Technologies and the Digital Transformation of Museums and Heritage Sites was conducted online during June 2–4, 2021. The conference was organized by the CYENS Centre of Excellence (formerly known as RISE), which constitutes a joint venture between the three public universities of Cyprus (University of Cyprus, Cyprus University of Technology, and Open University of Cyprus), the Municipality of Nicosia, the Max Planck Institute for Informatics (Germany) and University College London (UK). This was the first conference in a series of CYENS conferences focusing on Interactive Media, Smart Systems, and Emerging Technologies (IMET).

The first RISE IMET conference was dedicated to Emerging Technologies and the Digital Transformation of Museums and Heritage Sites. In particular, the conference was dedicated to the exploration of current practices in the use of emerging and interactive technologies such as augmented, mixed or virtual reality, holographic models, 3D models, artificial intelligence, sensors, and gamification in museums and heritage sites. The aim of this conference was to promote critical and interdisciplinary approaches and conversations between participants from diverse fields and to encourage dialogue between academics and professionals from various backgrounds on digital advances, innovation, and their impact on the field of cultural heritage. Thus, the conference was addressed to academics and professionals from the fields of museum studies, cultural heritage, computer science, heritage management, artificial intelligence, visual arts, and cognitive science, amongst others, and it aimed to provide an interdisciplinary platform to discuss state-of-the-art developments in academia and industry, as well as opportunities for networking and collaboration through a series of keynote addresses and presentations.

The conference offered a variety of themes, focusing on many different types of technologies as well as different key discussions, such as the advantages, challenges and limitations of emerging technologies, current theoretical and practical approaches in digital heritage, emerging trends in the digital presentation, interpretation and management of cultural heritage, issues of immersion and authenticity, and the application of emerging technologies in specialized areas of cultural heritage (e.g. contested heritage, cultural tourism, education and museum pedagogy, participatory practices, etc).

A total of 119 submissions were received from authors in more than 27 countries, including the USA, the UK, the Philippines, Estonia, Austria, Greece, France, Australia, Cyprus, Spain, Norway, Finland, the Netherlands, China, Sweden, Germany, Argentina, Israel, Russia, Mexico and Italy, amongst others. All submissions went through a rigorous review process to ensure that the best quality papers were selected for presentation.

This volume includes 23 selected papers from the conference. All full papers went through a rigorous double blind review process involving at least three independent reviewers. The Scientific Committee made a tremendous effort to ensure fairness and consistency throughout the review process.

The volume is structured around six main themes: Digital curation and visitor engagement in museums and heritage sites; VR, AR, MR, mobile applications, and gamification in museums and heritage sites; Digital storytelling and embodied characters for the interpretation of cultural heritage; Emerging technologies, difficult heritage, and affective practices; Participatory approaches, crowdsourcing, and new technologies; Digitization, documentation, and digital representation of cultural heritage. Through these themes, the proceedings volume covers many aspects of different applications of emerging technologies in museums and heritage sites, offering insights on both the technical aspects and challenges faced and the interpretive aspects of the museum experience, as well as on the visitor/user experience. The papers also cover and discuss a variety of different technologies such as VR, AR, MR, gamification, virtual humans (avatars), projections and holograms, 3D scanning and photogrammetry, digital archival practices and digitization tools, NKRL (Narrative Knowledge Representation Language) tools, and sonic practices, amongst others.

The collection of papers comes from authors from universities, research centres, and museums and heritage organizations, showcasing case studies and collaborative research amongst various actors and countries, and presenting different approaches and challenges found in different parts of the world. The selected papers are also indicative of the interdisciplinary nature of the conference, since many author groups consist of a mixture of collaborating scientists (coming from the fields of technology or computer science, museums and heritage, and digital humanities) showcasing interdisciplinary endeavors and research, which was the main aim of RISE IMET.

RISE IMET 2021 offered a virtual platform for its participants to share their experiences, knowledge, and insights and to exchange ideas on the future of emerging technologies in museums and heritage sites. The conference also included five keynote speeches from distinguished academics and professionals: Alan Chalmers (WMG, University of Warwick), Sarah Kenderine (Laboratory for Experimental Museology, eM+, École Polytechnique Fédérale de Lausanne), Jenny Kidd (Cardiff University), Nancy Proctor (Director, The Peale Center for Baltimore History and Architecture), and Roberto Scopigno (Director, ISTI-CNR, Italy). We would like to extend our gratitude to our keynote speakers for their contribution in the conference. We are also extremely grateful to our Scientific Committee for the valuable reviews and the time they invested in producing high-quality reviews and ensuring the high academic standard of all accepted papers. Their expertise and support constituted a bedrock for the success of this conference. We would also like to thank Springer for supporting us in the production of these proceedings and for providing us with the opportunity to publish the RISE IMET proceedings in their CCIS series.

Last but not least, the editors would like to take this opportunity to thank all conference participants for supporting and trusting RISE IMET, especially through the organizational difficulties faced because of the COVID-19 pandemic. Their high-quality contributions and vivid participation allowed RISE IMET to achieve the academic and public outreach goals set at the beginning of this journey.

June 2021   Maria Shehade
                                            Theopisti Stylianou-Lambert

Organization

General Chairs

Theopisti Stylianou-Lambert — Cyprus University of Technology/CYENS Centre of Excellence, Cyprus

Maria Shehade — CYENS Centre of Excellence, Cyprus

Scientific Committee

Georgios Artopoulos — The Cyprus Institute, Cyprus
Kostas Arvanitis — University of Manchester, UK
Nikolas Bakirtzis — The Cyprus Institute, Cyprus
Gareth Beale — University of Glasgow, UK
Agiatis Benardou — ATHENA Research Centre, Greece
Antonis Bikakis — University College London, UK
Chiara Bonacchi — University of Stirling, UK
Alexandra Bounia — University of the Aegean, Greece
Katherine Burton Jones — Harvard University Extension School, USA
Fiona Cameron — Western Sydney University, Australia
George Caridakis — University of the Aegean, Greece
Despina Catapoti — University of the Aegean, Greece
Alan Chalmers — University of Warwick, UK
Panagiotis Charalambous — CYENS Centre of Excellence, Cyprus
Angeliki Chrysanthi — University of the Aegean, Greece
Yiorgos Chrysanthou — University of Cyprus/CYENS Centre of Excellence, Cyprus
Loraine Clarke — University of St Andrews, UK
Costis Dallas — University of Toronto, Canada
Areti Damala — CNRS/Ecole Normale Supérieure, France
Daniela De Angeli — University of Bath, UK
Kirsten Drotner — University of Southern Denmark, Denmark
Maria Economou — University of Glasgow, UK
Haitham Eid — Southern University at New Orleans, USA
Anna Foka — Uppsala University, Sweden
Bernard Frischer — Indiana University, USA
Andreas Georgopoulos — National Technical University of Athens, Greece
Antigone Heraclidou — CYENS Centre of Excellence, Cyprus
Lily Hibberd — Université de Paris, France/EPFL, Switzerland
Eva Hornecker — Bauhaus-Universität Weimar, Germany
Marinos Ioannides — Cyprus University of Technology, Cyprus
Martin Kampel — Technische Universität Wien, Austria
Jenny Kidd — Cardiff University, UK

Volker Kuchelmeiste	University of New South Wales, Australia
Tsvi Kuflik	University of Haifa, Israel
Andreas Lanitis	Cyprus University of Technology/CYENS Centre of Excellence, Cyprus
Annette Loeseke	NYU Berlin, Germany
Paul Marty	Florida State University, USA
Franco Niccolucci	University of Florence, Italy
George Papagiannakis	University of Crete/FORTH Institute, Greece
Seamus Ross	University of Toronto, Canada
Maria Roussou	National and Kapodistrian University of Athens, Greece
Apostolos Sarris	University of Cyprus, Cyprus
Maria Shehade	CYENS Centre of Excellence, Cyprus
Colin Sterling	University of Amsterdam, The Neverlands
Theopisti Stylianou- Lambert	Cyprus University of Technology/CYENS Centre of Excellence, Cyprus
Elena Stylianou	European University Cyprus, Cyprus
Stella Sylaiou	Hellenic Open University, Greece
Hannah Turner	University of British Columbia, Canada
Giasemi Vavoula	University of Leicester, UK
Elena Villaespesa	Pratt Institute, USA
Sharon Webb	University of Sussex, UK
Tim Weyrich	University College London, UK
Andrea Witcomb	Deakin University, Australia

Organised by

The RISE IMET conference was organized by CYENS CoE through the RISE project that has received funding from the European Union's Horizon 2020 Research and Innovation Programme under Grant Agreement No 739578 and the Government of the Republic of Cyprus through the Deputy Ministry of Research, Innovation and Digital Policy.

Contents

Digitization, Documentation and Digital Representation of Cultural Heritage

Digital Curation and Visitor Engagement in Museums and Heritage Sites

Computational Archives for Experimental Museology

Sarah Kenderdine$^{(\boxtimes)}$, Ingrid Mason, and Lily Hibberd

Laboratory for Experimental Museology, EPFL, Rue des Jordils 41,
1025 Lausanne, Switzerland
sarah.kenderdine@epfl.ch, ingrid.mason@anu.edu.au,
https://emplus.epfl.ch/

Abstract. This article addresses the potential for computational practises within archival and museological domains by charting a positional shift occurring in digital archives; from working with an object orientation and containment – to computing with a dimension orientation, segmentation, analytics and visualization. Computational museology allows us to conceive new trajectories that link all forms of cultural materiality: objects, knowledge systems, representation and participation. Following key definitions, the authors: outline state of the art in archival access and museological engagement through a series of examples; examine advances in the computational analysis of archives exploring forward-looking trends for massive digital cultural archives; and introduce an upcoming project, *Narratives from the long tail: transforming access to audiovisual archives*.

Keywords: Museology · Audiovisual archives · Curatorial analytics · Visualization · Interaction · Immersion

1 Introduction

1.1 Definition

Experimental museology sited within cultural heritage emerges from the delicate interstices of technologies and interfaces, human interaction and experience, and culture and social spaces. As a fulcrum for translation experimental museology traces epistemic patterns of abstraction, documentation and reformulation of cultural heritage; and the systemic transitions of the archive and cultural interaction with the archive [1].

1.2 Computational Archives

A positional shift is occurring in digital archives; from working with an object orientation and containment delineated in documentation and high-level archival ontologies – to computing with a dimension orientation, segmentation and analytics. New semantics arising out of this systemic shift are yet to be grounded, interpreted, abstracted and formalised as informatics in cultural heritage documentation. Computational archives are new terrain upon which curators will reckon with heritage materiality and calculate and define new fine-grained archival ontologies and narratives [2]. Large-scale curated

M. Shehade and T. Stylianou-Lambert (Eds.): RISE IMET 2021, CCIS 1432, pp. 3–18, 2021.
https://doi.org/10.1007/978-3-030-83647-4_1

video archives serve as important social contexts for difficult questions arising in data science and computer science to be asked and answered—and also connect diverse audiences with their multimedia cultural heritage. Video archives can be oriented to enabling novel exploitation of new, curated, diverse and large data assets, for the purposes of public engagement e.g., examining the rules of cinematography [3] through computation and analytics.

An interdisciplinary approach to working with computational archives will aid with testing technological and epistemological assumptions underlying computer vision, audio-visual, archival, and media studies; and new media research [4, 5]. By harnessing the push for transparency in the reuse of scientific research methods to transform big cultural datasets into computational archives this can also serve as "…an open process of scrutiny [and] is one of the pillars of scholarship and, in the end, scholarship's claim to social legitimacy" [6, p. 75].

It is timely for a wide range of research disciplines and archivists that work with video, to work with computer scientists, to examine how this mix of disciplines and research methodologies can be effectively drawn together to deliver value to different industries and sectors – and – wider community. Work has already been undertaken to detect and identify notable figures in footage drawn from more homogenous video archives for the purposes of refinement and testing techniques [7] in laboratory settings to meet an organisation goal, monographic narratives and national agenda [8]. Multimodal computational methodologies are yet to be applied to heterogenous curated cultural video archives, across a multitude of cultures, periods, events, experiences, storylines and genre. Experimental museology aids with expanding, testing and linking together the work undertaken in research labs as scholarly labs and in museums as labs for civic engagement with scholarship and curatorship.

1.3   Experimental Museology

This essay focuses on the work of the Laboratory for Experimental Museology (eM+) at EPFL. Within its broad remit from computational imaging through to immersive visualization, part of its research is based on new modalities of access to digital archives. Bridging academia, archives, museums and society, eM+ focuses on the contemporary challenges of public access to the principal mnemonic records of the 20th and 21st centuries: large-scale audiovisual archives and the large-scale cultural datasets that are the foundation of museological archives. Through computational processes, eM+ sets out to address and resolve the gap between digital archives and the embodied, participatory world of museological experience encompassing machine learning, visual analytics, digital museology, and archival science. Taking a 'systems thinking' approach to incorporate all aspects of its dynamic structure, 'computational museology' builds upon digital archiving through interlocking methods that will allow audiences to meaningfully explore the semantically rich 'long tail' of audiovisual memory [9].

Computational museology lies at the intersection of artificial intelligence, data curation, experimental and speculative visualization and performative archives. It is grounded in novel approaches to digital museology and digital archives in conjunction with the application of participatory museology. The domain undertakes to innovate 'narrative visualization', where narrative is widely understood to arise from a rich philosophical background in time-based media (cinema, media art, gaming) and interactive visualization. The approaches taken in the examples in this essay, provide systematic attempts to solve the challenges of narrative coherence for visualization through its computationally enabled data mining, analytic and interactive visualization approach. As we attempt to address an interdisciplinary description, it is evident that some disciplinary boundaries overlap, while others are siloed. This summary reading underscores the challenges of our topic, as well as highlighting why these fields have to date been independently unable to resolve the impasse of public access to the 'long tail' of audiovisual archives.

2   Massive Cultural Data

2.1   Audiovisual Archives

Audiovisual archives face an impasse with multiple implications for culture, public history and society. The pressure for these repositories to be 'open' has increased with European Commission strategies of inclusiveness, accessibility to and reuse of public information. This is underscored in the promotion of research and innovation, through FAIR and Open Access policies, and the notion of shared value as invested in 'the Commons' [10]. For the world's moving image and sound archives, preservation and access are twofold aims with sometimes conflicting values: digital preservation seeking to safeguard collections, while access prioritizes societal and economic impact. Closed collections also entail perpetual high-cost maintenance yet have little civic value [11, p. 10, 22]. Archival scholars, such Fossati, have pointed to these distinctions; highlighting dichotomies of preservation versus the reuse of film archives, and the need for engagement with new performative frameworks [12], to provide a genesis for both archival practices and museological approaches.

In response, broadcast institutions, notably the Netherlands Institute for Sound and Vision (NISV), have been at the forefront of pioneering policy and research [13]. Indicating the nature of the challenge, with an investment of 100 + million euro, the Eye Filmmuseum and NISV project, Images for the Future (2007–2014) resulted in 20% of the Filmmuseum's collection being digitized. However, due to copyright restrictions, only 2% was made public [14, p. 48]. Several similar investments have been made including by EU Screen portal [15], the BFI's 'Unlocking Film Heritage' program [16, 17] and Europeana [18].

2.2   Curatorial Analytics

Archival practices are relitigated and reworked by the introduction of computation and operationalization [19]. Digital archives have long been managed as collections of objects with database and search as efficient functional mechanisms that use Cartesian documentation methodologies and information retrieval methods. Archives are containers for objects – and – a social construction of all that they signify and obscure. That is, disrespect or respect du fonds, arrangement and description—how archives are grouped, defined and represented; and appraisal and elision—what is retained and interpreted and why. Archival theory is freighted with social observation and practices of control asserting socio-political and semantic boundaries. Archives exist in multiverses [20] and are "deeply implicated in webs of affective relations" [21, p. 7].

Operationalizing the archive in a museological context triggers three significant positional shifts in archival theory and practice: (1) the archive moves out from sphere of object containment and archival system retrieval and into the social sphere of immersed experience; (2) the archivist moves into a new cultural mediation mode enabled by interdisciplinary dialogue with museology and media specialists and computer scientists; and (3) the multitude of cultural features embedded in the digital archive are reified in new spatiotemporal, social, affective and aesthetic semantics that enable new abstractions, political restructuring and narrative reimagining.

A computational archive is a continuation of the functional definitions of and interactions with the archive, but as "data source" rather than object store. The use of computer vision (as analytic tool) is a new approach yet to be embedded in archival practice and cultural heritage informatics. Operationalization of the archive as "data source" exposes the need for an end-to-end data flow from institutional metadata and content stores to new data repositories [22, 23]. Acts of data integration, transformation and restructuring in the generation of cultural analytics will also involve curatorial interpretation of archival objects, their dimensions, relationships and contexts. A "dimension" view of archival data as valent and affective, is a continuation of the precept that cultural signifiers emerge "from the archive" regardless of their material presence or absence, or promotion or elision. A computational archive is a refactoring not just of digital archives but also of curatorial practices of authority and interpretation and the philosophical and positional shifts required in digital transformation. A curatorial approach to selecting and formalizing analytics aligned with museological and archival interpretation and documentation and paratext practices can encompass multiple perspectives and explanations.

Curatorial analytics will build on cultural analytics (as material deconstruction of the archive through computation and generalization) [24] by maintaining a focus on semantic refinements, variation, contextualization and significance.

3   Archival Access in Museums

Museums have experimented with new technological forms and formats to enhance public engagement. Digital museology has been at the forefront of this trajectory more than a decade [25]. Within this field, a distinct approach of experimental museology has been taken by the Laboratory for Experimental Museology at EPFL to innovate at the intersection of immersive visualization technologies, visual analytics, aesthetics and cultural data. This area of research has advanced theoretical frameworks emerging from new museology since the early 1990s, redefining the boundaries of public and exhibitionary space. Through its tripartite speculative, applied and theoretical research, experimental museology engenders new modes of knowledge production arising from digital cultural archives, doing so through a participatory model focused on situating audiences and their experiences at the center of knowledge creation [26].

Significant to this latter pursuit is the overlooked role of 'embodiment' in creating meaningful museum experiences, specifically by amalgamating cultural heritage archives with interactive cinema to foster novel forms of embodied narrative [27, 28]. Experimental museology thus nurtures new forms of interpretation based on phenomenological and cognitive encounters as they emerge in relation to immersive, interactive visualization technologies [29]. Important theoretical shifts due to the impact of digital technologies on spectatorship and perception inform the experimental framework of eM+, among them the concepts of immediacy and remediation [30], interactive narrative, aesthetic transcription [31, p. 10], and modes of performance and creative reuse as a means of generating new narrative and memory.

In order to address the gap between audiovisual repositories and the public sphere, it is necessary to augment the data curation lifecycle at a systemic level [32] in a dual method that implements novel computational approaches to the archival collections themselves [33] in tandem with novel forms of in situ engagement for narrative making. We propose a major research effort to enable these new forms of expressive media through computational methods and analytics, thus enabling the enormous untapped potential for public 'history making' and promoting sustainable futures for audiovisual memories [34].

3.1 Narrative and Visualization

Kenderdine and her collaborators have been at the forefront of a major research trajectory in the creation of narrative through interactive systems and information visualization for cultural heritage materials (i.e., sites, objects and archives). The pioneers of this field have also conceived powerful interactive visualization environments, endowed with omnispatial and omnidirectional capacities in which participants are mobile and are able to look in any direction in the three-dimensional 360-degree virtual environments [35, 36]. Crucial to this present research, immersive framing notably helps to resolve problems of data occlusion and distribute the mass of data analysis in networked sequences revealing patterns, hierarchies, and interconnectedness, and data fusion [37] while hybrid approaches to data representation allow for the development of audio strategies to augment the interpretation of search results [38]. For instance, Panorama+, the 360-3D platform that is the basis of the experimental setting that has been shown to enhance cognitive exploration and interrogation of high-dimensional data, essential for big data while also providing powerful spaces akin to the real world for simulation [39].

A seminal media artwork in this domain is T_Visionarium II [31, 40] developed among other iterations between 2006 and 2014 (see, Fig. 1. and video at https://vimeo.com/2832411). Situated in a panoramic environment, its source material is a collection of 24 h of free-to-air broadcast TV footage from 7 Australian channels. Computationally segmented according to changes (i.e., edits or to camera angle cuts), and analyzed to assign these to metadata categories of emotion, expression, physicality and scene structure, and metatags such as speed, gender, color, in the final visualization, the viewer can both search and recombine 500 simultaneously looping video streams of 4 s each. The system is highly responsive: when one image is selected, all the other semantically similar clips flock to the opposite side, 180 of the 360-degree display screen. The entire search matrix can be weighted in favor of specific metatags chosen by the viewer, and the clips can be recombined to create a new filmic episode. This early experiment in spatialized video montage reveals the affordances of empowering the viewer to engage in actively re-conceptualizing a moving image collection. The dynamic re-sequencing of segments allows the user to create an emergent or 'transnarrative' version (i.e., traversing individual narratives).

Fig. 1. *T-Visionarium II*, iCinema Centre, UNSW 2009. Photo: iCinema, UNSW.

ECLOUD WWI is an interactive spatial browser for the exploration of cultural data collected in the Europeana 1914–1918 archive (Fig. 2). Presented in a 3D custom designed 9 m by 3 m projection screen, the installation contains more than 40,000 images of war memorabilia ascribed to 2,500 individual stories collected across Europe between 2009 and 2013 in an ongoing Europeana crowdsourcing project [103].

The installation instantaneously aggregates the digital imagery and its associative metadata to provide an immersive viewing experience. Museum visitors use an iPad tablet to navigate and direct the data that is displayed on the panoramic arc of its screen. Six satiric European maps of the period are entry points into the archive via specific images that represent particular stories chosen by the curators of Europeana. Selecting one of these images brings up its description and related articles, artifacts and objects. This story group then becomes the portal to other metadata-associated image groups that appear as 'clouds' of images rendered on a rotating 3-D cylinder. Selecting any image from this cylindrical cloud causes the picture, along with its description and associated themes and metadata, to expand, and this in turn provides the viewer with the opportunity to link to other such clouds of images with different themes [41].

With 40,000 images and 15 keywords, the contents of this Europeana digital archive can be dynamically recombined for extended non-linear exploration by the viewer. The visualization strategies engaged in ECLOUD WWI signal opportunities for new curatorial practices and embodied museography by redeploying Internet data in a situated museum setting. ECLOUD WWI applies an integrative pluralist approach to the juxtaposition of image and memory that signals a shift from traditional classification and organization to a newer search-and-remix paradigm; the emphasis here is on personal affective engagement with cultural memory and on interface.

Fig. 2. *eCloud WW1,* Applied Laboratory Interactive Visualization and Embodiment, 2012. Photo: Jeffrey Shaw.

Counter to the notion that databases and narratives are natural enemies [42], the dynamic segmentation and recombination of data has the potential to open up new realms of narrative coherence for participants, while also challenging conventions of meaning making. The world's first immersive 360-degree interactive data browser for museum collections *mArchive* (Fig. 3) was the result of an experimental application designed to develop emergent narrative arising from a museum collection. This research project was focused on 100,000 heterogenous image records from Museum

Victoria (with a total collection of 16 million items). The application uses extant collection metadata as the basis for an active interface to create the equivalent of a 'real-time curating machine'. It has been installed since 2015 in the Museum's visualization system, where it is available for up to 30 visitors at one time.

Fig. 3. *mArchive,* Museum Victoria, 2015. 100,000 objects distributed across a 360-degree 3D screen. Note: no text-based search engine is provided. Photo: Volker Kuckelmeister.

More recently, *Jazz Luminaries* (2019; Fig. 4, see video at https://vimeo.com/414654196, password: jazz), transforms the Montreux Jazz Festival archive into an interactive installation. Combining extant metadata and novel visualization, Jazz Luminaries enables viewers to cut, remix and replay over 13,000 videos of the 5,400 jazz greats recorded in the archive. Each musician is represented by a node, which is interconnected to other Festival artists based on their historic collaboration over the years. This interaction is enabled through a unique multimodal interface, under a fulldome where participants generate an experience of their own, illustrating the shift from a linear classification of objects within inventories to their remix, recollection, regeneration and reworking, interaction and serendipitous discovery [43].

3.2   Visualization – Searching Collections

A shift in the 'grammar' of the visual occurred from the end of the 1990s, as graphic and computational techniques were applied to visually represent and generate alternate insights into complex and large-scale collections of information [44]. Often referred to as the 'diagrammatic turn' [45], these new forms of information visualization, or InfoViz, are based on the notion that graphical representation can harness and augment

Fig. 4. *Jazz Luminaries* by eM+, *Infinity Room 2*, ArtLab EPFL 2019. Viewers reclined under the eM+ dome, navigating a social network constellation of the jazz greats in the Montreux Jazz Archive. Photos: Catherine Leutenegger/Sarah Kenderdine

basic powers of human perception, and that visual representations of data can further 'amplify cognition' [46].

The influence of data-driven visualization on search tools (i.e. networks, histograms) is evident in the consistent graphic and informatic logic of flatness, linear navigation [47]. With the advent of the Internet, from the mid-1990s public collection websites could have become a virtual counterpart for the in-situ, located archive. While information visualization and 'cultural analytics' have arguably altered how we view databases [48] tools for searching them remain rooted in archival conventions of 'grammato-centristic notions of data storage' [50, p. 117]. Access and engagement with a majority of these databases continues to rely on 'query-response' or text-driven single searches [50]. Critics highlight that the state-of-the-art in visualizing cultural heritage collections still hinges on this database paradigm and that the whole domain requires more 'generous' and expressive interfaces for in-situ access [51–53]. These questions are fundamental for audiovisual archives, which cannot be resolved in two-dimensional pictograms.

For researchers working in the recently defined domain of 'audio visual digital humanities' [54] the application of digital visualization techniques to cultural heritage datasets is a new and innovative research methodology [55, 56]. This progress has prompted a turn away from the tools made for textual digital humanities studies, towards new approaches for access, discovery and study of moving image and sound materials. There is also an awareness of the need to shift this research from an institutional framework, to address the crisis of public access [57]. Other research in this field has concerned how interaction and user creativity can be harnessed to enhance browsing environments, such as multimodal browsing or searching along multiple threads [58, 59].

3.3   Advances in Computational Video Analysis

Video retrieval, or the content-based retrieval of digital moving images in the computer vision research domain, has been a significant field for 20 years, see TRECVIC, for instance [60]. Central to online video platforms (YouTube, Vimeo) video retrieval is also one of the key tools that large moving image archives use to make their digital collections searchable online. Recent work on information retrieval and data analytics enabled by machine learning research has made an impact on broadcasting production discoverability [3, 61].

Advances in the visualization of video data, which began with visual abstractions of images in video as keyframes and evolved to incorporate different semantic information (features from text and sound), have also evolved to incorporate features into an informatics layer [62], such as video-slicing [63], and linking those slices along a timeline to connect features in space and time [64]. Visual analytics research has begun to refine methodologies through which the semantics derived from 'deep architectures to capture complex relationships among multimodal features', including gesture and emotion recognition [65]. Computer vision has seen noted breakthroughs since 2012 in convolutional neural networks – a deep learning technique that can detect objects in images with almost human-level accuracy [66]. There has been intense work on new neural network architectures for various perception tasks such as human detection, and activity classification [67]. Although pose estimation has been studied before the deep learning era, it is a significant cornerstone in the new work of Wei et al. [68].

In summary, a curatorial focus on data is maturing in computer vision research, to delineate datasets as fit for different tasks (instead of 'one size fits all'). There is also a growing interest in the evaluation of video data for the purpose of developing and testing algorithms, however the sources for this research is usually web accessible, camera or sensor imaging (readily available), or it is orchestrated and generated for the purpose of experimentation. Computer vision research using video has vastly diversified like its datasets, in tandem with machine learning techniques. Datasets with few or no labels have been used for unsupervised learning, and well-labelled datasets can also be used for supervised learning. The visualization of video data, however, tends to repeat the functional and illustrative forms of scientific visualization (i.e., networks, histograms, the use of snippets or derivatives are used to visualize features).

There is, to date, no discussion on data science challenges associated with video visualization for the purpose of engagement and this is the subject of an upcoming project *Narratives from the long tail: transforming access to audiovisual archives*, funded by the Swiss National Science Fund as a Sinergia grant (2021–2025) in collaboration with: EPFL, University of Zürich, University of Amsterdam and the archives of the International Olympics Committee (Olympics Museum), Montreux Jazz Archives, Swiss Television and Radio and the Eye Museum in the Netherlands. *Narratives* will transcend state-of-the-art across all its fields to initiate a groundbreaking visualization framework for interactively (re)discovering hundreds of thousands of hours of audiovisual materials. This is achieved through *Narratives'* highly novel 360-degree 3D Narrative Visualization Engine, that will dynamically reveal the spatial, temporal, social, affective and aesthetic patterns, phenomena and processes of archival collections, and ensure 'narrative coherence' for audiences as they navigate them. This scalable and participatory engagement model aims to situate audiences and their experiences at the center of knowledge production while also stimulating innovation in archival practices [69].

4 Conclusion

Artificial intelligence and computational video archives are already operationalized in broadcasting, film production and professional sports. Computational methodologies and visualization technologies, techniques, and analytics from industry that are taken up, translated and reworked with cultural heritage practice will impact on curation, pedagogy, aesthetics and the design of public exhibitions. Constraints and issues in computer and data science include a slow transition from machine learning enabled experimentation into the uptake and refinement of computational methods and their application in different loci. New challenges around data quality, scale, and accessibility, and the exposure of bias in data, algorithms, analytics and visualization methods have emerged and pose collective challenges. There is a call for more transparency, explainability and interpretability in data science, computational and AI methods and practices [70]. Multiple disciplinary interests are converging and opening out questions that expose issues with big data curation, human-computer interaction, ethics and social impact, visualization, and knowledge transfer [71]. Diverse perspectives are needed to challenge and critically evaluate computational methodologies and the use of artificial intelligence in cultural and social contexts, including museums.

The rise of audiovisual analytics addresses a need to get through content quickly and to search through databases for content and as a specialism has already positively impacted several domains e.g., broadcasting, sport, commerce, and science [72]. Video analytics, computational archives and AI however will all need to be critically evaluated, reinterpreted and potentially reconfigured to become a part of curatorial practice in cultural heritage. In a public space curatorial intention and public response involve social and dynamic human-machine interaction and dialogue, so multiple perspectives can be drawn together in the interpretation and representation of cultural and social knowledge [73]. Experimental museology contends very differently with the challenge of high dimensional data that contains a myriad of variables and correlations and multiple historiographic explanations and reinterpretations of cause, effect and consequence. Experimental museology is a driving force for diverse narrative and analytics and visualization that embrace curatorial determinations of cultural significance, individual and communal reassessments and redefinitions, variation and uncertainty [74].

References

1. French, A., Villaespesa, E.: AI, visitor experience, and museum operations: a closer look at the possible. In: Anderson, S., Bruno, I., Rao, S., Rodley, E., Ropeik, R., Hethmon, H. (eds.) Humanizing the Digital: Unproceedings from the MCN 2018 Conference, pp. 101–113 (2019)
2. Marciano, R., et al.: Archival records and training in the age of big data. In: Percell, J., Sarin, L.C., Jaeger, P.T., Bertot, J.C. (eds.) Re-envisioning the MLS: Perspectives on the Future of Library and Information Science Education. Advances in Librarianship, vol. 44B, pp. 179–199 (2018)
3. Wright, C., et al.: AI in production: video analysis and machine learning for expanded live events coverage. SMPTE Motion Imag. J. **129**(2), 36–42 (2018). https://doi.org/10.5594/JMI.2020.2967204
4. Van Gorp, J., Bron, M.: Building bridges: collaboration between computer science and media studies in a television archive project. Digit. Hum. Q. **13**(3) (2019)
5. Masson, E.: Humanistic data research: an encounter between epistemic traditions. In: Schäfer, M.T., Van Es, K. (eds.) The Datafied Society: Studying Culture through Data, pp. 25–38. Amsterdam University Press, Amsterdam (2017)
6. Röhle, B.R.T.: Digital methods: five challenges. In: Berry, D.M. (ed.) Understanding Digital Humanities, pp. 67–84. Palgrave Macmillan, London (2012). https://doi.org/10.1057/9780230371934_4
7. Mittal, T., Bhattacharya, U., Chandra, R., Bera, A., Manocha, D.: M3ER: multiplicative multimodal emotion recognition using facial, textual, and speech cues. Proc. AAAI Conf. Artif. Intell. **34**(2), 1359–1367 (2019)
8. Phillipson, G., Forman, R., Wossey, M., Wright, C., Evans, M., Jolly, S.: Automated analysis of the framing of faces in a large video archive. In: Proceedings of the Joint Workshop on Intelligent Narrative Technologies and Workshop on Intelligent Cinematography and Editing, AAAI Conference on Artificial Intelligence and Interactive Digital Entertainment, INT/WICED@AIIDE (2018)

9. Kenderdine, S.: Radical intangibles: materializing the ephemeral. In: Kostas, A., Chiara, Z. (eds.) Museums & Society. Special Issue: Digital (and) Materiality in Museums (2021)
10. Guidelines to the Rules on Open Access to Scientific Publications and Open Access to Research Data in Horizon 2020. http://ec.europa.eu/research/participants/data/ref/h2020/grants_manual/hi/oa_pilot/h2020-hi-oa-pilot-guide_en.pdf. Accessed 21 Mar 2017
11. Edmonson, R.: Audiovisual archiving: philosophy and principles - UNESCO Digital Library. United Nations Educational, Scientific and Cultural Organization, Bangkok (2016)
12. Fossati, G.: Found footage filmmaking, film archiving and new participatory platforms. In: Bloemheuvel, M., Fossati, G., Guldemond, J. (eds.) Found Footage: Cinema Exposed, pp. 177–184. Amsterdam University Press, Amsterdam (2012)
13. Kaufman, P.B.: Towards a New Audiovisual Think Tank for Audiovisual Archivists and Cultural Heritage Professionals. Netherlands Institute for Sound and Vision, Hilversum (2018). https://doi.org/10.18146/2018thinktank01
14. Keller, P., van Excel, T., Oosterwijk, M.: Images of the past, 7 years of Images for the Future. Netherlands Institute for Sound and Vision, EYE Film Institute, the National Archives and Kennisland (2015)
15. EU Screen. http://euscreen.eu/about.html. Accessed 24 May 2020
16. British Film Institute: Unlocking Film Heritage. https://www.bfi.org.uk/britain-on-film/unlocking-film-heritage. Accessed 2 May 2020
17. Fairall, C.: BFI film forever: unlocking film heritage. In: Sustainable Audiovisual Collections Through Collaboration: Proceedings of the 2016 Joint Technical Symposium, pp.10–15. Indiana University Press, Bloomington (2017)
18. Europeana: Europeana Pro Mission. https://pro.europeana.eu/about-us/mission. Accessed 24 May 2020
19. Underwood, W., Marciano, R.: Computational thinking in archival science research and education. In: 2019 IEEE International Conference on Big Data (Big Data), Los Angeles, CA, USA, pp. 3146–3152 (2019). https://doi.org/10.1109/BigData47090.2019.9005682
20. Gilliland, A.J.: Archival and recordkeeping traditions in the multiverse and their importance for research situations and situating research. In: Gilliland, A., McKemmish, S., Lau, A. (eds.) Research in the Archival Multiverse. Monash University Press, Melbourne (2017)
21. Cifor, M.: Affecting relations: introducing affect theory to archival discourse. Arch. Sci. **16** (1), 7–31 (2015). https://doi.org/10.1007/s10502-015-9261-5
22. Goodall, T., Esteva, M., Sweat, S., Bovik, A.C.: Towards automated quality curation of video collections from a realistic perspective. In: 2017 IEEE International Conference on Big Data (Big Data), pp. 2240–2245. IEEE, Boston (2017). https://doi.org/10.1109/BigData.2017.8258175
23. Fan, L., Yin, Z., Yu, H., Gilliland, A.: Using data-driven analytics to enhance archival processing of the COVID-19 hate speech twitter archive (CHSTA). LIS Scholarship Archive (2020). https://doi.org/10.31229/osf.io/gkydm
24. Manovich, L.: The science of culture? Social computing, digital humanities and cultural analytics. J. Cult. Anal. (2016). https://doi.org/10.22148/16.004
25. Eriksson, B., Stage, C., Valtysson, B.: Cultures of Participation: Arts, Digital Media and Cultural Institutions. Routledge, London (2019)
26. Kenderdine, S.: Experimental museology: immersive visualization and cultural (big) data. In: Achiam, M., Haldrup, M. (eds.) Experimental Museology in the Age of Experience. Routledge, London (2021)
27. Kenderdine, S.: Prosthetic architectures of the senses: museums and immersion. Screen **61**(4), 635–645 (2020)

28. Chao, H., Delbridge, M., Kenderdine, S., Nicholson, L., Shaw, J.: Kapturing Kung Fu: future proofing the Hong Kong Martial Arts Living Archive. In: Whatley, S., Cisneros, R.K., Sabiescu, A. (eds.) Digital Echoes, pp. 249–264. Springer, Cham (2018). https://doi.org/10. 1007/978-3-319-73817-8_13

29. Kenderdine, S.: Embodiment, entanglement, and immersion in digital cultural heritage. In: Schreibman, S., Seimens, R., Unsworth, J. (eds.) A New Companion to Digital Humanities, pp. 22–14. Wiley, Chichester (2015)

30. Bolter, J.D., Grusin, R.A.: Remediation: Understanding Mew Media. MIT Press, Cambridge (1999)

31. Bennett, J.: T_Visionarium: A User's Guide. UNSW Press/ZKM, Sydney/Karlsruhe (2007)

32. Brunow, D.: Remediating Transcultural Memory, Documentary Filmmaking as Archival Intervention. De Gruyter, Berlin (2015)

33. Ingravalle, G.: Remixing early cinema: historical explorations at the EYE Film Institute Netherlands. Moving Image **15**(2), 82–97 (2015)

34. Fickers, A., van den Oever, A.: Experimental media archaeology: a plea for new directions. In: Technē/Technology: Researching Cinema and Media Technologies - Their Development, Use, and Impact, pp. 272–278. Amsterdam University Press, Amsterdam (2014)

35. Kenderdine, S.: Prosthetic architectures of the senses: museums and immersion. Screen **61** (4), 635–645 (2020)

36. Kenderdine, S., Hart, T.: Cultural data sculpting: omnispatial visualization for large scale heterogeneous datasets. In: Proceedings of Museums and the Web 2011, Toronto, Canada. Archives & Museum Informatics (2011)

37. Lock, J.G., Filonik, D., Lawther, R., Pather, N., Gaus, K., Kenderdine, S., Bednarz, T.: Visual analytics of single cell microscopy data using a collaborative immersive environment. In: Proceedings of the 16th ACM SIGGRAPH International Conference on Virtual-Reality Continuum and its Applications in Industry - VRCAI 2018, Tokyo, Japan, pp. 1–4 (2018)

38. Kenderdine, S., Nicholson, J.K., Mason, I.: Modeling people and populations: exploring medical visualization through immersive interactive virtual environments. In: Holmes, E., Nicholson, J.K., Darzi, A.W., Lindon, J.C. (eds.) Metabolic Phenotyping in Personalized and Public Healthcare, pp. 333–367. Academic Press, Boston (2016)

39. Shen, H., et al.: Information visualisation methods and techniques: state-of-the-art and future directions. J. Ind. Inf. Integr. **16**, 100102 (2019)

40. T_Visionarium. http://www.icinema.unsw.edu.au/projects/t_visionarium/. Accessed 15 Mar 2020

41. Kenderdine, S., McKenzie, H.: A war-torn memory palace: animating narratives of remembrance. In: Proceedings of Digital Heritage International Congress, Marseille, pp. 315–322. IEEE (2013)

42. Manovich, L.: Database as a symbolic form. In: Parry, R. (ed.) Museums in a Digital Age, pp. 64–71. Routledge, London (2010)

43. Kenderdine, S.: Jazz luminaries. Photo Lond. Mag. **3**, 10–36 (2020)

44. Drucker, J.: Humanities approaches to graphical display. Digit. Hum. Q. **5**(1), 1–21 (2011)

45. Krämer, S.: Operative bildlichkeit: von der 'grammatologie' zu einer 'diagrammatologie'? re exionen über erkennendes sehen. In: Hessler, M., Mersch, D. (eds.) Logik des Bildlichen: Zur Kritik der ikonischen Vernunft. Verlag, Bielefeld (2009)

46. Clark, A.: Supersizing the Mind: Embodiment, Action, and Cognitive Extension. Oxford University Press, New York (2008)

47. Steele, J., Iliinsky, N.P.N. (eds.): Beautiful Visualization: Looking at Data Through the Eyes of Experts, 1st edn. O'Reilly, Sebastopol (2010)

48. Manovich, L.: Cultural analytics: visualizing cultural patterns in the era of 'More Media'. DOMUS, Spring (2009)

49. Ernst, W.: Dis/continuities does the archive become metaphorical in multi-media space? In: Kyong Chun, W., Keenan, T. (eds.) New Media, Old Media: A History and Theory Reader, pp. 105–123. Routledge Taylor & Francis, New York, London (2006)
50. Fairbairn, N., Pimpinelli, M.A., Ross, T.: The FIAF Moving Image Cataloguing Manual. Indiana University Press, Bloomington (2016)
51. Rahman, M.M.: Search engines going beyond keyword search: a survey. Int. J. Comput. Appl. **75**(17), 1–8 (2013)
52. Kenderdine, S., Chan, L.K.Y., Shaw, J.: Pure Land: futures for embodied museography. J. Comput. Cult. Heritage **7**(2), 1–15 (2014). https://doi.org/10.1145/2614567
53. Whitelaw, M.: Generous interfaces for digital cultural collections. Digit. Hum. Q. **9**(1), 1–16 (2015)
54. Windhager, F., et al.: Visualization of cultural heritage collection data: state of the art and future challenges. IEEE Trans. Visual Comput. Graphics **25**(6), 2311–2330 (2019). https://doi.org/10.1109/TVCG.2018.2830759
55. Olesen, C.G.: Towards a 'humanistic cinemetrics?' In: van Es, K., Schäfer, M.T. (eds.) The Datafied Society: Studying Culture through Data, pp. 39–54. Amsterdam University Press, Amsterdam (2017)
56. Flueckiger, B.: A digital humanities approach to film colors. Moving Image J. Assoc. Moving Image Arch. **17**(2), 71–94 (2017). https://doi.org/10.5749/movingimage.17.2.0071
57. Warwick, C., Terras, M.M., Nyhan, J. (eds.): Digital Humanities in Practice. Facet, London (2012)
58. Sauer, S.: Audiovisual narrative creation and creative retrieval: how searching for a story shapes the story. J. Sci. Technol. Arts **9**(2), 37–46 (2017). https://doi.org/10.7559/citarj.v9i2.241
59. de Rooij, O., Worring, M.: Browsing video along multiple threads. IEEE Trans. Multimedia **12**(2), 121–130 (2010)
60. TRECVID 2019 Guidelines. https://www-nlpir.nist.gov/projects/tv2019/index.html. Accessed 24 Feb 2020
61. Shih, H.: A survey on content-aware video analysis for sports. IEEE Trans. Circuits Syst. Video Technol. **28**(5), 1212–1231 (2018). https://doi.org/10.1109/TCSVT.2017.2655624
62. Truong, B.T., Venkatesh, S.: Video abstraction: a systematic review and classification. ACM Trans. Multimedia Comput. Commun. Appl. **3**(1), 1–37 (2007). https://doi.org/10.1145/1198302.1198305
63. Tang, A., Greenberg, S., Fels, S.: Exploring video streams using slit-tear visualizations. In: CHI 2009 Extended Abstracts on Human Factors in Computing Systems, Boston, M.A, pp. 3509–3510 (2009). https://doi.org/10.1145/1520340.1520516
64. Lay, S., Vermeulen, J., Perin, C., Donovan, E., Dachselt, R., Carpendale, S.: Slicing the Aurora: an immersive proxemics-aware visualization. In: Proceedings of the 2016 ACM Companion on Interactive Surfaces and Spaces, Niagara Falls, Ont., pp. 91–97 (2016). https://doi.org/10.1145/3009939.3009954
65. Olah, C., Mordvintsev, A., Schubert, L.: Feature visualization. Distill **2**(11), e7 (2017). https://doi.org/10.23915/distill.00007
66. Lin, T.-Y., et al.: Microsoft COCO: common objects in context. In: Fleet, D., Pajdla, T., Schiele, B., Tuytelaars, T. (eds.) ECCV 2014. LNCS, vol. 8693, pp. 740–755. Springer, Cham (2014). https://doi.org/10.1007/978-3-319-10602-1_48
67. Zhang, S., Benenson, R., Omran, M., Hosang, J., Schiele, B.: Towards reaching human performance in pedestrian detection. IEEE Trans. Pattern Anal. Mach. Intell. **40**(4), 973–986 (2018). https://doi.org/10.1109/TPAMI.2017.2700460

68. Ji, S., Xu, W., Yang, M., Yu, K.: 3D convolutional neural networks for human action recognition. IEEE Trans. Pattern Anal. Mach. Intell. **35**(1), 221–231 (2013). https://doi.org/10.1109/TPAMI.2012.59

69. EPFL: Narratives from the long tail: transforming access to audiovisual archives`. https://www.epfl.ch/labs/emplus/projects/narratives/. Accessed 06 Mar 2021

70. Baur, T., et al.: eXplainable cooperative machine learning with NOVA. KI - Künstliche Intelligenz **34**(2), 143–164 (2020). https://doi.org/10.1007/s13218-020-00632-3

71. Crawford, K., Paglen, T.: Excavating AI: the politics of images in machine learning training sets, 19 September 2019. https://excavating.ai/. Accessed 06 Mar 2021

72. Karpathy, A., Toderici, G., Shetty, S., Leung, T., Sukthankar, R., Fei-Fei, L.: Large-scale video classification with convolutional neural networks. In: IEEE Conference on Computer Vision and Pattern Recognition, Columbus, OH, pp. 1725–1732 (2014). https://doi.org/10.1109/CVPR.2014.223

73. Masson, E., van Noord, N.: Feature extraction and classification. https://sensorymoving imagearchive.humanities.uva.nl/index.php/2020/01/06/feature-extraction-and-classification/. Accessed 05 Jan 2021

74. Khulusi, R., Kusnick, J., Meinecke, C., Gillmann, C., Focht, J., Jänicke, S.: A survey on visualizations for musical data. Comput. Graph. Forum **39**(6), 82–110 (2020). https://doi.org/10.1111/cgf.13905

Machine Learning and Museum Collections: A Data Conundrum

Lukas Noehrer[1](✉) , Jonathan Carlton[1,2] , and Caroline Jay[1]

[1] The University of Manchester, Manchester, UK
lukas.nohrer@manchester.ac.uk
[2] BBC R&D, Salford, UK

Abstract. Museums contain vast amounts of information and knowledge, providing a vital source of engagement for diverse audiences. As society becomes ever more digital, museums are moving towards making their collections available online to the public. However, just providing a searchable interface to the entirety of the collection could be a barrier to successful engagement. Tremendous craftsmanship is put into creating interesting and informative in-person curations of selected items, and a challenge exists in replicating this online. One solution could be the application of recommender systems, which personalise information to the individual based on their previous interactions and tastes. These systems power many popular online services, but cannot be applied without considerations and decisions being made about the data that is given to the engine. As museum collections vary in their nature and content, particular care should be taken when handling the data – standard methods may not apply. In this paper, we present the challenges of data curation in the context of using machine learning techniques with museum collections, supported by two case studies.

Keywords: Data · Museum collection · Recommender system · Machine learning

1 Introduction

Museums, society's collecting and memory institutions, are holders of a vast amount of information and knowledge. As society progresses towards a *post-digital* [1] and on-demand life, where technology is ubiquitous, museums face an ever-increasing demand to digitise and disseminate their collections, particularly since the start of the COVID-19 pandemic [2]. This progression from off- to on-line entities does, however, provide an opportunity to make collections accessible and to engage a broad audience for education, entertainment, and scholarly purposes. Nevertheless, given vast collections, creating individually curated pathways online that capture the tastes and interests of users poses an additional challenge for museums. A potential solution is the automation of the curation process through the application of machine learning (ML).

As a research field dedicated to serving personalised content to individual users, recommender systems are a natural fit to the automation of the curatorial process. Recommender systems are used on a daily basis by millions of people in well-known media

M. Shehade and T. Stylianou-Lambert (Eds.): RISE IMET 2021, CCIS 1432, pp. 19–31, 2021.
https://doi.org/10.1007/978-3-030-83647-4_2

applications, such as Netflix [3] and Spotify [4], in e-commerce [5, 6], and in medical sciences [7], often without users knowing explicitly about their existence or functionality [8]. To serve personalised content to users, these systems use similarity between items (content-based), similarities between users and items (collaborative), or a combination (hybrid).

However, as with other modelling approaches, a model is only as good as the data it uses and recommendation models rely on good data quality, in a consistent format, and heavily engineered architecture to collect, process, and feed the data into the model. Hence, it is critical that, as museums move their collections online and make them available for new applications such as ML, careful consideration is made with regard to data collection and entry; two areas that often remain overlooked and not rigorously examined [9] or have been the cause of bias over the course of history [10].

Creating a ML model that is functional and fair – where the predicted user preference is accurate and unbiased – requires rigorous assessment of the available data and careful consideration of further engineering - should it be *required*, for example in the case of erroneous entries – such as misspelling, missing values, or wrongly labelled data - or *desired*, to curate existing entries according to certain aspects, as in the inclusion as well as exclusion of features. In the case of museums, such features can refer to all properties associated with an entry in the database, such as metadata and images. Engineering, manipulating, and removing such features needs careful consideration and knowledge about the database, as it could negatively impact personalisation and diversity downstream.

In this paper we reflect on the process and challenges of adopting a dataset for use in a museum recommender system: *MuseREC*. This is followed by a discussion of the challenges we faced in terms of data curation in digital collections, and the steps necessary to prepare the data to be used in a machine learning application, followed by two case studies of differently sized institutions: a local council-run museum in the United Kingdom (UK), and a national institution based in the United States (US). The contribution of this paper is a five-step framework to address data curation for ML techniques in the museum sphere. In doing so, we developed guidelines and highlighted the necessary steps and caveats of ML techniques for museum collections, and we further illustrate the necessary considerations of using such models.

2   Background

Recommender systems first appeared as an independent field of ML in the Nineties, mainly founded on cognitive research, approximation theory, information retrieval studies, and forecasting theory [11]. Based on algorithms that calculate similarities between data points, recommender systems can filter through an abundance of information and serve recommendations based on three main methods *(i) content-based filtering*, *(ii) collaborative filtering*, and *(iii) hybrid-recommender engines* as a combination of the first two techniques to increase performance.

The application of recommender systems has been trialled and investigated in museums and galleries, amongst others, for the personalisation of tours and visits

[12–18], in multimedia browsing systems [19–21], chatbots [22], and smart and edge-intelligent devices [23, 24].

Investigating the history of recommender system development for museums, it is evident that most systems were designed for in-house user experiences and on-site guided tours, focussed "either on gallery-like presentations and/or linear narratives" [25].

Recommender System MuseREC

To enable an audience to explore collections personalised to their tastes and recent activity, along with investigating the utility of an individual curatorial process, we built a content-based recommender system using collection data, which includes metadata and images. The system, formed of two components - the content-based model and the web system (with the latter creating a wrapper around the former) - serves recommendations to users based on their interactions with items in the collection, enabling personalised curations.

To construct the model, we used high-resolution digital images of the artwork and collection pieces and trained a convolutional autoencoder - a deep learning method that outputs a reconstructed input [26] - to learn low-dimensional feature representations. To utilise the rich information in the collection metadata, such as the title and description, we applied term frequency-inverse document frequency (TF-IDF) [27] – a technique that scores rarer words (often more valuable) higher than frequently appearing words. We then concatenated the two feature vectors to form a single feature vector for each item in the collection. As we have no target to optimise for, nor user preference information to construct a collaborative or hybrid model, we used k-means - an unsupervised clustering model - to produce recommendations of similar items. When using the unsupervised clustering model, we worked under the assumption that data which appear closer together in cluster space are items that would be of interest to the user.

To host the model, a web system was created that provided users with access to the collection database and served recommendations based on their interactions. With each item in the collection having its own webpage, the user can search and interact with the website to find items they are interested in - along with providing ratings for individual pieces. From these ratings and interactions, a performance evaluation can be carried out, and a comparison between users can be performed through A/B testing.

3   From Data to Curated Pathways

Databases in museums evolved over time, and how the data was entered and collected, has an impact on ML outcomes. A considerate process is therefore valuable in terms of avoiding the model delivering inaccurate results. It also elicits thinking about potential bias and possible future harms or the reinforcement of unwanted patterns in the data. Thus, this section introduces a *Recommender Life Cycle* in the context of using museum data for recommendations.

3.1   Recommender Life Cycle

We present five steps that consider the life cycle of a recommender pipeline, whilst explaining the implications and caveats of adopting and using a dataset for recommender systems. This process is inherently interdisciplinary and requires domain, data and technical knowledge. Future applications, for use in research or audience-centred, need standardisation and have to follow certain guidelines such as the ones proposed in the *FAIR Guiding Principles* [28] to make data in museums findable, accessible, interoperable, and reusable for a broad usership, and to avoid falling victim to the potential harms of ML applications [10], or the hype around a new technology leading to the inheritance, or even reinforcement, of power structures imprinted into collections, such as the misrepresentation of gender [29]. In the next section we therefore reflect on the pitfalls, obstacles, and considerations about using museum collection datasets in a recommender system and model our process with the help of established data science tools (Fig. 1).

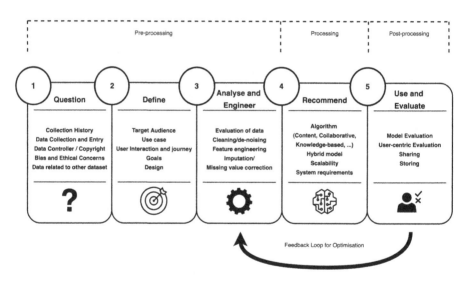

Fig. 1. Five steps of the *Recommender Life Cycle*

Questioning the Data

The first pivotal point towards good ML models are data collection and entry, two steps that define the outcome of the recommender system, but often remain unreflected or even neglected [9, 30]. In most scientific experiments, the collection of data is controlled and planned beforehand, whereas in the case of museum collections, data has already been collected - in some cases, centuries prior. We call this approach *reverse collecting*, as we need to look back in the timeline to understand how the collection was formed.

The creation of a useful dataset for the recommender and its users requires questioning the data and investigating how it became part of the collection, and under what circumstances it has been entered to improve the quality of the outcome and its accuracy. Over the last decades, museums have been prompted to critically address their "history of elitism and exclusion" [31, p. 7] causing issues, such as bias, racism, and inequalities to imprint into their collections. The ML community is just slowly picking up pace in considering ethical and fair applications; a practice that led to generalisations, misuse of terminology, and decisions that cause a *downstream harm* [10], or data being considered ethical just based on their availability [30]. On the other hand, computational methods can help museums to create new knowledge, around objects and beyond, supporting a "meaning making that engages affordances unique to data" [32]. This meaning making has to be made with careful consideration, being aware that the quantifiable processes of ML do not necessarily lead to a true interpretation of the collection. Using ML can therefore lead to fallacies, such as the implications of discovering the *ground-truth* of a collection, or technologies being impartial, ironing out all forms of bias inherently inscribed into the data. ML techniques will mean that institutions still have to face the troublesome and challenging parts of their collection [29], whilst ML practitioners need to trace back the evolution of the dataset, documenting the findings, i.e. as proposed by [33] in form of datasheets to enhance reproducibility and openness, acknowledging that if a recommender system returns satisfying results in one area of application, it cannot be taken for granted to work for another field.

Defining Target Audiences and Purpose

Most commercial data science models define their target audience in the first step of the development process [34]. Our recommender system, however, is aimed at exploring collections and creating pathways through an abundance of information through facilitated interaction. Hence, building a model that suits a certain customer group is not our highest priority, and we therefore rather define the target audience according to the collection data we have available and where it makes sense to include it in the pipeline. This approach mitigates against *data cosmetics*, the attempt to tailor and manipulate data to maximise profit whilst trying to suppress unwanted patterns or information. Target groups include museum professionals, researchers, and museum visitors. Assigned audiences are not mutually exclusive, but have different needs in terms of their information seeking behaviour [35] to be considered when building the recommender, regarding interface functionality and the overall design of the application. A web-based recommender system enables users to break the spell of the museum's authoritative voice and the fictitiously created neutrality, through facilitating outside the search box content interaction, acting as "contextualizing devices" [36, p. 236]. Developing audience-centred systems means further to rethink the, often divergent, understanding of data by professionals and non-expert visitors. Creating and trialling the recommender with direct input of future users through early pilots not just caters to the needs of the target audience, but also enables the system to provide much sought-after "personalized entry points that speak to people's individual needs" [37, p. 35] rather than an institutional one system fits all approach.

Analysing and Engineering

Rarely can data be used as input into models without first transforming the data into a usable state, engineering additional features or alternative representations, or both.

Additionally, steps are often taken to remove missing values and reduce noise, all of which have implications downstream.

Feature engineering, a method of transforming raw data into descriptive and usable features for modelling, presents challenges and complexities in this context. The process can be prescriptive to the data collected, but there exist common strategies that can be applied to the museum collection data. For example, metadata associated with items are often textual data which allows for natural language processing techniques to be applied, such as TF-IDF or WordtoVec [38].

However, missing values in some of these fields - namely description and title - can mean that items in the collection have to be removed, leading to the same problem as previously discussed; creating a lack of diversity in the dataset. In some cases, artworks can be more subjective - perhaps the artist has omitted a description to encourage the viewer to interpret the work in their way, this would be flagged as a missing value and could be lost, but it is a feature of the item itself.

Often, images can form one of the components of a collection dataset - these are digital photographics taken as part of the recording of items in the collection. Similar to metadata, there are established techniques for handling images in a feature engineering pipeline. Considerations and precautions should be taken when working with images to ensure that each item is included where possible, for example, the quality and age of the photographs could introduce complexities in the handling of the images. These nuances make feature engineering in this context challenging and ultimately rely on data being in a consistent format and of high quality, with descriptive fields included in the dataset.

Recommending

As much as all former steps influence the outcome of the recommendations served, so do the algorithms used in the system architecture. Thus, this step needs careful consideration, reflection, and awareness about the power and limitations of ML techniques. To create a personalised experience, recommender systems can use different data for various types of recommendation techniques.

The two overarching approaches used to serve recommendations are either prediction or ranking, with the common goal of delivering outcomes to users containing *(i) relevant objects*, that are *(ii) novel*, with a *(iii) serendipitous effect*, rather than recommending the obvious, and a *(iv) diverse range* of served recommendations [39].

The means to reach these goals further depend on what data has been chosen, or is available, to be used for the system. Whereas content-based systems use metadata of objects in the collection, such as artist names, descriptions, and tags, to serve recommendations based on a user's rating, collaborative filtering methods require the input of many users to function satisfactorily. The system faces a *cold start problem*, where little user interaction leads to statistical shortfalls of the algorithms, making accurate predictions impossible. A technique of interest in regard to expert curations in the museum field are knowledge-based recommender engines, requiring domain knowledge and a higher search specificity than explorative modes, such as knowledge-engineering and mapping, but enable feature-driven retrieval according to the user's needs [40]. A combination of two or more techniques is called a hybrid system and enables the recommender to use two or more models combined to usually enhance accuracy, and overall user-satisfaction. Although it sounds controversial to not automatically opt for a hybrid approach, it is to bear in mind that a combination of multiple ML models prerequisites the data required to power it, and factors, such as scalability and affordability play a considerable role.

Using and Evaluating the Data

Recommendations served by the engine can be evaluated with statistical methods observing properties of the systems, such as accuracy and model performance, in offline experiments and in-the-wild user studies [41]. In the case of a museum application, where knowledge production and discovery are in the foreground, the subjective user experience might be a better overall indicator, and a combined approach, as used by [42] is advisable, as trade-offs, i.e. having less accuracy but a more diverse collection sample might still be overall favoured by users. User-centric methods evaluating a museum recommender system include the system itself, the perception of the system, the user experience, and the interaction, where all but the system itself are influenced by personal and situational characteristics.

4   Case Studies

Setting up the *MuseREC* system, we approached our partner institutions to use their collection data for our ML model. These data are not just heterogeneous in their nature, containing metadata, images, 3D models, and other formats, but they also differ in the way data is stored, processed, and exported. The following two case studies prompted us to reflect about the challenges we faced in this paper, as we realised that there is no *one-model-fits-all* approach, and using a recommender system in a museum requires careful consideration rather than using an existing dataset to test the model, a practice quite common in the ML field [10].

The case studies are divided into a short introduction about the institutions, then we present how the data was exported, followed by the implications and thoughts this means for a ML model.

4.1   A Local Council-Owned UK Institution

One of our partner institutions is a council-owned museum in the United Kingdom with a collection size of less than 50,000 objects. The first export included metadata stored in tabular format in a Microsoft Excel spreadsheet. During the analysis of the dataset, we encountered several issues with the exported data. We used the vendor's system's uniquely assigned *Internal Record Number (IRN)* as our unique identifier - a unique key to retrieve values in the data store - to calculate the maximum amount of rows in the file. Over 82% of entries in *Medium: Technique and Material* were missing, about 74% of the section *Main Title*, and 56% in *Creator's Name* had empty values. Overall, there was just one section without missing values in the dataset, *Object Name*, descriptions of techniques and the materiality of objects, i.e. painting, etching, or dress. Other issues we encountered include imposed database restrictions (a restriction to not enter more than, in this case, 256 characters into a cell) leading to descriptions of objects being cut off, duplicate entries, and like-for-like entries where the same information was used interchangeably in different columns.

Missing values and errors in museum datasets are common [43, 44] but the number of missing values witnessed in this case would have a detrimental effect on the diversity of recommendations. Whereas the exported XLS files can be swiftly converted into CSV to make them more convenient to analyse, tabular formats are error prone and can lead, in the worst case, to a loss of information. To address the problem of the missing characters in the object descriptions, we requested the whole set as an XML export, a format that is used to serialise data in a structured, interchangeable format, that is highly favoured over tabular for the purpose of ML applications and to set up a relational database.

We further identified that the use of various systems - reaching from accession registers, card indices, and object files to digital databases and professional collection management software - increases the likelihood of mistakes with every transition from one system to another, with a variety of risks involving human and technological factors. Main problems in case of this institution were underfunding, delegating tasks requiring expert knowledge to volunteers, and human errors, such as incorrectly transcribed information, duplicates and non-entries [45].

Image files had to be directly downloaded in bulk through a time-limited access to the vendor's data transfer system. This meant the images were not directly associated with their metadata, but linked to it via *Identifier*, a key holding values in the form of image file names. To match the metadata accordingly required us to first clean the dataset by dropping the objects without any associated images, then to match the metadata to the images. A normally straight forward process, we encountered extremely verbose image identifiers, with highly repetitive sequences, and multiple values associated with the same cell, making it more difficult to separate one from another. Having finalised this step, we parsed all data into a JSON file.

4.2   A National US Institution

Our second partner is an institution comprising several national museums, a zoo, and research centres, based in the United States of America. The institution holds a collection of about 150 million items, and can be described as universal. Access to the collection information is managed through a RESTful Application Programming Interface (API), which lets us retrieve the necessary data through querying the institution's collections management system directly. The Data Science team further granted us access to an extended data corpus via a JSON file dump.

Using an API is a straight-forward process, but it often requires at least some computational knowledge for smaller queries, and more extensive expertise to enable its full power. The institution's data is further accompanied by an extensive metadata model for stored objects. A downfall of API queries is their restriction by the options made available by the API's owner, i.e. our freedom to query the DB in whatever format. In this case, the possible queries are extensive and a lot of information is openly available. If an object contains media it is both defined through a Boolean operator (media: true/false) and retrievable through URI (Uniform Resource Identifier) in the form of a URL (Uniform Resource Locator) on the World Wide Web. The institution uses ML applications in their Data Science Lab to handle big data projects and to create knowledge and insights. Whereas usage is mainly focussed on projects concerning genomics and pattern analysis, it certainly has a knock-on effect in terms of openness towards the use of ML for other collections and in terms of access to equipment and knowledgeable staff in-house, let alone having established data standards and policies in place. Another point enabling us to use data for MuseREC is the institution's mass digitisation programme, aiming to document the full breadth of all collections digitally.

Though this is commendable, it posed another level of decision-making for us, as such large amounts of data will need to be restrained in some way as the diversity and complexity of having all collections in a recommender system would exceed current ML capabilities. The institution actively promotes the use of their data for educational, and scholarly purposes, and has currently around five million of objects digitised and available freely under Creative Commons Zero (CC0).

5   Discussion

Setting up a successful recommender system requires careful consideration of multiple facets, not just in relation to the ML model itself, but also about the data curation beforehand.

The institutions' histories are tightly interwoven with the fabric of the data held by them, and a blind ingestion of collection data into a recommender model can lead to errors and is prone to return unsatisfying results.

Our case studies show that the museums' collections have naturally grown over time with records getting passed through many hands, from curators to registrars, and other stakeholders. Such practices led to barely identifiable records, and a loss of information or unfindable objects, as successors could not make sense out of the records, decipher or retrieve them, leading to backlogs of various kinds, from data entry and data tidying to a feeling of disregard toward inconsistencies [46], leading to a vast amount of uncatalogued items since the early advent of computers in museums [47].

The data deficiencies transferred into collection management systems may be partially compensated by professional users holding the required knowledge to find a way to fill the gaps, a work-around not applicable to ML technologies. The use of ontologies and common vocabularies is advisable, as it makes data understandable independent from an institution's subjective practice, and authoritative interpretation.

Errors and inaccuracies do not solely occur at the point of data entry, but can further arise during the use of the database. These include data degradation, errors whilst moving data, and incorrect entries.

Further obstacles observed on the way to a functioning model are copyright, and licensing issues with media data. It is beneficial to have free-to-use images for a recommender engine, which are shareable and downloadable by users, and it is recommended to make the whole dataset, containing collection metadata and images, available for reasons of reproducibility and interoperability. Such open practice would not just facilitate the formation of data partnerships, but it would further allow to compensate shortfalls of collections through the ability to cross-train with datasets of other institutions to overcome missing values, bias, and a lack of diversity. Image licensing is not returning high profits in the UK [48], and more and more art museums decide to abolish their copyright restrictions [49], enabling a broader access and usage to the favour of scholarship, education, and engagement with collections.

Vendors as intermediaries can pose further restrictions on the shareability and usability of data, with licences and legacy agreements [50] often keeping the institution's own data locked away - even for their own use - whilst especially making smaller institutions inflexible and unable to keep up pace with technological evolutions.

6 Conclusion

Museums and the ML community can certainly benefit from each other, leveraging lessons learned from shortfalls of their own fields through learning from one another, where the convergence of new technologies and exchange of domain knowledge leads to fairer and safer applications in the future. A well-engineered and functioning system has the ability to facilitate collection exploration, and can be used to retrieve data that would either not be discoverable with traditional means or would not be necessarily associated with each other in classic curations, i.e. thematic or chronological.

To date, 46% of UK museums surveyed for the Digital Culture Report 2019 state a lack of skills/knowledge as a barrier to realising digital projects, a number that increased from 2013 [51, p. 9] due to computational methods becoming ever more complex and the handling of big data structures posing a problem to companies and businesses, amongst them museums [52]. Creating unified approaches and developing guidelines for ML in museums will help to include smaller institutions. Further, the development of easy plug-and-play systems that can be used with little technological knowledge will enhance user engagement and promoting research. Thus, museums aiming to use ML on a broad scale rather than in-house experiments, need to adhere to data standards recommended by ML communities and professional bodies of the museum world, exercise rigorous documentation, and practice good data-housekeeping.

This will keep institutions up with the pace of digital advancements, and strengthen their digital profiles, whilst enabling inter-museum systems and exchange of collection data for a common benefit.

References

1. Berry, D.M.: The post-digital. the new aesthetic and infrastructural aesthetics. In: Bühler, M. (ed.) No Internet, No Art, 2nd edn. Amsterdam: Onomatopee (2018)
2. ICOM: Museums, museum professionals and COVID-19', International Council of Museums (2020). https://icom.museum/wp-content/uploads/2020/05/Report-Museums-and-COVID-19.pdf. Accessed 30 June 2020
3. Gomez-Uribe, C.A., Hunt, N.: The Netflix recommender system: algorithms, business value, and innovation. ACM Trans. Manage. Inf. Syst. 6(4), 1–19 (2016). https://doi.org/10.1145/2843948

4. Jacobson, K., Murali, V., Newett, E., Whitman, B., Yon, R.: Music personalization at spotify. In: Proceedings of the 10th ACM Conference on Recommender Systems, Boston, Massachusetts USA, p. 373, September 2016,. https://doi.org/10.1145/2959100.2959120

5. Rastogi, R.: Machine learning @ Amazon. In: The 41st International ACM SIGIR Conference on Research & Development in Information Retrieval, Ann Arbor MI USA, pp. 1337–1338, June 2018. https://doi.org/10.1145/3209978.3210211

6. Smith, B., Linden, G.: Two decades of recommender systems at Amazon.com. IEEE Internet Comput. 21(3), 12–18 (2017). https://doi.org/10.1109/MIC.2017.72

7. Oumaima, S., Soulaimane, K., Omar, B.: Latest trends in recommender systems applied in the medical domain: a systematic review. In: Proceedings of the 3rd International Conference on Networking, Information Systems & Security, Marrakech Morocco, pp. 1–12, March 2020. https://doi.org/10.1145/3386723.3387860

8. The Royal Society, Machine Learning: The Power and Promise of Computers that Learn by Example (2017)

9. Jo, E.S., Gebru, T.: Lessons from archives: strategies for collecting sociocultural data in machine learning. In: Proceedings of the ACM FAT* 2020 Conference, Barcelona, Spain, pp. 306–316 (2020)

10. Suresh, H., Guttag, J.V.: A framework for understanding unintended consequences of machine learning, February 2020 [cs, stat]. http://arxiv.org/abs/1901.10002. Accessed 27 Oct 2020

11. Adomavicius, G., Tuzhilin, A.: Toward the next generation of recommender systems: a survey of the state-of-the-art and possible extensions. IEEE Trans. Knowl. Data Eng. 17(6), 734–749 (2005). https://doi.org/10.1109/TKDE.2005.99

12. Benouaret, I., Lenne, D.: Personalizing the museum experience through context-aware recommendations. In: 2015 IEEE International Conference on Systems, Man, and Cybernetics, pp. 743–748, October 2015. https://doi.org/10.1109/SMC.2015.139

13. Keller, I., Viennet, E.: Recommender systems for museums: evaluation on a real dataset. In: Proceedings of the Fifth Conference on Advances in Information Mining and Management, Brussels, pp. 65–71 (2015)

14. Kontiza, K., Loboda, O., Deladiennee, L., Castagnos, S., Naudet, Y.: A museum app to trigger users' reflection. In: CEUR Wokshop on Mobile Access to Cultural Heritage, p. 8 (2018)

15. Koukoulis, K., Koukopoulos, D., Tzortzi, K.: Connecting the museum to the city environment from the visitor's perspective. Appl. Comput. Inform. S2210832719301991 (2019). https://doi.org/10.1016/j.aci.2019.09.001

16. Loboda, O., Nyhan, J., Mahony, S., Romano, D.M., Terras, M.: Content-based recommender systems for heritage: developing a personalised museum tour. In: Proceedings of the 1st International 'Alan Turing' Conference on Decision Support and Recommender Systems (DSRS-Turing 2019), p. 7 (2019)

17. Rossi, S., Barile, F., Galdi, C., Russo, L.: Recommendation in museums: paths, sequences, and group satisfaction maximization. Multimed. Tools Appl. 76(24), 26031–26055 (2017). https://doi.org/10.1007/s11042-017-4869-5

18. Ruotsalo, T., et al.: SMARTMUSEUM: a mobile recommender system for the Web of Data. Journal of Web Semant. 20, 50–67 (2013). https://doi.org/10.1016/j.websem.2013.03.001

19. Albanese, M., d'Acierno, A., Moscato, V., Persia, F., Picariello, A.: A multimedia recommender system. ACM Trans. Internet Technol. 13(1), 1–32 (2013). https://doi.org/10.1145/2532640

20. Semeraro, G., Lops, P., De Gemmis, M., Musto, C., Narducci, F.: A folksonomy-based recommender system for personalized access to digital artworks. J. Comput. Cult. Herit. 5(3), 1–22 (2012). https://doi.org/10.1145/2362402.2362405

21. Wang, Y., Stash, N., Aroyo, L., Gorgels, P., Rutledge, L., Schreiber, G.: Recommendations based on semantically enriched museum collections. J. Web Semant. **6**(4), 283–290 (2008). https://doi.org/10.1016/j.websem.2008.09.002

22. Colace, F., De Santo, M., Lombardi, M., Santaniello, D.: CHARS: a cultural heritage adaptive recommender system. In: Proceedings of the 1st ACM International Workshop on Technology Enablers and Innovative Applications for Smart Cities and Communities – TESCA 2019, New York, NY, USA, pp. 58–61 (2019). https://doi.org/10.1145/3364544.3364830.

23. Hashemi, S.H., Kamps, J.: Exploiting behavioral user models for point of interest recommendation in smart museums. New Rev. Hypermedia Multimed. **24**(3), 228–261 (2018). https://doi.org/10.1080/13614568.2018.1525436

24. Su, X., Sperlì, G., Moscato, V., Picariello, A., Esposito, C., Choi, C.: An edge intelligence empowered recommender system enabling cultural heritage applications. IEEE Trans. Industr. Inf. **15**(7), 4266–4275 (2019). https://doi.org/10.1109/TII.2019.2908056

25. Pavlidis, G.: Recommender systems, cultural heritage applications, and the way forward. J. Cult. Heritage **35**, 183–196 (2019). https://doi.org/10.1016/j.culher.2018.06.003

26. Zhang, S., Yao, L., Sun, A., Tay, Y.: Deep learning based recommender system: a survey and new perspectives. ACM Comput. Surv. **52**(1), 38 (2019)

27. Rajaraman, A., Ullman, J.D.: Mining of Massive Datasets. Cambridge University Press, New York (2011)

28. Wilkinson, M.D., et al.: The FAIR guiding principles for scientific data management and stewardship. Sci Data **3**(1), 160018 (2016). https://doi.org/10.1038/sdata.2016.18

29. Anderson, S.: Some provocations on the digital future of museums. In: Winesmith, K., Anderson, S. (eds.) The Digital Future of Museums: Conversations and Provocations, 1st edn., Routledge, pp. 10–25 (2020)

30. Boyd, D., Crawford, K.: Critical questions for big data: provocations for a cultural, technological, and scholarly phenomenon. Inf. Commun. Soc. **15**(5), 662–679 (2012). https://doi.org/10.1080/1369118X.2012.678878

31. Taylor, J.K.: The Art Museum Redefined: Power, Opportunity, and Community Engagement. Palgrave Macmillan, Cham (2020)

32. Padilla, T.: On a Collections as Data Imperative. UC Santa Barbara (2017). https://escholarship.org/uc/item/9881c8sv

33. Gebru, T., et al.: Datasheets for Datasets. arXiv:1803.09010 [cs], March 2020. Accessed 17 Nov 2020

34. Fayyad, U., Piatetsky-Shapiro, G., Smyth, P.: Knowledge discovery and data mining: towards a unifying framework. In: Proceedings of the Second International Conference on Knowledge Discovery and Data Mining, Portland, Oregon, pp. 82–88 (1996)

35. Skov, M., Ingwersen, P.: Exploring information seeking behaviour in a digital museum context. In: Proceedings of the second international symposium on Information interaction in context - IIiX 2008, London, United Kingdom, p. 110 (2008). https://doi.org/10.1145/1414694.1414719.

36. Murray, J.H.: Hamlet on the Holodeck. The Future of Narrative in Cyberspace. The Free Press, New York (1997)

37. Simon, N.: The Participatory Museum. Santa Cruz, CA: Museum 20 (2010)

38. Mikolov, T., Chen, K., Corrado, G., Dean, J.: Efficient estimation of word representations in vector space. arXiv:1301.3781 [cs], September 2013. Accessed 28 Nov 2020

39. Aggarwal, C.C.: Recommender Systems: The Textbook, 1st edn. Springer, New York (2016). https://doi.org/10.1007/978-3-319-29659-3

40. Burke, R.: Hybrid recommender systems: survey and experiments. User Model. User Adap. Inter. **12**, 331–370 (2002)

41. Gunawardana, A., Shani, G.: Evaluating recommender systems. In: Ricci, F., Rokach, L., Shapira, B. (eds.) Recommender Systems Handbook, pp. 265–308. Springer, Boston, MA (2015). https://doi.org/10.1007/978-1-4899-7637-6_8

42. Knijnenburg, B.P., Willemsen, M.C., Gantner, Z., Soncu, H., Newell, C.: Explaining the user experience of recommender systems. User Model User Adap Inter **22**(4–5), 441–504 (2012). https://doi.org/10.1007/s11257-011-9118-4

43. Green, H.E., Courtney, A.: Beyond the scanned image: a needs assessment of scholarly users of digital collections. CRL **76**(5), 690–707 (2015). https://doi.org/10.5860/crl.76.5.690

44. Nekola, J.C., Hutchins, B.T., Schofield, A., Najev, B., Perez, K.E.: Caveat consumptor notitia museo: let the museum data user beware. Glob. Ecol. Biogeogr. **00**, 1–13 (2019). https://doi.org/10.1111/geb.12995

45. Mitchell, E.S.: "Believe Me, I Remain...". The Mary Greg Collection at Manchester City Galleries. Manchester Metropolitan University, Manchester, UK (2018)

46. Shepherd, R.: Museum documentation: a hidden problem or something to shout about?. RegistrarTrek: The Next Generation (2014). http://world.museumsprojekte.de/?p=4023. Accessed 08 Nov 2020

47. Ellin, E.: Museums and the computer: an appraisal of new potentials. Comput. Humanit. **4**(1), 25–30 (1969)

48. Grosvenor, B.: How abolishing museum image fees could boost audiences. In: The Art Newspaper (2018). http://www.theartnewspaper.com/blog/how-abolishing-museum-image-fees-could-boost-audiences. Accessed 24 Nov 2020

49. Huang, P.H.: Managing digital image licensing services in art history museums. J. Arts Manage. Law Soc. **50**(4–5), 220–233 (2020)

50. Padilla, T.G.: Collections as data: implications for enclosure. C&RL News **79**(6), 296 (2018). https://doi.org/10.5860/crln.79.6.296

51. Bandopadhyay, S.: Digital Culture 2019: Museums, Nesta & Arts Council England (2020). https://media.nesta.org.uk/documents/DC2019-Museums-factsheet.pdf. Accessed 13 Nov 2020

52. Finnis, J., Kennedy, A.: The Digital Transformation Agenda and GLAMs. A Quick Scan Report for Europeana', Culture24, July 2020

Trails of Walking - Ways of Talking: The Museum Experience Through Social Meaning Mapping

Dimitra Christidou[1]([✉]) [iD] and Luise Reitstätter[2] [iD]

[1] Department of Computer Science, Norwegian University of Science and Technology, Trondheim, Norway
dimitra.christidou@ntnu.no
[2] Department of Art History, University of Vienna, Vienna, Austria

Abstract. This paper discusses the digital method Social Meaning Mapping (SMM) and its affordances to capture aspects of the museum visit. SMM, embedded in the Visitracker tablet-app, enables the annotation of visitors' movement and interactions in a particular gallery room post-visit. During a researcher-led session, visitors handle the tablet and annotate their experience on its screen while sharing their thoughts aloud. Both visitors' annotations and their voices are being recorded through the app. Each SMM can be accessed through Visitracker's portal as a video which re-creates visitors' 'trails of walking' (what they mark) and their 'ways of talking' (what they say) in synchronization. In this paper, we draw upon data collected at the Austrian Gallery Belvedere in Vienna to argue that SMM created by visitors can complement tracking and timing (T&T) data collected by researchers, allowing for a more holistic understanding of the museum experience. The analysis shows that SMM captures visitors' experiences in a multimodal way, both visual and verbal, enabling them to foreground aspects of their personal experience, spatial practices, co-experience and social realms of their visit.

Keywords: Informal learning · Visitor studies · Multimodal data · Collaborative mapping

1 Introduction

Museum professionals and researchers have been conducting tracking and timing studies (T&T) since the early 1930s in order to understand the behavior of museum visitors and inform the design of existing and future exhibitions. In T&T studies unobtrusive observations of visitors are carried out, with their movement, dwell time and other behavioral data being timed and tracked on printed copies of the museum's floor plan [1–4].

Over the past four decades, varied information and mobile sensing technologies such as Global Positioning System (GPS), Radio Frequency Identification (RFID), iBeacon and Bluetooth were incorporated in audience research methodologies. These technologies can track visitors as they move through an exhibition or site without the active involvement of a researcher [5, 6]. More recently, with Bring your Own Device

© Springer Nature Switzerland AG 2021
M. Shehade and T. Stylianou-Lambert (Eds.): RISE IMET 2021, CCIS 1432, pp. 32–46, 2021.
https://doi.org/10.1007/978-3-030-83647-4_3

approaches (BYOD), devices such as visitors' mobile phones can be used to install applications offered by museums that also allow the collection of data on visitors' movement and interaction with the exhibits. Others have also utilized mobile eye tracking technologies in the museum to collect and assess detailed accounts of visitors' viewing patterns [7–9]. While we acknowledge that knowing precisely where visitors are and what they look at is useful when designing exhibitions and interpretive resources, it does not tell us a lot about who our visitors are and how they subjectively responded to the displayed collections and why.

In order to learn more about the specifics of each museum visit from visitors' perspective, a tablet-based app called Visitracker was designed [10]. The app allows the data collection through three methods: T&T, survey and Social Meaning Mapping (SMM). SMM uses a digital copy of the floor plan along with a paint toolbox, which visitors use to recount their experience in the room verbally and visually by marking it on the digital floor plan [11]. The app records both the visual markings drawn on the screen and visitors' conversations unfolding during this activity.

In this paper, we draw upon data collected at the Austrian Gallery Belvedere in Vienna (N = 152) to argue that SMM provides us with a way of capturing aspects of their experience that complement the data researchers collect through T&T. In what follows, we outline the theoretical underpinnings of the SMM method and its affordances and discuss its use through a collaborative study conducted in late 2018. Through a representative case from our dataset, we exemplify the four layers of information that became visible and audible during SMM – the individual experience, spatial practices, co-experience and social realms. These layers render visible and audible more diverse aspects of the museum, offering new multimodal insights into the visualization of the museum visit and enriching existing research methodologies.

2   Social Meaning Mapping

Similar to T&T methods, SMM uses the image of the museum floor plan to record aspects of the museum visit. Whereas T&T takes place while visitors are in the room, SMM is used after the visit. During a researcher-led session, visitors in groups up to four are prompted to handle the tablet themselves and use this spatial representation along with a paint toolbox to share their movement ('trails of walking') and their own reflections as they recount their embodied experience in the museum space ('ways of talking') (Fig. 1a). The app records both visitors' trails of walking and ways of talking. The process of visitors' map making is rendered in the format of a video which allows its synchronized re-creation (Fig. 1b). By visualizing visitors' 'trails of walking' along with their 'ways of talking', each video functions as a representation of visitors' embodied experience in the specific room [12].

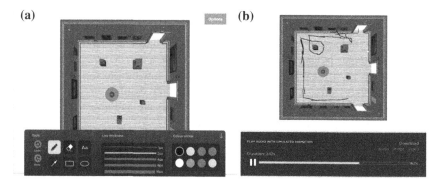

Fig. 1. (a) The SMM interface; (b) The SMM video on the Visitracker portal.

Similar to the narrative inquiry method [13], SMM draws upon audiovisual narration to capture aspects of visitors' personal (what the individual experiences) as well as social experiences (the individual interacting with others). As visitors collaborate during map making on the digital representation of the room, they are prompted to reimagine themselves in the room and share, re-create, negotiate and co-construct with their co-visitors and the researcher their experience in this room ('trails of walking'). While doing so, they also reflect on the personal and social memories of 'being' in the specific room ('ways of talking').

SMM was designed as a research method that is responsive to visitors' own agendas and experiences [14, 15]. By drawing upon visual data (both the digital floor plan and the drawing activity), SMM empowers visitors' agency in the shaping of their experience and facilitates their reflections without depending heavily on language. At the same time, as the floor plan depicts not only the room but also the artworks on display, it allows visitors to refer to these by marking them out, without requiring them to recall the names of the artists and the artworks.

Asking visitors to offer their input during SMM acknowledges their agency in meaning making and transforms them from map users into map-makers [12]. As visitors map their own experience on the official design of the museum (the floor plan and the collection), their engagement with SMM can be seen as a form of 'counter mapping' [16]; that is, making and sharing maps that rewrite official versions and offer spatial form of counter narrative that entails very personal versions of embodiment of the lived space. While being made, this counter mapping is also being shared with their co-visitors and the researcher [17], allowing the latter to return to features of the map and prompt visitors to expand on their 'trails of walking' and 'ways of talking'.

3   The Belvedere Visitracker Study

The Belvedere Visitracker study builds upon a pilot study conducted in 2017 at the National Museum of Art, Architecture and Design in Oslo, Norway, in which SMM was used for the first time. The objective of this pilot study was to test SMM and provide first insights into which aspects of the museum visit are rendered visible and audible when using this method. Aspects of visitors' personal context in relation to the physical context were marked visually and elaborated verbally, while aspects of their social context were rendered visible through their 'trails of walking'. Visitors tended to mark one trail of walking and finish each other's sentences when their visit was perceived as a joint social experience by them [11]. As the sample was small (9 groups of visitors), studies with a larger and more diverse sample were needed.

In designing the Belvedere Visitracker study, we wished to include a larger sample of visitors and explore the specific research question of how visitors in groups of two experienced the recently redisplayed collection in the Secession room at the Upper Belvedere in Vienna, Austria. The room, located on the first floor, showcases 13 paintings and three sculptures from around 1900, which represent the artistic work of the avant-garde movement Secession formed by Austrian painters, graphic artists, sculptors and architects who opposed traditionalism in style and sought international exchange (Fig. 2).

Fig. 2. The Secession room, Upper Belvedere.

3.1 Methods and Data Collection

Data collection took place during a week (Monday-Sunday) in late September 2018. Each of the five team members carried a tablet with the Visitracker app installed on it, a university identification card, a clipboard with a pen and consent forms in English and German. Each researcher approached visitors in dyads at the museum staircase and, after introducing herself, the project's objectives and the data collection stages, invited them to participate in the study. If the visitors agreed and were older than 18 years, they were handed the consent form to read and sign.

The data collection occurred in three consecutive stages, with a different method used during each stage: (1) T&T at the Secession room, (2) a short survey consisting of twelve questions on visitors' sociodemographic background and visiting practices (i.e., gender, age, nationality, country of residence, frequency of visiting museums, reasons for visiting the Belvedere), and (3) a SMM created by each pair. Both stage 2 and 3 took place immediately after visitors exited the Secession room. A near-by room reserved for small events called Oktogon was used in stages 2 and 3, allowing visitors to sit comfortably and share their reflections in a more private setting (Fig. 3). During the first two stages, the researchers registered the data whereas visitors handled the tablet on their own in the third stage. During SMM, they were only minimally instructed by the researcher on how to use the tool and prompted at times to elaborate. Once finished with their SMM, visitors were offered a thank-you card with the contact details of the two principal investigators, and a small gift donated by the museum. Upon visitors exiting Oktogon, each researcher filed a protocol reporting any issues encountered (i.e., technical, linguistic) and her own reflections on the general circulation in the room, the pair's interaction and other relevant information. Data collection for all three stages lasted on average 25 minutes.

We recruited 76 pairs of visitors (N = 152); 21 female, 8 male and forty-seven pairs of mixed gender. Based on the data collected through the survey in stage 2, our sample consisted of thirty-one nationalities, with almost all visitors (97%) coming to Vienna as part of a trip and visiting the Belvedere for the first time (90%), revealing that our sample consisted mainly of international tourists. This demographic complies with the dataset collected through the museum's ticketing system in 2018, allowing us to conclude that our sample was representative of the visitors to the Upper Belvedere. Acknowledging the international background of our sample and the linguistic abilities of the research team, visitors were given the opportunity to speak during SMM in the following languages: English, German, Danish, Swedish, Italian, French, and Japanese. Using a language they felt comfortable communicating in aimed at empowering the inclusion of visitors' voices in our study. To our knowledge, this is a study among few using multiple languages in data collection.

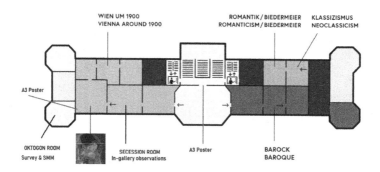

Fig. 3. The first floor of the Upper Belvedere.

3.2   Data Analysis

The dataset was accessed through Visitracker's online portal. We first transcribed the audio recorded for each SMM; when in a different language, we translated it into English. Although we could not identify our participants from the data collected, visitors often called each other by their names during the SMM. All such instances were altered to preserve anonymity. We then created a multimodal transcript for each SMM, with visitors' talk on the left side and screenshots from the accompanying marking activity on the right side. We chose to transcribe each SMM in such a way to illustrate *how* visitors communicated *and* represented meaning through their talk and sign making activities on the digital canvas [18].

We conducted inductive analysis, coding themes emerging from the dataset following Grounded Theory [19] and systematically marking their occurrence with the help of the NVivo 12 qualitative data analysis software. Codes such 'previous experience', 'previous knowledge', 'resource used', 'personal relevance' emerged from the analysis. To narrow down our themes, we grouped these codes into four thematic units that have been also foregrounded in previous research on visitors' experiences in museums. These thematic units are both grounded in the data as well as theoretically driven.

1. **Individual experience**: instances in which visitors refer to their individual perspectives on and expectations of their museum visit – what Doering & Pekarik [20] refer to as 'entrance narratives'. Here, we coded instances in which visitors referred to their personal expectations, experiences, emotions and memories related to the artworks and the museum visit and space.
2. **Spatial practices**: including references to visitors' ways of experiencing the space, their engagement with it and their navigation in it, including visiting practices [21, 22].
3. **Co-experience**: instances when visitors referred to interactions they shared and performed with a member of their own group [23, 24] and
4. **Social realms**: instances when visitors referred to interactions in relation to other groups of people and visiting conditions [23, 25, 26].

This methodological approach acknowledges the concept of "theoretical sensitivity" in Grounded Theory, for which the prior knowledge of the researcher is consciously used in the empirical exploration of the material [19].

4   Trails of Walking - Ways of Talking: A Case Study

In this section, we exemplify how these themes are grounded in our data by drawing upon one case study (nr. 69) involving a pair of female visitors (W and Wb) (Table 1). Based on the T&T data collected during stage 1, they spent fifteen minutes in the gallery room and their visit was highly collaborative, with both visitors staying in close proximity and interacting with each other. During the survey in stage 2, they mentioned that one of them was living in Prague and the other one was doing an internship in Vienna, which was an opportunity for them to meet there and visit, among others, the Upper Belvedere. They also mentioned that they often travel together and that they like to visit museums and other cultural institutions. Their experience of visiting museums became foregrounded also during the SMM in stage 3 when referring for example to their encounter with Mona Lisa (turns-in-talk 54–60).

Table 1. Transcript of case study nr. 69

Turn-in-talk	Ways of talking	Trails of walking
01	W: So, went around and we were discussing	
02	Wb: That we liked, that one [Early Spring]	
03	W: Yeah, we liked this one, I didn't know. I wasn't familiar with the artist. This one is kind of sad [Lost]	
04	Wb: Yeah, that one we thought it was really sad	
05	W: I mean he is pretty lonely (Wb and W laugh)	
06	Wb: We thought that this was beautiful [Emotion] but it was really beautiful	
07	W: This one also, I liked the way, it wasn't familiar	
08	I: Familiar?	
09	W: No, I wasn't familiar with the artist either but it's nice, I like the style and then of course, Van Gogh [Plain of Auvers] we were talking about	

10	Wb: We were talking about him. Never seen this one of course, about his life also (both laugh) I was kind of Oh yeah, I always forget that he killed himself (all laugh)	
11	I: Were you able to tell from that painting? Probably not	
12	W: No, probably not. Although it is kind of little sad cause it is, I mean it's lonely	
13	Wb: Yeah, it is compared to the other one	
14	W: It's lonely, cause it is, it is pretty but you are looking into the field and there is no one there. It is little bit	
15	Wb: Yeah, because it was one of the last ones, no? it was, yeah	
16	W: It said, yeah, his last one. And then, we went here we were discussing	
17	Wb: That was fun that one	
18	I: About?	
19	W: No, we were talking about yeah. We were trying to figure out where the actual Scream was, and there is four of them apparently. I didn't remember that either	
20	Wb: So, we opened Google for that (both laugh)	
21	I: Oh yeah you opened	

22	W: Yeah, we were googling things on our phone, and we didn't really look at this one [Adolescentia] cause we went straight to the Klimt [Judith]	
23	Wb: Yeah, we stopped there for a while	
24	W: We were looking and reading and	
25	Wb: Yeah, we commented how you can see the difference from the ones in the previous room and then this one	
26	I: In the room you walked in before	
27	Wb: Yes, they were	
28	W: The ones we saw earlier on, some early works yeah and I mean his style has changed	
[...]	[....] [transcript continued]	
51	I: I was going to ask you if it felt different the impression from the photograph or a reproduction when you see the original thing	
52	W: Yeah, I mean I am pretty sure I have seen this in a photograph before	
53	Wb: Yeah, in person that one looks super real	

54	W: It was very nice, and you know that gold kind of shimmers in the light, and it looks nice, it is a lot more impressive in person, yeah. I mean they already look good in the photos but when you see them in person (laughs) We were saying it is not like the Mona Lisa, when you go and you are disappointed (laughs)	
55	I: Were you disappointed by the Mona Lisa?	
56	W: Yeah, I mean everyone is disappointed and then also you are getting pushed by a hundred other tourists	
57	Wb: Yeah, it is like the situation	
58	W: Taking photos, it is not a good situation, yeah	
59	I: The environment kind of shapes the way you look at and enjoy art	
60	W: If there are too many people, too crowded, so here is perfect cause there is not too many, it is quieter	

5 Findings

The pair engaged with SMM for five and half minutes. From the transcript, we see that W is leading both the marking of the 'trail of walking' and the sharing of her 'ways of talking'. Nonetheless, W used the pronoun 'we' in 35 instances, signaling that she is depicting and discussing their collective experience of the room. In the rest of instances in which the personal pronoun "I" was used by W, these reflected upon her prior knowledge – what she knew about the artists, personal evaluation of the artworks, and expectations on the exhibition visit, and not the experience on site. During the whole duration of their SMM, Wb also contributed with her own comments, either elaborating upon or prompting further the reflections shared by W.

Similar to the findings of the 2017 pilot study [11], the highly collaborative experience of the Secession room was also manifested through the single trail line drawn for both visitors. In this particular example, the pair did not elaborate on their 'trail of walking' visually as much as they did verbally. Nonetheless, their 'trail of walking' (Fig. 4a) was a very accurate representation of their movement in the room when contrasted to the movement map created through T&T (Fig. 4b).

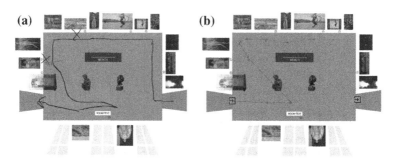

Fig. 4. (a) The SMM created by the pair; (b) the movement map created through T&T.

In turn 03, W shared that she "liked this one, I didn't know. I wasn't familiar with the artist". A few lines below (turn 07), she mentioned again that she liked a painting without knowing its artist. This hints perhaps at her linking her likeness of an artwork to knowing the artist who created it. This interpretation is supported by other turns in which prior knowledge of the artist often informed the pair's interactions with the artworks ("of course, Van Gogh"). In the case of Munch's painting, it triggered the pair to wonder about another famous painting by him ("we were trying to figure out where the actual Scream was"), a question to which they found the answer after browsing the internet on their phones ("and there are four of them apparently. I didn't remember that either. We were googling things on our phone").

In the rest of the turns in talk, W described the artworks in terms of emotional attributions (i.e., "this one is kind of sad", "although it is kind of a little sad cause it is, I mean it's lonely"). At times, the museum's interpretational resources seemed to elicit the pair's prior knowledge. For example, the text accompanying van Gogh's artwork introduces the painting as 'an unusually wide landscape painted shortly before van Gogh's suicide', a piece of information that made the pair look closer, contrasting this information to the painting's visual characteristics. Both visitors elaborated on their embodied encounter with the painting by linking the label's suicide reference to the emotions the painting triggered ("it's lonely, cause it is it is pretty but you are looking into the field and there is no one there", turn 14; "yeah, because it was one of the last ones, no? it was, yeah", turn 15).

In designing SMM, we wished to use the tool to capture visitors' embodied experience in the specific room [12]. As it can be seen in the transcript, visitors mentioned several of the embodied practices they performed while in the room. These included (a) stopping at certain artworks ("yeah, we stopped there for a while", turn 23), (b) skipping artworks in order to explore others in depth ("and we didn't really look at this one [Adolescentia] cause we went straight to the Klimt [Judith]", turn 22), and (c) the combined activities of looking at art and reading labels ("we were looking and reading", turn 24).

Especially in turn 22, W named the artist which is considered a part of visitors' personal and co-experience context. Upon looking at Klimt's painting, the pair shared that they discussed the differences between the painting in this room ("Judith") and the ones they encountered earlier during their museum visit ("we commented how you can see the difference from the ones in the previous room and then this one", turn 25). This comparison allowed the pair to conclude that "his style has changed" (turn 28). They also discussed the embodied experience of encountering the actual painting compared to looking at it in a photograph ("in person that one looks super real", turn 53) as their visit to the Secession room allowed them to notice "that gold kind of shimmers in the light, and it looks nice, it is a lot more impressive in person, yeah. I mean they already look good in the photos but when you see them in person" (turn 54).

Interestingly, the social realm of their visit came into play both imaginatively as well as on site when the pair started discussing their personal encounter with "Judith" at the Belvedere in comparison to the "Mona Lisa" at the Louvre ("we were saying it is not like the Mona Lisa, when you go and you are disappointed", turn 54). In this reflection, both visitors introduced their past into the present by comparing a previous encounter with a famous artwork to their encounter with Klimt's "Judith" in terms of how the social realm affected their experiences. They both mentioned that they preferred encountering paintings when there are not many people sharing the same space with them, as crowds seem to be obstructing their experience ("pushed by a hundred other tourists taking photos", turn 56). Here, the embodied experience of being at another museum came into contrast with the embodied experience of being at the Secession room.

6 Conclusions

There has been strong criticism on the validity of data collected through T&T based on researchers' observations and interpretations of what visitors did and what they looked at [27, 28]. The findings of the study presented here exemplify how SMM can complement third person observations conducted through T&T by introducing visitors' own reflections on their experience, the space, the interpretive resources that became, or not, relevant during their visit to the Secession room.

In our given example, the pair represented their visit as a sequential line. Our analysis did not focus on the interactions visitors had with each artwork displayed in the room; rather, we collected, represented and analyzed the museum experience as a trail since "the unit of analysis is not a work of art [...] it is the collection of the works of art that a person encounters in a museum visit" [29, p.35]. While marking their 'trail of walking', several aspects related to their personal and social context were shared through their 'ways of talking', including interactions unfolding between them and others in the same room. Their map making was highly collaborative, with each finishing the other's sentences and sharing the same reflections on the artworks, the artists and their techniques. There were many layers of information revealed during the SMM, with visitors discussing other experiences they had in different museums in the world, their previous and extended knowledge of art and artists, and their interpretations being based on the artworks' characteristics or the emotions emerging when looking at them.

Despite the richness of the dataset we collected through SMM, the design features of SMM imposed a number of restrictions and challenges. For example, we decided that each pair was assigned to one researcher taking care of all three study stages for reasons of clarity and trust. As the data collection for all stages lasted on average thirty minutes (but in some cases even much longer as the researcher was waiting for visitors to show up in the Secession room), it imposed demands on the workforce used during the study both in terms of time and physical involvement. Moreover, as we collected data in one gallery room, we avoided having more than two researchers present at the same time. This decision restricted the number of pairs we could recruit per day. When it comes to using SMM, visitors found sometimes hard to identify which room was represented in the digital floor plan, while the small size of the tablet's screen restricted both visitors from map-making simultaneously. This could impact the degree and the ways in which visitors collaborated, or not, during SMM.

Nonetheless, the multiple layers of information we collected through T&T and SMM can inform the arrangement of the collection and the design of interpretive resources, including the label text, audio guide, and museum brochures. By looking at the pattern of movement of all visitors, the curatorial team can easily identify areas and artworks which visitors approach or avoid. In this case, the two sculptures positioned in the middle of the room seem to be neglected by visitors. At the same time, most of the artworks that visitors talked about during their SMM seemed to be those displayed at the top left corner of the room. Displaying popular artworks in the same space partly led to instances of crowding, which has been mentioned during SMM as a factor affecting negatively visitors' art experience. Combining art-historical knowledge and empirical evidence on visitors' responses to specific artworks and gallery settings as provided through SMM can inform the development of curatorial practices. It could even be possible to integrate SMM in a procedural and participatory exhibition development offering visitors to embed visual and verbal responses to different pro-totyped exhibition constellations.

Our focus in this paper was to present SMM as a participatory method and its capacity to facilitate, evoke as well as collect visitors' collaborative and personal reflections on the recent visit to a gallery room as a temporally and spatially embodied activity. Contrary to place-based digital technologies that do not take into consideration the social nature of the museum visit [30, 31], SMM allows visitors to work collab-oratively and "write themselves" on the map by "seeing themselves" in the room represented in the digital floor plan [12]. Thus, SMM collects and represents their experience by mobilizing both their memories about their overall experience and their embodied memories about being in the room. Aspects of embodiment contribute to a better understanding of the experience they had and allows multiple layers of infor-mation to emerge in relation to the physical, social and personal context of their visit. More research is needed to explore the potential of using SMM as an interview method in different museums and in more than one rooms, foregrounding how the design of the museum space and the juxtaposition of the collections informs visitors' experience and meaning making.

Acknowledgements. We would like to thank the Austrian Gallery Belvedere, the generous visitors participating and the following researchers: Karolin Galter, Anna Miscenà, and Jan Mikuni who participated in data collection, and Anna Fekete, Mark Elias Napadenksi, Rebekah Rodriguez, Lena Syen, Clara Swaboda, Daniel Teibrich, and Sophie Wratzfeld who assisted in data preparation. Data collection and research was partially supported by the Cultural Heritage Mediascapes: Innovation in Knowledge and Mediation Practices project at University of Oslo, Norway. The Visitracker app was developed by EngageLab at the Faculty of Education, University of Oslo.

References

1. Bitgood, S.: An analysis of visitor circulation: movement patterns and the general value principle. Curator **49**(4), 463–475 (2006)
2. Chiozzi, G., Andreotti, L.: Behavior vs. time: understanding how visitors utilize the Milan natural history museum. Curator Museum J. **44**, 153–165 (2001)
3. Serrell, B.: The aggregation of tracking-and-timing visitor-use data of museum exhibitions for benchmarks of "thorough use." Visitor Stud. **23**(1), 1–17 (2020). https://doi.org/10.1080/10645578.2020.1750830
4. Yalowitz, S., Bronnenkant, K.: Timing and tracking: unlocking visitor behavior. Visitor Stud. **12**(1), 47–64 (2009)
5. Moussouri, T., Roussos, G.: Examining the effect of visitor motivation on visit strategies using mobile computer technologies. Visitor Stud. **16**(1), 21–38 (2013)
6. Yoshimura, Y., et al.: An analysis of visitors' behavior in the louvre museum: a study using bluetooth data. Environ. Plann. B Plann. Design **41**(6), 1113–1131 (2014). https://doi.org/10.1068/b130047p
7. Garbutt, M., East, S., Spehar, B., Estrada-Gonzalez, V., Carson-Ewart, B., Touma, J.: The embodied gaze. Exploring applications for mobile eye tracking in the art museum. Visitor Stud. **23**(1), 82–100 (2020)
8. Reitstätter, L., et al.: The display makes a difference. A mobile eye tracking study on the perception of art before and after a museum's rearrangement. J. Eye Move. Res. **13**(2), Article 6 (2020)
9. Walker, F., Bucker. B., Anderson, N.C., Schreij, D., Theeuwes, J.: Looking at paintings in the Vincent Van Gogh Museum: eye movement patterns of children and adults. PLoS ONE **12**(6), e0178912 (2017). https://doi.org/10.1371/journal.pone.0178912
10. Pierroux, P., Steier, R.: Making it real: transforming a university and museum research collaboration into a design product. In: Svihla, V., Reeve, R. (eds.) Design as Scholarship. Case Studies from the Learning Sciences. pp. 115–129. Routledge (2016)
11. Christidou, D.: Social Meaning Mapping as a means of exploring visitors' practices in the museum. Visitor Stud. **23**(2), 162–181 (2020). https://doi.org/10.1080/10645578.2020.1773708
12. Christidou, D., Reitstätter L.: From map using to map making: the museum experience through social meaning mapping. In: Gresalfi, M., Horn, I.S. (eds.) The Interdisciplinarity of the Learning Sciences, 14th International Conference of the Learning Sciences (ICLS) 2020, vol. 2, pp. 1087–1094. International Society of the Learning Sciences, Nashville, Tennessee (2020)
13. Clandinin, D.J., Connelly, F.M.: Narrative Inquiry: Experience in Story in Qualitative Research. Jossey-Bass, San Francisco (2000)

14. Prosser, J., Loxley, A.: Introducing Visual Methods, ESRC National Centre for Research Methods Review Paper, NCRM/010 October (2008)
15. Emmel, N.: Participatory social mapping: An innovative sociological method. Working paper (2008). http://eprints.ncrm.ac.uk/540/2/2008-07-toolkit-participatory-map.pdf
16. Wood, D.: Rethinking the Power of Maps. Guilford Press, New York (2010)
17. Christidou, D.: Social Meaning Mapping: a digital tool for visitors to map their museum experience. In: Lund, K., Niccolai, G.P., Lavoué, E., Hmelo-Silver, C., Gweon, G., Baker, M. (eds) A Wide Lens: Combining Embodied, Enactive, Extended, and Embedded Learning in Collaborative Settings, 13th International Conference on Computer Supported Collaborative Learning, vol. 2, pp. 763–765 (2019)
18. Kress, G., van Leeuwen, T.: Reading Images: The Grammar of Visual Design. Routledge, London (1996)
19. Corbin, J., Strauss, A.: Basics of Qualitative Research Techniques and Procedures for Developing Grounded Theory. Sage, Thousand Oaks (2008)
20. Doering, Z.D., Pekarik, A.J.: Questioning the entrance narrative. J. Museum Educ. 21(3), 20–23 (1996)
21. Reitstätter, L.: Die Ausstellung verhandeln. Von Interaktionen im musealen Raum (Negotiating the exhibition: On social interactions in the museum space). Bielefeld: transcript (2015)
22. Kirchberg, V., Tröndle, M.: The museum experience: mapping the experience of fine art. Curator Museum J. 58(2), 169–193 (2015)
23. vom Lehn, D., Heath, C., Hindmarsh, J.: Exhibiting interaction: conduct and collaboration in museums and galleries. Symbolic Interact. 24(2), 189–216 (2001). https://doi.org/10.1525/si.2001.24.2.189
24. Christidou, D., Steier, R.: Embodying artistic process in art gallery visits. In: Knutson, K., Okada, T., Crowley, K. (eds.) Multidisciplinary Approaches to Art Learning and Creativity: Fostering Artistic Exploration in Formal and Informal Settings, pp. 22–46 (2020)
25. Jafari, A., Taheri, B., vom Lehn, D.: Cultural consumption, interactive sociality, and the museum. J. Market. Manage. 29(15–16), 1729–1752 (2013). https://doi.org/10.1080/0267257X.2013.811095
26. Pelowski, M., Liu, T., Palacios, V., Akiba, F.: When a body meets a body: an exploration of the negative impact of social interactions on museum experiences of art. Int. J. Educ. Arts 15 (14) (2014)
27. Adams, M., Falk, J.H., Dierking, L.D.: Things change: museums, learning and research. In: Xanthoudaki, M., Tickle, L., Secules, V. (eds.) Researching Visual Arts Education in Museums and Galleries: An International Reader, pp. 15–32. Kluwer Academic Publishers (2003)
28. Rose, G.: Visual Methodologies, 3rd edn. Sage, Thousand Oaks (2012)
29. Smith, J.: The Museum Effect: How Museums, Libraries, and Cultural Institutions Educate and Civilize Society. Rowman & Littlefield, Lanham (2014)
30. Bowers, J., et al.: From the disappearing computer to living exhibitions: shaping interactivity in museum settings. In: Streitz, N., Kameas, A., Mavrommati, I. (eds.) The Disappearing Computer. LNCS, vol. 4500, pp. 30–49. Springer, Heidelberg (2007). https://doi.org/10.1007/978-3-540-72727-9_2
31. Ciolfi, L., Bannon, L.: Learning from museum visits: shaping design sensitivities. In: Proceedings of HCI International 2003, Crete, June 2003, pp. 63–67 (2003)

Why is This Exhibit Digital? – Dimensions of Digital Exhibits in the Museum Space

Pille Runnel[1]([⊠])[iD], Pille Pruulmann-Vengerfeldt[2][iD],
and Krista Lepik[3][iD]

[1] Estonian National Museum, Muuseumi tee 2, 60532 Tartu, Estonia
Pille.runnel@erm.ee
[2] Malmö University, 20506 Malmö, Sweden
[3] University of Tartu, Ülikooli 18, 50090 Tartu, Estonia

Abstract. Digital objects have controversial roles in the exhibition space [1, 2], ranging from being a vague 'must be' element at the exhibitions signifying their contemporaneity, to being a crucially important design tool shaping museum experience. Departing from the museum communication studies, this article seeks to provide an analytical framework about the digital exhibits within the exhibitions. Based on an iterative reflexive process whereby the empirical data in the form of exhibits at the Estonian National Museum and literature are in a circular dialogue with each other, we look at the potential role of the digital exhibits by using analytical dimensions, which have been strategically, although not always consciously utilized in the exhibition development. We start with 1) Spatiality, involving potentials and limitations of space-bound digital elements, and 2) Temporality, concerning dilemma between stability and changeability of the content. Next, approaching digital exhibits from the perspective of 3) private-public dimension as well as 4) single-multi-user aspects allows for a better understanding of the previously discussed sociability dimension [1, 3]. 5) Increasingly, narrating the past depends on the fusion of fictional-documentary formats. Finally, considering the critical perspective, we will also look at the dimensions of 6) authoritative-collaborative voice and 7) openness or determinedness of the interpretation. Outlining some of the theoretical underpinnings through concrete examples, we argue for the heuristic value of these dimensions in understanding visitor engagement.

Keywords: Digital exhibits · Museum engagement · Exhibition design · Spatiality · Temporality · Social exhibitions

1 Introduction

Contemporary exhibitions embrace different media, which afford experiences scaling from information retrieval to complex multisensory experiences. When combined with other materials, digital media offers potential for creating unique environments and visiting experiences. Often, the focus is on understanding space as a primary context contributing to the potential of technological interventions rather than discussing the

© Springer Nature Switzerland AG 2021
M. Shehade and T. Stylianou-Lambert (Eds.): RISE IMET 2021, CCIS 1432, pp. 47–60, 2021.
https://doi.org/10.1007/978-3-030-83647-4_4

affordances of the digital media in the spatial context. As a result, lacking a clear frame and direction, visitor engagement with interactives is often chaotic, impulsive, and depthless [4]. The media ecology of museums and exhibitions is part of the wider media ecosystem, therefore, discussions of developing media for museum purposes (museum communication, exhibitions) should be understood in a broader context.

This article uses the digital exhibits displayed at the Estonian National Museum's (ENM) permanent exhibition "Encounters" [5] as the empirical material for the analysis. The exhibition opened in 2016 invites the visitor to pursue Estonian cultural history and everyday life in this region in a backward chronological order starting from the recent past and finishing around the first human settlements. The national museum of the tech-savvy nation invites visitors to the exhibition space where both digital and analog exhibits have been merged in a coherent narrative. When developing the design concept, the exhibition team rejected the approach of adding digital elements to the exhibition as mere interactives, seeing the rich opportunities provided by the technologies to experiment with.

The digital exhibits were introduced as independent exhibits early in the production process. Using the content (knowledge, stories, collections) as the primary guideline, the exhibition team assigned certain qualities and needs to the digital exhibits. These included a need to translate texts into many languages; a need to demonstrate large bodies of data, such as databases; a need to address abstract topics; and a need to let the audiences take the lead in meaning-making. The goals included narrating personal stories to show different viewpoints regarding the historical events and restoring the context to the exhibited objects by introducing and compiling various documentary sources.

The evolving exhibition design concept split these needs into five distinct types of digital exhibits: a) curator's texts on e-ink screens; b) displaying historical originals (objects, documents, photos, documentary films etc.) on horizontal interactive multimedia touch-screens; c) interactive multimedia touch screens for showing large amounts of data: collections, databases, visualizations of researcher's hypothesis etc.; d) audiovisual exhibits (both fictional and documentary film); e) hands-on exhibits combining material and digital elements. While all these types of exhibits were designed as location-specific – to be accessed only at the exhibition space – an additional digital layer called "Take a museum home with you" is a work in progress, and the plan is to link the onsite exhibition experience with online content made accessible with the smart ticket.

The media technology centered typology of digital exhibits serves well when the exhibition team strives toward linking content-related goals to particular digital solutions. However, it does not support understanding the interrelations and synergies between different properties of digital exhibits and invisible consequences behind particular design decisions.

The aim of this article is to outline seven analytical dimensions we identified in the analysis of the digital exhibits developed for the "Encounters" exhibition, which operate as scales rather than poles. We rely on reflexive and iterative qualitative analysis [6] whereby we iterated reflections between our own experiences of being part of the exhibition team [7] with the experiences of being visitors at the exhibition with our reading of the relevant literature. We contribute to the academic explorations for understanding the potential of the digital technologies in the exhibition space [8, 9] as well as to the ongoing discussions of distributed museum [10, 11]. The dimensions introduced are set in a broader framework of museum engagement, which can be seen as a link between the performance of a museum and the experience of the audience, covering emotional, intellectual, social, and other forms of engagement. We see the dimensions also as a tool for museum practitioners to expand the digital technologies in the museum through careful considerations of their role in audience engagement. Our goal is not to work towards a model of impact assessment of the digital design solutions, but towards a formative, generative mindset in seeing the potential of different digital elements and discussing their synergies in support of an engaging exhibition narrative. Before outlining the dimensions, we introduce four exhibits, which exemplify the dimensions later.

2 Exhibits

2.1 "The Baltic Way"

In the evening of 23 August 1989, at 7 pm, about 2 million people held hands and formed a continuous human chain 600 km long, from Tallinn to Vilnius. It was a peaceful political demonstration for the 50th anniversary of the Molotov-Ribbentrop Pact which secret protocols divided Europe between Germany and The Soviet Union, annexing independent Estonia to the latter. The exhibit, presenting the event from the perspective of the participants, consists of two screens: a horizontal interactive screen and a vertical screen with original archival documentary footage from the event. The screens are complemented by the e-ink screen, displaying text. The horizontal screen is designed for both personal and multi-user experience: private browsing or collaboration and co-learning. Visitors can find and mark their location at the historical event or contribute with photos by contacting the museum, triggering remembrances of personal experience, nostalgia, and sharing. The interaction between the participants becomes a joint memory work. The exhibit addresses recent times, allowing for more open interpretation. The database, presented in the form of the chain across the countries, contains 3000 photos across three Baltic countries.

2.2 "The Synthesizer of Freedom"

Fig. 1. "The Syntheziser of Freedom" enables both single and collaborative uses. Photo by Berta Vosman.

"The Synthesizer of Freedom" (Fig. 1) represents the emergence of freedom of expression in Estonia since the 1980s. Slogans legendary for the locals, along with pieces from radio shows, music videos, politician's speeches, and familiar symbols from 1990s can be revisited at the large table-shaped installation with a round display in the middle of it [7]. At the edges of the table, box-shaped cavities with up to 20 floppy disks (3,5″) in each with different colors to signify different topics and available content. Placing a disk in an appropriate slot will start a visual (e.g., a logo), text, moving image, or sound on the central screen, and combining one of each will allow for a remix of different cultural artefacts.

The contemporary remix culture inspired representation of the media of the 1990s enables the users to mix different media formats. While mixing sound, video/photo, or text-based, the results of their activity are visible in real time at the center of the table. Depending on the age and experience the visitor can mix slightly familiar faces, music videos, or graphic images, or also recognize the phrases, words, and titles of the songs in their original historical context. Visitors can explore the table on their own, or with friends, or join strangers already exploring the table. Remix culture builds on practices where the boundaries between media production and play are not distinguishable from each other. Visitor's use of the mixer results in new, but ephemeral pieces: when mixing the content, the users can produce and reconstruct, but not save or share the result of their activity.

2.3   "The Twitterscape"

One of the sub-themes of the permanent exhibition "Encounters" is exploring the mediated urban experiences of youth. Produced in collaboration with children and youth [12], the section includes a touch-screen based exhibit "Twitterscape." The screen displays a map of geo-tagged tweets, based on real-life data flow. This exhibit was first designed in the ENM's Exhibition Lab for the exhibition on urban youth. While closely linked to the everyday experiences of the visitors, the exhibit has been easy to engage with, thus changing the ways in which youth and children relate to the museum. "Twitterscape" allows young visitors to become the active agents of the visit shaping the situated dynamics of talk and interaction among the participants, actively leading and shaping the visiting experience of the adults (for example, teachers attending the school group) by explaining the touch-screen, which represents their knowledge and experiences.

2.4   "The Smart Bed"

Fig. 2. Schoolchildren experimenting with the uses of "The Smart Bed". Photo by Anu Ansu.

A contemporary bed in the area of the "Encounters" exhibition (Fig. 2) introducing the domestic change in the 20th century and beyond by displaying the bedrooms also debates the balance of public and private in these, seemingly most private spaces. The bed, surrounded by a semi-transparent curtain, invites a visitor or group of visitors to lie on the bed, only to understand that the system takes a snapshot of those who dared to lay down. The visitor can raise and look at oneself lying on the bed on a space-bound image, but unable to remove it or take it with them, as it disappears in a mere 20 s. "The

Smart Bed" invites people to think about how the private habit of sleeping in a private bedroom has been made public for everyone passing by. The group members' social support is appreciated to dare to undertake the experience of lying down in public space making the exhibit work better for a group even if the technology is usable also alone.

3 Mapping the Analytical Dimensions of the Digital Elements of Exhibits

We will now continue with the seven dimensions, which can be used to plan and design as well as to understand existing exhibits or evaluate their capacity to engage visitors. The notion of affordances [13] makes it clear that the digital exhibits are not always under the control of the curators and designers as the interpretations by the visitors will differ. The dimensions are intertwined: tweaking one of these dimensions can affect others in terms of what audiences perceive and how they engage with the digital exhibit. The prominence of these dimensions depends on the content and context of the particular exhibition space - hence it is possible that not all dimensions are immediately detectable. The process of conceptualization of the dimensions was informed by the iterative reflexive process based on the digital layer of the Estonian National Museum and the ways the onsite spatial context links with the user experience.

3.1 Spatiality

Spatiality, often intertwined with other dimensions. In investigating user experiences within media platforms, we usually focus on single user sessions on/with personal devices. In the exhibition context, we need to understand both single- and multi-user sessions on public devices, recognizing that the exhibits are simultaneously physically fixed within a spatial design. In studying digital exhibits, their engagement potential is often precisioned by adding the user journey's physical trajectory. Thus, the spatial dimension of the exhibits makes the task of understanding their engagement potential a more complex one.

On the one hand, many digital elements are present for the duration of the visit, making them available only within the museum space, as they are imagined enriching the museum-going experience. This means exhibits are spatially bound, functioning in specific places on specific trajectories. On the other hand, the spatial dimension can also be unbound, characterizing the digital elements that can be accessed pre- or post-visit, supporting the museum engagement also outside the physical location of the museum. Here, the trajectories surrounding the engagement with the exhibit are outside the museum's control. Museums are increasingly investing in specifically designed apps, companion-websites that support post-visit engagement, QR-codes inside the exhibition opening websites in mobile phones, etc. When investigating digital exhibits within the museum context, we need to understand that some of the digital elements are intended for only local consumption, others mainly to be used locally, but can also function as follow-ups, and some are specifically designed to support engagement after the visit.

To bring an example, "The Syntheziser of Freedom", playing with the symbols of the 1990s is a purpose-built concrete "table" placed in the museum space with touchscreen and RFID readers, offers an experience that could not be transferred online in a similar manner. The collaborative possibilities are spatially bound to the museum, thus are fully functioning and can only be experienced on site. This is perhaps contrary to many other situations, where the digital elements are used to extend and expand the visit outside the museums. Newly emerging in the COVID-19 situations, the digital elements which would have been otherwise intended for on-site use only (e.g. listening to a sound-clip with headphones) are now sometimes made more transposable by the museums. Instead of listening with the museum headphones, visitors could scan QR codes and access these sound-clips with their phones in order to reduce the spread of the virus by touching museum exhibits. Such an approach makes the sound-clip less spatially bound while the engagement is still primarily imagined within the exhibition space. Opening sound files on the phone makes them mobile and allows for follow-up listening outside the museum as well, even if this is not the purpose of the engagement from the designers' perspective. The dimension of spatiality is not limited to being bound or unbound, but it designates a property, which can be utilized by design by approaching it as a slider to help to plan, analyze and understand both more or less spatially bound digital exhibits.

3.2   Temporality

A digital exhibit can be built to showcase existing, fixed (and most likely carefully studied and prepared) content, which is not to be altered in any way. For example, the purpose of the exhibit can be providing access to the archival documents, to a completed database, or exhibiting finished, authored visual or textual works. The stability of such exhibits depends on the museum and curators. These exhibits might be interactive (selecting, zooming in and out, scrolling, speeding up and down etc.), but the dimension of temporality is not part of the affordances allowing for different kinds of visitor engagement.

At the same time, it is possible to display materials as intentionally incomplete, dependent on the interventions by the visitors, including content that can be altered or added by the visitors. The content, modified or created by the users, can be made temporarily or permanently accessible also for the next visitors. For example, the exhibit "The Baltic Way" enables the visitors to choose their level of interaction with the content and has the potential to be always a temporary work in progress. The underlying database is designed to be a contributory database with no clear narrative, except the actual trajectory of the chain across the Baltic countries, despite depicting a seemingly stable event fixed both in terms of space and time. Each following visitor can potentially access a new, more complete version of the exhibit if visitors before them have decided to add their photos to the collection.

"The Smart Bed" illustrates an exhibit where temporality becomes the main affordance for engagement. A photo, taken of the visitor(s) lying on the bed, disappears again in just a few seconds. The temporary quality protects the privacy of the users as well as allows for playful experimentation created based on original contents. In this example, temporality is the most dominant property as the image is ephemeral, not shared with the next visitors, and entirely disappearing from the museum (unless captured with the visitor's camera).

Although not part of the intended consequences in these examples, they highlight the varying degrees of curatorial power. The temporality of the digital exhibits supports more "letting go of control" as the curators can allow for more uncontrolled material when its presence in the museum is briefest. In those cases, the exhibits afford more collaborative voices to emerge (see also Sect. 3.6).

3.3   Between Public and Private

Digital technologies alter and transform the complex set of social practices that interweave memories, material traces, and performative enactments to give meaning and significance in the present to the lived realities of our past [14]. The public-private dimension looks at how digital exhibits facilitate meaning-making. On the one hand, this dimension is about how contributing private experiences or knowledge potentially contributes to the public, collective representations and identities. On the other hand, engaging with collective representations at the exhibitions potentially helps to make private, individual experiences meaningful in new ways.

Traditional collections-based engagement on digital heritage has been about transforming content from one format into another, describing artefacts or synthesizing knowledge. Previous studies have demonstrated the importance of such activities on communities, but the meaning to the individual/participant group, such as volunteers engaged with the heritage work, has been neglected [15]. "The Baltic Way" exhibit regularly produces encounters where users who were part of the now historical event themselves, find familiar persons in the photos when browsing. Thus they, as well as everybody else who contributes to the exhibit by adding new content (photos or tags), can address other visitors or general audiences. Also, their private experience is being both musealized and made part of public representation about the event through this exhibit. Users not only give their photos to the museum but also participate in a process where personal experience and memories become collective representation.

"The Twitterscape" works in a similar way where you can see other people's posts and add your own. You can share a private moment in public and make it visible in the museum exhibit. At the same time, tweets fail to generate joint memory work as there is less of a distinct shared moment and display of tweets is temporally bound. For "The Twitterscape" to support shared memory work the time and space need to meet, e.g. there is an event which invites tweeting and tagging, so it becomes visible in the map like a concert in the museum or class visit.

"The Smart Bed" also pushes on the experiences between public and private as it aims to work as a cultural critique of the illusion of privacy, offering the possibility to personally experience blurring of the boundaries. In "The Smart Bed", such sharing of the moment of lying down becomes public twice - while in the bed and then in the 20-s recording of it. Daring to experiment and lay on the bed thus exposing oneself to the public even temporarily has been accepted as a playful encounter where the temporality supports public sharing of the private moment. In short, the public dimension can include both collective and individual experiences, or it can invite sharing private experiences to the public.

3.4   Between Single User and Multi-user

Digital exhibits can be used alone, or in some cases, by multiple users simultaneously. For example, the E-ink exhibition labels displaying texts in multiple languages can be read by several people at once, but these are generally intended for single-use. This intention is expressed both in the size and location of the labels and the basic assumption that reading the written text is nowadays primarily a solitary experience. The E-ink labels offer no user intervention other than changing the language with a personal ticket. Other digital exhibits allow collaborative sessions for multiple users. Touchscreen-based exhibits displaying databases (photos, texts), can be used in the company of others even simply by browsing, as it may trigger collective meaning-making. Elsewhere collaborations between users can be activated solely around the attempt to learn to operate the exhibit to access the content, such as "The Twitterscape." And finally, the exhibits inviting collaborative multi-user sessions (games, databases, media mixer "The Synthesizer of Freedom") can trigger both problem-solving (how to use) and improvisational content creation: one visitor making a step, the other adding her interpretation, answering or directing the possible uses and joint interpretations, resulting in a collaborate meaning-making. This kind of collaboration sets them apart from exhibits such as "The Baltic Way" or "The Twitterscape" which can also be used and made sense when operating them alone.

The use and interpretation of the (digital) exhibit cannot always be limited to single- or multi-user dynamics. Firstly, in terms of meaning-making, the single user – multi-user dimension becomes interwoven with the public or private dimension. Both "The Baltic Way" and "The Twitterscape" work as melting pots of thoughts and experiences of single users, potentially expanding beyond the walls of the museum because of their weight or scope. Secondly, the exhibition is situated in a mediated society and the meaning can be given by the general public, who is not even physically attending the exhibition nor using any of the exhibits, but the meaning is introduced to the exhibits through media representations. We point this out, as the curators and designers working on the exhibition and conceptualizing different exhibits, usually only consider the direct, spatial presence of the visitors and work toward offering solutions and inviting engagements of the onsite visitors. Their starting point is working with different modalities and opportunities offered by the digital technology at the level of the exhibition as a designed environment, rather than at the level of the exhibition as a part of larger media ecology.

3.5   Between Documentary and Fiction

As digital exhibits often rely on the audio-visual (AV) materials, then increasingly, to tell the story of the past, the AV used at the exhibition navigates at the documentary-fictional scale, similar to how the clear distinction between these genres is challenged in contemporary cinema. At the "Encounters" exhibition, the goal is to facilitate emotional engagement, but also to give visitors the freedom of interpretation [16]. AV-based digital exhibits present invisible, personal and mundane stories, both as visual documents and as interventions to the narrative. They are also used for presenting the times, when the film did not yet exist. The AV used at the exhibition ranges from newly made fictional films and anthropological documentaries to archival film footage, being more than a mere illustrative, educational or entertaining element in the exhibition space.

According to visual anthropologist Paul Henley [17], cinema should be treated as a medium of suggestion and implication rather than of statement and description. In this way, one ensures that a film remains not just an act of discovery for the maker but also for the viewer, who thereby participates actively in the construction of the meaning of the film. The distinction between the fictional and documentary approaches is not strictly set at the exhibition. On the one hand, the contemporary visual anthropological approach to creatively record, interpret and present daily life is not so different from a fiction film in terms of its potential to engage people when compared to the conventional documentary film built on explanations about the presented images in the form of the voiceover or experts' opinions. On the other hand, the fiction films at the exhibition, used solely for presenting the time periods, when filming had not yet been invented, are not entirely fictional, as they are based on archival sources, such as original court protocols. The fiction-based AV-exhibits use original artefacts displayed at the exhibition, creating an explicit link with the time period. Yet, a strong artistic aesthetic approach applied to the fictional AV-exhibits ensures that the visitors would not interpret the films as reconstructions of historical events.

In our examples of digital exhibits, "The Synthesizer of Freedom" allows the audiences to experiment on the scale of documentary and fiction by combining symbols of the 90s (including documentary video and sound footage) in new formations, creating fictional mash-ups. While the interpretations are clearly open and playful, the elements in the underlying database are documentary evidence of the time.

3.6   Between Authoritative and Collaborative

The museums are known for their capacity to provide interpretations about the exhibits to their visitors [18], thus having an authoritative voice about the contents of the museum. Nevertheless, as Tatsi [3 p.18] argues, "hegemonic authority position does not have to contradict the principle of individual choice fundamentally, so the museum as an authority can also choose to collaborate with its visitors, including via various exhibits". The authoritative/collaborative dimension enables us to analyze how the design of the digital exhibits targeted the goal of museum as a dialogical and open public space, to what extent it succeeded in involving or presenting diverse voices and in which ways the digital exhibits embraced this approach.

All material artefacts, displayed at the exhibition have been selected by the curators' team. At the same time, there is a scale in which the digital exhibits can be seen incorporating the voices of the visitors. For instance, "The Synthesiser of Freedom" is based on the images and media clips from the 1990s, selected by the curators, thus representing an authoritative curatorial choice. The users of this exhibit cannot add sounds, images, or symbols to the database or the piece they are currently mixing. The exhibit, however, enables creative combinations and does not need to adhere to any historical accuracy, thus bringing the collaborative voice of the participants to the fore. However, the exhibition welcomes contributing from the eyewitnesses' position to temporally passing events with other exhibits such as the "The Baltic Way" to avoid framing the event, and to enable eyewitnesses to contribute. As the museums are also engaged with contemporary collecting, attempts to document the present times, supported by digital exhibits, such as "The Twitterscape", would require a collaborative approach. It is up to the museum to leave the meaning-making process to the visitors or use its expertise to filter and analyze the created content, using its authoritative viewpoint.

3.7 Between Open and Closed

Side by side with interpreting the exhibit in terms of authority or collaboration, we can analyze whether or to what extent the exhibit is open for the interpretations provided by the visitor - whether the exhibit can be approached as an open or a closed text [19]. Even more, the activity related to the exhibit may also be approached in terms of its openness or closedness. The open activity can be modified, changed or expanded by a participant [20], while the closed activity is scripted or explicitly organized for a participant [19]. Hence, in terms of openness, the exhibit can both guide the thoughts and actions of visitors or invite them to use and interpret the exhibit freely. Such a decision is part of the curatorial decision-making, and it is up to the audiences to recognize invitations of openness of the interpretation.

The digital exhibits afford diverse degrees of freedom when it comes to interpretations. What does laying in "The Smart Bed" mean, is left for the visitor to decide. Interpretations can emerge from different contexts, such as how we are taught to act on a bed (such as not jumping on it) or how we are taught to act in a museum (for example, not touching the exhibits). "The Synthesizer of Freedom" acts as a set of building blocks that enables to produce unique combinations of textual, audial, and visual elements and interpret this combination at one's own will. However, at the level of actions, all digital exhibits present a fixed set of technical possibilities to interact with the exhibit and attempts to use them differently might not succeed. Despite fairly open creative possibilities, the technology still does not afford everything and hence justifies the use of scales when talking about the extent in which digital exhibits provide open activities.

4   Implications of the Dimensions for Visitor Engagement

Digital exhibits in the museum can fill several different purposes - they can add, enhance or replace museum objects in their traditional sense. Moreover, digital technologies allow museum content to leave the museum building and facilitate distributed museums [10] to reach more people, so the perceived benefits are related to boosting the public profile and reaching bigger audiences [21]. As we use digital technologies in everyday life in different ways and purposes, it is challenging for the museums to offer digital tools which facilitate engagement, being both original and unique while remaining familiar enough so that they do not reject visitors with different skills and perceptions. Familiarity is an important consideration especially if digital exhibits have been designed as equal to the tangible layer of the exhibition, thus containing crucially important content in terms of completing the exhibition narrative.

Our focus in this paper has been on looking at how the choices we make in designing different digital exhibits in museums afford engaging with existing audiences [21] onsite, at the exhibition space. Here we can see that tweaking different characteristics of the digital objects can support different types of engagement just as the tangible layer of the exhibition does. Morris Hargreaves Mcintyre [22] categorizes engagement on the basis of human needs – intellectual, emotional, spiritual, and social engagement. Apart from educating [23] or informing [24] the visitor, the exhibit can also be designed with purposes of evoking emotions or socialization/acculturation [23], as well as inviting the visitor to consult (i.e. debate or provide feedback), collaborate, or connect with the museum both as a lay visitor or a professional in some specific field of the museum [24]. The seven dimensions of the digital exhibits support one or another of these modes of engagement. For example, the dimensions of private/public or single-user/multi-user may support social engagement, while the authoritative/collaborative dimension of a digital exhibit may support various forms of informing, learning or collaborating. Depending on a particular digital exhibit, different dimensions can facilitate unique constellations. In further work, investigating these constellations will be the next step in understanding how digital exhibits support visitor engagement.

Modes of engagement offered by the museum and picked up by the audience explicitly shape their visit to a museum. For example, when designing dynamic, open digital solutions, inviting visitor contributions, also access to constantly evolving knowledge, memories, and interpretations of previous visitors is provided. Yet, it is difficult to foresee whether this invitation to share and do joint memory work is accepted and met by immediately disappearing attention, or a more in-depth engagement. Hence digital exhibits have to be designed and included with sensitivity and openness to uses not entirely predictable during the design process. The seven dimensions outline here can support such a reflection process for museum design teams.

The dimensions of digital exhibits reveal, on their scales, characteristics that are lacking in tangible exhibits such as artefacts or documents. The distributed museum as such poses challenges that are not always discussed in museums' code of ethics or collection policies: how to protect the privacy of the contributing visitor or what to do with the big data-like collaboratively born digital content that is being updated on a constant basis. The dimensions proposed in our paper provide critical aspects that set apart the digital exhibit from a traditional tangible exhibit, and demand the curators' attention when working on a new digital exhibit.

References

1. Hornecker, E., Ciolfi, L.: Human-Computer Interactions in Museums. Morgan & Claypool (2019)
2. Hossaini, A., Blackenberg, N.: The Manual of Digital Museum Planning. Rowman & Littlefield (2017)
3. Tatsi, T.: Transformations of museum-embedded cultural expertise. Doctoral dissertation. University of Tartu Press, Tartu (2013)

4. Huhtamo, E.: Freedom, control and confusion in the art museum: why we need 'exhibition anthropology'? In: Henning, M. (ed.) Museum Media. The International Handbooks of Museum Studies, pp. 259–277. Wiley-Blackwell (2015)

5. Rattus, K.: Dialoogilisus Eesti Rahva Muuseumi püsinäitusel "Kohtumised". In: Runnel, P., Aljas, A. (eds.) Eesti Rahva Muuseumi aastaraamat, pp. 143–161. Eesti Rahva Muuseum, Tartu (2016)

6. Srivastava, P., Hopwood, N.: A practical iterative framework for qualitative data analysis. Int. J. Qual. Methods 8(1), 76–84 (2009)

7. Runnel, P., Pruulmann-Vengerfeldt, P.: Producing a media-rich permanent exhibition for the Estonian National Museum as arts-based research. Communicazioni Sociali 1, 124–131 (2021)

8. Annhernu, P.: The Assembly of museum media: Tracing the adoption of novel forms and formats of communication technology into museum media production. Ph.D. dissertation. School of Museum Studies, University of Leicester, Leicester (2019)

9. Ntalla, I.: The interactive museum experience. Investigating experiential tendencies and audience focus in the Galleries of Modern London and The High Arctic Exhibition. Ph.D. dissertation. City University of London, London (2017)

10. Bautista, S.S., Balsamo, A.: Understanding the distributed museum: mapping the spaces of museology in contemporary culture. In: Boddington, A., Boys, J., Speight, C. (eds.) Museums and Higher Education Working Together. Challenges and Opportunities, pp. 55–70. London, Routledge (2016). https://doi.org/10.4324/9781315596471

11. Rodley, E.: The distributed museum is already here–it's just not very evenly distributed. In: Lewi, H., Smith, W., vom Lehn, D., Cooke, S. (eds.) The Routledge International Handbook of New Digital Practices in Galleries, Libraries, Archives, Museums and Heritage Sites, pp. 81–92. Routledge, London (2020). https://doi.org/10.4324/9780429506765.

12. Pruulmann-Vengerfeldt, P., Runnel, P.: The museum as an arena for cultural citizenship: exploring modes of engagement for audience empowerment. In: Drotner, K., Dziekan, V., Parry, R., Schroder, K.C. (eds.) The Routledge Handbook to Museum Communication, pp. 143–158. Routledge, Taylor & Francis Group (2019)

13. Norman, D.: The Design of Everyday Things. Basic Books, New York (2013)

14. Giaccardi, E. (ed.): Heritage and Social Media: Understanding Heritage in a Participatory Culture. Routledge, London (2012)

15. Reinsone, S.: Searching for deeper meanings in cultural heritage crowdsourcing. In: Hetland, P., Pierroux, P., Esborg, L. (eds.) A History of Participation in Museums and Archives. Traversing Citizen Science and Citizen Humanities, pp. 186–207. Taylor and Francis. (2020). https://doi.org/10.4324/9780429197536-14

16. Leivategija, K.: Filmid Eesti Rahva Muuseumi püsinäitusel "Kohtumised". In: Runnel, P., Aljas, A. (eds.) Muuseumid tänapäeval: väljakutsed ja võimalused, pp. 89–110. Eesti Rahva Muuseum, Tartu (2020)

17. Henley, P.: Putting film to work: observational cinema as practical ethnography. In: Alfonso, A. I., Kurti, L., Pink, S (eds.) Working Images: Visual Research and Representation in Ethnography, pp 101–119. Routledge, London (2004)

18. Lord, B.: Foucault's museum: difference, representation, and genealogy. Museum Soc. 4(1), 1–14 (2006)

19. Eco, U.: The Role of the Reader. Indiana University Press, Bloomington (1979)

20. Myrzcik, E.P.: Digital Museum Mediation in Denmark: A critical exploration of the development, practice, and perceived outcomes. Doctoral dissertation. University of Copenhagen, Copenhagen (2019)

21. Proctor, N.: The Museum as Distributed Network, a 21st Century Model. Museum ID Magazine. https://museum-id.com/museum-distributed-network-21st-century-model-nancy-proctor/. Accessed 03 Apr 2021
22. Morris Hargreaves McIntyre: Ready to Engage: Deepening public engagement with Newcastle Gateshead Cultural Venues (report) (2010). https://mhminsight.com/files/ngcv-pe-research-report-v2-q5dR-100-2612.pdf
23. Smith, L.: Visitor emotion, affect and registers of engagement at museums and heritage sites. Conserv. Sci. Cult. Heritage **14**(2), 125–132 (2014)
24. Lotina, L.: Conceptualizing engagement modes: Understanding museum–audience relationships in Latvian museums. Doctoral dissertation. University of Tartu Press, Tartu (2016)

Mapping Sonic Practices in Museum Exhibitions – An Overview

Foteini Salmouka[(⊠)] and Andromache Gazi

Department of Communication, Media and Culture, Panteion University
of Social and Political Studies, 136, Syngrou Avenue, 17671 Athens, Greece
f.salmouka@panteion.gr

Abstract. Museums are increasingly incorporating sound in their exhibitions both as an exhibit and an interpretative medium. This paper traces the relationship between sound and museums, and then focuses on the integration of sound into the exhibition space. It is noted that, although the functional aspects related to the use of sound in museum exhibitions have been scrutinised, the exploration of sound as an interpretive medium is rather overlooked. To fill in this gap, the paper discusses sonic practices in contemporary museums and suggests a new classifying scheme for studying sound in museums. The proposed classification focuses on the three main roles accorded to sound in the exhibition environment: informative, interpretive, immersive. The various examples discussed provide ample evidence of the potential of sound in revitalising the museum experience.

Keywords: Museum sound design · Sensory museology · Interpretation · Immersion

1 Introduction

Sound is an integral part of the environment; it shapes the surrounding atmosphere, influences interpersonal relationships and mental states and, thus, becomes a determining factor in perceiving and interpreting the world around us [1]. Conceptual developments in the field of sound along with artistic practices developed since the 1960s led to the emergence of a new sound culture in both academia and the artistic field, which has promoted sound as an alternative interpretive medium - that is, a medium aimed at helping museum visitors interpret the objects and/or themes presented at an exhibition.

In response to this emerging trend museums have begun to incorporate sound into their exhibitions, either as an exhibition object or theme, or as a means of interpretation. Sound exhibitions and sound art exhibitions are on the rise and have contributed significantly to the development of a close association between museums and sound, however, the use of sound as an interpretive medium is rather limited in museum exhibitions and not sufficiently studied in academia.

This paper attempts to map, classify and propose a novel categorisation of audio practices incorporated in museum exhibitions according to the role accorded to sound in the exhibition environment, in order to discuss best practices and highlight current trends in the field for further research.

© Springer Nature Switzerland AG 2021
M. Shehade and T. Stylianou-Lambert (Eds.): RISE IMET 2021, CCIS 1432, pp. 61–75, 2021.
https://doi.org/10.1007/978-3-030-83647-4_5

2   From the Visual to the Audiovisual

The creation of the museum as a visual mechanism and the primacy of vision in Western culture are institutionalised perceptions, which were shaped by the system of aesthetic values of the 19th century, had prevailed until the mid-20th century and are present even to this day [2, 3]. The establishment of the first public museums in the 18th century and the subsequent admission of the public to collections that were until that time accessible only to people from the upper classes [4], limited visitors' sensory interaction with the exhibits as was practiced in Medieval and Renaissance collections [5]. During the 19th century sound and the senses in general (except from vision of course) were almost expelled from the museum environment, due to the emergence of two views. Firstly, aesthetic theories of art enhanced the aesthetic perception of art through the gaze, thus leading to the development of a hands-off culture and the establishment of visual perception as the predominant means of appreciation [5, 6]. Secondly, the view of the museum as a means of governance, discipline, control, and personal self-improvement led to the emergence of a new protocol of behaviour for the museum visitor [4, 7–9]. According to this protocol, exhibits are turned into objects of contemplation, the visitor becomes an observer, and the museum turns into a space of meditation and isolation [7, 9–11]. These perceptions had a great impact on the way museums used various interpretive media to frame the visual experience of the visitor.

However, new artistic practices, the introduction of new technologies in museums, the turn from the object-centred to the people-centred museum [4] as put forward by the New Museology[1] and the emergence of new scientific fields - such as the anthropology of the senses (e.g. [13–15]), and sensory museology (e.g. [16, 17]) - challenged western views of a hierarchical taxonomy of the senses and led to the "multisensory turn" of the last 30 years in museums [18, 19]. The incorporation of multisensory stimuli in the exhibition environment (e.g. tactile exhibits, interactive installations, historic odours etc.) which began in science, ethnographic, open-air and folk museums, gradually extended to other, more "traditional", types of museums, such as art museums and historical museums [5]. The multisensory museological approach is further supported by the rise of the performative view of cultural heritage in the beginning of the 21st century, which emphasises heritage as a process and as a performance, and not (or not merely) as a product [20].

The study of the museum's relationship with sound is part of the broader context of expanding the museum's sensory spectrum. Sound has been present in museums since their initial conception; nevertheless, its perception and use as a means of valuing objects has gradually given way to the practice of silent browsing, the restriction of human sounds, and the general view of silence as a cultural practice of knowledge production [21–23]. However, sound remained present in the museum environment in two ways: unintentionally, through the human and atmospheric sounds that make up

---

[1] The term was coined by Peter Vergo [12] in order to describe a "state of widespread dissatisfaction with the 'old' museology, both within and outside the museum profession [...] I would retort that what is wrong with the 'old' museology is that it is too much about museum methods, and too little about the purposes of museums".

the museum soundscape [24] and music iconography[2]; or intentionally through collections of sound objects and collections of musical instruments, and through artistic practices developed during the 20th century highlighting the close relationship between the visual arts and the arts of sound. From the 1960s onwards the presence of audio-visual stimuli in the museum was greatly enhanced with the development of new art forms (e.g. video art, performance, sound art, digital art) that resulted in a drastic change in the museum soundscape. Audio and audio-visual works of art, along with the creation of collections of sound recordings that are not the result of artistic production (e.g. oral history, field recordings, audio-visual heritage), made sound a collection object for museums. During the same period, a new sound culture has emerged through the study of hearing, auditory perception, and sound as a carrier of messages [25]. In addition, the recent interest of the social sciences in the study of sound as an indicator of social and cultural differences has led to the creation of exhibitions focusing on sound, especially from the beginning of the 21st century onwards (e.g. *Sonic Boom: The Art of Sound,* Hayward Gallery, 2000; *Bruits*, Musée d'ethnographie de Neuchâtel, 2010–2011; *Soundtracks*, SFMOMA, 2017–2018). However, as Howes [11 p. 294] argues "while the incorporation of non-Western elements into Western art has contributed significantly to the development of new artistic styles, it has not done much to expand the sensory repertoire of Western art works or alter their mode of display within the museum". What is more, the presentation of sound as an autonomous artistic practice carries the risk of further marginalising the sound and widening the gap between the senses [26]. In conclusion, new multi-sensory artistic practices, the introduction of new interpretive technologies in the exhibition environment, and museums' turn to enriching the visitor's experience laid the ground for rethinking the role of sound in the 21st century museum.

3   Sound in Exhibitions

The integration of sound in museum exhibitions, where sound is not the central theme, poses significant curatorial challenges. This section focuses on the possibilities offered by the comprehensive integration of sound in the exhibition environment and hints to possible avenues for further research in this field.

Sound has a variety of roles in contemporary museums: it is a museum object, an interpretive tool, a means of attracting visitors, an element of architectural design, a creative opportunity for artists, a conceptual model for studying the relationship of the individual with his/her environment, a means of immersion in or creation of a mood, and an opportunity for dynamic multi-sensory engagement with the exhibits [23, 27, 28]. Sound may be used to modify the semantic context of an exhibition, to update its content, to incorporate new information, and to link the exhibits together [29]. These possibilities arise from sound characteristics such as its ephemeral nature, its ability to highlight invisible relationships between reality, possibility and materiality, or between

---

[2] Music iconography includes works of visual arts that illustrate musicians, musical instruments, music performance etc.

moments, people and places, and the fact that acoustic space has no limits [30]. The presence of sound in the exhibition environment significantly affects the entire exhibition experience as it creates a new framework for connecting present and past, individual and collective experience, object and observer unlike what happens in other immersive environments such as cinema [22][3].

Research on the integration of sound in museum exhibitions includes a wide variety of issues ranging from ontological questions to guidelines for exhibition sound design. Kannenberg [24], for example, looks at the ontological questions involved in conceptualising sound as a museum object and explores sound as an object and as an event in the museum.

Different research approaches are adopted in relation to the interaction between sound and elements of the museum environment. Based on the use of sound in cinema, Bubaris [21], for instance, makes a distinction between *diegetic* (sounds incorporated into the exhibition: sounds of objects, sound of the exhibition space, multimedia installations etc.) and *non-diegetic* exhibition sounds (sounds that complement the exhibits such as audio guides). Stocker [29], on the other hand, based on the psychoacoustics of the exhibition space, perceives sound as either *useful* (sounds enhancing the visual perception of exhibits, e.g. music, narrative, ambient sound) or *useless* (sounds perceived as noise). Angliss [34] divides exhibition sounds into *foreground* (e.g. speech) and *background* (e.g. music, ambient sounds). Zisiou [35] examines the functional role of sound in the exhibition environment under the light of acoustic communication, and distinguishes three strategies for developing museum soundscapes: three-dimensional sound environments (3D soundscapes), "sound-recording" of the exhibition narrative, and special techniques of content development. Finally, research approaches to the integration of sound in exhibition design include a quest for best practices in acoustic design and the endorsement of guidelines to this end (e.g. [36, 37]).

We, therefore, note that research on the integration of sound in the exhibition environment focuses on either the functional/operational integration of audio elements in it, or on practical issues pertaining sound optimisation. Yet, the exploration of the role of sound as an interpretive exhibition medium is largely overlooked. In an attempt to start remedying this lacuna, the next section maps sonic practices in contemporary museum.

4 Mapping Sonic Practices in Museum Exhibitions

In this section we identify and map the various ways in which museums use sound to enrich an exhibition's meaning and enhance visitors' overall experience by offering multisensory stimuli. We propose a novel categorisation of sonic practices in museum exhibitions according to one of the three main roles accorded to sound in the exhibition

---

[3] Sound may also contribute to enhancing accessibility for blind and visually impaired visitors through the use of interpretive tools such as audio descriptions and audio guides. However, this goes beyond the scope of this paper as the use of sound for blind and visually impaired visitors requires special guidelines in terms of design and content. Recent research in this field includes interpretation practices (e.g. [31]), design issues (e.g. [32]), evaluation of accessibility strategies (e.g. [33]) etc.

environment: informative, interpretive, immersive. We also discuss good practices and highlight contemporary trends through a wide range of examples that demonstrate the diversity involved in the use of sound in museum exhibitions.

4.1   Informative Role

The integration of sound in museum exhibitions in order to transmit information highlights the informative role of sound as a means of enhancing the cognitive context of museum objects. Sonic practices with an informative role are based on the support, enhancement, or replacement of written text by textual elements read aloud by a narrator [38]. This allows the incorporation of a larger amount of information than that which may be integrated in the typical exhibition text (which has a number of specific limitations such as space constraints and the ability of visitors to read lengthy text). In this case, the spoken word prevails, and the act of reading is complemented by or replaced by the act of hearing. Sonic practices that highlight the informative role of sound include audio captions, audio guides and audio tours.

The term *audio captions* refers to sonic practices in which the spoken word is used for enriching the information about exhibits or exhibition themes. Audio captions enrich an object's textual data with the element of narration (dramatised or not) of stories and events from the historical, social and/or cultural context of the object. Audio captions have become one of the most popular practices for enriching an exhibition's informative material and are found in several permanent museum exhibitions. One such example is the Topography of Terrors Museum in Berlin, where the visitor encounters numerous listening options through one-ear headphones (Fig. 1). This practice allows the visitors to engage with the information available at the exhibition on different levels, depending on the time they can devote and their special interest in the exhibition subject matter.

Fig. 1. Audio station in Topography of Terrors Museum, Berlin. ©Topography of Terror Foundation

Audio guides are another established practice of incorporating sound in museums. Firstly, launched in the 1950s, they developed along the technological advances of the 20th century. Initially, they had the form of massive portable devices that used radio broadcasting. In the 1960s and the 1970s they evolved into portable media players (e.g. Walkman, Fig. 2), while now audio guides are available as either digital media devices available at the museum, or as applications in which the visitor has access via a smartphone. Today museums employ different forms of audio guides, which will be explored later.

In this section we examine conventional audio guides, henceforth termed *audio tours*, where a real person has been replaced by an electronic device guiding the visitor through the exhibition; the guiding voice has a didactic and informative character, like exhibition texts, the exhibition catalogue, or the guided-by-a-person tour [39]. In contemporary audio tours, visitors may choose informative material according to their age, special interests, and time available for the museum visit. Common types of audio tours are guided tours of selected exhibits (Fig. 3), thematic tours (Fig. 4), audio tours for families and children, and first-person narrative by historical figures. In brief, audio tours are an established and popular means of transmitting information which enhances the accessibility of exhibition content. Their widespread use in contemporary museums ensues from their being an auxiliary means of integrating sound into the exhibition environment without resorting to major interventions in the exhibition space. Moreover, the use of audio tours does not affect the acoustic properties of the space, or the experience of the exhibition by other visitors. Therefore, audio tours are favoured by even the most "traditional" and "silent" museums in which visitors do not normally encounter sound interventions in the exhibition space.

Fig. 2. Two visitors use LecTour audio tour system, National Gallery of Art, Washington, 1958. Courtesy of National Gallery of Art, Washington, DC, Gallery Archives.

Fig. 3. Collections' highlights of the Louvre. Source: Smartify application

Fig. 4. Thematic tour available at the British Museum. Source: Smartify application

4.2 Interpretive Role

The interpretive role of sound is highlighted by acoustic media aimed at strengthening an exhibition's conceptual framework. In fact, all the media used in an exhibition are interpretive, inserted as they are between the visitor and the exhibits and thus affecting his/her reception. The ability of sound to convey information and knowledge is recognised as one of the key functions that sound can perform in the exhibition environment [27–29, 34]. In this sense, the sound practices discussed in this section were created to deliver unique interpretive content [27] and to communicate key exhibition messages. The interpretive role of sound derives from the correlative and representational possibilities it entails, as a carrier of messages, ideas and situations, which, when employed in the exhibition environment, can highlight aspects that often remain invisible during a museum visit. The sonic practices discussed in this section are narrating objects, sonic references, sound heritage and sound exhibits.

Narrating objects are sonic practices in which the exhibits themselves are protagonists in narratives about their history, their social, historical, and cultural role and influence. Common methods of delivery include dramatised narration, where the narrator may be either an object or a character inspired by depicted forms, while the narrative plot is often complemented by relative sounds. Storytelling in first-person narratives has a strong personal tone, which enhances the emotional involvement of visitors through the immediacy it conveys and, at the same time, evokes memories from a collective history. Dramatised narration is also employed as a tool for "giving voice" to written sources in museum collections, a practice that is very useful in the case of ancient languages, as well as in placing written sources within a broader conceptual context and developing a dialogue with other exhibitions elements. In conclusion, *narrating objects* are a dynamic and creative medium, both educational and entertaining, for enhancing an exhibition's context.

Sonic references are sonic practices in which sound is used to supplement an object with audio elements that are either implied, or refer to the wider historical, social, and cultural background of the object's life. A first category of such practices are sonic references to the sound of objects that have lost their functionality during their museification process (e.g. musical instruments, objects with musical notation, etc.). Sonic references also try to explore the acoustic properties of objects in order to create new perceptual experiences for visitors. Examples of such practices include the acoustic guide *Musical Instruments: Mapping the Art of Music*[4] available at the MET in New York for a guided tour in the collection of musical instruments, and the interactive sound tables at the Music Gallery of the Horniman Museum in London (Fig. 5).

Fig. 5. Sound tables at the Music Gallery of the Horniman Museum in London. Music Gallery, 2015, Sophia Spring, ©Horniman Museum and Gardens

Another example of sonic references is *sonic representations* in which depicted elements (in works of art for instance) are activated through relevant sounds. Sonic representations as interpretive media are usually found in art museums: they activate

---

[4] https://soundcloud.com/metmuseum/sets/musical-instruments-mapping-the-art-of-music.

latent sonic cues to create a sonic representation of the artwork. They are original musical compositions for selected exhibits. A representative example is the acoustic guide *Sounds of the Gallery* (National Gallery, London)[5], for which original compositions were recorded along with soundscapes to explore the ways in which painters imply the presence of sound in their works.

Yet another example of sonic reference is *contextual sonic references* that encourage links between objects and their wider conceptual context through sound. Contextual sonic references connect the object with its historical, social, and cultural milieu or/and the themes linked to the object. Such was the case of the research project *Listening Galleries* (V&A Museum and Royal Academy of Music, 2008–2010) for the production of music for the exhibition *Baroque 1620–1800: Style in the Age of Magnificence* and for the redisplay of the Medieval and Renaissance collections at the V&A in 2009 (Fig. 6) [40]. Consequently, sonic references are a dynamic interpretive tool, which encourages visitor engagement through the creation of links between the exhibition milieu and the objects' original context.

Fig. 6. Audio point in Room 10a at the V&A. Source: [40]. Photograph by Stuart Frost.

---

[5] https://www.nationalgallery.org.uk/visiting/audio-tours/sounds-of-the-gallery.

Sound heritage refers to sonic practices that use recorded sound and audio, or audiovisual documents as an interpretation medium in museum exhibitions. Sound heritage may be used to significantly enhance an exhibition's content, documentation, and authenticity. At Churchill Museum in London, for example, visitors can hear Churchill's voice from excerpts of his speeches. This method enriches the content of the exhibition and helps boosting national memory and triggering emotions [41]. Oral history and personal testimonies are also significant interpretive media for enriching an exhibition's content and enhancing visitor engagement because they offer first-person authentic life stories that represent a wide range of experiences and multiple points of view [42]. As Gazi [42 p. 47] points out "what is gained when oral history takes center stage (or the only stage) in museum exhibitions is far greater than what is ostensibly 'lost' – that is, the prevalence of objects and conventional means of content delivery". A case in point is personal memories of pilgrims to Mecca incorporated into *Hajj: Journey to the Heart of the Islam* 2012 exhibition at The British Museum.

Finally, the interpretive role of sound is highlighted through *sound exhibits* that are normally commissioned specifically for an exhibition, like sound art installations, multimedia installations etc. In these cases, sound as an artistic practice enriches an exhibition's conceptual context. Such an example of a sound installation that enriches an exhibition's content is *Lydian Bells* by Brian Eno, commissioned for the exhibition *Treat Yourself: Health consumers in a medical age* (Science Museum London and Wellcome Trust, 2003), which explored alternative medicine practices and self-healing. For *Lydian Bells*, Eno created an ambient soundscape based on the so-called Lydian mode, a seven-tone musical scale, which is associated with relaxing and revitalising properties, aimed at exploring sonic therapy.

4.3 Immersive Role

This section presents sonic practices in which sound is deliberatively used for creating an atmosphere, a mood, and/or immersion [27]. In these cases, the use of sound emphasises experience rather than learning by offering a deeper engagement with artworks and a new way to experience art in the museum context. Working on a more subconscious level, sound and music are used to create mood, to increase and, also, direct affect so that it can determine our feelings upon what we see, to influence the pace of the tour and visitors' attention, and even to elicit emotions [43][6]. The practices discussed below include historical or cultural soundscape reconstruction, exhibition soundtracks, immersive audio guides, audio walks and sonic responses to artworks. In all these practices sound still holds its interpretative role, but the main purpose is to create an immersive, and in many cases augmented, environment that is more personal than institutional. Having said that, we must stress that drawing a line between the informative and the immersive role of sound is rather difficult, and perhaps even problematic, as information is present even in a completely immersive environment.

---

[6] The study of sound/music and affect is a subject of psychoacoustics, a field that examines how humans interpret and react to sound. Groundwork research in this field includes acoustics and acoustic engineering (e.g. [44]), perception (e.g. [45]), consumption studies (for a literature review on the topic see Gustafsson [46]), media studies (e.g. [47]) etc.

A case in point is *historical* or *cultural soundscape reconstruction,* which refers to sonic practices aimed at reviving a historical and/or cultural soundscape. This practice is usually found in historical and ethnological museums. The purpose of reconstructing a historical soundscape is double: On the one hand it connects museum visitors to a certain historic period, a historic fact, or a cultural group, and on the other it positions them within the acoustic environment of a past era or culture that differs significantly from our contemporary acoustic surroundings. Linking past eras, cultures, social classes, and even sexes, through sound is thus encouraged. An example is *Soundscapes of the Dam Square* which in 2013–2014 was installed opposite the painting *View of the Dam* (1895–1898) by George Hendrik Breitner in Amsterdam Museum. The installation consisted of three virtual soundscapes that reconstructed three different acoustic images of the square in three different points in time: 1895, 1935 and 2012. Through these *acoustic images*[7] visitors were able to observe changes in the city's soundscape along with the sounds dominant in each period [49]. Sound's informative role was, thus, successfully intermingled with its immersive power.

Exhibition soundtracks mainly employ music, and only partially sound, to differentiate exhibition sections, to create sonic zones, and to highlight specific exhibits. Often, though, exhibition soundtracks are of poor quality and instead of enriching visitors' experience, they may result in an uncomfortable one. On the contrary, high quality and carefully curated exhibition soundtracks can set the tone for the visit and help visitors experience a period, a location, or an environment[8].

Immersive audio guides refer to museum audio guides that create an immersive sonic environment through a combination of sounds, music and narrative, and the use of innovative audio technologies; this environment complements and works together with the visual elements of the exhibition. Lately, immersive audio guides are increasingly preferred by museums as a new and innovative audio technology (e.g. binaural recording, 3D soundscapes etc.) used to create high-quality original content. As an example, the MET's audio guide for the 2018 exhibition *Visitor to Versailles*[9] combined sound recordings on-site, scripted narration, narration of personal experiences, music, and relational sounds to create a fresh and authentic experience for visitors.

Audio walks refer to artistic audio guides that "walk" the visitor through the exhibition space. Audio walks are created by artists, but also recently a burgeoning number of cultural heritage producers, to provide a unique experience of museum and exhibition space. In audio walks, the guiding voice overshadows the acoustic space, while embedded sound effects create a cinematic atmosphere. Audio walks expand the space and blend the reality experienced by the visitor with that experienced by the narrator at an earlier stage. As a result, an illusionary sonic world is formed while visitors move around the space. The work of Janet Cardiff stands out in this field.

---

[7] The term *acoustic image* is defined as "an 'internal' image that is not necessarily attached to the 'external' visual of a sound's source or material origin". Acoustic images instantiate a network of semiotic associations [48 p. 6].

[8] A case in point is LACMA's exhibition soundtracks that are available on the museum's website https://www.lacma.org/athome/listen/exhibition-soundtracks.

[9] https://soundcloud.com/metmuseum/sets/visitors-to-versailles.

Cardiff has created numerous museum audio walks that combine personal narration by the artist with evocative sounds. The binaural recordings create an intimate acoustic environment, whereas narration stimulates imagination and sensation [39]. Both immersive audio guides and audio walks create an augmented environment that expands the space in which art is experienced, a practice that can be further exploited by museums.

Finally, *sonic responses to artworks* include original compositions inspired by visual works of art. Visual arts and music have always had a dialogic relationship, both at a theoretical level through common conceptual visions[10], and at the level of artistic production, through the exchange of artistic practices, as in the works of the Italian Futurists at the beginning of the 20th century. Works of visual art are an important source of inspiration for composers and sound artists, as illustrated by the rich list of relevant music works[11]. Commissioning new musical compositions as a response to objects in the museum collection is an emerging practice, which is increasingly explored in the context of temporary museum exhibitions. For example, new musical and acoustic pieces were commissioned for the 2015 *Soundscapes* exhibition at the National Gallery of London to explore new ways of presenting and experiencing art. Although in many cases sonic responses to artworks activate sonic cues from the artworks, the difference between sonic representations and sonic responses is that the latter have an abstract rather than a descriptive relation with the visual artwork. In conclusion, sonic responses to artworks promote the interaction between visual arts and music and leads to the development of a new conceptual framework for experiencing art in museums.

5   Conclusions

Over the last decades the presence of sound in museum exhibitions has significantly been enhanced and has been implemented in different ways according to the goals set at the design stage. The variety of sound practices discussed in the previous sections demonstrates that, in the context of museums' multi-sensory turn-evident in an increasing number of museums-sound can play a leading role in a so far merely visual environment and contributes to revitalising a museum visit.

Research so far has led to a number of observations that may facilitate further discussion on the challenges and opportunities from the inclusion of sound in museum exhibitions. To begin with, sonic practices that require intervention in the exhibition space are more often included in temporary exhibitions, as the modification of space is difficult in permanent exhibitions. In permanent exhibitions, on the other hand, there is a preference for audio guides and audio captions or for interactive audio stations; that is, practices that favour individual over collective hearing. Consequently, sound is still considered as an auxiliary medium, treated with hesitation in terms of its interpretive possibilities. This in turn results in its fragmentary and limited application.

---

[10] For a thorough exploration of this interplay see Vergo [50].

[11] Some notable examples are Sergei Rachmaninov's symphonic poem *Island of Death* inspired by Arnold Böcklin's homonymous painting, *Five Klee-Pictures* by Peter Maxwell Davies and Tōru Takemitsu's *All in Twilight* inspired by Paul Klee's homonymous painting.

Concerns over the presence of sound in museums include both the optimization of practical issues arising from its inclusion in the exhibition and the ways in which it affects the museum visit. In terms of operational functionality, frequent problems are noise "pollution" of the exhibition space, sound-bleeding in places where sound is not meant to be provided, inadequate maintenance of sound installations, poor sound quality, wrong location of the sound sources etc. All these may turn sound into a problem instead of a new prospect of enriching the museum experience, but this is also a problem with other interventions in the museum space, like for example visual effects, etc.

The contribution of experts in the acoustics and psychoacoustics of exhibition spaces is particularly important for optimising the functionality of sound practices. Moreover, new audio technologies such as directional speakers, sound shower speakers, binaural recording, augmented reality soundscapes, etc. have significantly helped resolve operational problems and improve the acoustic experience in the museum.

Regarding the effect of sound on the museum visitor, there have been serious concerns about visitors' distraction from the exhibits and their context, and the transformation of a visit's character from a didactic to an entertaining one. This, of course, is not a problem only with sound. However, the full integration of sound in an exhibition through careful planning from the early stages of the exhibition design (which should also involve specialised professionals) can highlight sound as a dominant conceptual and interpretive means that enriches museum narratives.

If planned during the earliest stages of an exhibition project, sound design cannot only help document museum objects but, more importantly, it can enrich their interpretation. At the same time, the incorporation of sound in an exhibition brings about changes in the relationship between visitors and exhibits; in fact, this relationship may become more personal through emotional involvement as evidenced in several of the sound practices discussed previously in this paper.

In conclusion, the use of sound as a means of interpretation in the museum is still poorly studied. The reasons can be traced in the fact that the arts of sound, sound research and the respective artistic and academic community are up until today distant from developments in the museum field. Bridging the gap requires initiatives aiming at the production of audio material for exhibitions and the development of synergies between the two fields. This, in turn, will help develop methodological tools and cultivate a new museum sound culture that will further advance the museum experience of visitors.

References

1. Rodaway, P.: Sensuous Geographies: Body, Senses and Place. Routledge, London & New York (1994)
2. Bal, M.: Visual essentialism and the object of visual culture. J. Vis. Cult. 2(1), 5–32 (2003)
3. Cox, R.: There's something in the air: sound in the museum. In Henning. M. (ed.) The International Handbooks of Museum Studies: Museum Media. Wiley, New York, pp. 215–234 (2015)
4. Hooper-Greenhill, E.: Museums and the Shaping of Knowledge. Routledge, London and New York (1992)

5. Classen, C.: The Museum of the Senses: Experiencing Art and Collections. Bloomsbury, New York (2017)
6. Classen, C., Howes, D.: The museum as sensescape: western sensibilities and indigenous artifacts. In: Edwards, E., Gosden, C., Phillips, R.B. (eds.) Sensible Objects: Colonialism, Museums and Material Culture, pp. 199–222. Berg, Oxford (2006)
7. Bennett, T.: The Birth of the Museum: History, Theory, Politics. Routledge, London & New York (1995)
8. Giebelhausen, M.: The architecture is the museum. In: Marstine, J. (ed.) New Museum Theory and Practice: An Introduction, pp. 41–63. Blackwell Publishing, Oxford (2006)
9. Marstine, J.: Introduction. In: Marstine, J. (ed.) New Museum Theory and Practice: An Introduction, pp. 1–36. Blackwell Publishing, Oxford (2006)
10. Bennett, T.: Civic seeing: museums and the organization of vision. In: Macdonald, S. (ed.) A Companion to Museum Studies, pp. 263–281. Wiley, New York (2006)
11. Howes, D.: The secret of aesthetics lies in the conjugation of the senses: reimagining the museum as a sensory gymnasium. In: Levent, N., Pascual-Leone, A. (eds.) The Multisensory Museum: Cross-Disciplinary Perspectives on Touch, Sound, Smell, Memory, and Space, pp. 285–300. Rowman & Littlefield, Lanham, Maryland (2014)
12. Vergo, P.: Introduction. In: Vergo, P. (ed.) The New Museology. pp. 1–5. Reaktion, London (1989)
13. Classen, C.: Foundations for an anthropology of the senses. Int. Soc. Sci. J. **49**(153), 401–412 (1997)
14. Cox, R.: Senses, Anthropology of. In: Callan, H. (ed.) The International Encyclopaedia of Anthropology, pp. 5411–5422. Wiley, New York (2017)
15. Howes, D.: Sensual Relations: Engaging the Senses in Culture and Social Theory. University of Michigan Press, Ann Arbor (2003)
16. Howes, D.: Introduction to sensory museology. Senses Soc. **9**(3), 259–267 (2014)
17. Howes, D., Clarke, E., Macpherson, F., Best, B., Cox, R.: Sensing art and artifacts: explorations in sensory museology. Senses Soc. **13**(3), 317–334 (2018)
18. Edwards, E., Gosden, C., Phillips, R.B.: Introduction. In: Edwards, E., Gosden, C., Phillips, R.B. (eds.) Sensible Objects: Colonialism, Museums and Material Culture, pp. 1–31. Berg, Oxford (2006)
19. Levent, N., Pascual-Leone, A. (eds.): The Multisensory Museum: Cross-Disciplinary Perspectives on Touch, Sound, Smell, Memory, and Space. Rowman & Littlefield, Lanham, Maryland (2014)
20. Haldrup, M., Bærenholdt, J.O.: Heritage as performance. In: Waterton, E., Watson, S. (eds.) The Palgrave Handbook of Contemporary Heritage Research, pp. 52–68. Palgrave Macmillan, New York (2015)
21. Bubaris, N.: Sound in museums – museums in sound. Mus. Manag. Curatorship **29**(4), 391–402 (2014)
22. De Visscher, E.: Music in museums - A model for the future? In: Meyer, A. (ed.) Musikausstellungen - Intention, realisierung, interpretation, pp. 13–22. Folkwang University of the Arts, Essen, Olms (2018)
23. Wiens, K., De Visscher, E.: How do we listen to museums? Curator **62**(3), 277–281 (2019)
24. Kannenberg, J.: Listening to museums: sound mapping towards a sonically inclusive museology. Museol. Rev. **20**, 6–17 (2016)
25. Cox, C., Warner, D.: Introduction: music and the new audio culture. In: Cox, C., Warner, D. (eds.) Audio Culture: Readings in Modern Music, pp. xiii–xvii. Bloomsbury, New York (2015)
26. Belinfante, S.: Listening. In: Kohlmaier, J., Belinfante, S. (eds.) The Listening Reader, pp. 5–28. Cours de Poétique, London (2016)

27. Everrett, T.: A curatorial guide to museum sound design. Curator **62**(3), 313–325 (2019)
28. Hjortkjær, K.: The Sound of the past: sound in the exhibition at the Danish Museum Mosede Fort, Denmark 1914–18. Curator **62**(3), 453–460 (2019)
29. Stocker, M.: Exhibit sound design. Mus. Int. **47**(1), 25–28 (1995)
30. Voegelin, S.: Soundwalking the museum: a sonic journey through the visual display. In: Levent, N., Pascual-Leone, A. (eds.) The Multisensory Museum: Cross-Disciplinary Perspectives on Touch, Sound, Smell, Memory, and Space, pp. 119–130. Rowman & Littlefield, Lanham, Maryland (2014)
31. Hutchinson, R., Eardley, A.: The accessible museum: towards an understanding of international audio description practices in museums. J. Vis. Impairment Blindness **114**(6), 475–487 (2020)
32. Vaz, R., Freitas, D., Coelho, A.: Blind and visually impaired visitors' experiences in museums: increasing accessibility through assistive technologies. Int. J. Inclusive Mus. **13**(2), 57–80 (2020)
33. Mesquita, S., Carneiro, M.J.: Accessibility of European museums to visitors with visual impairments. Disability Soc. **31**(3), 373–388 (2016)
34. Angliss, S.: Sound and vision. Mus. J. **57**, 26–29 (2005)
35. Zisiou, M.: Ηχητικός μουσειολογικός σχεδιασμός: το μουσειακό ηχοτοπίο και η λειτουργία του [Sonic museological design: the museum soundscape and its function]. Unpublished doctoral thesis, Ionian University, Greece (2014)
36. Angliss, S.: Sound advice. Mus. Pract. Autumn **2005**, 32–35 (2005)
37. Weatherhead, A.: Sound advice: acoustic considerations for exhibit design. ASTC Dim. **2007**, 3–4 (2007)
38. Schoer, H.: The sounding museum: box of treasures. Transcript Publishing, Bielefeld, Germany (2014)
39. Kelly, C.: Gallery Sound. Bloomsbury, London & New York (2017)
40. Frost, S., Nuti, G.: Another dimension: integrating music with the Medieval & Renaissance Galleries. V&A Online Journal (2012). http://www.vam.ac.uk/content/journals/research-journal/issue-no.-4-summer-2012/another-dimension-integrating-music-with-the-medieval-and-renaissance-galleries/. Accessed 24 Oct 2020
41. Watson, S.: Myth, memory and the senses in the Churchill Museum. In: Dudley, S. (ed.) Museum Materialities: Objects, Engagements, Interpretations, pp. 204–223. Routledge, London & New York (2010)
42. Gazi, A.: Oral testimonies as independent museum exhibits. A case-study from the Industrial Museum in Athens. Oral Hist. Rev. **46**(1), 26–47 (2019)
43. Agrawal, S., Simon, A., Bech, S., Baerentsen, K., Forchhammer, S.: Defining Immersion: Literature Review and Implications for Research on Immersive Audiovisual Experiences. Audio Engineering Society, New York (2019)
44. Cowan, J.: The Effects of Sound on People. Wiley, New York (2016)
45. Warren, R.: Auditory Perception: An Analysis and Synthesis. Cambridge University Press, New York (2008)
46. Gustafsson, C.: Sonic branding: a consumer-oriented literature review. J. Brand Manag. **22**, 20–37 (2015)
47. Chion, M.: Audio-Vision. Columbia University Press, New York (1994)
48. Filimowicz, M., Stockholm, J.: Towards a phenomenology of the acoustic image. Organised Sound **15**(1), 5–12 (2010)
49. Bijsterveld, K.: Ears-on exhibitions: sound in the history museum. Public Hist. **37**(4), 73–90 (2015)
50. Vergo, P.: The Music of Painting: Music, Modernism and the Visual Arts from the Romantics to John Cage. Phaidon, Berlin (2010)

VR, AR, MR, Mobile Applications and Gamification in Museums and Heritage Sites

Interdisciplinary Design of an Educational Applications Development Platform in a 3D Environment Focused on Cultural Heritage Tourism

Stavros Vlizos[1,4]([⊠]), Julia-Anna Sharamyeva[2],
and Konstantinos Kotsopoulos[3]

[1] Ionian University, Corfu, Greece
vlizosst@ionio.gr
[2] National and Kapodistrian University of Athens, Athens, Greece
jamsharamy@arch.uoa.gr
[3] University of Patras, Patras, Greece
kkotsopoulos@upatras.gr
[4] Amykles Research Project, Sparta, Greece
research@amyklaion.gr

Abstract. This paper is intertwining the technology, education and public archaeology sectors in a case study approach of the archaeological site of the Sanctuary of Amyklaion, an important center of human activity in ancient Sparta, Greece. The creation of an innovative digital platform for the development of educational applications focused on cultural heritage tourism with the use of extended reality and gamification elements is presented. The applications are designed to be managed by a central documentation platform in a 3D environment produced by the digitization of the archaeological site, the excavation and archaeological finds. The main goal in the creation of this platform is to enhance the experiential learning of visitors of the archaeological site and the involvement of communities in the production and consumption of knowledge through new media, using educational methodologies and a human-centered ambient intelligence approach.

Keywords: Amyklaion · Digital humanities · Mixed reality · Augmented reality · Ambient intelligence · Gamified education applications

1 Introduction

In recent years, archaeology has unprecedently crossed its academic boundaries, forming interdisciplinary collaboration opportunities to further research regarding the preservation and presentation of archaeological data, and the interaction of cultural heritage sites with their communities. Particularly the technology sector has broadened the spectrum of possibilities offered to cultural heritage managers in overcoming challenges characteristic to ancient sites, while the education sector is crucial in providing methodologies for public archaeology programs.

© Springer Nature Switzerland AG 2021
M. Shehade and T. Stylianou-Lambert (Eds.): RISE IMET 2021, CCIS 1432, pp. 79–96, 2021.
https://doi.org/10.1007/978-3-030-83647-4_6

This research proposes an innovative approach to the design of scenarios for education applications on a digital platform using augmented and mixed reality in archaeological sites, guided by quantitative and qualitative methods. The goal is to transfer the experiential learning experience through focused methodology of the excavation of the archaeological site of the Sanctuary of Amyklaion in Sparta, Greece, to students and "cultural" tourists. The section State of the Art will cover the theory on the interdisciplinary collaboration between the broad archaeological, technological and educational sectors, and highlight some approaches that will be used in the following research. Subsequently, the section Methodology will add substantially to our understanding of focused quantitative and qualitative methods that are utilized in the creation of educational scenarios for augmented and mixed reality applications.

In the main section of the Case Study, the reader will find, after a brief presentation of the archaeological site, a detailed description of the augmented reality educational platform that is currently under development, with emphasis given on the individual components that the platform integrates for serving its purpose. We elaborate on the educational scenarios incorporated in the platform and we demonstrate via a showcase example the platform's operation. To ensure the usability of the platform, we carried out a user survey in which we record the familiarity of end users with the technologies being embedded in the platform as well as their needs with respect to the services offered. The results of the user survey along with their implications to the deployment of the platform are thoroughly discussed in the Results section, where we also outline the educational scenarios that serve the project objectives. We conclude the article (Conclusions and Future Work) with a summary of the work in progress and we outline open issues in this ongoing research that merit further study.

2 State of the Art

Over the last few years, a close cooperation has been developed between the technology and culture sectors to create useful tools for the preservation and presentation of cultural heritage [1, 2]. Augmented reality technology has opened new avenues and created unique opportunities in the field of culture. Visitors now have the opportunity of a unique and novel experience in museums and cultural heritage sites as through augmented reality they can "process" exhibits and cultural goods in another way [3, 4]. Thus, the public is actively involved in history through the provision of virtual stories and information offered by museums and cultural institutions to enhance its experience [5, 6]. The educational community has also developed a keen interest in the use of electronic tools to further educational goals. A three-dimensional virtual environment can be used as an educational tool bringing people from different locations to interaction with the purpose of gaining knowledge [7]. Moreover, gamification creates new approaches to historical experience as the visitor becomes actively involved. The concept of gamification, in using game design elements and mechanics in non-game or serious contexts to engage people and enhance learning, problem-solving and action

[8, 9], is directly related to the possibilities offered by the digital space. The digital in its various forms, websites, applications, etc. dominates as a medium in almost every aspect of human activity. Flexible, malleable, without the limitations of the analog space, it also draws most of human creativity. It is very important, however, not to turn digital into an end, for that would widen the gap between the digital and the analog/physical world. In that direction, gamification is viewed as a valuable concept applied within a variety of contexts [10] to varying degrees of success [11]. Serious or applied games with historical content are one of the most popular forms of public history and, in combination with their historical content choices, become particularly effective as narratives experienced in informal settings [12]. Gamification applications are essentially a new form of historical text that offers the opportunity to change the ways in which history is perceived by the public, as they possess properties that precede their content and simultaneously shape it [13].

The holistic approach of the following case study combines studies about interactive narratives through augmented reality [14, 15], the prospect of creating fun experiences with AR [16], the self-determination of the applications' user via gamification [17], the transition of extrinsic gamification types of users to their relative intrinsic types of users [18], the enabling of active participation and learning processes through new realities [19–21], the creation of narrative scenarios and rich material for the enhancing of the user's learning [22–24] and the logic of creating alternative narratives in case the user chooses it [25, 26]. Finally, there are also studies that cover parts of the suggested framework, e.g., the HoloMuse, that offers a complete experience interaction with museum exhibits through mixed reality [3].

3   Methodology

A case study approach was used in the archaeological site of the Sanctuary of Apollo Amyklaios which involved the collection and analysis of primary data specific to this site. For the purposes of better evaluation of the community's acquaintance with the proposed new technologies, quantitative and qualitative methods were combined in the form of a questionnaire and accompanying short interviews. To combine the two kinds of data needed the options of parallel data gathering and integrated design of the survey were chosen, providing more insightful understandings [27, 28]. The specific methods are explained in detail in the respective section of the Case Study below and the subsection Community Inquiry.

On the development of the scenarios on the digital platform, bibliographical research was conducted. Bruner's [29] theory of discovery learning was decided as the core pedagogical philosophy. A key element of this theory is the belief that for the subject of the learning process to discover new aspects in an already pre-existing form of knowledge, it is necessary to have stimuli. Through an exploratory process the essential understanding of new knowledge will be achieved. As a continuation of the above understanding, the constructivist theory of knowledge approach was selected.

According to the theory, learning effectiveness is inextricably linked to one's ability to creatively understand and assimilate knowledge, through a process of interacting with various stimuli [30]. Proponents of this educational model believe that subjects of the learning process, when actively involved in the receival and construction of information and knowledge, are then able to understand it in depth as well as maintain it [31]. In more detail, this approach highlights the effectiveness upon learning processes of play, discovery, mobilization of the subject's imagination, and interaction and interactivity with the information provided [30]. Specifically, the parts missing from traditional learning environments are what the research attempts to cover using augmented and mixed reality and gamification techniques.

4   Case Study

4.1   The Archaeological Site of Apollo Amyklaios

At a distance of 5 km south of Sparta in the Peloponnese, Greece, and on the hill of the church of Hagia Kyriaki, near the settlement of Amykles, lie the remains of the ancient Sanctuary of Apollo Amyklaios [32, 33]. According to ancient written sources [34], the sanctuary constituted the most significant religious center of the Lacedaemonians in the ancient era. The site is host to several monuments from a variety of chronological periods, most notably the unique Throne of Apollo, a temple in the form of a seat for the colossal xoanon (wooden statue) of the Olympian god Apollo, that can be undoubtedly considered the most impressive and yet enigmatic architectural monument of the end of the Archaic period. Besides the important architectural and material remains, the archaeological site is connected to major historical events and the cultic festival of Hyakinthia, celebrated annually in honor of local hero Hyakinthos and Apollo [35]. Thus, the archaeological site has sparked the interest of various distinguished scholars since the late 19th century and since 2005 it is the subject and raison d'être of the Amykles Research Project [36]. The archaeological site of the Amyklaion incorporates a series of values and offers significant benefits of scientific, historical, educational, aesthetic, local and economic character to society but also to the individual groups connected to it, for example the neighboring settlements, the scientific community, the local students etc. The evidenced continuous use of the location since the Early Helladic period, ca. 2200 BC. until today, expresses the timelessness of the archaeological site, while the presence of the church of Hagia Kyriaki since the 19th century is a component of the past and present social life of Amykles, connected to the collective memory of the inhabitants. Finally, the place offers a multi-sensory experience as it is located in a panoramic position with rich natural beauty and a vast view to the south valley framed by the mountains of Taygetos and Parnonas. All these characteristics that make the hill an archaeological, religious and natural landmark need to be shared in a direct and experiential way with its community and visitors [35].

However, there are many limitations in that direction: the site faces different difficulties, some common to other cultural spaces, such as the lack of original material due to its reuse in local constructions since late antiquity, the constraints of its rural location and ongoing systematic excavations which inhibit visitation, as well as the fact that the site remains largely unknown or indifferent to the public despite its importance. In general terms, the antiquities and the past of the area have always been a point of reference for the inhabitants, to the extent that they influence and define, to a certain extent, the modern cultural life of the area. Nevertheless, their connection to the present is mainly limited to attracting tourists, to the sterile invocation of a glorious past, and to the sometimes-unhistorical highlighting of specific aspects of a long-standing local history. These challenges present an opportunity to research existing and create innovative ways of resolving obstacles that cultural heritage sites in general may face.

4.2 Augmented and Mixed Reality Educational Platform

The present project aims to highlight the above issues and focus on the community and visitors of the site, enabling them to interact in a direct way with the monuments, the environment and the cultural heritage, and to utilize their cultural content by cultivating intuitive understanding and learning. The architecture of the digital platform for the creation of education applications consists of a central documentation platform with 3D support (CDP), an educational narrative applications development subsystem (END) and a mixed reality training modules development subsystem (MRT). The 3D content produced from the digitization of the archaeological site, the excavation and archaeological finds is imported and managed from the central documentation platform. Dynamic virtual educational narratives that intend to enrich the visitor's experience through their presentation via augmented and mixed realities are followingly developed by the archaeologists in the two subsystems of the platform. Thus, the platform will be able to unite the digital and analog cultural space through gamification interventions that activate the physical space through imagination and creative composition. Through a programming interface (API) the content of the CDP and the processes of the END and the MRT are offered to an augmented reality application (AR-App) for mobile devices which support ARCore and to a mixed reality application (MR-App) designed for HoloLens 2. With its human-centered ambient intelligence approach utilizing the location awareness from GPS location and beacons, it will enhance the experiential learning of visitors of the site, such as students and cultural tourists and demonstrate the idea that archaeological sites and their material should not only be the subject of scientific study and then just admirable by the public, but actively engaged with.

CDP, END and MRT are web applications and were developed with NET Framework. Unity, a popular cross-platform game engine, was used for presenting the documentation of 3d content utilizing its WebGL build option. Unity and C# were used for the development of the AR-App in iOS and Android and for the MR-App in HoloLens 2. One of the final goals of the project is to tangibly share the results and methods of the research with the people of the archaeological service and other cultural institutions, so that it can be utilized in other heritage sites through customization.

4.3 Proposed Objectives

Considering the prior research and outcomes of similar digital platforms, and the results of the brief analysis of weaknesses and opportunities present in the archaeological site of the Amyklaion, some key principles were proposed for the design of the educational scenarios and the user interaction of the educational applications. These principles can be sorted in two main categories, the first relating to operational objectives specific to those who will create the educational scenarios in the application environment, and the second is objectives pertaining to the way the content can be presented to the visitors.

The operational objectives include (1) the ease of configuration and detail modification of the scenarios in the END and MRT subsystems so that they can be adapted to different heritage sites through the proposed methodological analysis of their visitors, and (2) the utilization of the ambient intelligence features (GPS, beacons, etc.) of the educational applications accustomed to a heritage site so that to improve the personal experience of the user.

On the side of the content presentation modes, objectives involve (a) ensuring that the visitor can get acquainted with the key narratives of the site, (b) the use of gamification elements where possible in the learning process and (c) the use of comprehensive content for people of all social and age groups to cultivate genuine interest towards archeological material as cultural goods capable of conveying meaning to everybody and not exclusively the specialists. Finally, (d) special care must be taken to preserve interaction with the natural environment, for a direct and grounded, albeit multi-sensory, communication with the traces of history.

The development of the digital platform for the creation of educational applications followed an interdisciplinary route. For the past two years, during the excavation seasons the archaeological site, as well as specific excavation trenches have been digitized as 3D models with photorealistic textures with the use of photogrammetry terrestrial photographs and unmanned aircraft systems (drones) at regular intervals (per excavation strata). The generated 3D models of the site were imported into the content management system (CDP). The descriptive and three-dimensional information about the excavation and the findings that was stored in the CDP constitutes the basic material for the development of the educational applications. These applications take the form of a narrative with game elements utilizing augmented and mixed reality and positioning technologies (GPS and beacons). In its subsystems, the CDP allows the creator to incorporate georeferenced 3D models of the archaeological site, excavation strata and findings and cross reference them along with supportive material, such as text, images, video, audio, quizzes etc.

4.4 Community Inquiry

For the purposes of this stage of development of the educational applications in the digital platform environment, to deduce the level of user familiarity with the new technologies and based on that to fine-tune the platform's usability, a survey in the form of a questionnaire and accompanying short interviews was chosen. A focus group of 24 participants visited the archaeological site accompanied by the research team. The participants were locals who had either visited the site multiple times prior to the survey or had knowledge of it through proximity. Before the conduction of the survey, the participants were self-guided around the site with the help of temporary informational signs, placed by the research team as part of a separate study (not outlined here) regarding the best placement of the necessary permanent signage of the archaeological site which is currently in its final stages. The questionnaire contained closed questions and the accompanying interview expanded on the answers providing some open questions so as to combine the quantitative and qualitative methods of research and get the insightful results needed in this phase of the case study.

Beside demographic data, the survey included questions on the familiarity of the participants with smart devices and their type of use, as well as with the technologies of virtual, augmented and mixed reality, establishing a baseline of the participants' rudimentary expertise, or lack thereof, on the subject matter. Regarding the level of familiarity with the use and trends of smart devices, 29.17% assessed themselves as being moderately and 37.50% as being very familiar. This self-assessment seems to reflect the number of smart devices the partakers own, with 37.50% possessing 3–4 devices. Among users of smart devices, the majority (85.71%) reported needing them for both personal and professional reasons. Coming to the subject of VR, AR and MR technologies, 66.67% had knowledge of at least one prior to the survey, with the most well-known being VR (75%). From thereon, the survey focused on the use of the above-mentioned technologies in archaeology and cultural settings and their perceived usefulness in the visitors' experience and learning. Of all partakers, 75% agreed to the new technologies assisting in the visit of an archaeological site and the learning process. Regarding the possibility of experiencing the Amyklaion using extended reality technologies, the participants reported being moderately (18.18%), very (31.82%) and extremely (40.91%) interested.

Finally, the participants were asked to contribute their thoughts on which monuments of the Amyklaion would be most advantageous in their presentation through the new technologies or should be highlighted and what other parameters they believe are important for the research team to consider. Regarding the best monuments to engage digitally, out of the 24 members of the survey, 21 indicated the Throne of Apollo as the most representative of the site and the one hardest to fully understand architecturally without any visual aid. Following, with 18 mentions, was the Hyakinthia festival as a good opportunity to witness and better understand the rituals of this extremely important to the ancient Spartans annual fest. Of average interest were the altar and the *peribolos* with 16 and 10 mentions respectively, probably since they have been recently partially restored, while the remains of the Roman and Byzantine periods gathered the least suggestions (4 and 6). In addition to the monuments, some participants felt that the excavation process itself and its most important milestones through time are interesting and vital, even, to communicate through the digital application. In this context, the wish for seeing the findings of the excavation in situ, by way of 3D models of pottery and metal objects, came up as a companion mode of learning to visiting the archaeological museum that is situated in the center of Sparta. The interview yielded satisfactory results as to its initial goal, since the participants opinions and directives coincide with those of the research team: most of the participants stressed the importance of having a complete overview of the archaeological site, as well as learning from a specialist, i.e., an archaeologist, but in comprehensive terms for visitors. Additionally, many concluded that they would find the use of quizzes a fun and memorable way of learning, echoing, unbeknownst to them, the concept of gamification [8]. Finally, highlighting the landscape alongside the archaeological content was also a point that the participants thought of as ideal. The survey findings are used to better understand the end user's needs and to modify the user experience designed in the platform deployment.

5 Showcasing Current Results

To better showcase the features and use of the digital platform and its subsystems, a sample of two of the developed scenarios is followingly presented, the first one for the educational narrative applications development subsystem (END) and the second for the mixed reality training modules development subsystem (MRT).

Considering the key thematic units of the archaeological site, mentioned above, and used for the placement of informational panels throughout the site to facilitate a plain visit (Fig. 1), the research team devised an educational scenario about the Hyakinthia festival. The creator can set and categorize each task and subtask by difficulty, duration, degree of immersion, as well as define which positioning technology will be used for each one to activate (Fig. 2). In this scenario (Fig. 3), the visitor is presented with information about the festival while being in the starting position near the church (Fig. 3, 2.1). After the completion of quizzes (Fig. 4) and static tasks related to learning about the phases of the festival, they are invited to gain "rights" or an invitation to "participate" in the Hyakinthia. To do so, with the guidance of the AR-App, they must complete the task of preparation, which is comprised by subtasks of locating items they need. One example subtask is the discovery of the hidden flute by solving quizzes and following hints towards its location near the altar (Fig. 3, "Flute" point near the center). A beacon corresponding to the item has been concealed there and once the visitor approaches it during the specific scenario, it is considered found and collected. The same applies to the rest of the items. Once all the subtasks are complete, the visitor can then "participate" in the Hyakinthia festival. They are prompted to go towards the Throne of Apollo (Fig. 3, 2.2) and once the application device is positioned correctly (with the use of GPS position and a marker on the sign), corresponding to the preset viewing point of the location where the temple was situated, the visitor is rewarded with a 3D model of the Throne (Figs. 5, 6) represented in antiquity and augmented in real size.

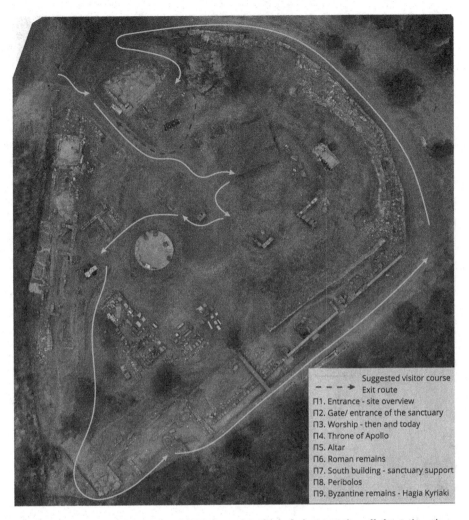

Fig. 1. The main stations of a visit to the archaeological site, covering all thematic units

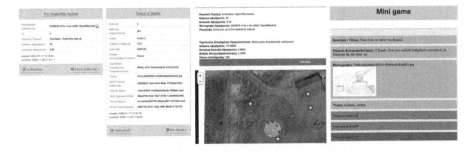

Fig. 2. The digital platform during the creation of the scenarios in the education application (END subsystem)

Fig. 3. An overview of the complete END scenario, containing points of interest and tasks for the visitor/user

Fig. 4. The AR-App during the first scenario

Fig. 5. Indicative 3D models (in progress) of monuments that will be used in augmentations in the relative scenarios

Fig. 6. AR-App augmentation lab tests

Next up, in the mixed reality subsystem a scenario was devised to show the methodology of an archaeologist and the progress of the excavation. The research team combined the above-mentioned theory, the excavation documentation, and the findings, the most important of which were digitized, with the 3D models of the strata in one of the excavation's trenches (Fig. 7) as the basis of the scenario. In the MRT subsystem one can create scenes for a scenario, where each scene contains a trench layer 3D model, and in turn for each scene create different findings groups (Fig. 8) where the appropriate objects are integrated from the CDP and visualized at their finding point accompanied with their documentation in the MR-App.

After the creation of the scenario in the MRT, the presenter sets in the archaeological site, with the use of MR-App in HoloLens 2, in placing mode, the position of the 3d excavation layers and its relative 3D objects (Fig. 9). The positions of the 3D holograms were saved in Azure Spatial Anchors so that the information can be used across multiple HoloLens, iOS, and Android devices. When the locations of all 3D holograms in the real world of the scenario are set up, the presenter uses the presenter mode of the MR-App. The MR-App recognizes the environment, and the first holograms of the scenario are appearing at their original placements (Fig. 10), so the presenter starts the interaction with them and gradually proceeds to the next steps of the presentation of the phases of the specific excavation scenario.

Fig. 7. An overview of the 3D models of excavation strata that are used in the MRT scenario

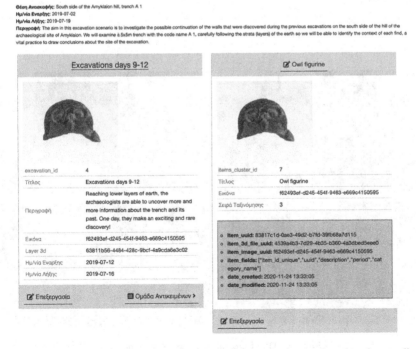

Fig. 8. The digital platform during the creation of the scenarios in the education application (MRT subsystem)

Fig. 9. HoloLens lab tests, placing mode

Fig. 10. HoloLens lab tests, presenter mode

That way, with the use of appropriate MR optical media, e.g., Microsoft HoloLens, the users can navigate a simulation of the real trench's excavation layer by layer, accompanied by the appropriate information to understand and experience the process and joy of discovery of the excavation. The AR-App and the MR-App will be thoroughly tested in the upcoming excavation season.

The elements of gaming [37] that are incorporated in the education application to engage visitors as players, relate to notions of progression, investment and the cascading information theory: with each subtask completed the users gather points and when they have amassed the needed number of points they level up and earn new badges. This adds an elementary incremental success and progression visualization. Achievements are awarded as a recognition for completing each scenario unit, which deepens the sense of pride for the work done in the application. Additionally, as new game scenarios can be easily created through the subsystems of the digital platform, a potentially infinite amount of them may be generated by the specialists, either easy and simple or more complex. In this aspect, the community will regularly receive new challenges and so will be inclined to check in periodically and thus cultivate feelings of investment and loyalty. Throughout the experience, the visitors navigate the learning environment, i.e., the archaeological site, to discover snippets of knowledge, a practice related to the cascading information theory which posits that information should be released gradually to gain the appropriate level of understanding at each point during a narrative. Special care has been taken not to overwhelm the visitors, so as not to distract them from the physical space, but instead to find new ways of connecting to it. Finally, it should be noted that the highlighted scenarios are only an example of the variety of narratives one can create in the platform subsystems utilizing different aspects of the platform's possibilities.

6   Conclusions and Future Work

The present case study proposed a design methodology of educational scenarios for digital platforms which utilize augmented and mixed reality elements based on the user needs and understanding of the environment, the topography and the narratives of the site. It is showcased in an innovative digital platform for the creation of educational applications for the archaeological site of the Amyklaion using augmented and mixed reality and gamification methods. While the aim of the platform is to revive ancient Amyklaion as a living museum, which visitors can enter and understand [38], it should be made clear that the restoration of the entire past of the archaeological site is impossible, despite all technological applications. Moreover, the composition and interpretation of the past is influenced by the ideological perceptions and experiences of the modern age [39]. Nevertheless, even with these unavoidable constraints in mind, the digital platform is a unique tool that will increase the ability to create easy and impressive results for original educational applications.

Further research of the output of the presented application, specifically on the design of the scenarios and serious games using an established assessment framework [40], and on the perception of it by its users, both creators and final users by way of quantitative and qualitative research methods, is in order. As the archaeological site is undergoing excavations and is essentially unvisitable for long periods of time, the research and feedback loop for the survey and the scenarios will be completed in the coming excavation season. This would potentially contribute to the wider research on the theoretical foundation that can explain the positive effects of gamification and new technologies [41]. Additionally, the adaptation of the digital platform and its resulting education applications on other archaeological sites or cultural settings such as museums and open-air art exhibitions is seen as a necessary long-term addition to the project by the research team.

Acknowledgment. The current research is based on the project «Digital platform for the development of educational applications focused on cultural heritage tourism with the use of augmented reality, mixed reality and gamification» (ACRONYM: AMREP - Augmented - Mixed Reality Educational Platform), which is co-financed by the European Union and Greek national funds through the Operational Program Competitiveness, Entrepreneurship and Innovation, under the call RESEARCH – CREATE – INNOVATE.

References

1. Cassidy, B., et al.: A virtual reality platform for analyzing remote archaeological sites. In: Proceedings of the 32nd International BCS Human Computer Interaction Conference. BCS Learning & Development Ltd., Swindon (2018). https://doi.org/10.14236/ewic/HCI2018.171
2. Liritzis, I., et al.: Digital technologies and trends in cultural heritage. Mediterr. Archaeol. Archaeom. **15**(3), 313–332 (2015). https://doi.org/10.5281/zenodo.33832
3. Pollalis, C., et al.: HoloMuse: enhancing engangement with archaeological artifacts through gesture-based interaction with holograms. In: Proceedings of the Eleventh International Conference on Tangible, Embedded, and Embodied Interaction, pp. 565–570. ACM, New York (2017). https://doi.org/10.1145/3024969.3025094
4. Saborido, A.E., Castanò, F., Buono, M.: Review on new technologies in art and archaeology: the Vesuvian cities. In: IOP Conference Series: Materials Science and Engineering. Florence Heri-Tech – The Future of Heritage Science and Technologies, vol. 364 (2018). https://doi.org/10.1088/1757-899X/364/1/012051
5. Papagiannakis, G., et al.: Mixed reality, gamified presence and storytelling for virtual museums. In: Lee, N. (ed.) Encyclopedia of Computer Graphics and Games. Springer, Cham (2018). https://doi.org/10.1007/978-3-319-08234-9_249-1
6. Petrelli, D.: Making virtual reconstructions part of the visit: an exploratory study. DAACH **15**, e00123 (2019). https://doi.org/10.1016/j.daach.2019.e00123
7. Arya, A., et al.: Collaborating through space and time in educational virtual environments: 3 case studies. J. Interact. Technol. Pedagogy **2** (2012). https://jitp.commons.gc.cuny.edu/collaborating-through-space-and-time-in-educational-virtual-environments-3-case-studies/
8. Deterding, S., et al.: From game design elements to gamefulness: defining gamification. In: Proceedings of the 15th International Academic MindTrek Conference: Envisioning Future Media Environments, pp. 9–15. ACM, New York (2011). https://doi.org/10.1145/2181037.2181040
9. Kapp, K.M.: The Gamification of Learning and Instruction: Game-Based Methods and Strategies for Training and Education. Pfeiffer, San Francisco (2012)
10. Zichermann, G., Linder, J.: The Gamification Revolution. McGraw-Hill Education, New York (2013)

11. Nacke, L.E., Deterding, S.: The maturing of gamification research. Comput. Hum. Behav. **71**, 450–454 (2017). https://doi.org/10.1016/j.chb.2016.11.062
12. Chapman, J., Rich, P.: The design, development and evaluation of a gamification platform for business education. In: Academy of Management Annual Meeting Proceedings, vol. 2015, no. 1 (2017). https://doi.org/10.5465/AMBPP.2015.185
13. Dougherty, J., Nawrotzki, K. (eds.): Writing History in the Digital Age. University of Michigan Press, Ann Arbor (2013). https://doi.org/10.3998/dh.12230987.0001.001
14. Shilkrot, R., Montfort, N., Maes, P.: nARratives of augmented worlds. In: Proceedings of the IEEE International Symposium on Mixed and Augmented Reality - Media, Arts, Social Science, Humanities and Design. IEEE, Munich (2014). https://doi.org/10.1109/ISMAR-AMH.2014.6935436
15. Viana, B.S., Nakamura, R.: Immersive interactive narratives in augmented reality games. In: Marcus, A. (ed.) DUXU 2014. LNCS, vol. 8518, pp. 773–781. Springer, Cham (2014). https://doi.org/10.1007/978-3-319-07626-3_73
16. Yovcheva, Z., et al.: Empirical evaluation of smartphone augmented reality browsers in an urban tourism destination context. IJMHCI **6**(2), 10–31 (2014). https://doi.org/10.4018/ijmhci.2014040102
17. Hammady, R., Ma, M., Temple, N.: augmented reality and gamification in heritage museums. In: Marsh, T., Ma, M., Oliveira, M.F., Baalsrud Hauge, J., Göbel, S. (eds.) JCSG 2016. LNCS, vol. 9894, pp. 181–187. Springer, Cham (2016). https://doi.org/10.1007/978-3-319-45841-0_17
18. Kotsopoulos, K., et al.: An authoring platform for developing smart apps which elevate cultural heritage experiences: a system dynamics approach in gamification. J. Ambient Intell. Human. Comput. (2019). https://doi.org/10.1007/s12652-019-01505-w
19. Bacca, J., et al.: Mobile augmented reality in vocational education and training. Procedia Comput. Sci. **75**, 49–58 (2015). https://doi.org/10.1016/j.procs.2015.12.203
20. Dunleavy, M., Dede, C.: Augmented reality teaching and learning. In: Spector, J.M., Merrill, M.D., Elen, J., Bishop, M.J. (eds.) Handbook of Research on Educational Communications and Technology, pp. 735–745. Springer, New York (2014). https://doi.org/10.1007/978-1-4614-3185-5_59
21. Ellenberger, K.: Virtual and augmented reality in public archaeology teaching. Adv. Archaeol. Pract. **5**(3), 305–309 (2017). https://doi.org/10.1017/aap.2017.20
22. Huang, T.C.: Seeing creativity in an augmented experiential learning environment. Univ. Access Inf. Soc. **18**, 301–313 (2019). https://doi.org/10.1007/s10209-017-0592-2
23. Matsuo, M.: A framework for facilitating experiential learning. HRDR **14**(4), 442–461 (2015). https://doi.org/10.1177/1534484315598087
24. Rousou, M., et al.: Engaging visitors of archaeological sites through "emotive" storytelling experiences: a pilot at the Athenian Agora of Athens. Archeologia e Calcolatori **28**(2), 405–420 (2017). https://doi.org/10.19282/AC.28.2.2017.33
25. Mott, B.W.: Decision-theoretic narrative planning for guided exploratory learning environments. Dissertation, North Carolina State University (2006)
26. Riedl, M., Saretto, C.J., Young, R.M.: Managing interaction between users and agents in a multi-agent storytelling environment. In: Proceedings of the Second International Joint Conference on Autonomous Agents and Multiagent Systems, pp. 741–748. ACM, New York (2004). https://doi.org/10.1145/860575.860694
27. Caracelli, V.J., Greene, J.C.: Crafting mixed-method evaluation designs. New Dir. Eval. 19–32 (1997). https://doi.org/10.1002/ev.1069
28. Greene, J.C.: Mixed Methods in Social Inquiry. Jossey-Bass, San Francisco (2007)
29. Bruner, J.S.: The act of discovery. Harv. Educ. Rev. **31**, 21–32 (1961)
30. Papert, S., Harel, I.: Constructionism. Ablex Publishing, Norwood (1991)

31. Winn, W.D.: A conceptual basis for educational applications of virtual reality. HITL technical report R-93-9, Human Interface Technology Laboratory, Seattle, WA (1993)
32. Vlizos, S.: Das Heiligtum und seine Beigaben: Bronzestatuetten vom Amyklaion. In: Frielinghaus, H., Stroszeck, J. (eds.) Kulte und Heiligtümer in Griechenland: Neue Funde und Forschungen. Beiträge zur Archäologie Griechenlands, Mainz, vol. 4, pp. 71–95 (2017)
33. Vlizos, S.: Metallwerkstätten, Produktion und Infrastruktur des Heiligtums: der Fall des spartanischen Amyklaions. In: Lo Monaco, A. (ed.) Spending on the Gods. Economy, Financial Resources and Management in the Sanctuaries in Greece. Annuario della Scuola Archeologica di Atene e delle Missioni Italiane in Oriente, Supplementum, Athens, vol. 7, pp 37–46 (2020)
34. Amykles Research Project (n.d) Testimonia. https://amyklaion.gr/en/sanctuary/testimonia. Accessed 29 Nov 2020
35. Amykles Research Project (n.d). https://amyklaion.gr/en. Accessed 29 Nov 2020
36. Delivorrias, A., Vlizos, S. (eds): Amykles Research Project: Works 2005–2010, vol. 11–12, pp. 73–191. Benaki Museum (2012)
37. Salen, K., Zimmerman, E.: Rules of Play: Game Design Fundamentals. The MIT Press, Cambridge (2003)
38. Jacobsen, J., Holden, L.: Virtual heritage: living in the past. Techné **10**(3), 55–61 (2007)
39. Champion, E.: Heritage role playing: history as an interactive digital game. In: Pisan, Y. (ed.) Proceedings of IE 2004: Australian Workshop on Interactive Entertainment. University of Technology, Sydney (2004)
40. Mitgutsch, K., Alvarado, N.: Purposeful by design? A serious game design assessment framework. In: Proceedings of the International Conference on the Foundations of Digital Games, pp. 121–128. ACM, New York (2012). https://doi.org/10.1145/2282338.2282364
41. Sailer, M., et al.: How gamification motivates: an experimental study of the effects of specific game design elements on psychological need satisfaction. Comput. Hum. Behav. **69**, 371–380 (2017). https://doi.org/10.1016/j.chb.2016.12.033

Cultural Heritage Documentation: The Case Study of the Ottoman Bath in Apollonia, Greece

Stella Sylaiou[1]([✉]), Paschalis Androudis[1], Maria Tsiapali[2],
Nikolaos Trivizadakis[2], Dimitrios Ramnalis[3], Vassilios Polychronos[3],
Vassilios Efopoulos[4], and Konstantinos Evangelidis[5]

[1] Department of History and Archaeology, Aristotle University of Thessaloniki, 54124 Thessaloniki, Greece
[2] Ephorate of Antiquities of Thessaloniki City, 546 46 Thessaloniki, Greece
[3] GEOSENSE IKE, Terma Proektasis Maiandrou Str., P.O. Box 352 - 57013, Oraiokastro, Thessaloniki, Greece
[4] TESSERA S.A., Dardanellion 11, 57010 Pefka, Thessaloniki, Greece
[5] Department of Surveying and Geoinformatics Engineering, International Hellenic University, Serres Campus, 62124 Serres, Greece

Abstract. This paper presents a cutting-edge application, namely, "Mergin'-Mode" (https://merginmode.com/), on the basis of its first pilot implementation which took place within a project aiming at the accurate visual documentation and innovative reconstruction of a specific cultural heritage building. Prior to this, it presents the primary mapping techniques and provides a comparative analysis and a benchmarking based on features that are considered critical in the cases of Cultural Heritage (CH) sites digital documentation. The ability of "Mergin'Mode" to represent monuments by merging their actual image with a detailed and accurate virtual reconstruction of their initial condition, overlaid with the use of Mixed Reality (MR) is demonstrated. Moreover, the archeological characteristics of the specific site, as well as background information on the technologies employed and the documentation protocols are provided. The application, which relies on Geoinformation technologies, is able to provide stunning on-site MR experiences by combining state-of-the-art digital recording technologies (mainly Photogrammetry and laser scanning), as well as input from archeologists and other specialists. More specifically the case study presented, regards the reconstruction and representation of an Ottoman Bath in Apollonia, Greece. The paper begins with the provision of background knowledge and context, giving a description of the technical processes involved in the pilot implementation of "Mergin'Mode". The architecture of "Mergin'Mode", i.e., its components and the characteristics of its authoring tool are described, thereby outlining the applications' vast ability to adapt, expand and provide meaningful, exhilarating, and informative experiences to on-site (or remote) visitors. "Mergin'Mode" is presented as an example of a cutting-edge application that brings to life archeological sites fusing the actual with the virtual, the present and the past, by incorporating diverse interaction modalities, multimodal content, dynamic input with the use of Geoinformatics, thus adding value to the experience of CH sites' visitors.

© Springer Nature Switzerland AG 2021
M. Shehade and T. Stylianou-Lambert (Eds.): RISE IMET 2021, CCIS 1432, pp. 97–110, 2021.
https://doi.org/10.1007/978-3-030-83647-4_7

Keywords: Digital heritage · Geoinformatics · Mixed Reality

1 Introduction

In spite of provisions made by international agreements, conventions and protocols, Cultural Heritage (CH) is still vulnerable not only to natural or man-made disasters, but also during recovery and reconstruction phases. CH is at risk and needs protection from: Time and lack of adequate funds for its preservation, natural factors such as earthquakes, extreme weather conditions, acts of intentional destruction caused by people, e.g., wars, conflicts, and terrorism, accidents such as fire etc. New technologies offer the opportunity to record and directly render monuments in minute detail, creating 3D digital 'twins' of the original buildings or artefacts, thereby facilitating preservation and conservation efforts, especially in the case of damage occurring after the digitization process. Moreover, emerging technologies, especially Virtual (VR) and Mixed Reality (MR) generate vast prospects with respect to monuments' promotion, through historically accurate and impressive visual reconstructions of the past. These visualisations of monuments in specific junctures of the past with the use of MR/VR applications, bring history to life. Therefore, users, be them cultural tourists, or locals, gain insights on CH sites' history, as such applications transform their visiting experience, with spectacular as well as informative representations that enable them to better understand the appearance, function and significance of CH buildings.

Promotion of CH sites is key for the Cultural tourist industry, and the development of such applications, especially those launched by hand-held devices (smartphones or tablets) can offer a non-intrusive tool for fostering visitors' experience and understanding through virtually reconstructing the past, without seeking recourse to intrusive and often controversial physical interventions on monuments that seek to re-construct or extend existing structures in order to give a better sense of a site's past.

This paper presents such a cutting-edge application, namely "Mergin'Mode" (https://merginmode.com/) which demonstrates monuments by merging their actual image with virtual reconstruction of their initial/past appearance, overlaid with the use of Mixed Reality, with efficacy and accuracy. This MR application relies on Geoinformation technologies and it is able to provide exiting as well as informative on-site experiences by combining state-of-the-art digital recording technologies, input from archeologists and other specialists for historically correct reconstructions.

In his paper, the pilot implementation of "Mergin'Mode" that delivered the reconstruction and representation of the Ottoman Bath in Apollonia is presented, while a description of context and processes leading to this implementation are provided. More specifically, the following section (i.e., 'Background'), provides an overview of the three major mapping techniques used for CH buildings, their advantages, and weaknesses, thereby providing context and background information before outlining the methods employed in this pilot implementation in the third section of this paper (in Sect. 3.3). Likewise, in Sect. 2 ('Background'), contextual information is given on the internationally established guidelines pertaining to the recording of CH monuments (i.e., covering topics such as location, typology) before describing the project's respective approach, based on the adaptation of existing norms (in Sect. 3.2). Section 3 presents the "Mergin' Mode" pilot project starting from an overview of the site's history and characteristics (Sect. 3.1) from an archeological standpoint. Then, Sub-Sect. 3.2 provides an outline of the elements included in the documentation procedure adopted by this project, with emphasis on the key areas/topics that are covered. Section 3.3 presents the methods employed from a technical perspective, with regard to data acquisition (visual documentation), 3D rendering and monuments' reconstruction. In Sect. 3.4, the two main components (managers' and end-users') of "Mergin' Mode" are outlined. Namely the 'manager's component' that relates to administrators who e.g., manage or deposit digital material, and the end-user component. Finally, the "Mergin' Mode" authoring tool is presented along with the capabilities it includes for enriching the presented content with customized, adaptable material and its provisions for input.

2   An Overview of Mapping and Digital Documentation Methods

Various initiatives have stressed the need for setting principles for monuments and sites' recording. More specifically, International organisations, such as ICOMOS that in 1996 published the Principles for the Recording of Monuments, Groups of Buildings and Sites[1] have tried to address this need. Likewise, the Council of Europe in 2012 published 'Guidelines on Cultural Heritage: Technical tools for heritage conservation and management'. Moreover, at a national level, there have been various initiatives from the Greek Ministry of Culture, such as POLEMON[2]; furthermore, the Greek Archaeological Cadastre has set guidelines about the types of information that have to be recorded.

For many years, topographic surveying based on TDS (Total Data Stations) or GNSS receivers was the key mapping method for producing accurate measurements both 2D and 3D. However, the results were not rich enough in content and additional effort had to be spent to highlight picture details. Furthermore, classic TDS mapping was time consuming and the larger and more varied the site was, the more complex and time consuming the workflow was. Finally, the produced documentation was inconsistent as it was a sum of free-standing, and not systematically interconnected drawings, notes, designs, images, and pictures.

During past decade, the LiDAR or Laser Scanning, a contemporary active sensor technique was introduced as the ultimate mapping tool for archaeological purposes. A LiDAR system measures distances by sending laser pulses at an object and receives the reflected pulses with a sensor. By applying basic trigonometry rules, it is possible to calculate accurate distances and by receiving pulses from thousands or millions of reflecting points it is possible to reconstruct a point-based model. LiDAR is able to scan large scale sites accurately. However, this is an expensive task and the whole process proves to be relatively slow since every object must be scanned from different angles in

---

[1] https://www.icomos.org/charters/archives-e.pdf.

[2] http://nam.culture.gr/portal/page/portal/deam/erga/nam.

order to be reconstructed in 3D. For a new scene of an object to be captured, the equipment must be moved and set up to a new position and many times it must be lifted with crane or with a very expensive drone. Complex ruins like temples and sculptures require a very time-consuming workflow but in the end the documentation is accurate, rich, and consistent.

Photogrammetry is nowadays considered as the ultimate mapping technique, boosted by the technological progress noted in DSLR (Digital single-lens reflex), pocket cameras, smartphone cameras, drone cameras etc. Photogrammetry is a process for extracting accurate 3D models, reconstructed from 2D images. Being a passive sensor mapping technique, it can be applied in any case where reflectance exists. That is the one of the basic differences between Photogrammetry and LiDAR [1]. As the reflectance varies due to light or material, Photogrammetry performance varies too. Been cost effective, easily available, and versatile Photogrammetry makes an appealing option for certain types of surveying. Add to this the stunning performance of modern drones with cameras, you have a robust, efficient, cost effective, content rich and accurate mapping technique.

Mapping is a cornerstone of systematic archaeological documentation and interpretation. Table 1 provides a comparison matrix a benchmarking of the three methodologies:

Table 1. Comparing CH mapping methods

Characteristics	TDS/GNSS mapping	LiDAR mapping	Photogrammetry mapping
Initial investment, hardware and software	Moderate	High	Low
Portability	Moderate	Moderate	Excellent
Acquisition workflow	Hard	Hard	Easy
Processing workflow	Moderate	Moderate	Moderate
Time cost workflow	High	High	Low
Content rich deliverables	Low	High	High
Accuracy	High	High	High
Distance dependence	Moderate dependence	High dependence	Low dependence
Light dependence	High dependence	Independent	High dependence
Cost Benefit	Low	Moderate	High
Versatility	Low	Moderate	High

Applications that use VR, AR and MR have been developed for personalised heritage exhibitions [2] or for personalised cultural heritage indoor and outdoor experiences [3], for enhancing virtual museum experiences [4]. However, before 4G's introduction, it was not possible to support a MR-based scene on a mobile smart device, due to the limited bandwidth and Internet speeds in the Global System for Mobile Communications (GSM) networks. A survey about MR systems in indoor and outdoor applications in cultural heritage is provided in [5] and [6]. A MR smart guide provides information about historical buildings and relevant 3D contents can be overlapped with the real monuments [5]. In our case, "Mergin' Mode" project aims at monument demonstration through the merging of the real with the virtual, assisted by geoinformatics technologies with the help of MR providing an open-source platform that relies on location-based data and services, as well as geospatial functionalities [6].

3 Mergin' Mode Project

"Mergin' Mode" (https://merginmode.com/) is a Cultural Information System aiming to demonstrate monuments by merging real with virtual, in a Mixed Reality, assisted by Geoinformation technologies. The system makes use of cutting-edge technologies in the field of Geoinformatics for creating digital surface models of high accuracy, through the usage of unmanned aerial vehicles and worldwide recognized contemporary photogrammetric tools. It comprises an authoring tool and an app that with the help of a GPS can support overlaying of (a) highly detailed virtual terrain environments and three-dimensional models representing animate or inanimate objects, placed, or moving over these environments and (b) the real world as captured by the camera of a smart device [6].

3.1 Study Area and Monumental Complex

The *mahallah* of Pazargah (in Greek Παζαρούδα, act. Apollonia) was settled by the southern shore of lake Beşik (present-day Volvi). It belonged to the *nahiye* of Pazargah under the *Kaza* of Thessaloniki. The site enjoyed a special status and prosperity during the Ottoman period, with an important bazaar that lasted for many days [7].

This prosperity during the 16th century was probably linked to the great patronage of the Ottoman Grand Vizier Sokollu Mehmed Paşa, who built and endowed there a big complex of pious character, which served mainly as a station post [8–12]. The ruins of this grandiose complex still stand close to the Via Egnatia axis and could give us just a glimpse of the great area in which they extend. They form a rectangular complex (overall dimensions approximately: 47 × 20, 40 m), from which are now preserved a small mosque, a longitudinal ruined inn (khan) and in a much better condition its bath (hamam). Ioli Vingopoulou, linking the construction of the monuments with Grand Vizier Sokollu, proposed as foundation date the period 1566–1574 [10], while Heath Lowry suggested as possible date of construction the period 1565–1579 [8]. It seems that the area around the lake Beşik (Volvi), was a pious foundation (*vaqf*), the revenues of which were destined to the maintenance of the Royal Library at the Palace of Topkapı in Istanbul. The complex is mentioned in the sources by the Venetian officer Gabrielle Cavazza in 1591 [8], as well as by the Ottoman travelers of the 17th c. Katip Çelebi [13] and Evliya Çelebi [14].

The hamam is a representative Ottoman building of the type that is still preserved in present-day Greece [15–18]. This important and historic building of Apollonia needs a careful and detailed maintenance, in order to stop further collapses and decay of the existing structural building material and mortar. The pavement and the system of hypocausts also need consolidation and restoration.

The hamam was built with stones of medium size, bricks, and mortar. In its upper parts, the vaults are constructed with bricks and were once covered with tiles. Once it was a longitudinal structure, with all its constructive parts built along the N-S. axis. First it was the so called "cold room" (a vestibule, in Turkish *Camekan*), a high and almost square room, once covered with a four-sided wooden tiled roof, then the intermediate room (*soğukluk*) and finally the hot section (*sıcaklık* or *iç hamam*) with its heating system (*külhan*).

From the hamam that stands in a semi-ruined condition, today remain the section with the vaulted hot room built on hypocausts, the intermediate vaulted room, and a small room of secondary use. The "cold" section of the bath, where its entrance was opened is in ruins. According to scholars, there are two building phases in the remaining parts of the hamam, the second one possibly dating to the 18th of 19th c.

The vault of the *sıcaklık* of the bath is resting on its corners on five-sided squinches, a building practice that is very common in the Ottoman architecture of the 16th c. A quite similar practice was used in the Sokollu Mehmed Paşa hamamı in Edirne, as well as in Yeni hamam in Thessaloniki. The interior of the hot section, as well as of the intermediate room of our hamam, are lightened by holes with symmetrical arrangement which are opened at the highest parts of the vaults.

Judging by the type of its ground plan, the hamam of Apollonia could be classified in the group of Ottoman baths with a polygonal hot section adorned with niches (in fact there are several sub-classifications of the types of Ottoman hamams that are already proposed by Greek and foreign scholars).

3.2   Monument's Documentation

Initially we have defined the scope and the methods of recording. The scope was to record in detail the monument in its current condition not only for reasons of digital preservation, but also to be virtually reconstructed and presented in the Mergin'Mode platform. For the needs of the monument's documentation the following information has been recorded:

- Its name
- Its type
- Its location with coordinates
- Its chronological period
- If it can be visited or not
- If it is connected to other monuments or not
- Its dimensions
- Its materials
- Its special characteristics (e.g., ornaments, decorations, inscriptions)
- The name of the Ephorate of Antiquities that has its responsibility
- The name of the recording organization
- Its (short) description

- Cross-references to related monument's documentation concerning texts, photographs, studies, archaeological publications, archaeological reports

The information that corresponds to the above topics will be presented in the application in the end-users' component as contextual data that will expandable and navigable in a non-intrusive way. However, the information provided is regarded as key, because it relates to the integrity and dependability of the background information given for each and every monument that will be (re)presented through "Mergin'Mode". The flexible nature of the authoring tool and overall architecture of "Mergin'Mode" allows for the inclusion of multimodal material describing e.g., special characteristics and explanatory information on the monuments' type, thereby providing context beyond a mere archival-style taxonomical description of the CH buildings main data. Data sets organised in a consistent and standardized way, do not function as reference information or some kind of meta-data only, but can play a significant role on issues of interoperability, cross-referencing as well as enable search of contents along searchable terms or key words, especially as the application will cover more monuments, as discussed in the fourth section.

3.3 Data Collection/3D Data Acquisition

To meet the project's requirements, two different techniques with identical outputs in terms of deliverables were selected. These were a) Photogrammetry, for the monument exterior and surrounding area and b) laser scanning (LiDAR), in the interior due to lack of light. Those two independent workflows deliver same type of outputs that can be easily aligned together to produce a highly accurate and content rich total 3D reconstruction.

For the Photogrammetry workflow the Parrot Anafi [19] drone was employed. It utilizes a 20 mpixel camera on a 3-axis stabilization system and produces high quality images. Parrot Anafi is a small yet very capable camera drone. It weights 320 gr and its size can fit and maneuver easily in narrow paths between the construction and surrounding trees and poles. Furthermore, its size and low weight makes it safe to operate. Image acquisition has been done manually as the shape and the size of the construction could not be supported by automatic mission planning. A total number of 229 images were captured in different heights and angles.

For image processing, the industry leading photogrammetry software Pix4Dmapper was employed[3]. Through a flexible three-step processing workflow it provides high capabilities of assessing and enhancing a model's accuracy and image calibration. That is considered very critical for highly accurate models when images are oblique and not at nadir. Figure 1a, depicts the output, after image calibration and Fig. 1b the resulting 3D textured mesh.

---

[3] Pix4Dmapper, https://www.pix4d.com/product/pix4dmapper-photogrammetry-software.

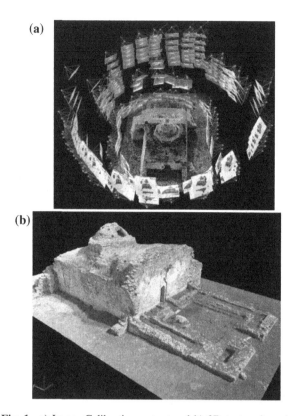

Fig. 1. a) Image Calibration output and b) 3D textured mesh.

For the monument interior a LiDAR approach was adopted, as the ambient light was minimal and Photogrammetry methodology could not be applied. The Laser Scanner employed was the FARO FOCUS M70. It is a state-of-the-art laser scanner device being capable of mapping up to 70 m. In terms of speed and productivity FOCUS M70 has a maximum speed of 488,000 points per second. Its accuracy is 3 mm and utilizes an on-board GNSS receiver and altimeter and a camera that can capture panoramas up to 165 Mpixel resolution. The camera is used to enhance 3D points with texture.

To map every aspect of the monument's interior a network of target spheres and checkerboards was set up to assist the post processing alignment of the different scans. A total of eight scenes (scans) with a mean duration of 8 min each were planed and captured. During each scene acquisition, artificial flood lighting was employed, to enhance the scanned textures and details of the surfaces (Fig. 2).

Fig. 2. Target Spheres network

Post processing was necessary as all the different scenes had to be aligned and cleaned from noise in order to produce one unique output 3D model. The software employed was the FARO Scene[4]. The three-step workflow that was adopted included 1) importing of the different scans, 2) aligning and merging of the scans using the target registration method by utilizing the target spheres and checkerboards and 3) 'dressing'/overlaying the model with textures. The final output was the 3D model both as a 3D point cloud and as 3D textured mesh.

Figures 3a and b illustrate a view of the 3D reconstruction of the Ottoman bath made for the needs of the project. For the 3D reconstruction of the heritage building, we have used: (a) reality-based data collected with the aid of laser scanning for indoor and photogrammetry for outdoor mapping [20], and (b) 3D reconstructions based on historical documentation provided by the managing authority of the monument e.g., analogue and digitized material: maps, archival documents, photographs, etc. and created with the help of 3D Studio Max software.

The 3D reconstructions will be enriched in the future, in order to include complex architectural and structural elements in the interior of the monument, as well as historical information especially in connection to the bath's functions with the use of MR. Thus, the geometric modeling of the industrial buildings was conducted with real data that will also be useful for their preservation, and the monitoring of possible changes, and in case of eventual damages, will also assist to their reconstruction.

---

[4] FARO's 3D Documentation Software for terrestrial and handheld Scanners, https://www.faro.com/products/construction-bim/faro-scene/.

(a)

(b)

Fig. 3. Views of the Ottoman bath's virtual reconstruction

3.4   Presentation with Mixed Reality App

"Mergin' Mode" comprises two software components: (a) the Manager component used for preparing the cultural content and (b) the end-user component concerning the visitor of the site which will be perceiving the digital content merged with the real world captured by the smart device camera, experiencing that way a MR.

The end-user component was developed fully in open source Javascript libraries. It takes advantage of the state-management supported by React.js and Redux.js, which makes rendering fast and responsive. For the development of 3D geospatial worlds with animated and inanimate georeferenced models Three.js was employed. For any transformation between coordinate reference systems Proj4.js was employed. The software was tested for a mean content size of 100 MB, on a mean mobile device (octa core processor, 4 GB RAM). The computational load depends on the content size; however, the processing capacity of an average mobile device seems to respond satisfactorily.

For demonstration purposes a custom virtual geospatial world was prepared. The creation of the custom virtual geospatial world of the monument practically means to put 3D models, along with motion effects to produce a 3D scene of the monument. The

Manager component offers for the capability of easily: a) importing 3D point clouds, DTM/DSM and 3D textured meshes of the area, b) specifying or importing points, paths, and polygons, for placing other 3D models (animate or inanimate), and c) specifying motion paths. The objects of a 3D scene of a custom virtual geospatial world can be exported and served via geospatial web services during navigation on site or may be downloaded offsite, for offline use. A demo platform of the Manager component with the Ottoman bath's virtual reconstruction along with its photogrammetrical mapping is available online[5] and is also demonstrated.[6]

As the user lies and navigates inside the "influence area" of the site and observes it, and as the position and the angle of view of his smart device are being modified, virtual events and storytelling are appropriately enabled and visualized. The end-user component is a typical app that handles the satellite navigation system, the gyroscope, and the camera of a smart device, merging the real with the virtual to present the content in an MR mode (Fig. 4). In the final version of Mergin'Mode app we expect that relationships between the 3D reconstruction of the monument and the representation of its content will contribute to visitors' engagement via interactivity and the use of narratives [21].

Fig. 4. Virtual reconstruction in the mobile app

The key component of MR that differentiates the end-user experience from that of an AR/VR setting, is the implementation of occlusion [22] between virtual and real

---

objects. That way, whenever a virtual object is behind a real object (or vice-versa) the app renders appropriately the mixed reality scene by hiding the virtual object (or part of it) behind the real object. Occlusion is achieved through Mixed Object implementation. A Mixed Object is the result of linking a real object captured by a camera with a set of digital properties [23]. In our case the digital properties include a three-dimensional georeferenced digital model of the real object. The digital model is rendered with a transparent mask over the real object and its exact positioning in relation with other virtual objects implements occlusion. Figure 5 shows the three steps for the Mixed Object implementation. The Ottoman bath photogrammetrically mapped transformed to a virtual object presented with a textured mesh, is partially covering a virtual tree (left picture). Applying typical image processing techniques (blackening, additive blending) a transparent mask is applied, however the virtual Ottoman bath still covers the virtual tree (middle picture). The two pictures analysed were developed offsite. Onsite -in the field- the end-user app renders the real Ottoman bath as this is captured by the camera, but it has already been transformed to a Mixed Object, since its transparent digital model still covers the virtual tree (right picture).

Fig. 5. Implementing a Mixed Object to achieve occlusion

4   Conclusions and Future Prospects

"Mergin'Mode" is a cutting-edge application of emerging technologies, bound to move beyond its first implementation in the Apollonia Ottoman complex which essentially provided an opportunity to develop and test its characteristics. The technologies available today for gathering and rendering data in 3D, offer in conjunction with MR applications, unprecedented capabilities to CH organisations to promote monuments and draw the attention of large audiences, e.g., cultural tourists or students, and raise awareness about such sites. The lowering of costs in hardware as well as software that allow easy fusion of data and 3D rendering, with the ability to enable highly enjoyable and meaningful MR experiences at handheld/portable devices, democratizes knowledge and offers a fulcrum for bolstering cultural tourism. Likewise, conservation efforts benefit directly (through detailed documentation) and indirectly by increasing public/organizational interest. "Mergin'Mode" has been implemented at a relatively small monument that lies off the beaten (tourist) track. However, special interest groups are already visiting the site and the existence as well as provision of such an application would drastically increase the level of interest and could function as incentive for more visits. A study of users' reception of the app would be an adequate complement to this research with the use of mixed method tools. Moreover, this could take the form of expert/user evaluation thereby gaining insights by analyzing the data in a comparative manner. Moreover, the real potential of "Mergin'Mode" lies in its use within urban spaces such as Thessaloniki, Rome, or Athens where existing monuments could not only come to life, but a vast number of users could incorporate into their everyday lives the use of a specialized and user-friendly MR application for hand-held devices, in order to gain insights and look anew CH buildings that surround them. The availability of applications such as "Mergin'Mode" can increase the attraction of cities where present and past merge, with the use of innovative technologies.

Funding. This research has been co-financed by the European Regional Development Fund of the European Union and Greek national funds through the Operational Program Competitiveness, Entrepreneurship, and Innovation, under the Special Action "Open Innovation in Culture" (project code: T6YBΠ-00297).

References

1. Barsanti, S.G., Remondino, F., Visintini, D.: Photogrammetry and Laser Scanning for archaeological site 3D modeling–some critical issues. In: CEUR Workshop Proceedings, 2nd Workshop on the New Technologies for Aquileia, vol. 948, pp. B1–B10 (2012)
2. Liarokapis, F., Sylaiou, S.: Experiencing personalised heritage exhibitions through multimodal mixed reality interfaces. In: Proceedings of the 5th International Workshop on Ubiquitous and Collaborative Computing in Conjunction with the 24th BCS Conference on Human-Computer Interaction, 7 September 2010, pp. 28–37. University of Abertay, Dundee (2010)
3. Liarokapis, F., Sylaiou, S., Mountain, D.: Personalizing virtual and augmented reality for cultural heritage indoor and outdoor experiences. In: Proceedings of the 9th International Symposium on Virtual Reality, Archaeology and Cultural Heritage, Eurographics, Braga, Portugal, pp. 55–62 (2008)
4. Sylaiou, S., Kasapakis, V., Gavalas, D., Dzardanova, E.: Leveraging mixed reality technologies to enhance museum visitor experiences. In: Proceedings of the 9th IEEE International Conference on Intelligent Systems, Madeira Island, Portugal, pp. 595–601 (2018)
5. Bekele, M.K., Pierdicca, R., Frontoni, E., Malinverni, E.S., Gain, J.: A survey of augmented, virtual, and mixed reality for cultural heritage. ACM J. Comput. Cult. Herit. **11**, 1–36 (2018)
6. Evangelidis, K., Sylaiou, S., Papadopoulos, T.: Mergin' mode: mixed reality and geoinformatics for monument demonstration. Appl. Sci. **10**(11), 3826 (2020)
7. Dimitriadis, V.: Tax categories of the villages of Thessaloniki during the Turkish occupation. Makedonika **20**, 375–462 (1980). (in Greek). [Δημητριάδης, Β.: Φορολογικές κατηγορίες των χωριών της Θεσσαλονίκης κατά την Τουρκοκρατία. Μακεδονικά **20**, 375–462 (1980)]
8. Mertzios, K.: Μνημεία Μακεδονικής Ιστορίας, Thessaloniki (1947)
9. Hatzitrifonos, E.: Οθωμανικό λουτρό στην Απολλωνία της Βόλβης. Μακεδονικά **26**, 139–168, 1–11 (1988)
10. Vingopoulou-Papazotou, I.: Η χρονολόγηση του Οθωμανικού συγκροτήματος στην Απολλωνία (1566–1574). Μακεδονικά **27**, 409–411 (1990)

11. Vingopoulou-Papazotou, I.: Δίκτυο αρχαιολογικών χώρων και μνημείων Κεντρικής Μακεδονίας (Νομοί Θεσσαλονίκης-Κιλκίς-Πιερίας). Πρόσωπο και Χαρακτήρας (2007)

12. Androudis, P.: Η πρώιμη Οθωμανική τέχνη και αρχιτεκτονική στην Ελλάδα. Barbounakis Editions, Thessaloniki (2016)

13. Rumeli und Bosna geographisch beschrieben von Mustafa ben Abdalla Hadschi Chalfa. (aus dem türkishen übersetzt von Joseph von Hammer), Wien, 83 (1812)

14. Moschopoulos, N.: Η Ελλάς κατά τον Εβλιά Τσελεμπή. Μια τουρκική περιγραφή της Ελλάδος κατά τον ΙΖ΄ αιώνα. Κριτική ανάλυσις και έλεγχος του «Οδοιπορικού» (σεγιαχατναμε) του Τούρκου περιηγητού. Επετηρίς της Εταιρείας Βυζαντινών Σπουδών 14, 497–498 (1938)

15. Kanetaki, E.: Συμβολή στη μελέτη των οθωμανικών λουτρών στον ελλαδικό χώρο. Μνημείο και Περιβάλλον 6, 49–75 (2000)

16. Kanetaki, E.: Οθωμανικά λουτρά στον ελλαδικό χώρο. Technical Champer of Greece Editions, Athens (2004)

17. Kanetaki, E.: Οθωμανικά λουτρά στον ελλαδικό χώρο. Τυπολογία και επανάχρηση αυτών. In: Ήπιες επεμβάσεις και προστασία ιστορικών κατασκευών. Proceedings of the Mild Interventions for the Protection of Historic Structures Conference, Thessaloniki, pp. 257–266 (2004)

18. Stefanidou, E.: Τα χαμάμ στην Ελλάδα: τύποι και εξέλιξή τους. In: Βέλος του Χρόνου, pp. 85–109. University Studio Press, Thessaloniki (2004)

19. Ackerman, E.: Parrot's new drone reclaims a niche: the Anafi marks the company's return to the consumer space-[Resources_Review]. IEEE Spectr. 55(9), 21 (2018)

20. Patias, P., Grussenmeyer, P., Hanke, K.: Applications in cultural heritage documentation. In: Li, Z., Chen, J., Baltsavias, E. (eds.) Advances in Photogrammetry, Remote Sensing and Spatial Information Sciences. ISPRS Book Series. ISPRS Congress Book, vol. 7, pp. 363–384. CRC Press, Taylor & Francis Group (2008)

21 Sylaiou, S., Dafiotis, P.: Storytelling in virtual museums: engaging a multitude of voices. In: Liarokapis, F., Voulodimos, A., Doulamis, N., Doulamis, A. (eds.) Visual Computing for Cultural Heritage. SSCC, pp. 369–388. Springer, Cham (2020). https://doi.org/10.1007/978-3-030-37191-3_19

22. Wloka, M.M., Anderson, B.G.: Resolving occlusion in augmented reality. In: Proceedings of the 1995 Symposium on Interactive 3D Graphics 1995, Monterey, CA, USA, pp. 5–12 (1995)

23. Coutrix, C., Nigay, L.Q.: Mixed reality: a model of mixed interaction. In: Proceedings of the Working Conference on Advanced Visual Interfaces, pp. 43–50 (2006)

Development of Design Protocols in the Use of Virtual Reality for Cultural Heritage Representation

Gamaliel J. Domingo[✉]

De La Salle University, Manila, Philippines

Abstract. In the Philippines, there are currently no design protocols for appropriate cultural heritage representation using VR. Hence, this study collated inputs from literature concerning the concepts of Authenticity and Aura; the factors affecting heritage representation; and lastly, the solicited views from connoisseurs through focus group discussions, interviews and content analysis of their historical VR projects. Results of the study found that Authenticity and Aura can be conceptualized in non-materials terms through Mode of Production, Authorship, Ownership, and Performance. These understandings may help resolve issues related to historical accuracy of representing cultural heritage objects.

Keywords: Virtual heritage · Authenticity · Aura

1 Introduction

1.1 Overview

Heritage sites across the Philippines are being converted to 360-degree VR for a more immersive experience. Cultural agencies such as the National Museum, National Historical Commission of the Philippines (NHCP) and Ayala Museum have partnered with VR development companies to adopt VR technology in their exhibits as well as to digitize all important built heritage in the country. The increasing popularity of VR, especially in cultural heritage representation, needs to be accompanied by the establishment of measures to mitigate, if not wholly eliminate, the risk of misrepresentation, like giving false impressions of heritage sites and distorting historical records. Such misrepresentations could influence viewers' perception in a negative sense and could take a toll on the historical and cultural significance of a site. Technologies are deeply interwoven with our perceptions and practices; therefore, designers need to take responsibility for the inevitable mediating influence of VR on the viewers. Verbeek's theory of technological mediation explains that technologies when they are used, help to shape human actions or practices.

This justifies the need for a targeted design protocol that would safeguard appropriate cultural heritage representation in VR while providing guidelines for a holistic balance of what experts from different disciplines deemed necessary in an immersive experience:

M. Shehade and T. Stylianou-Lambert (Eds.): RISE IMET 2021, CCIS 1432, pp. 111–124, 2021.
https://doi.org/10.1007/978-3-030-83647-4_8

Historians and archeologists defend the primacy of accuracy and precision of the information delivered. Educators and psychologists stand up for the benefit of experience and clarity of the instructional goals. Computer Specialists and 3D artists champion the importance of attractiveness and engagement...[1].

A design protocol would aid in identifying what constitutes an acceptable historical representation that would address other challenges such as lack of meaningful and cultural content, lack of later interpretation, lack of engagement, lack of sense of place, technological limitations, etc. A well-designed protocol would also help in resolving technical issues of VR during deployment because it anticipates issuses and suggests suitable solutions. Considering these challenges and consequences of misrepresentations, the researcher found it important to investigate the following research questions:

1. What are the factors affecting heritage representation in VR?
2. What are the different VR approaches to heritage representation?
3. What are the proper design protocols in the use of VR for the representation of historical/cultural subjects?

2 Review of Related Literature

2.1 Authenticity

With the growing adoption of VR for cultural heritage, a demand for an increased 'Authenticity' of representation was put forward [2–4]. Authenticity can be defined as the quality of being authentic, truthful, or genuine [5]. In conservation, it is examined in terms of the structure, material fabric, and composition [6, 7]. But in this study, the researcher examined Authenticity in terms of (a) Mode of Production, b) Authorship, c) Ownership, and d) Performance.

Mode of Production. In order to enhance the Authenticity of a heritage representation in VR, it is essential to have rigorous methods and precise documentation of information sources and hypotheses [8]. The London Charter underlines the need for intellectual accountability and data transparency to ensure the methods and outcomes are accurate, reliable, based on facts, and authentic [9]. Others argue that Authenticity depends on the credibility of research, accessibility of data, as well as the analytical and decision-making processes used [8–10].

Authorship. This refers to who created the content or representation [11]. In order to enhance the authenticity of a heritage representation, the creators have to be acknowledged [11]. Presenting it as anonymous in favor of the host organization dehumanizes it and only shows the power relationships between who created the data and who has the institutional authority [11]. Explicit authorship is important as the process involves decision-making among the creators (technological authority) [11]. While other authors argue that a focus on Authorship is a lazy and restrictive way to interpret a creative work, it is still relevant to the experience and negotiation of people of Authenticity [12].

Ownership. This refers to who legally controls the content [11]. One of the simplest ways a viewer can associate with a heritage object and feel closer to the creator of representation, is to own a copy of it as it binds the content, conceptually as well as legally, to its owner [11]. Even when that copy is freely available for download, one can still experience the sense of closeness to the creator [11]. Too much restrictions could hinder this closeness implied by ownership and could be disempowering for the viewer.

Performance. Interaction with cultural heritage is possible in VR through 'immersivity' and 'presence' [13]. Immersivity is defined as the measure of a technology's ability to induce immersion as a mental state [14]. Performance in VR is possible since no director decides where the viewer should look, and they have the freedom to explore the virtual world [14, 15]. However, if the system relies on a narrative script, the viewer might focus only on the points of interest and restrict the viewer [14]. This problem, also known as 'interactive paradox,' can only be addressed by either giving the control to the user and sacrifice narrative form or to the computer to create a coherent narrative [14]. Therefore, it is important to consider the viewer's instinctive tendencies and desire to exercise freedom when designing heritage representations.

2.2 Aura

The notion of Authenticity is connected to 'Aura.' People seek out objects with an Auratic quality [11]. Aura refers to the work of art's presence in time and space, its uniqueness at the place where it happens to be [16]. This concept state that reproduction detaches the reproduced object from the time and place in which it was made.

However, Costello argues that "Aura is not a predicate attaching to one category of artwork at the expense of another, but rather picks out a quality held in common—or not at all—by art in general at any given moment in history" [17]. Abbing further argues that instead of diminishing the 'Aura' of art, reproduction helps to extend the Aura of the works reproduced [18]. These arguments counter the notion that the work of art's Aura withers through reproduction.

Depending on how well-executed and immersive the VR is, the sense of sharing the same space as the digital object can be achieved [19]. Aura can migrate to the copy depending on the efforts, costs, techniques employed in reproducing it [20]. However, it still does not overcome the lingering issues of immateriality and sanitization, as pointed out by Benjamin's concept of 'Aura.' This can be attributed to the lack of physical markers such as dirt, bacteria, oil, and other various substances [11].

Visitors interact with the artifacts and institution for a variety of reasons. It is argued that Aura is not necessarily intrinsic to the objects themselves but must be constituted in Performance [21]. When the replica allows Performance with heritage, the Aura of the original partly migrates, and new meanings help to regenerate the original Aura [13]. It is also argued that the process of reconstruction is a performance that enhances the migration of Aura through cognition or affective bodily interaction [13].

In literature, 'Aura' is used in such a way that suggests a definition of cultural presence. In VR, cultural presence is a feeling that people with a different cultural perspective have occupied that virtual environment as a 'place' [22]. It happens instantly, like being teleported to a virtual environment, without the ritual of passage or arrival [22].

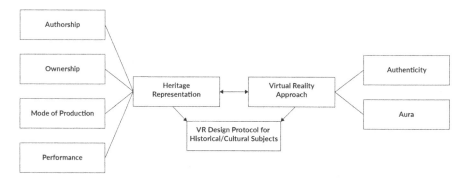

Fig. 1. Conceptual framework of the study

In order to design the protocol, the researcher drew from two interrelated factors: heritage representation and VR approaches (see Fig. 1). Specifications for heritage representation are used to define the framework within which designers have to consider in developing heritage representation in VR. On the other hand, VR approaches are Authenticity and Aura.

3   Methodology

3.1   Data Gathering and Analysis

The researcher used purposive sampling in choosing participants for the study. Purposive sampling, also known as judgment sampling, is a nonrandom technique in selecting participants based on their knowledge and experience [23]. In this study, the researcher selected thirteen participants, composed of historians, museum curators, production designers, 3D artists, Virtual heritage developers, and a head official from a cultural agency that has the institutional authority in the presentation of cultural heritage in the Philippines to stretch the diversity of data on the category of heritage representation. There are three methods of data collection tools the researcher used. A chart outlining these methods and the corresponding data collected is presented below (see Table 1).

Table 1. Methods of data collection

Method	Collected data
Content analysis	Written analysis
Focus group discussion	FGD transcripts
In-depth interview	Interview transcripts

These methods were used to determine the presence of the concepts of Authenticity and Aura and to identify the intentions, focus, or communications trends of their organizations. Their feedback (primary source) based on their experiences, will add more insights and empirical evidence for the research questions being investigated. The researcher used thematic analysis to highlight the most frequent opinions enumerated by the respondents.

3.2 Scope and Limitations

Given that the study aims to define the parameters for an acceptable historical representation and the recommended approach for utilizing VR in cultural heritage representation, input from renowned experts in the field were consolidated and aggregated into an easily understandable criterion. The validation and characterization of audience experience were beyond the scope of the study and were thus no longer conducted and collected.

The continues outcomes of VR projects on cultural heritage representation are useful to identify other important design considerations. The design protocols developed in the study can be altered and not in any way aim to be the norm.

4   Presentation of Results

4.1   Case 1 – Ayala Museum

The Ayala Museum opened its first immersive VR experience dubbed *Future of History: Dr. Jose Rizal's Execution* on June 19, 2017, in celebration of the 156th birth anniversary of the national hero. Through this, visitors can experience history by being present during the execution of Dr. Rizal in Bagumbayan (now known as Luneta Park) on December 30, 1896. He was executed by firing squad by the Spanish colonial authorities for his advocacy for reforms in the Philippines [25]. The museum's audience development manager claimed that the initiative to utilize VR was motivated by the desire to satisfy Filipinos hunger for history and to stimulate the interest of those who are indifferent. Meanwhile, the museum's chief historical consultant asserts a different motivation, saying that the *The Diorama Experience*, handcrafted in the 1970s, was "tired and old, and they are static," so they decided to involve newer, younger and generate more visual engagements. To this, they agreed and recognized that the younger generation is a "touch generation" whose learning is different; hence, there should be a more immersive experience.

The development started with research, utilizing a team of historical consultants complemented with the support and efforts of the board of trustees and the museum staff. While they value Authenticity and Accuracy in depicting Dr. Rizal, they also had to make subjective and interpretative decisions. The chief historical consultant also admitted that they cannot be completely accurate with their representations.

The VR provides alternative experiences of embodiment by placing viewers in entirely different bodies, which they can activate through the movements of their heads. The viewer can assume the role of a bystander, of a firing squad soldier, or Dr. Jose Rizal himself. It was shot from different perspectives because according to them history is experienced from different perspectives. For example, as a soldier, the viewer faces the moral dilemma of whether to shoot Rizal or not.

A year after the positive reception of the pilot, the museum launched another VR content entitled *Emergence of the Filipino Nation*, which featured Filipino independence leaders Emilio Aguinaldo and Andres Bonifacio. The 10-min-long VR experience allows visitors to witness four historical events, including the 'Cry of Pugad Lawin', the beginning of the Philippine Revolution against the Spanish Empire; the Tejeros Convention, the first election of officers of the new government [28]; the trial of Filipino revolutionary leader Andres Bonifacio in Maragondon; and the Proclamation of Philippine Independence in Kawit, Cavite. The writer explained that they valued accuracy from the established historical facts; however, they also had to make subjective and interpretative decisions they call as "creative license."

4.2   Case 2 – National Historical Commission of the Philippines

The NHCP launched its first immersive VR experience dubbed as *Ramon Magsaysay* on August 31, 2018 in line with the celebration of the 111th birth anniversary of the late president in Castillejos, Zambales. Ramon Magsaysay was the seventh president of the Philippines. He was well-known as the 'Champion of the Masses', having opened the presidential palace to the general public [26]. He also pioneered election jingles during his run for office. In 1957, months before finishing his term, his plane crashed in Cebu, killing him and 26 other passengers [26]. Through the VR experience, visitors can witness him announcing the opening of the Malacanang to the Filipino people, his land reform program to the press, known as the National Resettlement and Rehabilitation Administration (NARRA), and by watching him and his wife Luz dancing to the tune of his signature campaign song, the *Mambo Magsaysay*, while talking about the Japanese war reparations and his WWII exploits.

The ancestral house-turned-museum of Magsaysay is wholly geared towards the youth (see Fig. 2). The shrine curator claimed that their interactive exhibits were designed with young people in mind. The immersive VR experience is the latest addition to their existing museum technologies, which include a touch screen kiosk, a magic mirror, and a short audio-visual presentation of the legacy of Pres. Magsaysay. The NHCP Historic Sites Development Officer admitted that they adopted VR because it attracted the younger generation to go to the museum.

Fig. 2. Visitors of all ages trying the *Ramon Magsaysay 360-degree VR Experience* from Gaton, Noel, curator. Museo ni Ramon Magsaysay, 31 Aug. 2018

The proponents of the project also admitted that they wanted to enhance the museum experience of their visitors. The NCCA Cultural Heritage Section Head agreed that VR was designed for the enhancement of museum experience. However, he cautioned that the adoption of new technologies does not guarantee enhanced museum experience. He suggested consulting the target audience when determining the appropriateness of adopting such tools to ensure that it is necessary, responsive, and inclusive.

According to the NHCP, in portraying a scene in the life of a hero or any era in Philippine history, one needs to consider the clothing, the usual hairstyle, and the accuracy of the place. Problems usually arise when the research was not intensively conducted, as it could lead to historical inaccuracies. For example, the first VR video was shot entirely at the Quirino Council of State Room of the Malacanang Palace, where, historically, essential meetings of Pres. Magsaysay took place. The actor donned the classic and signature side part haircut of Pres. Magsaysay and his tailored barong and slacks pants.

It was not long after their initial release of the *Ramon Magsaysay; the* NHCP launched their second VR content dubbed as *Battle of San Juan Del Monte*. This battle, also known as the Battle of Pinaglabanan, took place on August 30, 1896 and is considered as the first major battle of the Philippine Revolution, which sought Philippine independence from Spain. Members of the group called the 'Katipunan', founded by Filipino revolutionary leader Andres Bonifacio, gave up their lives for the freedom of the Philippines [27]. The VR was launched at the newly opened and modernized Museo El Deposito on February 20, 2019. Visitors can experience critical events during the Battle of San Juan del Monte by joining Andres Bonifacio and Emilio Jacinto, the commander in chief of the 'Katipunan'.

4.3   Case 3 – DigiScript Inc.

DigiScript Inc. has extended their assistance to cultural agencies by providing 3D laser scanning and photogrammetry services. Its president shared that their pilot project was the Minor Basilica of San Sebastian in 2012. He saw the importance of 3D data capture in the conservation of heritage sites and admitted that this method of documentation could be a tool to connect and supplement other conservation efforts. He also claimed that the data could be used to reconstruct the historical site and could help everyone connect closer to "essential issues in our history" through VR.

The company works closely with architects, engineers, parish priests, and cultural agencies like the NHCP and the National Museum in documenting and preserving digitally all-important built structures in the Philippines. Their other 3D survey and as-built projects include the Manila Cathedral, Taal Basilica, Rizal Monument, and Bonifacio War Tunnel. They also provided detailed engineering studies for heritage structures and churches damaged by the 2013 Bohol earthquake & typhoon Yolanda.

They have been posting some of their works online, like 3D models of church statues and artifacts, to allow remote access, interaction, and up-close inspection of these digitized cultural objects. However, the president of the company finds some disadvantages of VR when it comes to cultural heritage representation. First, it is costly to develop one, and second, the risk of misrepresentation can be very high for an artist rendering or visualizing a cultural heritage compared to a laser scanned documentation. He gave a caveat that, at the initial phase of the creation, one should be clear of the purpose for the VR.

5   Discussions of Results

5.1   What are the Different VR Approaches in Heritage Representation?

The different VR approaches to heritage representation are Authenticity and Aura. Authenticity refers to the quality of being authentic, truthful, or genuine, while Aura refers to the unique existence of the original object in space and time [5, 16]. For DigiScript, Authenticity in heritage representation is attained by stating early in the development, the purpose and nature of visualization. If the visualization claims to be the 'real' thing or as close as possible to the original, it should be careful not to give a wrong impression of the original. For the NHCP, Authenticity is attained by conducting extensive research and by consulting subject matter experts. Ayala Museum agrees with NHCP but adds that the artistic or subjective decisions of the designer should also be controlled in light of Authenticity. Other literature suggests the importance of data transparency, ensuring the credibility of information sources, acknowledging the names of individuals responsible in it, and selecting appropriate interactivities that enhance immersion and sense of presence in attaining Authenticity.

While Benjamin claims that Aura is lost during reproduction, other authors argue that it can partially migrate to the copy depending on the quality of reproduction, the effort or technique employed by the designer, and the selection of appropriate inter-activities that allow interaction between the viewer and the representation. Compared to Authenticity, data transparency, the credibility of sources, and acknowledgment of creators are not as critical in Aura because the focus is always on the finished product and the technology used. DigiScript mitigates the risk of subjectivity by using 3D laser scanning and photogrammetry to capture the exact appearance of the historic site/structure or cultural object and convert it to a 3D digital copy. The NHCP, on the other hand, shoots at the actual place where the historic event took place to lessen the influence of the production or set designer over the final product. In contrast to the first two organizations, Ayala Museum allows the influence of the designer to be more apparent in the finished product by creating life-size replicas of historical sites/structures in the set to represent its original appearance during the historic event.

5.2   What are the Factors Affecting Heritage Representation in VR?

Heritage representation in VR consists of four interrelated factors: (1) Authorship, (2) Ownership, (3) Performance, and (4) Mode of Production. Rather than a quest for Authenticity and Aura in the object themselves, which somehow have already been sacrificed, they can be conceptualized in non-material terms. In this study, the per-spective of 'authenticity' is defined by the Mode of Production (transparency of sub-jective and objective decisions to the audience), Authorship (recognizing the producer/creator of representations), Ownership (accessibility of the content), and performance (engagement and experience of the audience with the representation as a source of truth). This view follows the theory of technological mediation which rec-ognizes the role of designers in shaping/influencing the mediation of technology to the perception of human beings of the real world.

As VR becomes a means of public history and communicators of cultural heritage, the number of audiences who are given access to information is growing rapidly. This immersive technology has become a valuable tool in conveying stories about the past and in valuing cultural heritage among the public. Thus, it is also important to examine the role of audience in VR.

According to Beale, authenticity cannot be said to reside in the representation itself but in the interplay between the creator, representation, and the audience. Jeffrey claimed that immateriality of digital objects creates new forms of relationships between the representation and the audience as they engage or experience them. In the material world, this consumption is as valid as the Performance of heritage. Tourists interact with the cultural heritage for a variety of reasons and in a variety of ways.

On Authorship, creative outputs most often explicitly reference an author and this in turn allows their audience to situate the work in the context of an author's other works, perhaps helping them to understand nuances, but also allowing them to attach notions of authenticity to the work irrespective of whether it is a copy or not. This could also mean that audience attributes a level of authority to the producer or creator of representation [24]. Authorship enhances the authenticity of the digital object by connecting its audience with its creators while simultaneously acknowledging the creative nature of the process.

On Ownership, the possibility to own a version or to freely use and re-use for any purpose is one of the easiest ways to feel closer to its creator.

On Mode of production, documentation of the evaluative, analytical, deductive, interpretative, and creative decisions made in the course of production should be disseminated in such a way that the relationship between research sources, implicit knowledge, explicit reasoning, and visualization-based outcomes can be understood. Failing to do so deprives those who want to understand the production.

5.3   What Are the Proper Design Protocols in the Use of VR for Heritage Representation?

Given the varied contexts of VR deployment, the design protocol consists of several options for each component identified– design goal, design process, and deployment (see Fig. 3).

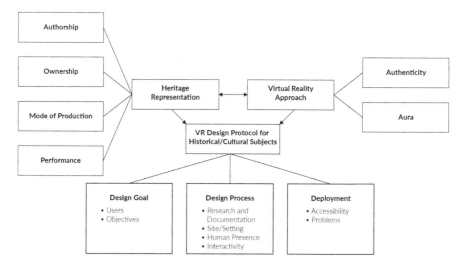

Fig. 3. Expanded conceptual framework of the study

Design Goal. Before diving into VR development, designers should identify their users, and specify the objectives of the project. Users are defined as anyone who will access the VR. They are generally grouped into two: The In-House Team and the End-Users.

In-House Team. This group is comprised by people who are part of the research, development, and validation of the VR. This includes consultants, constituents of the host institution, and people who will give the final approval for the deployment of the VR.

These people need to be identified to ensure that their specifications will be incorporated in the design and their requirements are met for approval.

End-Users. This group refers to the audience. They can be narrowed into a target demographic (i.e. age group) to ensure the effectiveness and appeal of the VR. This includes on-site and off-site viewers.

Objectives refer to the things the producer/creator plan to achieve. By defining the objectives of the VR, it can help focus their efforts and increase the chances of attaining them. Heritage representation in VR serves main two purposes: for research and for entertainment.

Design Process. Research and documentation are integral parts of the design process and the overall Authenticity of heritage representation in VR. During the research, the designer should gather as much data as possible regarding the historical/cultural subject. These data would inform the design of historical/cultural subjects in VR.

Designers must document their sources of information by creating a list and online storage of data. The list names the historical or cultural subject and states its source, whereas online storage contains all photos, videos, and other data collected from various sources. Designers may use file storage services to store and share their collected data to the team. By merely saving them on the computer, the risk of loss is high in case of a virus, breakdown, theft, or other problems that occur. A Good practice in doing research is to always maintain an organized system. In case any questions arise, the designer should be able to find the references here. On the other hand, the list must be accessible to the users in order for them to see the basis of the designer. This would enhance the Authenticity of representation because of data integrity and transparency. However, access to storage is subject to restrictions for safety reasons.

Currently, there are no specific guidelines on how to present the list of sources to the end-users. Museums and exhibition fairs do not display this information to the general public because of a lack of space and lack of appeal. Even so, they do not incorporate these into the content because they want to limit the time of using VR, given the number of visitors who want to try it. There is also the problem of nausea or dizziness experienced by some users, which might worsen when presented with too many texts. Instead, they make use of an introduction label that describes the VR content in general, typically large, placed on a wall, and sometimes accompanied by a LED TV showing its teaser.

Regardless if the user is not or interested to look at it, it is still essential to make a list accessible to the user for the sake of Authenticity. To do that, the curator may consider adding a QR code to the introduction label to enable visitors to easily access them from their website without the hassle of manually entering the address (URL). In other countries, they create a website for the VR project alone.

Site/Setting. This is the environment where VR takes place. In heritage representation, it is usually the site that is associated with important historical events, figures, or relations with other countries. This may include groups or clusters of buildings or structures whose significance is seen in the entirety of the setting, unit, or space rather than in its individual elements or characteristics. This may include the houses of ethnic/indigenous tradition, and of the Spanish colonial, American colonial, Post-war periods and/or mixed historical styles. It can be a designed through the following methods: a) physical recreation, b) actual site/setting, c) 3D reconstruction, d) 3D laser scanning. To enhance the Authenticity and sense of presence, the site/setting must represent the architectural style, characteristics, and form of the period and must convey the historical and cultural significance of the place to the viewer.

Costumes and Hairstyles. These should also be taken into consideration when designing heritage representations with human presence. It requires some degree of innovation and imagination. For 360-degree/VR films, when creating costumes, designers may look for alternative (cheaper) materials that the camera will capture as if they are real. Authentic textiles materials are hard to find and can be very expensive. Another important reminder in designing period costumes, the silhouette of the given period takes primary consideration before the texture and color. There is leeway for interpretation in color because there were only black and white photos. Nevertheless, designers should stick to what has been written or photographed in order to avoid the risk of misrepresentation.

Deployment. The problems encountered today by cultural agencies with VR are the following:

Cost. It varies depending on the specifications of the project. Usually, the specifications for a 3D VR are the type of system, platforms, headset, engine, environment, number and quality of 3D models (low or high polygon), animation, server, backend, and extra features. For 360-degree/VR videos, the specifications include the cast, crew, production design, and other elements. Aside from the cost of developing VR, there is much more than that initial spend to consider – the cost of deployment. This includes the number of headsets to be used, the design of VR booth/exhibit, promotion, and maintenance, which includes repair, replacement of unit, batteries, cord, and charger.

Wear and Tear. Due to the number of visitors using the VR headsets, the units are very much prone to wear-and-tear. When left unattended, visitors who are not familiar with VR would make their way to get the device working. Because of excitement and lack of viewing devices, kids may fight over whose turn it is to use the VR. During peak days, the prolonged use of VR headset can cause it to heat up substantially. This can put a strain on the Museum's annual budget.

Lack of Manpower. Due to a very limited headcount manning the Museum's simultaneous exhibitions, curators could not look after every visitor using the VR. Visitors are left with an instruction on how to use the VR. Although it helps the user make his/her way to get the headset working, it also poses a risk of damage. Usually, 360/VR contents run between two minutes and 10 min, excluding the time to wear and adjust the headsets. Curators would have difficulty assisting hundreds of visitors, such as bulk tours.

Hygiene. With the high standard of hygiene in the post-lockdown world, VR headsets on display in museums might be removed. This pandemic poses a significant problem not only on the current VR exhibitions but also on the use of VR technology in museums and heritage sites.

6 Conclusions and Recommendations

The factors discussed in the study are all present in each VR approach. The design protocol combines Authenticity and Aura and provides specific guidelines for each factor. For example, in terms of Authorship, the design protocol insists on explicit Authorship to enable users to identify the creators. Ownership should also be determined early in the design process. By identifying the target users, and the objective of the project, the control on accessibility can be determined. For the Mode of Production, the design protocol insists on the transparency of all the processes. It will show the extent of subjectivity and objectivity of the representation. Lastly, Performance with cultural heritage is ensured by guidelines for selecting appropriate interactivities in VR to allow users to understand the significance of the cultural object, to empathize with the characters, or to feel a sense of presence in a historical site.

The design protocol also adheres to the approaches used by providing guidelines in 1) gathering research, 2) documenting and sharing sources, 3) disclosing processes from design to production, 4) designing the environment, and 5) designing the costumes. Given that the design protocol was aggregated from consolidated literature and interview with experts, the study could be extended by exposing the design protocol to field practitioners and collecting their feedback for refining the protocol. Further research on users and their needs is recommended in order to understand better how they interpret or give meaning to identity, memory, story and knowledge. After refining, the resulting design protocol can be forwarded to the National Historical Commission of the Philippines for review and dissemination.

References

1. Sideris, A.: Re-contextualized antiquity: interpretative VR visualization of ancient art and architecture. In: Mikropoulos, T., Papachristos, N. (eds.) International Symposium on Information and Communication Technologies in Cultural Heritage, p. 163. The University of Ioannina (2008)
2. Frischer, B., Stinson, P.: The importance of scientific authentication and a formal visual language in virtual models of archaeological sites: the case of the House of Augustus and the Villa of the Mysteries, pp. 49–83 (2002)
3. Bakker, G., Maulenberg, F., de Rode, J.: Truth and credibility as a double ambition: reconstruction of the built past, experiences and dilemmas. J. Vis. Comput. Animat. **14**(3), 159–167 (2003)
4. Bentkowska-Kafel, A., Denard, H.: Paradata and transparency in virtual heritage. Ashgate Publishing, Ltd. (2012)
5. Jones, S.: Experiencing authenticity at heritage sites: some implications for heritage management and conservation. Conserv. Manag. Archaeol. Sites **11**(2), 133–147 (2009)
6. Pye, E.: Caring for the Past: Issues in Conservation for Archaeology and Museums, p. 65. James & James, London (2001)
7. Phillips, D.: Exhibiting Authenticity. Manchester University Press, Manchester (1997)
8. Lopez, L.: Authenticity and realism: virtual vs. physical restoration. In: Authenticity and Cultural Heritage in the Age of 3D Digital Reproductions, pp. 25–33. McDonald Institute for Archeological Research (2018)

9. Hermon, S., Niccolucci, F.: Digital authenticity and the London charter. In: Authenticity and Cultural Heritage in the Age of 3D Digital Reproductions, pp. 37–47. McDonald Institute for Archeological Research (2018)

10. Damnjanovic, U., Hermon, S., Iannone, G.: Documentation of the decision-making process in the analysis of digital heritage objects. In: Digital Heritage International Congress, pp. 743–746 (2013)

11. Jeffrey, S.: Digital heritage objects, authorship, ownership and engagement. In: Authenticity and Cultural Heritage in the Age of 3D Digital Reproductions, pp. 49–56. McDonald Institute for Archeological Research (2018)

12. Barthes, R.: The death of the author. In: Image Music Text, pp. 142–148. Fontana Press (1977)

13. Di Franco, P., Galeazzi, F., Vassallo, V.: Why authenticity still matters today. In: Authenticity and Cultural Heritage in the Age of 3D Digital Reproductions, pp. 1–9. McDonald Institute for Archeological Research (2018)

14. Ryan, M.: Narrative in VR? Anatomy of a Dream Reborn. Facta Ficta J. Narrat. Theory Media 2(2), 93–111 (2018)

15. Pimentel, K., Teixeira, K.: VR: Through the New Looking Glass, 1st edn, pp. 1–301. Intel/Windcrest (1993)

16. Benjamin, W.: The Work of Art in the Age of Mechanical Reproduction. Penguin Books (2008).

17. Costello, D.: Aura, face, photography: re-reading Benjamin today. In: Walter Benjamin and Art, pp. 164–184. Continuum (2005)

18. Abbing, H.: New techniques, mass consumption and mass media help demystify the arts. In: Why are Artists Poor? The Exceptional Economy of the Arts, pp. 306–309. Amsterdam University Press (2002)

19. Jeffrey, S.: Challenging heritage visualization: beauty, aura, and democratization. Open Archaeol. 1, 144–152 (2015)

20. Latour, B., Lowe, A.: The migration of the aura or how to explore the original through its facsimiles. In: Switching Codes: Thinking Through Digital Technology in the Humanities and the Arts, pp. 275–297. University of Chicago Press (2010)

21. Joy, J.: Biography of a medal: people and the things they value. In: Schofield, J., Johnson, W., Beck, C. (eds.) Material Culture: The Archaeology of Twentieth-Century Conflict, pp. 132–142 (2002)

22. Champion, E.: Virtual places. In: Champion, E. (ed.) Playing with the Past, pp. 27–62. Springer , London (2011). https://doi.org/10.1007/978-1-84996-501-9_3

23. Tongco, M.: Purposive sampling as a tool for informant selection. Ethnobot. Res. Appl. 5, 147–158 (2007)

24. Shanks, M.: Photography and archaeology. In: The Cultural Life of Images: Visual Representation in Archaeology, pp. 73–107. Psychology Press (1997)

25. Rizal, J.: Center for Philippine Studies. http://www.hawaii.edu/cps/rizal.html. Accessed 11 Mar 2021

26. Magsaysay, R.: Official Gazette of the Republic of the Philippines. https://www.officialgazette.gov.ph/banner-artwork/ramon-magsaysay/. Accessed 11 Mar 2021

27. E.O. No. 394. https://lawphil.net/executive/execord/eo1972/eo_394_1972.html. Accessed 11 Mar 2021

28. Andres Bonifacio and the Katipunan. https://nhcp.gov.ph/andres-bonifacio-and-the-katipunan/. Accessed 11 Mar 2021

Digital Storytelling and Embodied Characters for the Interpretation of Cultural Heritage

Place-Based Digital Storytelling. The Interplay Between Narrative Forms and the Cultural Heritage Space

Angeliki Chrysanthi[1](✉) ⓘ, Akrivi Katifori[2,3] ⓘ, Maria Vayanou[2] ⓘ,
and Angeliki Antoniou[4] ⓘ

[1] Department of Cultural Technology and Communication,
University of the Aegean, 81100 Mytilene, Greece
a.chrysanthi@aegean.gr
[2] Department of Informatics and Telecommunications,
National and Kapodistrian University of Athens, 15784 Athens, Ilissia, Greece
[3] Athena Research Center, Artemidos 6, 151 25 Marousi, Greece
[4] Department of Archival, Library and Information Studies,
University of West Attica, Ag. Spyridonos, 122 43 Egaleo, Greece

Abstract. Digital storytelling has been extensively used in cultural heritage sites with the aim to construct knowledge about the past and promote its significance to the present. From the body of research and practical implementations that are concerned with hybrid forms of storytelling in cultural heritage sites, only a few systematically explore the interplay between narrative form and space. Focusing on the interactive paradox as it manifests in the connection between the narrative structure and the physical space of heritage sites, this paper explores the theory and practice of place-based storytelling and provides an analytic and comparative discussion based on best practice examples in an attempt to identify current challenges and lessons learnt.

Keywords: Digital storytelling · Hybrid experiences · Cultural heritage sites · Interactive narrative theory · Place-based experiences

1 Introduction

For more than two decades, several technologies have been extensively used in cultural heritage sites under broader interpretative programmes with the aim to present the past to contemporary audiences in an engaging way. Experimentations, old and new, have employed a variety of techniques attempting to combine the physical (the site, its features and relevant interpretative material) with the virtual (reconstructions and digital storytelling), seamlessly in an experience. This has led to a variety of such "hybrid" approaches which have utilised available technologies to create storytelling experiences situated in physical spaces [1–3]. With the use of the term "hybrid" we attempt to encompass all such approaches, shifting the focus more to the visitor felt experience rather than to the individual enabling technologies.

© Springer Nature Switzerland AG 2021
M. Shehade and T. Stylianou-Lambert (Eds.): RISE IMET 2021, CCIS 1432, pp. 127–138, 2021.
https://doi.org/10.1007/978-3-030-83647-4_9

It is, however, a truism that even the most recent applications are outdated from an experience design point of view since they largely ignore the interpretative origins and current developments in digital heritage theory and practice [4]. At the same time, from the majority of existing scholarly work that is concerned with hybrid forms of storytelling in cultural heritage sites, only a few systematically explore the interplay between narrative forms and the cultural space in an interactive place-based experience. In the best-case scenario, current implementations oscillate between prioritising the virtues of a basic narrative structure (e.g. exposition, climax/peak of plot and resolution) or the interactive capabilities of enabling technologies and their novelty effect in providing onsite interpretation.

Thus, there remains an important gap in research and practice for the effective design of such hybrid place-based storytelling experiences. Also, the impact that stories can have in presenting aspects of the past to the public in an appealing way remains largely unexplored [5].

The aim of this work is to extend a much-needed discussion on the role of hybrid storytelling in cultural spaces, such as heritage sites, and its connection to the narrative form. To do so, we first provide a brief introduction on hybrid digital storytelling for heritage sites. We then describe the interactive paradox in the context of this type of storytelling experiences, which has been the motivation for our work, before moving to an analytic and comparative discussion on best practice examples from the domain. In the last sections of this paper we attempt to identify important challenges and lessons learnt.

2 Hybrid Digital Storytelling in Heritage Sites

Digital storytelling has been extensively used as an interpretative tool in museums and places of cultural significance and provides visitors with stories where the material remains meet with immaterial customs and traditions, as well as the local meets with the global and the transcultural aspects of the past.

Employing a variety of enabling technologies and design approaches, these "hybrid" applications are particularly popular among visitors because of their ability to combine the physical properties of a place, with impressive digital overlays – whether visual or acoustic. As a result, heritage is experienced in environments emerging from linking the physical site with either digital visual representations, narrations, soundscapes, interactive and playful activities or a combination of the above.

In this broader frame, storytelling through innovative interpretive design and cutting-edge technologies aims to enhance the embodied, multisensory [6, 7] and the interactive characteristics of a visit [8, 9]. Recent examples also shift attention to adaptive storytelling, taking into account movement and interests to personalise the visitor experience [10–12].

Furthermore, storytelling that emerges from visitor interaction with the physical properties of space and cultural objects through sensory input seems to be a promising direction of research [13, 14]. This research in the field of cultural heritage aligns with theoretical multimodal approaches for knowledge construction, where different elements in digital and physical form function as multiple gates for perceiving, interacting and ultimately understanding aspects of the past [15, 16]. Another important branch in this area of research focuses on the interactive properties of digital storytelling in order to augment the social aspects of cultural experiences [17, 18] and reveal the emotional baggage that may be triggered during a visit in an archaeological site [19].

3   Interactivity in Place-Based Experiences and the Interactive Paradox

"Digital storytelling" and "interactive digital storytelling" are terms encompassing a wide variety of applications, which do not always involve "interactivity" with the strict narrative-related definition of the term [20, 21]. The narrative structure, as the framework that defines the order of presentation of the story to its audience, including also the plot and setting, can be characterized as "interactive" where there is at least a basic amount of user agency in relation to how the narrative unfolds. In this sense, interactivity has been used to characterize a wide spectrum of narrative types; on one end of the spectrum there are those with a fully interactive story plot, where the user may affect in fact the story outcome, while on the other end, there are those with a linear, fixed plot, where the user in some cases might be offered pseudo-choices that may provoke reflection and engagement, or offer additional content, auxiliary to the main plot.

An inherent problem of interactive storytelling has been identified in the literature as the interactive paradox [22] and refers to "the integration of the unpredictable, bottom-up input of the user", in our case into supporting the visitor free movement, while at the same time maintaining a predefined, fixed narrative structure. To illustrate this better in the context of a digital heritage experience, we provide a short scenario:

Imagine roaming freely in a rural archaeological site, marveling at the monuments and the surrounding nature while lingering at will over anything that attracts your attention and interacting with travel companions. At the same time, you experience a seductive story through your mobile device that guides you throughout the site. The story hooked you from the first moment when it presented the site as a place shrouded in mystery until you kept experiencing a climax of the interactive story through the various choices you made. In the end you had two options to end the story and both appeared to be very enticing.

As is illustrated in the above scenario, the system supporting interactive storytelling must integrate the user's unpredictable movement and choices (user-agency) in a series of events happening both in the physical and the digital world in a way that the rules of the narrative are met, to ensure a coherent story. Such rules and structure, however, presuppose a top-down design of the experience and a relatively fixed sequence of events defined in the story (writer-control) thus, turning the whole endeavour into an impossible mission; in other words, a paradox [22, 23]. The more a design focuses on enabling multiple user interaction with the story plot, the harder it is to maintain a coherent narrative structure.

In other domains, such as narratology, this realisation brought about a major disbelief for the developments in interactive digital narrative [24], while ludology scholars even doubted the compatibility of interaction and narrative [25]. Overcoming such binary views expressed in an infamous debate between narratologists and ludologists, more balanced approaches to the issue at hand, defined narrative as a "forgiving, flexible cognitive frame for constructing, communicating, and reconstructing mentally projected worlds" [26]. This paves the way for interactive narrative to be defined as a form of expression which is activated and defined by the digital medium used each time while at the same time it functions as a flexible platform bringing interaction and narrative into creative synergies [21].

Despite the more recent developments in the field aiming to create memorable cultural experiences with hybrid storytelling experiences, a series of questions unfold offering fertile ground for debate and further research. To what extent can we combine a meaningful and complex narrative structure with an experience where the user walks and interacts freely with the physical cultural heritage site? Is this a desirable approach for cultural heritage interpretation and presentation and if so, how can this be achieved? What kind of consequences might we expect from a heritage management and protection of the cultural environment point of view?

3.1   Free Exploration vs Following the Narrative Structure

According to Roussou, Ripanti, and Servi [19], at an abstract level, all interactive storytelling applications in cultural heritage sites fall under two broad categories. The first is more concerned with maintaining a fixed, linear narrative structure. The narrative may foresee choices for the user as part of its structure, however in every case, the structure is ordered and guides the user sequently from one part of the plot to the next. This approach necessarily limits visitor's freedom to explore the physical space. In other words, the requirements for maintaining narrative structure take precedence over visitor interaction with the heritage site itself.

The second category aims to offer emergent digital narratives through storyworlds with well-defined story characters and rules which define the visitor interaction with the narrative. The storytelling experience is designed to unfold organically through place-based discoveries taking place during the user interaction with the narrative itself or the physical space (e.g. lingering, choosing pathways and pace of discovery), both governed by strict rules [27]. These independent interactions can be characterised as "micro narratives" that ultimately fit into an overarching narrative structure aiming to highlight the site's cultural and historical value. This second category mainly encompasses game-related storytelling approaches in which the meaning of narrative is adjusted according to the visitor interaction with the hybrid experience, and overall, it has a more entertaining purpose.

This simple categorization may constitute an important conceptual and methodological tool for consideration while designing hybrid storytelling in environments of cultural significance. However, it is important to extend this categorization by considering the main objectives of the experience itself alongside the specific design aims of the place-based storytelling experience. To this end, Azuma [28] proposed a tripartite strategy framework by considering the practical requirements and purpose of use as well as the enabling technologies (Table 1).

Table 1. Azuma's strategies on location-based mixed and augmented reality storytelling.

Storytelling type	Function	Result in space
Reinforcing	Enhance the interpretative affordances of a place	The spatial experience is more attractive than its component parts
Reskinning	Emphasis on the story presentation	The space is redefined based on storytelling requirements
Remembering	Emphasis on externalising memories	Empowering space through personal stories

The first strategy, called reinforcing, aims to highlight the interpretative value of a place of cultural or historical significance with digital augmentations. In this case, the final hybrid result is considered significantly more attractive from the individual physical and virtual elements that comprise it. The second strategy, called reskinning, puts emphasis on the story and the ways to present it. In result, the physical space is redefined and negotiated each time based on the storytelling requirements. The third category refers to augmenting the physical space with memories and personal stories so that the hybrid experience can leave a more powerful, emotional, impression of the space to the user. This paper is more concerned with the first two categories. The third category, being about empowering spaces through personal stories, falls out of the scope of this analysis.

4   Structured Narrative and Interaction in Cultural Heritage Sites: Three Cases Studies

In order to further explore the interaction between the narrative structure and the cultural site in current applications in the field, in this section we focus on the analysis of three case studies that fall under the first two strategies in Azuma's framework (Table 1), Reinforcing and Reskinning. The selection criteria for the specific projects include: a) a robust theoretical background reflected in the design of the relevant applications, b) significant body of work progressing during the last decade as a result of multiple gradual experimentations, and c) technological and methodological innovations as a result of theory, experimentation, and impact cross-fertilization. They all commonly share an understanding of the importance of maintaining a basic plot as a way of offering to visitors of cultural heritage sites engaging and emotional interactive experiences. In the remainder of this section, we present the selected innovative approaches and design solutions in an attempt to frame and initiate a discussion on the subject.

4.1   Situated Simulation

The situated simulation approach refers to the use of virtual environments which adapt according to visitor movement and interactions in the physical space. This type of storytelling is implemented mainly through virtual scenes which are activated by the visitor and progress as she makes her way in the site.

This approach has been developed by Sitsim lab, which has been experimenting for almost a decade with a type of storytelling that uses a combination of sensors to register and adapt the virtual environments to the user's location and perspective with satisfying results [5, 29]. After exploring different approaches, the lab focused on designing place-based narratives. In the project called Via Appia Antica, the lab developed an application that creates a simple interaction between time and movement in space in one of the most well-known ancient roads of Rome. The natural and unobstructed movement of the user along this road activates the visualisation of historic scenes with references to Rome's ancient history [30]. The interface was designed to offer additional playful activities such as taking snapshots of the scenes during the hybrid experience.

In a more recent work presenting the historical landing of allied forces on Omaha Beach during the Second World War, they explored specific narrative functions. Firstly, they represented the timeline of the landing events in the physical space, then, in parallel to the main narrative plot, they enriched the experience with in-depth information activated at certain nodes, including historical images, oral histories and other details relevant to the main plot [5]. The design was informed by Genette's theory on pause which is formed by the relationship between story time and discourse time [31].

In this frame, the narrative experience is divided in scenes and summaries. The latter refer to the compression of real time events (of the story) which in this example correspond to Allies bombardment. This event lasted in reality half an hour and was "compressed" in order to be represented in a narrative lasting two minutes. The reconstructed scenes are connected both with the sequence of events as well as the physical space where they occurred. The whole mixed reality scene is combined with storytelling which completes the dramaturgy of the experience.

Another example utilises the concept of "pause" in order to introduce a different type of activity in the narrative structure which falls outside the main plot. During the pause which interrupts temporarily the flow of the main plot, the user can explore the hybrid space in the application by clicking on the hotspots designed to appear on the screen of the device. When this exploration finishes, the user can continue with the main plot of the interactive story.

In this experience, the main plot is predefined, offering no option of choosing between alternative storylines. In this case, both the user's movement in the battlefield and interactions with the hybrid story are controlled by the designed structure, with the exception that the user can affect the pace of the experience.

4.2   Turning Point Interaction

A different approach is offered by the research project Crossroads, in the frame of which fifteen narratives were created, influenced by historical events, which also took place in the Second World War in the province of Brabant in the Netherlands [32]. The design of the storytelling approach was based on the exploration of themes and events under a narrative structure model which followed five stages [33, 34]: a) defining the setting, which includes defining space, time, main characters and other introductory events, b) defining the moment when events are set in motion and activate the next steps, c) defining the turning points, where decisions on the storyline and acceleration of action happens, and e) defining the ends/or resolution to a drama.

Each narrative is designed for a single location, and visitor interaction with the progression of the story plot is only allowed in the "turning point" of the plot, allowing the user to influence the end of the story. According to the conceptual model defined, the user experiences the story from a first-person perspective and is invited to make certain choices which will impact the lives of the story characters.

On the technical side, this experience utilises the use of augmented video. Recorded scenes of actors performing a drama in the physical space are mixed with virtual scenes to create a hybrid experience that travels the user to the past. The application uses geolocation technologies to register the experience in the physical space and make the content visible to visitors. It does not foresee movement in space at the same time as the story progresses. Although the user in this case does not have much control in either moving in space or in the story plot is nevertheless considered as an active observer of a story unfolding in space. Contrary to the Omaha beach example, the user is able to control the plot by making a choice at particular turning points.

4.3   Linking Exhibits with Narrative Plot

The third category of examples examined in this work originate from the European research projects CHESS and EMOTIVE which developed a series of tools and experiences for interactive storytelling, exploring and experimenting with its social and emotional dimensions. These experiences focus mainly on maintaining a coherent narrative plot throughout the visit by linking informational content relevant to the various points of interest in space with the narrative plot. Most of the experiences were initially designed for museum and exhibition spaces [10, 35, 36], while some were adapted to the requirements of place-based storytelling, such the archaeological sites of Çatalhöyük, in Turkey, and Ancient Agora, in Greece [19, 37]. Apart from developing a set of tools for authoring and presenting hybrid storytelling [8, 35, 38], the basic conceptual narrative model presents a very interesting case.

Following a story-centered approach, the points of interest in a cultural space are integrated in the plot of a fiction. This way, micro-narratives on different subjects and possibly difficult to link under a single coherent plot, in the strict sense, are presented under an overarching narrative [19]. This narrative functions as a vehicle for enabling the presentation of micro-narratives [39], is fictional and is not confused with the presentation of documented historical and interpreted archaeological evidence of the site. This approach is similar to a known narrative model which was introduced by Cohan και Shires [40] and combines a kernel story with satellite events. The user can experience micro-narratives, can interact with them and the physical space without jeopardizing the cohesion of the background fictional narrative.

Another characteristic of the project's approach is the character-centered design of the main narrative plot. Characters appear as protagonists of the stories or as a type of virtual guides. In certain cases, the characters involved in the same plot and the relationship they develop as the story unfolds are the basic elements of driving the plot forward [19] In other cases, several main characters narrate the same events from a different perspective thus, providing different interpretations through the technique of multiple angles and promoting historical empathy for the people of the past [17].

5 Towards a Typology of Place-Based Storytelling in Cultural Sites

The analysis of the three case studies may provide insight on what types of hybrid interactive storytelling works best according to the type of experience we wish to offer each time. In this section we provide a synthesis of the lessons learnt from this analysis by attempting to expand on the aforementioned categorizations by Azuma and, Roussou and Servi (see Table 2). The aim of this synthesis is to describe hybrid place-based experiences based on the type of storytelling adopted in relation to the desired visiting style. The latter is largely defined by whether designed interactions put emphasis on the physical or the virtual space, as well as the movement restrictions applying on each specific site.

For example, if the design brief concerns an archaeological site with impressive but sensitive remains and a picturesque surrounding view with the requirement to prioritise the experience of the physical space while controlling visitor movement, then perhaps the first category would be more appropriate. The hybrid storytelling experience should prioritise attention to the physical space while the narrative structure should guide the visitor in a predefined manner in order to protect sensitive areas from mechanical erosion.

In a different vein, when a historical place lacks impressive physical remains there are opportunities to provide more impressive visual and acoustic augmentations, so choosing between the second and fourth category would only be a matter of whether curators wish to create a structured story or provide multiple emerging narratives in a more playful experience.

Table 2. Developing a typology for hybrid place-based storytelling experiences in cultural heritage

Type of place-based storytelling	Style of visit	Result of the hybrid experience
Emphasis on interactive narrative structure and attention to physical space	Controlled movement in the cultural space and minimal interaction with story plot	The interpretation of the physical space is led by the interactive story
Emphasis on maintaining narrative plot and attention to virtual space	Flexible movement in the cultural space and controlled interaction with the story	The physical space is used as a vehicle to tell a story with fixed plot
Emphasis on the rules defining the story plot and attention to the physical space	Flexible movement and micro narratives controlled by rules applying to the physical space	Micro narratives, loosely connected to one other, emerge from exploring a physical space
Emphasis on the rules defining the story plot and attention to the virtual space	Free roaming and emergent narratives controlled by rules applying to the virtual space	Micro (satellite) narratives loosely linked to the physical space emerge as a result of progressing an overarching (kernel) story

This typology is by no means exhaustive, but it provides a useful methodological tool for defining the storytelling of places that bear significant cultural, historical, and archaeological values. Most importantly, our synthesis addresses the important aspect of the type of spatial experiences that can be offered with the right type of hybrid storytelling. The analysis of the chosen case studies presents different solutions for experiencing space and reports clear limitations which can impact the visitor perception of heritage sites. For instance, the sequence in which a user visits an archaeological site is very crucial for understanding its function in the past and may directly link up to the narrative that curators may choose to develop.

At the same time, designing an overarching structured narrative – whether fictional or based on historical events – and linking it either with in-depth information or satellite micronarratives may be an effective solution to overcome the interaction paradox in structured narratives.

6   Conclusions and Future Work

We believe that we are still away from being able to formulate a robust typology that addresses both theoretical and methodological considerations as highlighted in this paper. Such frameworks are important to understand how novel digital technologies impact existing forms of expression while generating new ways to tell stories. However, it is still early days of experimenting with stable versions of technologies that enable hybrid and rich cultural storytelling, and it is believed that it will take more time until a comprehensive standardisation occurs [5, 41].

Although, the technique of emergent narratives discussed in Sect. 3.1 has not been examined in detail, it is not considered by the authors as less important but rather as less relevant to the main focus of this paper. In this type of digital storytelling, a significant part of creating successful spatial experiences comes down to finding resourceful ways of integrating micronarratives in the environment (physical or virtual) without imposing a structured narrative on the overall experience of space [25]. Afterall, moving within a culturally significant place and going through an embodied interaction with the remains or the surrounding nature; choosing to linger in order to marvel at a view or to increase the pace of walking as a result of the eagerness to discover more things around the site; these are all part of the cultural experience and need to be considered when designing hybrid interactive storytelling. On the other hand, due to the continued technological advancement, new genres of storytelling shall emerge and shall be renegotiated under the lens of cultural curation in a fruitful and creative cycle which no doubt will give birth to new paradigms in the field.

Our paper attempted to frame emerging types of hybrid storytelling for Cultural Heritage spaces, as well as to reveal and summarise a series of challenges that curators face, which do not necessarily relate to the technology itself. These include among others: a) defining the level of user control and the flexibility in experiencing digital storytelling, b) successfully linking fiction with facts, c) presenting complicated layers of the past on fragile physical grounds, and d) considering visitor movement in relation to synchronous or asynchronous, structured, or unstructured narratives.

To conclude, further work is required in order to advance this interdisciplinary topic from a point of converging theoretical, methodological, technical and technological requirements and create even more fruitful venues for effective place-based storytelling experiences.

Acknowledgments. This research has been co-financed by the European Union and Greek national funds through the Operational Program Competitiveness, Entrepreneurship and Innovation, under the call Special Actions AQUACULTURE – INDUSTRIAL MATERIALS – OPEN INNOVATION IN CULTURE (project code: T6ΥΒΠ-00123).

References

1. Pletinckx, D., Silberman, N., Callebaut, D.: Heritage presentation through interactive storytelling: a new multimedia database approach. J. Visual. Comp. Animat. **14**(4), 225–231 (2003)
2. Vlahakis, V., et al.: Archeoguide: an augmented reality guide for archaeological sites. IEEE Comput. Graph. Appl. **22**(5), 52–60 (2002)
3. Noh, Z., Sunar, M.S., Pan, Z.: A review on augmented reality for virtual heritage system. In: Chang, M., Kuo, R., Chen, G.D., Hirose, M. (eds.) Edutainment 2009. LNCS, vol. 5670, pp. 50–61. Springer, Cham (2009). https://doi.org/10.1007/978-3-642-03364-3_7
4. Kenderdine, S.: PLACE-Hampi, ancient Hampi and Hampi-LIVE - an entanglement of people-things. In: Forte, M. (ed.) Cyber-Archaeology. Archaeopress, Oxford (2010)
5. Liestøl, G.: Augmented reality storytelling – Narrative design and reconstruction of a historical event in Situ. Int. J. Interactive Mobile Technol. **13**(12), 196–209 (2019)
6. Kenderdine, S.: Embodiment, entanglement, and immersion in digital cultural heritage. In: Schreibman, S., Siemens, R., Unsworth, J. (eds.) A New Companion to Digital Humanities, pp. 22–41. John Wiley & Sons, New York (2016)
7. Kenderdine, S., Shaw, J.: A cultural heritage panorama: trajectories in embodied museography. In: Din, H., Wu, S. (eds.) Digital Heritage and Culture – Strategy and Implementation, pp. 197 – 218. 1st edn. World Scientific Publishing Company, Singapore (2014)
8. Roussou, M., Pujol-Tost, L., Katifori, A., Chrysanthi, A., Perry, S., Vayanou, M. The Museum as Digital Storyteller: Collaborative Participatory Creation of Interactive Digital Experiences. MW2015: Museums and the Web (2015). http://mw2015.museumsandtheweb.com/paper/the-museum-as-digital-storyteller-collaborative-participatory-creation-of-interactive-digital-experiences. Accessed 12 Mar 2021
9. Roussou, M., Katifori, A.: Flow, staging, wayfinding, personalization: evaluating user experience with mobile museum narratives. Multimodal Technol. Interaction **2**(2), 32 (2018)
10. Pujol, L., et al.: From personalization to adaptivity. Creating immersive visits through interactive digital storytelling at the acropolis museum. In: Museums as Intelligent Environments Workshop (MasIE), Proceedings of the 9th International Conference on Intelligent Environments, pp. 541–554 (2013)
11. Antoniou, A., et al.: Capturing the visitor profile for a personalized mobile museum experience: an indirect approach. In: CEUR Workshop Proceedings, vol. 1618. Halifax, Canada (2016)
12. Ardissono, L., Kuflik, T., Petrelli, D.: Personalization in cultural heritage: the road travelled and the one ahead. User Model. User-Adap. Inter. **22**(1–2), 73–99 (2012)

13. Petrelli, D., Ciolfi, L., Van Dijk, D., Hornecker, E., Not, E., Schmidt, A.: Integrating material and digital: a new way for cultural heritage. Interactions **20**(4), 58–63 (2013)
14. Keil, J., et al.: A digital look at physical museum exhibits: designing personalized stories with handheld augmented reality in museums. In: Addison, A., de Luca, L., Pescarin, S. (eds.) Proceedings of the International Conference Digital Heritage (2013)
15. Hooper-Greenhill, E.: Museums and their Visitors. Routledge, London, New York (1994)
16. Falk, J.H., Dierking, L.D.: Enhancing visitor interaction and learning with mobile technologies. In: Tallon, L., Walker, K. (eds.) Digital Technologies and the Museum Experience: Handheld Guides and Other Media, pp. 19–33. Altamira Press, Lanham (2008)
17. Katifori, A., et al.: Let them talk! Exploring guided group interaction in digital storytelling experiences. J. Comput. Cultural Heritage (JOCCH) **13**(3), 1–30 (2020)
18. Katifori, A., et al.: Cultivating mobile-mediated social interaction in the museum: towards group-based digital storytelling experiences. In: Museum and the Web (2016)
19. Roussou, M., Ripanti, F., Servi, K.: Engaging visitors of archaeological sites through 'emotive' storytelling experiences: a pilot at the ancient agora of Athens. Archeologia e Calcolatori **28**(2), 405–420 (2017)
20. Katifori, A., Karvounis, M., Kourtis, V., Perry, S., Roussou, M., Ioanidis, Y.: Applying interactive storytelling in cultural heritage: opportunities, challenges and lessons learned. In: Rouse, R., Koenitz, H., Haahr, M. (eds.) ICIDS 2018. LNCS, vol. 11318, pp. 603–612. Springer, Cham (2018). https://doi.org/10.1007/978-3-030-04028-4_70
21. Koenitz, H.: Towards a specific theory of interactive digital narrative. In: Koenitz, H., Ferri, G., Haahr, M., Sezen, D., Sezen, I.T (eds.) Interactive Digital Narrative, pp. 91–105. Routledge, New York (2015)
22. Ryan, M.-L.: From narrative games to playable stories: toward a poetics of interactive narrative. Storyworlds J. Narrative Stud. **1**, 43–59 (2009)
23. Aylett, R., Louchart, S.: Narrative theories and emergent interactive narrative. In: Proceedings of the Narrative and Interactive Learning Environments Conference, NILE04, pp. 25–33. Edinburgh, Scotland (2004)
24. Brenda, L.: Computers as Theater. Addison Wesley, London (1993)
25. Jenkins, H.: Game design as narrative architecture. Computer **44**(3), 118–130 (2003)
26. Herman, D.: Story Logic: Problems and Possibilities of Narrative. University of Nebraska Press, Lincoln, Nebraska (2002)
27. Avouris, N., Yiannoutsou, N.: A review of mobile playful narratives for learning across physical and virtual spaces method of research. Artif. Intell. **18**(15), 2120–2142 (2012)
28. Azuma, R.: Location-based mixed and augmented reality storytelling. In: Fundamentals of Wearable Computers and Augmented Reality, pp. 259–76, 2nd edn. CRC Press, Boca Raton (2015)
29. Liestøl, G.: Situated simulations: a prototyped augmented reality genre for learning on the IPhone. Int. J. Interactive Mobile Technol. (IJIM) **3**, 24 (2009)
30. Liestøl, G.: Along the Appian way. Storytelling and memory across time and space in mobile augmented reality. In: Ioannides, M., Magnenat-Thalmann, N., Fink, E., Žarnić, R., Yen, A.-Y., Quak, E. (eds.) EuroMed 2014. LNCS, vol. 8740, pp. 248–257. Springer, Cham (2014). https://doi.org/10.1007/978-3-319-13695-0_24
31. Genette, G.: Narrative Discourse. An Essay on Method. Cornell University Press, Ithaca (1980)
32. Calvi, L., Hover, M.: Crossroads: life changing stories from the second world war. A (transmedia) storytelling approach to World War II heritage. VIEW J. Eur. Television Hist. Culture **5**(10), 55–66 (2016)
33. McDonald, B.: Invisible Ink. A Practical Guide to Building Stories that Resonate. Libertary, Seattle (2010).

34. Philips, A.: A Creator's Guide to Transmedia Storytelling. McGraw Hill, New York (2012)
35. Vayanou, M., et al.: Authoring personalized interactive museum stories. In: Mitchell, A., Fernández-Vara, C., Thue, D. (eds.) ICIDS 2014. LNCS, vol. 8832, pp. 37–48. Springer, Cham (2014). https://doi.org/10.1007/978-3-319-12337-0_4
36. Katifori, A., et al.: Exploring the potential of visually-rich animated digital storytelling for cultural heritage: the mobile experience of the Athens university history museum. In: Liarokapis, F., Doulamis, N., Doulamis, A., Voulodimos, A. (eds.) Visual Computing in Cultural Heritage. Springer Series on Cultural Computing, pp. 325–345. Springer, Cham (2020b). https://doi.org/10.1007/978-3-030-37191-3_17
37. Katifori, A., Roussou, M., Kaklopoulou, I., Servi, K.: Mobile interactive storytelling in the Athens ancient Agora: exploring the right balance between the Site and the App, XVII. In: Culture and Computer Science, Konzerthaus, Berlin (2019)
38. Vrettakis, E., Kourtis, V., Katifori, A., Karvounis, M., Lougiakis, Ch., Ioannidis, Y.: Narralive – Creating and experiencing mobile digital storytelling in cultural heritage. Digit. Appl. Archaeol. Cultural Heritage **15**, e00114 (2019)
39. Vanoverschelde, F.: No Story without a backstory: the role and importance of the backstory in an augmented reality application for cultural heritage. In: NHT 2019 (2019)
40. Cohan, S., Shires, L.: Telling Stories: A Theoretical Analysis of Narrative Fiction. Routledge, New York (1988)
41. Miller, C.R.: Genre innovation: evolution, emergence, or something else? J. Media Innov. **3**(2), 4 (2016)

Bridging Past and Present: Creating and Deploying a Historical Character to Engage Audiences Through AR and VR

Juilee Decker$^{(\boxtimes)}$ ⓘD, Amanda Doherty ⓘD, Joe Geigel ⓘD, and Gary D. Jacobs ⓘD

Rochester Institute of Technology, Rochester, NY, USA
jdgsh@rit.edu

Abstract. This article describes the creation and deployment of a virtual tour guide to deliver content and enhance the visitor experience at the third-largest living history museum in the United States. Our work differs from other museum applications in AR and VR by: focusing on narrative storytelling from the point of view of an historical character embodied by a conversational digital avatar; employing place-based engagement within a historical context; and showcasing a historical figure who has an authentic connection to the museum environment he inhabits. Our goals with the project are three-fold. First, we provide an overarching narrative about life in western New York during the 19th century through the telling of five digitally-rendered characters whose stories are recounted in short-form vignettes shared with audiences. Second, we endeavor to develop "thinking dispositions" that encourage visitors to gauge and construct the significance of historical narratives that have the capacity to motivate reflection upon these stories on a personal, local, and global level. Third, we create a tripartite deployment that offers a common experience and supports a variety of delivery methods that respond directly to the health safety concerns raised by COVID-19. In sum, our project offers first-person accounts of the past mediated via XR, a blending of past and present to enhance the visitor experience.

Keywords: Digital storytelling · Interpretation and management of cultural heritage · Museums · COVID-19 · Visitor experience · Historical narrative

1 Introduction

Our project, Digital Docents: Historical New York Stories in Virtual and Augmented Reality (hereafter DIGITAL DOCENTS), involves students and faculty—in the colleges of liberal arts, art and design, and computer science at Rochester Institute of Technology—working in partnership with museum staff to deliver historical content in the form of a digital docent, modeled after a resident of western New York in the 19th century, who will guide visitors online and onsite at Genesee Country Village & Museum (hereafter GCV&M), the third-largest living history museum in the United States and the largest in New York state.

© Springer Nature Switzerland AG 2021
M. Shehade and T. Stylianou-Lambert (Eds.): RISE IMET 2021, CCIS 1432, pp. 139–155, 2021.
https://doi.org/10.1007/978-3-030-83647-4_10

1.1 Research Team, Collaborators, and Progress to Date

Our collaboration began in 2018 between museum studies and computer science faculty (Decker and Geigel) who wanted to site a research problem at the museum, employ technology as a possible solution, and engage our students in the research and scholarship around this project. Over the summer 2019, we added two collaborators from fine arts and digital design to our team (Doherty and Jacobs). Together, as our research team of four faculty, we decided to dive deeply into researching and developing one person from history to develop as a "character" who would become our first "digital docent." For this, we also enlisted the help and support of faculty from performing arts, one of whom remains regularly involved in our project.

By the close of the Fall 2019 semester, our team reached a significant milestone of creating a character who delivers a short-form narrative (less than 6 min) and responds to voice commands from the user. We presented this very early stage character at our university's annual XR symposium in 2019 with the caveat that we displayed the character within an entirely virtual environment to simulate how the character would appear at the museum in the museum building where he would be activated upon a visitor's entry into the historic building [1]. Anecdotal evidence captured at that time indicated a desire to learn content from a digitally rendered character who spoke of historic events as if in conversation, rather than delivering historical content directly as stated facts [2].

In 2020, we expanded our team to include students and faculty from performing arts, particularly music. See Figs. 1 and 2. We have also, consistently, engaged the expertise and advice of the museum staff, most notably the museum director and curator of collections, as well as museum interpretation staff (who were slated to begin performing narratives in the spring 2020, although this has been delayed due to COVID-19).

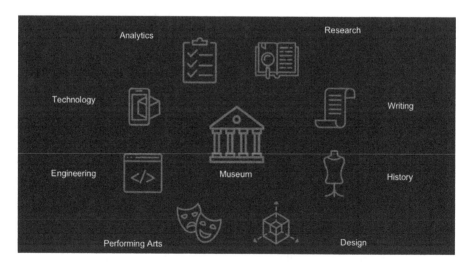

Fig. 1. DIGITAL DOCENTS research team which involves faculty and students from several disciplines, noted below. Created by authors.

Count of semester

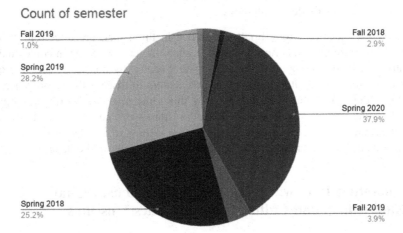

Fall 2019
1.0%

Fall 2018
2.9%

Spring 2019
28.2%

Spring 2020
37.9%

Spring 2018
25.2%

Fall 2019
3.9%

Fig. 2. Participants per semester ranging from 3 in the fall of 2018 to 39 in the spring 2020 (pre-COVID-19). Student involvement varies based upon teaching schedules and overlap with our project aims for a given semester. More than 100 individuals from across the university as collaborators and contributors to our project since spring 2018. Created by authors.

As of March 2020, our progress came to a screeching halt in terms of the development of digital assets, audio and motion capture, and archival research due to the COVID pandemic, the closure of all campus facilities, the closure of our museum partner, and the constraints on primary research. After several bi-weekly team meetings, we decided to expand our modes of delivery to include offsite VR. Our expanded content delivery plan enables various levels of accessibility while responding directly to the health safety concerns raised by COVID-19. In addition, the project offers an opportunity for an immersive and interactive educational experience, even at an unstaffed location within the museum complex.

1.2 Overview of Project Goals

Our research is framed by three goals for this project. First, we provide first-person accounts during the 19th century with regard to the technological, political, cultural, agricultural, architectural, and personal transformation over time in this geographical region. These changes are made visible through the perspective of five individuals whose stories are recounted in short-form vignettes delivered by a virtual guide. Second, we endeavor to develop "thinking dispositions" [3] that encourage visitors to gauge and construct the significance of historical narratives that have the capacity to motivate reflection upon these stories on a personal, local, and global level. Third, we outline our foundation for a tripartite deployment that enables various levels of accessibility while responding directly to the health safety concerns raised by COVID-19. DIGITAL DOCENTS aims to meets visitors where they are: whether online at home or onsite at the museum using one's own device or a museum provided device.

1.3   Overview of Project Outcomes

Our intended outcomes, only briefly described in this paper, are three-fold as well. First, visitors will gain historical knowledge about the past based upon contextualized narratives delivered digitally online and onsite. Second, by posing open-ended questions to visitors, the digital docents will ask visitors to discern the significance of a situation, topic, or issue, and consider why this topic might be worth investigating further. Third, our (in-development) evaluation framework and refinement will yield data about the likelihood and interest of museum visitors to use digital interactives to enhance their learning experiences online and onsite at cultural heritage institutions.

2   Literature Review: Living History Museums, Digital Storytelling, and Cultural Heritage Sites/Museums

Our project framework is digital storytelling sited to a living history (also known as "open air") museum in Western New York with 68 historic buildings that have been assembled in a village format, consisting of structures from the late 18th to the early 20th centuries (Fig. 3). This setting provides the environment for our virtual characters to tell their personal stories which are broadly applicable to the broader context of 19th century America. We chose storytelling for this museum application because it affords visitors the opportunity to make connections with the content and the entire experience [4].

Fig. 3. Aerial photo of historic village. Photo taken by authors.

2.1 Living History Museums and Visitor Experiences

Living history museum interpretation takes its cues from Freeman Tilden's treatise of interpretation, which impacted natural and cultural interpretation in the US since its initial publication in 1957 [5]. Tilden argues that interpretation should aim to extend far beyond the mere recitation of factual information: it should engage. Tilden's work, along with key texts and a range of approaches to living history and visitor experience, are summarized in Table 1 below.

Table 1. Living history museums & visitor experiences. Table created by authors.

Source	Findings
Tilden 1957; reprinted 2007 [5]	Defines interpretation as an educational activity which "aims to reveal meanings and relationships through the use of original objects, by first hand experience, and by illustrative media" (33)
Anderson 1982 [6]	Defines living history as "the simulation of life in another time."
Bennett 1985 [7]	Makes historical connection between museums and popular culture as well as other leisure sites, arguing that museums are places of education and moral instruction
Handler and Saxton 1988 [8]	Argue that history practitioners are keenly concerned with authenticity and that the role of the interpreter is to bridge past and present
Rosenzweig and Thelen 1998 [9]	Examining public perceptions of "history" and "the past," authors found that the public was engaged with the past and participated in past-related activities and that family past mattered most. They call these individuals "popular historymakers."
Cameron and Gatewood 2000 [10]	Argue that much is unknown as to what visitors actually want when they go to historical sites. They point to visitor studies that identify motivations for visits, such as anxiety about the future and nostalgia for the past in addition to gaining information, having fun, or creating memories, people often seek a deeper, more meaningful connection with a place or time period (as if spiritual, from above, i.e., numinous)
Dicks 2003 [11]	Brings together ethnographic and qualitative research involving globalization, heritage, and consumerism to examine how public places take on aspects of "visitability," meaning they are consumer-friendly, accessible, interactive, performative, and safe
Gordon 2008 [12]	Combines approaches from museum studies, tourism, and ethnography to propose a typology of exhibition and institutional frameworks for academic, corporate, community, entrepreneurial, and vernacular museums
Skinner et al. 2012 [13]	Define engagement as "constructive, enthusiastic, willing, emotionally positive, cognitively focused participation in learning activities." Ultimately, they see engagement is its own characteristic of the visitor experience, not an addendum to participation

(*continued*)

Table 1. (*continued*)

Source	Findings
Falk and Dierking 2013 [14]	Amplifying a contextual model of learning, the authors propose studying the interaction between personal, physical, and sociocultural contexts of a museum visit
Johnson 2015 [15]	Highlights the participatory, embodiment aspects of re-enactment and living history as having potential as a form of historical discourse
Shukla 2015 [16]	Shows how costumes, as visible representations of heritage, are set apart from everyday dress and, as such, mark a division between the ordinary and extraordinary
Allison 2016 [17]	Offers three case studies and argues that "museums are most effective when they provide entertaining experiences that excite curiosity and foster learning" (96)
Kelleher 2019 [18]	As crafts are an important part of Old Sturbridge Village's identity and are a major attraction for visitors, the author traces one museum's identity from a "historic crafts village" into a "historic village with crafts."

This body of literature points to the "letting go" of authority on the part of museums overall and, in particular, the framing of visitor experiences at living history museums. Invoking this release of authority, we also tethered our approach to Tilden's call for engagement while acknowledging the ways in which our digital docent might, still, simulate life in another time, even if not delivered in means of the past. Thus, as a research team we were informed, even in incremental and divergent ways, by the approaches noted above, which come from scholars and practitioners in the space of living history and audience research.

In particular, we sought both to simulate [6] and to contradict through the creation and delivery of digital experiences that address the engagement criteria defined by Skinner above [13] for the purpose of developing opportunities for the museum to connect with its visitors in meaningful ways so that they achieve an effectiveness outlined by Allison [18] as providing "entertaining experiences that excite curiosity and foster learning" (96).

2.2 Examples of Digital Storytelling at Cultural Heritage Institutions

In addition to a theoretical framework, our research was informed by examples of storytelling in museums and cultural heritage institutions abound. In particular, we look to an early example of digital storytelling that saw pedagogical dimensions of such practices, when used in partnership with museum experiences. Such practices can be learner-centered [19]. Building upon the work of CHESS (Cultural Heritage Experiences through Socio-Personal Interactions and Storytelling) which strived for rigorous academic integrity as part of storytelling, DIGITAL DOCENTS takes its cues from work done at the Acropolis Museum in Greece, Çatalhöyük in Turkey, and the

Stedelijk Museum in Amsterdam where stories were developed along three focal areas: plot, persona, and theme [20].

However, our work differs from other digital storytelling in museums due to our focus on narrative storytelling from the point of view of individual characters, in contrast to applications involving the layering of animations to enhance visitors' experiences with objects. Such object-focused AR experiences include expanded content for museum exhibit items, as in the case of The Franklin Institute's *Terracotta Warriors* [21] AR app that includes far more content than the onsite exhibition about the warriors excavated from the burial chambers of Emperor Qin Shihuangdi, China's first emperor. Other object-focused uses include the animation of skeletons of extinct animals from the past, exemplified by the Smithsonian Museum of Natural History's *Skin and Bones* exhibit [22, 23]. Moreover, the creation of historical narratives, embodied by digital characters situated in a placed-based contexts, further distinguish the project.

2.3 Conceptual Framework for Storytelling

DIGITAL DOCENTS aims to center the importance of storytelling at the museum and extend its potentialities by introducing digital characters gleaned from history who offer a means of learning about history through place-based narratives. The project ultimately contradicts assumptions about the ways in which living history museums—which by their very nature, are associated with historical tradition, hands-on, and analog experiences—might enhance visitor experiences through Augmented Reality (AR) and Virtual Reality (VR).

To center storytelling, we had to synthesize facets of living history museum interpretation, which is often mediated through the costumed interpreters who may take on a particular role, often with the premise that they are conveying what it was like to live in the past and the modern visitor has encountered them in their daily life as they speak informatively, usually while demonstrating a skill or trade [24, 25].

Digital Storytelling by Digital Docents as a Complement to Costumed Interpreters

To extend the museum's storytelling apparatus, we developed a protocol for creating digital docents who present their story in first-person who engage the visitor through voice recognition, question, and answer. The project thus supports and extends the museum's interpretation program in the historic village by rendering individuals who engage with visitors through the delivery of richly textured series of narratives derived from personal letters, journals, documents, autobiographies.

Place-Based Narratives

Our digital storytelling is place-based: visitors learn from a digitally rendered individual who is rooted to specific geographic locations of Western New York. Close approximation may be found with historical figures, keyed to sites, in an AR environment as employed through the app *England's Historic Cities*, which uses AR at 12 sites across England with historical figures, including William Shakespeare, as tour guides [26]. While *England's Historic Cities* uses an historical character as part of AR experience, he is a celebrity, as opposed to a less famous individual, as our project illustrates. Moreover, the site is the narrative driver—with *Cities* being invoked in the title of the app itself—rather than the biography of the individual. In contrast, our stories are driven by a personal narrative that is shared with the visitor in a location that has personal significance for the character.

Personal Significance with a Particular Museum Environment
The third way that DIGITAL DOCENTS differs from other museum applications in AR and VR is through its showcase of a historical figure who has an authentic connection to the museum environment he inhabits. In addition to offering storytelling from the point of view of an historical character and focusing on place-based engagement within a historical context, the digital docents are site-based on a micro-level, often inhabiting a structure that they could have encountered in their life time. Thus, as the museum visitor crosses the threshold of the doorway to the structure, they are greeted by a character who is geographically sited to a place that is not only authentic to this region, but of personal significance, as well.

3   Methods

By creating a method for visitors to interact with digital re-creations of historical characters who have ties to the geographic region during the 19th century and are sited to a particular location that is both place-based and personally-relevant, this supports our inquiry around three conceptual project goals, outlined below, which are informed by our technical methods.

3.1   Goal 1: Telling the Stories of Western New York

Conceptually, all characters developed in DIGITAL DOCENTS support our framing of narrative storytelling from the point of view of an historical character; place-based engagement within a historical context; and an authentic connection to the museum environment. The individuals include: reform advocate and New York State Senator Frederick Fanning Backus (1794–1858); Candace Beach (1790–1850), a teacher at a one-room schoolhouse who lived through the historic "year without summer" that occurred in 1816 as a result of the explosion of Mt. Tambora in Indonesia the year earlier; John Carlin (1813–1891), a poet and painter who graduated in 1825 from Pennsylvania Institute for the Deaf and Dumb; Austin Steward (1793–1869), who was born to enslaved parents in Virginia before moving to New York and becoming engaged in antislavery and temperance; and Lavinia Fanning Watson (1818–1900), a socialite who was the first woman to commission a naval ship. Each of the aforementioned had ties to this region and offers ways to understand the past. Through their stories they seek to engage audiences who are interacting with digital representations of historical persons.

The content and context are presented in recorded branching narratives that are broken down into topics that allow for pauses and verbal prompts from the user. Visitors can direct the "conversation" with the digital docent through their choices within the applications.

Through user-selected branching narratives, the characters guide the visitors through their lives and locations, allowing guests to have an immersive, entertaining, and informative experience. The five narratives trace the history of this region and its import in the national context. By building upon these rich secondary sources and scholarship explicating the wealth of primary sources related to celebrated individuals and, further, by creating branching narratives, DIGITAL DOCENTS excavates the lives and times of lesser-known individuals whose stories are bound to archival materials and presented digitally through our storytelling, as noted above. By linking these personal stories to broader narratives, we extend the characterization of these individuals as worthy, agents of change and thus include more perspectives and, in turn, ask the visitor to see themselves in these stories.

3.2 Goal 2: Developing "Thinking Dispositions"

During the concept and discovery phase, a digital avatar of Frederick Backus was created and placed in the entry foyer of the Livingston-Backus house at the GCV&M. We tested the concept using a HoloLens™ [2]. Feedback gleaned from this preliminary test indicated a desire for more interaction with the digital character.

To increase the engagement and to foster discoverability and multiple learning pathways, we decided to move from a "monologue" to a "dialogue" format that involves the digital docent and the museum visitor.

We also engaged the concept of "thinking dispositions" as a mode of inquiry and visitor engagement. Developed by Harvard Graduate School of Education, "Thinking Dispositions" can be employed in museums through the use of storytelling, in order to present the content conversationally, in a first-person interactive narrative [3]. The "dispositions" encourage learners to ask questions of themselves and their world by tiering their understandings by asking learners to ponder the following questions:

(1) Why might this [topic, question] matter to me?
(2) Why might it matter to people around me [family, friends, city, nation]?
(3) Why might it matter to the world?

This method encourages visitors to gauge and construct the significance of historical narratives. In our application, through the dialogues we create for our characters, we engage visitors to motivate reflection upon the stories of our characters on a personal, local, and global level.

For Backus and the other four characters in development, we structured the conversation as branching narratives devised into topics, as demonstrated in Fig. 4. The digital docents present information. The docents can also pose open ended questions to the museum visitors and allow them to create their own unique experience through a series of questions and prompts. The conversational presentation allows visitors to discern the significance of a situation, topic, or issue, and consider why a topic might be worth investigating further. Each topic has voice and interface prompts that will allow the user to choose how they engage with the character, providing a greater level of interactivity. The storytelling also offers a space for reflection and development of "thinking dispositions" to motivate reflection upon these stories on a personal, local, and global level.

This "thinking disposition" interaction and reflection, prompted by interaction with the digital docent, fosters the kind of experiential authenticity Penrose identified as possible through personal identification with museum content delivered via story-telling. Such scaffolded authenticity, in turn, Penrose argues enhances visitors' receptivity to the experience [27].

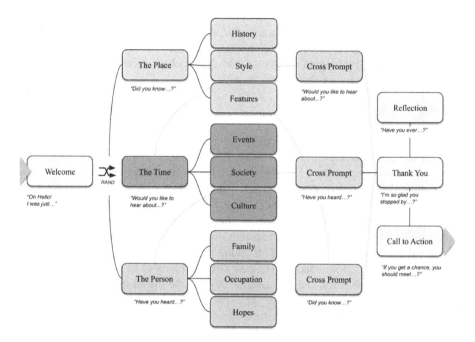

Fig. 4. Typical narrative branching map. Created by authors.

In practice, the conversation elements are encountered in two ways: by selecting and verbally articulating the next dialogue conversation (spoken word) or by scanning an object within the historic property to unlock dialogue options so that users are encouraged to explore various parts of the museum.

3.3   Goal 3: Tripartite Deployment and the Challenges Presented by COVID-19

DIGITAL DOCENTS offers visitors online and onsite the opportunity to understand the historical past and to learn first-person accounts from those who lived them. While initially we conceived of the project as deliverable through AR devices or AR mobile onsite at the museum, with the halt of all facets of social, educational, and entertain-ment based outside of the home due to the COVID-19 pandemic, our team began to re-think our strategy.

In March and April 2020, in the midst of "lock-down" due to the COVID-19 pandemic, we were forced to halt our development. While unfortunate in terms of our project timeline, the abrupt cessation afforded us the opportunity to reflect on the impact of COVID-19 on museum visitation, the likelihood of returning to open-air museums, and visitor needs in a post-COVID world.

Building upon the robust audience research from Wilkening Consulting and the American Alliance of Museums, who have released data stories surrounding visitor needs and desires in a post-COVID museum landscape, we redefined our project to develop a continuum of offerings across three platforms (in-museum AR, mobile AR, web-based VR). Moreover, our project meets the needs of visitors who will feel more likely, according to Wilkening, to visit outdoor attractions and less inclined to pursue hands-on activities [28]. However, living history museums are a conundrum in that they are open spaces (often situated as historic villages) that offer a plethora of hands-on activities; thus, DIGITAL DOCENTS now, in a post-COVID world, positions itself as an outdoor experience—and an indoor one— as well as an onsite and offsite one that can still meet visitors needs for tactility and engagement although now mediated through the digital characters and environments that we create. See Fig. 5.

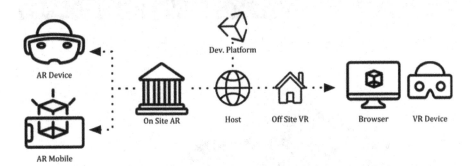

Fig. 5. Content distribution map. Created by authors.

Onsite AR. Visitors to the Genesee Country Village & Museum currently experience a historical village setting with buildings assembled from locations around western New York (none is from further than 100 miles away) and restored or otherwise made visitable and, in some cases, serving their original function or repurposed for a new, yet historically-relevant context [29]. As the visitor enters the doorway, with the AR device enabled, the virtual character welcomes the visitor and tells their story in first-person, in contrast to the costumed interpreters, and offering opportunities for the visitor to ask questions and answer them as well.

Offsite VR. Users offsite can experience the character in a Virtual Reality (VR) context, where a VR device creates the environment background as well as the digital docent, and delivered to cross platform web-browsers via WebGL [30]. This modality allows the museum to extend its interactive reach to homes and classrooms in addition to the onsite experience. The character content for both of these experiences is identical, with the primary difference being whether the background environment is displayed on the device. See Figs. 6, 7.

Fig. 6. Offsite VR. See https://www.cs.rit.edu/~jmg/Backus/. Created by authors.

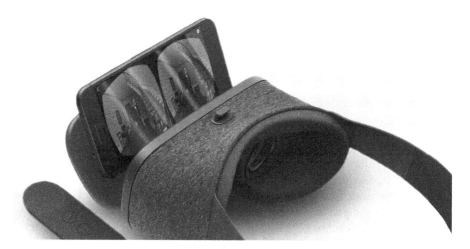

Fig. 7. Offsite VR headset mockup using Google Cardboard™· Created by authors.

With modes of access that include onsite at the museum using a museum-supplied AR device, a mobile AR app employed from a visitor's phone, or online through a Web based VR experience, DIGITAL DOCENTS engages visitors through multiple points of entry.

3.4   Design and Technical Specifications

DIGITAL DOCENTS combines and enables presentation of three sets of assets. The character is a 3D model. Its captured (and cleaned) animation are stored in FBX files. The monologue is read from a script, which is then used as part of the speech-to-text application, is captured as .mp3 files. The monologue also functions as the source for captions as well. Elsewhere we address the target application and libraries for translation of speech to text [31].

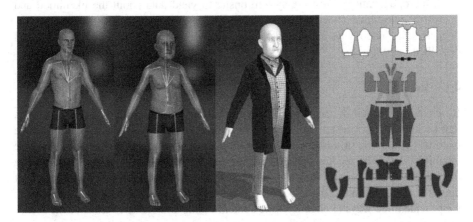

Fig. 8. Digital character modeling, rigging, and clothing design. Created by authors.

Character Creation

Historical research and documents are used to guide the appearance of the character, both regarding physical and facial features as well as proper costuming that reflects the time period in which the character is presented (Fig. 8). Our attention to historical accuracy supports the museum's ongoing mission of exhibiting historic clothing, as evidenced by their recent displays and from the Susan Greene Costume Collection featuring more than 3,500 rare, 19th-century garments and accessories, which also serve as source material for our project [32]. Our character creation process is described in more detail elsewhere [1, 2].

Development Platform

With DIGITAL DOCENTS, we focused on the one character to create a model and costume and dialogue, all of which were informed by historical research. We employed full-body motion capture to guide the creation of a rigged and animated 3D character model that was joined with an audio recording, imported into Unity and combined with the monologue script in text form.

Deployment

Deployment occurs on output devices including the HoloLens™, mobile device apps (both iOS and Android) and WebXR (a standard for deploying 3D and VR applications on a Web browser).

4   Results and Discussion

Our intended outcomes, as mentioned above, are three-fold. First, visitors will gain historical knowledge about the past based upon contextualized narratives delivered digitally online and onsite. Second, by posing open-ended questions to visitors, the digital docents will ask visitors to discern the significance of a situation, topic, or issue, and consider why this topic might be worth investigating further. Based upon our limited user-testing to date (pre-COVID), we have achieved these outcomes [1]. We await the opportunity to test the system onsite to yield data about the likelihood and interest of museum visitors to use digital interactives to enhance their learning experiences online and onsite at cultural heritage institutions. A timeline for this testing is described below.

4.1   Results

By creating a digital docent informed by the history of the building and general area that he inhabits, in western New York, the project offers the opportunity to place the historical character, in this case Dr. Frederick Fanning Backus, in the home he once inhabited, where he recounts stories in short-form vignettes for visitors. In delivering the content and allowing visitors to pause and reflect, we encourage visitors to reflect upon the stories of Western New York on the personal, local, and global level. Third, we provide three ways to encounter the content online and onsite to enhance the visitor experience.

The system is multi-modal and deployed on three platforms: an onsite AR device version; a mobile version that can be used onsite and offsite; and an offsite web browser/virtual reality version. Users access content and interact using a head-mounted device—which was, initially, our primary method of delivery, though that has changed since COVID-19 when we realized that we needed to adhere to health and safety concerns during the pandemic. Moreover, as offsite and virtual events became more common due to restrictions of COVID-19, we realized the value and potential of developing an offsite framework for the experience. To this end, we developed a Web app that could be accessed through the browser and additionally via VR device.

Due to COVID restrictions, we have been unable to test this system onsite at the museum to date. Prior to this, however, we received informal feedback from users in two phases in 2019 [2]. While we had planned to develop and conduct formalized user testing at the museum in the summer of 2020, COVID restrictions prevented us from doing so onsite. However, our first user-testing will take place in March 2021, involving two cohorts: nine museum staff and a larger number of volunteers. Pre-visit and post-visit surveys catered to the online experience as well as the onsite experience will provide quantitative and qualitative data on the extent to which the system and its delivery enhanced the visitor experience, as determined by the three facets noted above. The results will be shared in a forthcoming publication.

4.2 Discussion

In terms of measuring the success of our three goals, we are currently developing an evaluation framework for this experience. We build upon the work of Damala et al. [33] who focus their evaluation framework on the perspectives of cultural heritage professionals, the institution, and the museum visitor. We have begun the process of gaining insight from the museum professionals at Genesee Country Village & Museum, through an onsite user experience testing in March 2021. While that experience consists of three facets (pre-experience survey, post-onsite-experience survey, and post-offsite experience survey), we endeavor to use this feedback as a first step in benchmarking the perspectives of the institution and cultural heritage professionals, just as we seek to benchmark with our visitor surveys. We will use these quantitative and qualitative data to inform our next steps, in keeping with the MUSETECH matrix outlined by Damala et al. who propose the idea of limiting key questions related to a museum technology program. Our key question, as it has been throughout this research, has been focused on the enhancement of the visitor experience, predicated upon the delivery of a narrative by a historical character in a location where they have an historical tie, the framing of narratives that engage visitors in thinking dispositions, and three points of entry for this AR and VR experience.

5 Conclusion

By excavating stories from the past and delivering first-person narratives DIGITAL DOCENTS demonstrates how digital tools can be used to engage visitors through storytelling. Deeply-researched historical and archival material are translated into dialogues delivered onsite AR and offsite VR experiences at a living history museum.

Nevertheless, as living history institutions exalt hands-on elements as critical to the visitor experience, we seek to extend the possibilities to include digital immersive experiences without detracting from the hands-on, analog, onsite opportunities at the museum. Visitors onsite, in particular, have the best of both worlds: they have opportunities to engage with costumed interpreters at some locations of the museum in addition to learning from a digitally rendered character that serves as a guide on the side, an enhancement to the traditional museum experience.

The entire apparatus of storytelling thus encourages visitors to reflect on the content and to gauge and construct the significance of historical narratives, thereby tying together historical research with contemporary issues. Moreover, by employing immersive technologies with tripartite delivery that enables various levels of accessibility, our project responds directly to the health safety concerns raised by COVID-19. Our work is ongoing as we continue our research and design (during COVID-19 restrictions) and will begin motion and audio capture of the remaining narratives beyond Frederick Backus (Summer/Fall 2021).

Ultimately, our hope is that DIGITAL DOCENTS contradicts assumptions about Augmented Reality and Virtual Reality at living history (or open-air) museums which, by their very nature, are associated with historical tradition, hands-on, and analog experiences in order to show how creating and delivering historical narratives via AR and VR can yield authentic experiences that bridge past and present.

Acknowledgements. The authors are grateful to the staff of Genesee Country Village & Museum, in particular Becky Wehle and Peter Wisbey. At RIT, we thank students Lizzy Carr, Hannah Chase, Brienna Johnson-Morris, Kunal Shitut and Hao Su as well as a number of students from the following courses: Visitor Engagement and Museum Technologies, Museums and the Digital Age, Fundamentals of Acting, Costume Hair and Makeup, Character Design and Rigging, and Applications in Virtual Reality. In addition, we are grateful to faculty colleagues in fine arts at RIT including Andy Head, David Munnell, and Yunn-Shan Ma.

References

1. Jacobs, G.D., Decker, J., Geigel, J., Doherty, A.: Virtual docent for a living history museum. Frameless **2**(1) (2020). Article 18 in the 2019 Symposium Proceedings, in Decker, J. and Halbstein, D. (eds.) Frameless Symposium 2019, RIT Scholar Works, Rochester, NY, USA, vol. 2, Article 18. https://scholarworks.rit.edu/frameless/vol2/iss1/18/
2. Decker, J., Doherty, A., Geigel, J., Jacobs, G.: Blending disciplines for a blended reality: virtual guides for a living history museum. J. Interact. Technol. Pedagogy 17 (2020). https://jitp.commons.gc.cuny.edu/blending-disciplines-for-a-blended-reality-virtual-guides-for-a-living-history-museum/
3. Harvard Graduate School of Education: Project Zero: Three Ys. (2019)
4. Bedford, L.: Storytelling: the real work of museums. Curator Mus. J. **44**(1), 27–34 (2001). https://doi.org/10.1111/j.2151-6952.2001.tb00027
5. Tilden, F.: Interpreting Our Heritage, 4th edn. University of North Carolina Press, Chapel Hill (2007)
6. Anderson, J.: Living history: simulating everyday life in living museums. Am. Q. **34**(3), 290–306 (1982)
7. Bennett, T.: The Birth of the Museum: History, Theory, Politics. Routledge, London (1985)
8. Handler, R., Saxton, W.: Dyssimulation: reflexivity, narrative, and the quest for authenticity in 'living history.' Cult. Anthropol. **33**, 242–260 (1988)
9. Rosenzweig, R., Thelen, D.: The Presence of the Past: Popular Uses of History in American Life. Columbia University Press, New York (1998)
10. Cameron, C.M., Gatewood, J.B.: Excursions into the un-remembered past: what people want from visits to historical sites. Public Hist. **22**(3), 107–127 (2000)
11. Dicks, B.: Culture on Display: The Production of Contemporary Visitability. Open UP, London (2003)
12. Gordon, T.S.: Heritage, commerce, and museal display: toward a new typology of historical exhibition in the United States. Public Hist. **30**(3), 27–50 (2008)
13. Skinner, E.A., Chi, U., The Learning-Gardens Educational Assessment Group 1: Intrinsic motivation and engagement as "active ingredients" in garden-based education: examining models and measures derived from self-determination theory. J. Environ. Educ. **43**(1), 16–36 (2012). https://www-tandfonline-com.ezproxy.rit.edu/toc/vjee20/43/1
14. Falk, J.H., Dierking, D.: The Museum Experience Revisited. Left Coast Press, Walnut Creek (2013)
15. Johnson, K.M.: Rethinking (re)doing: historical re-enactment and/as historiography. Rethink. Hist. **19**(2), 193–206 (2015)

16. Shukla, P.: Costume: Performing Identities through Dress. Indiana University Press, Bloomington (2015)
17. Allison, D.B.: Living History: Effective Costumed Interpretation and Enactment at Museums and Historic Sites. Rowman & Littlefield for AASLH, Lanham (2016)
18. Kelleher, T.: Crafts and living history: old sturbridge village. In: Burke, C., Spencer-Wood, S.M. (eds.) Crafting in the World, pp. 193–212. Springer, Cham (2019). https://doi.org/10.1007/978-3-319-65088-3_10
19. Springer, J., Kajder, S., Brazas, J.B.: Digital storytelling at the national gallery of art. In: Museums and the Web 2004. Archives & Museum Informatics (2004). https://www.museumsandtheweb.com/mw2004/papers/springer/springer.html
20. Roussou, M., et al.: The museum as digital storyteller: collaborative participatory creation of interactive digital experiences. In: MW 2015: Museums and the Web 2015, 31 January 2015. https://mw2015.museumsandtheweb.com/paper/the-museum-as-digital-storyteller-collaborative-participatory-creation-of-interactive-digital-experiences/. Accessed 9 Sept 2019
21. Coates, C.: Virtual Reality is a big trend in museums, but what are the best examples of museums using VR? Museum Next, 17 July 2020. https://www.museumnext.com/article/how-museums-are-using-virtual-reality/
22. Ding, M.: Augmented Reality in Museums. Arts Management & Technology Lab, Carnegie Mellon University (2017)
23. Smithsonian Institution: Smithsonian Brings Historic Specimens to Life in Free "Skin and Bones" Mobile App. News Release, 13 January 2015. https://www.si.edu/newsdesk/releases/smithsonian-brings-historic-specimens-life-free-skin-and-bones-mobile-app
24. Thierer, J.M.: Telling History: A Manual for Performers and Presenters of First-Person Narratives. AltaMira for AASLH, Lanham (2010)
25. Roth, S.F.: Past Into Present: Effective Techniques for First-Person Historical Interpretation. University of North Carolina Press, Chapel Hill (2005)
26. England's Historic Cities: England's Historic Cities App – Main Video (2017). https://vimeo.com/210243815
27. Penrose, J.: Authenticity, Authentication and Experiential Authenticity: Telling Stories in Museums. Soc. Cult/ Geogr. 21, 1245–1267 (2018)
28. Wilkening Consulting: Data Stories Regarding Museums and the Pandemic (2020). http://www.wilkeningconsulting.com/datamuseum
29. Genesee Country Village & Museum (GCV&M): Mission Statement (2018). https://www.gcv.org/about/
30. Web-based VR is viewable here. https://www.cs.rit.edu/~jmg/Backus/
31. Geigel, J., Shitut, K., Decker, J., Doherty, A., Jacobs, G.: The digital docent: XR storytelling for a living history museum. In: 26th ACM Symposium on Virtual Reality Software and Technology, VRST 2020, pp. 1–3. Association for Computing Machinery, New York (2020). Article no: 74. https://doi.org/10.1145/3385956.3422090
32. Genesee Country Village & Museum: Susan Greene Costume Collection. https://www.gcv.org/explore/gallery/susan-greene-costume-collection/
33. Damala, A., Ruthven, I., Hornecker, E.: The MUSETECH model: a comprehensive evaluation framework for museum technology. ACM J. Comput. Cult. Herit. 12(1), 1–22 (2019). Article 7

Realistic Humans in Virtual Cultural Heritage

Alan Chalmers[1]([⊠]), Joseph Parkins[1], Mark Webb[2],
and Kurt Debattista[1]

[1] WMG, University of Warwick, Coventry, UK
alan.chalmers@warwick.ac.uk
[2] Medieval Coventry Charity, Coventry, UK

Abstract. The presence of people plays a key role in how an environment, both now and in the past, is perceived. While there have been numerous computer reconstructions of cultural heritage sites, many, if not most, of these do not contain people. One reason for this is the so called "uncanny valley" affect. Despite huge efforts to create highly realistic looking virtual humans, because we humans have evolved to fully recognise other humans with all our imperfections, computer representations never look "quite right". This can have a significant negative impact on how we perceive a virtual environment, despite all the efforts to accurately simulate the past. This paper investigates the inclusion of real humans in virtual cultural heritage applications. These humans are captured in 3D in ancient costumes and re-enacting relevant tasks. Care is taken to ensure that the lighting during the real capture and the lighting in the virtual environment match. The results of this approach are demonstrated for a number of ancient industries in a reconstruction of medieval Coventry.

Keywords: Realistic humans · Virtual reality · Cultural re-enactment · Medieval Coventry

1 Introduction

For over 30 years there has been significant research to improve the realism of virtual reconstructions of cultural heritage sites. From the early 3D models of IBM's Reilly [1] to the latest multisensory reconstructions, e.g. [2], improved physical simulation of the material properties of the environment and factors such as how light and other senses, audio, feel, and smell propagate within an environment including the presence of any participating media, such as dust and smoke, have driven the increase in realism. As Fig. 1 shows, the presence of participating media can have a significant impact on the perception of an environment. While the physical fidelity of reconstructed cultural environments is now at a very high standard, e.g. Figure 1, what is often very conspicuous in most reconstructions is the absence of people. When in use, an environment is never "empty", it contains the people who need to be in the environment either for work or for leisure.

High-fidelity simulation of virtual humans, including in virtual archaeology, has been a topic that has been active for many years [4, 5]. Despite all this effort, virtual humans in any environment still don't look "quite right". Termed the "uncanny valley effect" [6], virtual humans can elicit a substantial negative emotional response in the

© Springer Nature Switzerland AG 2021
M. Shehade and T. Stylianou-Lambert (Eds.): RISE IMET 2021, CCIS 1432, pp. 156–165, 2021.
https://doi.org/10.1007/978-3-030-83647-4_11

viewer. This can significantly affect the level of immersion that the viewer may feel in the virtual environment [7]. In this paper we consider the inclusion of real humans in the cultural heritage reconstructions. Human re-enactors, dressed in period costume and undertaking the ancient tasks in an accurate manner, are captured in high-fidelity in 3D and then incorporated into the virtual environment. This enables the ancient sites to be populated while avoiding any "uncanny valley" effects.

Fig. 1. Computer reconstruction of the temple of Kalabsha in Egypt showing the visual impact of the physically accurate simulation of dust in the environment [3]

The rest of the paper is structured as follows. Section 2 describes the system used to capture the re-enactors in 3D and the challenges faced in doing so. Section 3 provides the context for the cultural heritage case study considered in this paper; industries in Medieval Coventry in the UK. Section 4 presents the results of this work so far, and Sect. 5 discusses the remaining issues that need to be addressed and provides details of what the next steps for this research will be.

2 High-Fidelity 3D Capture

Recent advances in depth-capturing technology, such as the Microsoft Kinect Azure [8] and photogrammetric techniques, e.g. [9], have made it now possible to capture and subsequently display in great detail, volumetric videos (VVs); 3D volumes of dynamic activity. Such VVs are being increasingly used in a number of applications, including entertainment [10], sports [11], etc. Unlike stereoscopic video, VV includes all the detail of an object in 3D, enabling a viewer to examine it from any angle. Key challenges though are that capturing a dynamic object, such as a human undertaking a task, in 3D results in a lot data, and existing graphics pipelines are not well equipped to handle dynamic 3D point clouds.

2.1 The 3D System

Two different 3D capture systems have been used for this work: (1) Microsoft's Kinect V2s and (2) their Azure Kinects. The Kinects are Time of Flight 3D sensors. Originally developed as an aid for controlling games for Microsoft's Xbox, the Kinect and later the Kinect V2, quickly found alternative applications in capturing 3D environments. The Kinect V2 includes a 1920 × 1080 resolution RGB camera, a 512 × 424 pixels infrared camera, and an infrared emitter.

The weaving case study, Sect. 3.1 was captured with only 2× Kinect V2s. This was because the space in the actual environment was very limited, see Fig. 3, and thus it was only possible to capture one view of the weavers. The dyeing case study was captured with 3× Kinect V2s. The limited resolution of the RGB and infrared cameras meant that fine detail in the scene, such as the threads in the loom, were not captured. Furthermore, the Kinect V2s require an independent USB 3.0 controller per device, meaning that without adding PCI expansions, the control computer can only operate a single device. This is not helpful when a scene needs to be simultaneously captured from multiple locations. Indeed, the official API does not support multiple devices. Although open source APIs exists to support multiple devices, there is no means to automatically synchronise or timestamp the devices; this has to be done manually after the capturing process. Microsoft discontinued the Kinect V2 in November 2018.

Released in March 2020 (although only in the US and China), the Microsoft Azure Kinect is a low-cost ($399) 3D capture device which includes a 12 megapixel RGB camera, a 1 megapixel-depth camera, 360-degree seven-microphone array, and an orientation sensor [12]. Although the framerate of the Kinect Azure, 30 fps, is still relatively low, the high resolution of the cameras make the device well suited to capturing relatively slow forms of human motion, such as those involved in re-enacting medieval tasks. The official Azure API supports simultaneous capture from multiple devices and a hardware frame capture synchronisation is included. A major unsolved issue – to-date – is the lack of an officially supported cable of longer than 1m. Cables longer than this result in lost or corrupted frames, which have to be dealt with after the capturing process. In addition, despite having an array of 7 microphones on each device, there is currently no official means for accessing this data correctly, with only one audio feed per device being visible when using 3rd party libraries.

Four Kinect Azures were used to capture the tanning process in 3D, Fig. 5.

2.2 Challenges When Capturing Real Activities

Microsoft states quite clearly in their documentation that the Kinect Azure includes a global shutter that enables the device to be used in any ambient lighting condition [13]. This was simply not the case when we attempted to capture 3D data outside, even on a cloudy day. As Fig. 5 shows, it was necessary to enclose the area of capture in a "tent" in order to reduce the ambient lighting to a level that would not saturate the IR camera and thus avoid highly noisy or even no depth data.

Temporal and spatial alignment are critical when combining dynamic scenes from multiple devices. Spatial alignment is achieved by ensuring there is a static reference object in the scene that can be seen by all devices. As mentioned, temporal alignment in the V2s had to be done manually, whereas with the Azures, there is a mechanical link cable that ensures the temporal alignment.

Another important issue that has to be considered when incorporating captured VVs into a virtual environment, is the lighting conditions under which the objects were captured, and the lighting conditions that will be used within the virtual scene.

Capturing the real lighting with, e.g. a 360° HDR camera, enables this "lighting balance" to be achieved, e.g. [14].

3 Medieval Coventry

Originally a small Saxon settlement, by the late 14th century Coventry had grown to be one of the largest and most important towns in England and was the regional capital of the Midlands. Its success was based on the sale of raw wool, and later manufactured and finished woollen cloth, supplemented by other important industries including leather making and metalworking [15].

Coventry was particularly noted for its blue cloth, using imported woad for the colour and alum to fix the colour. Blue cloth was used in finished broadcloth or as the basis for expensive fabrics including 'scarlets' [16, 17]. The phrase "True as Coventry Blue" refers to the fact that the cloth retained its colour, despite the harsh laundry practises of the time. Coventry dyers were therefore important craftsmen, along with others in cloth 'finishing' including shearers and tailors. Some of Coventry's drapers and mercers, those who sold the wool and cloth, were amongst the wealthiest merchants in the country [17]. The city authorities rigorously controlled the quality of the city's cloth, packaged and sealed with the city's Elephant and Castle emblem [18].

Spon Street, to the west of Coventry's medieval walls, was a suburban area noted for its concentrations of weavers, dyers and tanners. It was conveniently located for access to the River Sherbourne, upon which tanners and dyers in particular depended for a supply of running water. Remaining tanning workshops inside the walls were required to re-locate to the suburbs due to the noxious character of preparing leather, as demonstrated by surviving documentary evidence for local regulations, for example in 1461 and 1473 [18].

Many of the surviving medieval buildings in Coventry were destroyed during the war or taken down during post-war reconstruction. A relatively large number survived in Spon Street due to its location away from the town centre, although the construction of the ring road across the street in the 1960's involved further losses. In 1967 the City Council launched a scheme to restore some of the remaining Spon Street buildings and other medieval buildings were relocated here having been taken down from other parts of the city [19]. Figure 2 shows some of the restored buildings today which are now used as shops, restaurants and a museum.

Fig. 2. Surviving medieval buildings in Spon Street, Coventry

3.1   Medieval Industries

English wool and woollen cloth were in high demand in Europe and made up the lion's share of the country's exports in the medieval period [16]. Coventry grew as a wool-producing town using flocks around the city owned by religious institutions, including the Benedictine priory of St Mary and the Cistercian foundations at Coombe and Stoneleigh. By the 14th century, Coventry was also manufacturing broadcloth for the overseas and domestic markets and this turned the city into a fast-growing 'boom town' attracting migrant workers to work in the textiles industry [17]. The process of producing broadcloth required a large workforce, especially large numbers of lower status weavers and spinners. By the late 15th century about a third of the city's workforce, including children, was employed in textiles and textiles-related industries and over a half of the population was engaged in low status wage-earning activities.

Natural ingredients were used to make dyes of various colours in the middle ages, e.g. madder for red, woad for blue, much of it imported from Europe or further afield. The dyed cloth or thread was dipped in a warmed dye bath containing a mordant solution such as alum to fix the colour evenly [16].

The leather industry was essential for everyday life in the middle ages, e.g. for clothing, shoes and boots, tents, saddles, gloves, purses and for carrying wine. Leather making was largely for the local domestic market, although the industry's importance has been under-estimated [20]. The leather trade worked closely with the town's butchers. The smells from the tanning establishments were particularly noxious as warm bird or dog droppings were used to loosen the hair and fat from the hides, before they were scraped off. They were then treated with urine and soaked for up to 12 months in deep vats. Finally, then the hides could be dried and worked into leather [21].

3.2   Project Aims

In 2021, Coventry will be City of Culture in the UK. Held every four years, after stiff competition, one city is chosen to showcase its cultural uniqueness. For a whole year, the city and its region put on a wide variety of cultural events, including music, dance, theatre and exhibitions. The work described in this paper will form an important part of Built Environment exhibition within Coventry's City of Culture activities. Held in the former Draper's bar in the city centre, this exhibition will run the whole year of the celebrations and is expected to attached many thousands of visitors (subject to any pandemic restrictions). After the year of the Coventry City of Culture finishes, the results of the project will be used to explain the importance of medieval industries to school children as part of the Medieval Coventry Charity's outreach activities.

4   Realistic Humans

Accurately simulating human appearance and actions in virtual environments remains a challenging problem [4], which is exacerbated by the "uncanny valley" affect [6]. To avoid this problem, and the negative impact unrealistic humans have on the perception of a virtual environment, real human activities were captured in 3D and incorporated into the virtual models. This is facilitated by the fact that across the UK there are a number of people and organisations that carry out, and indeed teach people, traditional medieval skills, such as weaving, dyeing and tanning, e.g. [22, 23]. These re-enactors play a key role in helping to preserve and pass on these skills.

4.1   Weaving

Re-enacted weaving was captured in 3D at The Weaver's House, 122 Upper Spon Street [24]. One of the houses in a terrace of five cottages that was built in 1455, the Weaver's House, has been carefully restored as to how it would have been in 1540 when it was inhabited by a narrow-loom weaver, John Croke and his family [25]. In addition to a medieval garden at the back of the house with plants that would have been grown for food, flavouring, medicine and household use, the house also includes a detailed replica of the loom that would have been used at the time.

(a)   (b)

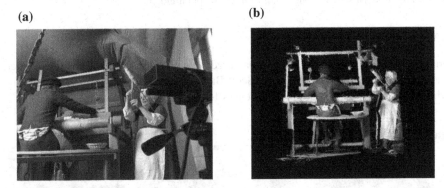

Fig. 3. Medieval weaving (a) capturing the re-enactors, (b) the resultant point cloud. Note the different colours on the captured weaver's back due to differences in the colour as seen by the two Kinect V2s.

The small room in which the loom is, was covered in green cloth to make the extraction of the loom and re-enactors easier and several minutes of weaving were captured using two Microsoft Kinect V2s, Fig. 3(a). Weaving re-enactors, Ruth Gilbert and Tim Jenkins operated the replica narrow loom.

4.2   Dyeing

Medieval dyeing was re-enacted by Debbie Bamford, of The Mulberry Dyer [22]. Established in the early 1990's, The Mulberry Dyer uses meticulous research in order to accurately recreate the dyeing process in a number of periods of history, including the middle ages. Examples of her work can be found in the V&A Museum, Hampton Court Palace, the Globe Theatre and other Museums and Historic Houses across the UK and Europe [22]. The dyeing process was captured using three Kinect V2's in an office, Fig. 4. (This was a mistake, as the smell of the dyeing process, which uses horse urine, remained in the office for several days).

(a)   (b)

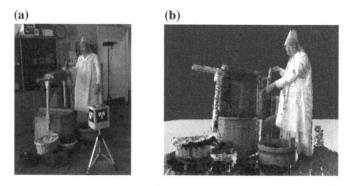

Fig. 4. Medieval dyeing (a) capturing the re-enactor, (b) the resultant point cloud. Note the box on a tripod to assist with the alignment of the three point clouds.

4.3   Tanning

Four different tanning processes were captured: washing, scraping, working the leather, and rinsing, Fig. 5. The tanners were Scott Baines and Liv of Rewild, Forest of Dean, who teach ancient skills to build awareness for sustainable rural living [23].

(a)   (b)   (c)

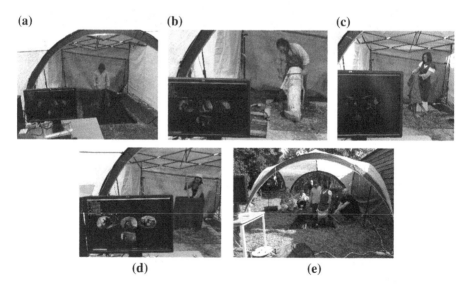

(d)   (e)

Fig. 5. Medieval tanning (a)–(d) the four captured processes (e) the challenging outdoor environment. The computer screen shows what is being captured from each Kinect Azure.

Capturing the different tanning processes in 3D produced some particular challenges. While weaving and dyeing could be captured in-doors, the tanning processes had to be captured outside, in particular because of the pit in which the hides are soaked, as Fig. 5 shows, it was necessary to enclose the capture area in a tent to reduce the ambient light levels, as explained in Sect. 2.2.

Fig. 6. Tanning point clouds

5 Discussion and Conclusion

Once the VVs have been captured and the virtual environment modelled, the VVs need to be incorporated into the virtual environment. This is still "work in progress" in this project. Figure 7 shows an early result with the model of the dyeing house, and the VV of the actual dyeing process relit with the virtual lighting.

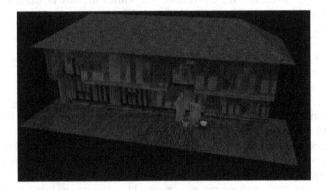

Fig. 7. Early results of combing the real captured human into the virtual environment.

Work is on-going to reduce the noise in the point clouds and to develop high quality compression methods to enable the dynamic points clouds to be viewed in real time during a live walk-through of the environment, e.g. using a HMD, rather than as pre-computed animations.

One restriction of the current approach is that all the activities, although appearing realistic, are fixed and simply play on a loop. This prevents the viewer from interacting with the virtual character in order to find out e.g. more details of the process. Future work will investigate having some chosen interactions so that the virtual humans can respond to certain pre-defined questions, and even the possibility of having a live interaction. In this case the re-enactors will be carrying out the activity in a remote location. The point cloud will be streamed live to the virtual environment and the viewer can interact directly with the re-enactor.

Future work will also carry out a detailed user study in order to compare the perceived realism of incorporating VVs of real people in to virtual cultural heritage environments with the traditional use of computer generated virtual humans.

Acknowledgments. We would like to thank Suzanne Psaila for creating the model of the medieval house and all the re-enactors for giving their time to this project.

References

1. Reilly, P., Shennan, S.: Applying Solid Modelling and Animated Three-dimensional Graphics to Archaeological Problems. IBM UK Scientific Centre (1989)
2. Dong, Y., Webb, M., Harvey, C., Debattista, K., Chalmers, A.G.: Multisensory virtual experience of tanning in Medieval Coventry. In: Eurographics Workshop on Graphics and Cultural Heritage, October 2017
3. Gutierrez, D., Sundstedt, V., Gomex, F., Chalmers, A.G.: Modeling light scattering for virtual heritage. ACM J. Comput. Cult. Herit. **1**(2), 1–15 (2008)
4. Magnenat-Thalmann, N., Thalmann, D.: Virtual humans: thirty years of research, what next? Vis. Comput. **21**, 997–1015 (2005)
5. Machidon, O., Dugulean, M., Carrozzino, M.: Virtual humans in cultural heritage ICT applications: a review. J. Cult. Herit. **33**, 249–260 (2018)
6. Mori, M.: The uncanny valley (Translated by K.F. MacDormanand and N. Kageki). IEEE Robot. Autom. **19**, 98–100 (2012)
7. Schwind, V., Wolf, K., Henze, N.: Avoiding the uncanny valley in virtual character design. ACM Interactions **25**(5), 45–49 (2018)
8. azure.microsoft.com/en-us/services/kinect-dk/. Accessed 14 Jan 2021
9. Nebel, S., Beege, M., Schneider, S., Rey, G.: A review of photogrammetry and photorealistic 3D models in education from a psychological perspective. Front. Educ. **5**, 144 (2020)
10. d'Eon, E., Harrison, B., Myers, T., Chou, P.: 8i voxelized full bodies-a voxelized point cloud dataset. ISO/IEC JTC1/SC29 Joint WG11/WG1 (MPEG/JPEG) input document WG11M40059/WG1M74006 (2017)
11. Intel true view for immersive sports experiences. https://newsroom.intel.com/news-releases/arsenal-fc-liverpool-fc-manchester-city-bring-immersive-experiences-fans-intel-true-view. Accessed 17 Jan 2021
12. Microsoft Kinect Azure. azure.microsoft.com/en-us/services/kinect-dk/. Accessed 14 Jan 2021
13. Microsoft Kinect Azure documentation. docs.microsoft.com/en-us/azure/kinect-dk/depth-camera

14. Happa, J., et al.: Virtual relighting of a Roman statue head from Herculaneum: a case study. In: AFRIGRAPH 2009, pp 5–12. ACM (2009)
15. Phythian-Adams, C.: Desolation of a City: Coventry and the Urban Crisis of the Late Middle Ages. University of Cambridge (1979)
16. Walton, P.: Textiles. In: Blair, J., Ramsay, N. (eds.) English Medieval Industries London, Hambledon, pp. 319–354 (1991)
17. Hulton, M.: 2nd Edition True as Coventry Blue. Coventry & County Heritage Series No.21, Coventry, Historical Association (2000)
18. Dormer Harris, M.: The Coventry Leet Book or Mayor's Register Parts II & III. Early English Text Society, London, Keegan Paul (1907-9)
19. Gill, R.: From the black prince to the silver prince: relocating Medieval Coventry. In: Harwood, E., Powers, A. (eds.) The Heroic Period of Conservation. Twentieth Century Architecture 7. The Twentieth Century Society, London (2004)
20. Swanson, H.: Medieval Artizans: An Urban Class in Late Medieval England. Blackwell, Oxford (1989)
21. Cherry, J.: Leather, pp. 295–318. English Medieval Industries, Hambledon, London (2001)
22. The Mulberry Dyer. https://mulberrydyer.com. Accessed 14 Jan 2021
23. The Rewild Project. www.therewildproject.com. Accessed 14 Jan 2021
24. The Weaver's House. https://theweavershouse.org/. Accessed 14 Jan 2021
25. Meeson, B., Alcock, N.: Black Swan Terrace, Upper Swan Street, Coventry: a comparison of Medieval Rentiers. Vernacular Architect. **47**, 1–19 (2016)

REVAthens: Bringing Athens of the Revolution to Life Through Museum Theatre Methodology and Digital Gamification Techniques

Andromache Gazi[1], Thodoris Giannakis[2], Ilias Marmaras[3],
Yiannis Skoulidas[3], Yannis Stoyannidis[4], Foteini Venieri[1],
and Stewart Ziff[3(✉)]

[1] Panteion University of Social and Political Sciences, 136, Syngrou Avenue,
17671 Athens, Greece
[2] Athens, Greece
[3] Personal Cinema, Athens, Greece
[4] University of West Attica, Agiou Spiridonos, Egaleo, 12243 Athens, Greece

Abstract. REVAthens is a project that lies at the intersection of history, public history, museum theatre, gamification, and digital narration. It aims at creating alternative readings of the Revolution and at highlighting different approaches to it through the narrative of historical characters who lived at the time. REVAthens aims to renegotiate banal narratives of the Revolution by highlighting new perspectives on historical events and historical subjects that may challenge and/or break down previous perceptions and/or stereotypes. The project utilizes the methodology of museum theater with the aim of shaping examples of historical subjects who lived during the Revolution of 1821 in Athens and who mediate their experiences to a contemporary audience through a digital application with game elements.

Keywords: Museum theatre · Gamification · Digital narration · Public history

1 Introduction

Funded by the Hellenic Foundation for Research & Innovation, within the frame of a large-scale research action for the bicentenary of the 1821 Greek Revolution, REVAthens aims at creating alternative readings of the Revolution and at highlighting different approaches to it through the stories of historical characters who lived at the time.

More specifically, REVAthens is an interactive digital "tour" of historical events that took place during the siege of Athens by Kioutachis in 1826–1827. Selected

Thodoris Giannakis-3D Artist, Game Developer. Ilias Marmaras-Game Developer and Researcher, Member of the Personal Cinema Collective. Yiannis Skoulidas-Programmer, Game Developer, Member of the Personal Cinema Collective. Foteini Venieri-Post-doc Researcher. Stewart Ziff-Artist, Game Developer, Educator (New and Emerging Media), Independent Researcher, Member of the Personal Cinema Collective.

M. Shehade and T. Stylianou-Lambert (Eds.): RISE IMET 2021, CCIS 1432, pp. 166–183, 2021.
https://doi.org/10.1007/978-3-030-83647-4_12

characters represent historical subjects who lived in Athens at the time "share" their personal experience with contemporary visitors of the city and present their view of the events. Their stories and narration are based on contemporary historiographical and museological approaches, and will be activated through a digital interactive application, which will make use of gamification and museum theatre techniques.

The application is targeted to a large audience and offers users the ability to connect visible material remains and/or specific historic events with first-person evidence as narrated by different characters who experienced the 1826–1827 siege. In this way, we intend to offer an understanding of the multiple influences (social, economic, and cultural) that the Revolution had on the daily life of the inhabitants of Athens (both Christian and Muslim) and to provide a new interpretive approach to historic events and/or biographies of the period. Our goal is to help a present-day audience to view this significant period in Greek history under new light and to comprehend the changes that such an upheaval brought to the lives of common people. Through the example of Athens, we aim to direct the audience's attention to the microhistory of a national revolution. By choosing the 1826–1827 siege of the Acropolis, in particular, we also want our audience to see the classical monuments through the prosaic eyes of the commoner, an illiterate soldier for example, or a housewife of the early 19th century.

By incorporating contemporary academic research into an application targeted to non-specialists, the project aims at heightening historical consciousness through processes that encourage a renegotiation of the past and, at the same time, a new perspective on the present and the future [1–3].

2   The project's Rationale and Theoretical Grounding

The Revolution of 1821 was a milestone in the formation of the Greek nation-state, the subsequent construction of the official national narrative and identity. This was an ideologically charged period, which in recent decades has been re-framed theoretically and methodologically, resulting in the creation of new readings [e.g. 4–9 p. 233–234, 10, 11]. These new readings have formed a framework within which the dominant historical narrative begins to recede under the weight of the acceptance of alternative stories and interpretations. Traditionally, the historical biographies of the period constitute in their vast majority "an image of unreal heroes, an image of emblematic and timeless figures of the Greek nation" that "the biographers do not integrate organically into the society of their time"; so, they have become "heroes" with non-historical characteristics" [9, p. 234]. On the contrary, social history allows the exploration of how everyday people experienced the Revolution [12–15]. This view is informed by contemporary developments in the fields of history and museum studies and is associated with the emergence of "invisible" aspects of the subjects' experience. It is part of the general context of "history from below" that contrasts itself with the stereotype of traditional political history and its focus on the actions of "great men" [see, among many, 16]. It is also firmly associated with the development of public history as the study and presentation of historical research to non-specialist audiences, in a variety of forms, most often (but not always) falling outside the realm of academic history.

In terms of presentation, public history exploits a broad range of deliverables including museum exhibitions, film, historical fiction, and virtual products [17 p. 50, 18].

Furthermore, the turn towards a more inclusive history goes hand in hand with the trend towards the democratization and "humanization" of museum narratives [19–23]. This view does not aim at a "representation" of the lived past, but at the production of knowledge about it [18, p. 274–282]. In the field of museology, in particular, this trend is accompanied by the search for interpretive tools, able to mediate not only verbally but also tangibly the multi-layered character of experience [see, for example, 24], linking the specific to the general.

This need is well met by museum theater, a form of interpretive theater that can condense and communicate directly multiple levels of historical narrative. Museum theater includes a range of methodological tools that allow for the creative management of narrative material, going beyond the limits of other communicative and interpretive approaches. In particular, it can encourage reflection on the tangible, emotional, aural and visual dimensions of memory [25, 26]. Besides historically, theatre does not merely supply information; it contextualizes information (or objects) "intellectually, emotionally, socially, politically, spiritually and aesthetically" [27, p. 13].

Museum theater has also proven to be a valuable tool for interpreting difficult and sensitive topics [28, 29]. A prerequisite, however, for activating these possibilities is that appropriate planning has preceded it. Museum theater is a medium that can serve a wide variety of purposes and approaches: it can create a "closed" and/or nostalgic image of the past or, conversely, raise questions and reflections about historical narratives, emphasizing the complexity of historical processes [30, 31]. In recent decades, the approach to broader historical and social issues through museum theater has developed significantly, morphologically, and functionally, because of the social and cultural role that contemporary museums[1] and heritage sites are called upon to fulfill. The recognition of the multiple meanings and functions of cultural heritage has led to the formation of an ethical framework, linking culture and society and, consequently, the museum to the social environment to which it belongs [32–37]. This recognition was followed by an investigation of the role of museums "in tackling specific manifestations of inequality, such as racism and other forms of discrimination", and the impact of museum activities in the lives of individuals and communities [36, p. 3].

The methodological utilization of museum theater in our project allows for the creation of digital material, based on primary and secondary research on the experience of protagonists of the 1821 Revolution and residents of Athens at that time. The main merit of this method is that it allows the interpretation of the attitudes, expressions, perceptions, linguistic and extralinguistic codes, and the cultural practices and beliefs that accompany the material remnants of the past. In this way, we may challenge canonized narratives and acknowledge the inherent controversy and dissonance in what is accepted as historical heritage [38]. The following example, which refers to the first

---

[1] The term "museum" is used in accordance to the definition provided by the International Council of Museums: "A museum is a non-profit, permanent institution in the service of society and its development, open to the public, which acquires, conserves, researches, communicates and exhibits the tangible and intangible heritage of humanity and its environment for the purposes of education, study and enjoyment" [39].

siege of the Acropolis in 1821, is presented here as indicative of historical accounts that undermine embedded popular beliefs on national history and the national self.

2.1   An Example - The Siege of Athens

Source: [40, p. 8–13][2].

> "In May 1821, the Muslim inhabitants of Athens were fortified inside the Acropolis. The besiegers were determined to persevere until the siege ended. For this reason, the imprisoned concluded that the only way was to seek military help from other cities. Thus, on the night of May 15, they managed to advance through Greek troops 15 of their fellow citizens who boarded a ship and traveled to Karystos. Finally, they informed the local authorities of Chalkida and requested the sending of military aid. The prospect of the assistance of Ottoman troops revived the morale of the besieged.
> On May 27, with the start of the Muslim holiday of Ramadan, the besieged released 30 Greek women who were being held hostage and asked that they be exchanged with their fellow believers. The fighters welcomed their compatriots but did not comply with the request of the besieged, as they considered it [the request] a sign of weakness and physical exhaustion from hunger. Finally, on May 30, the rebels' estimates were vindicated, as some Ottomans left the castle and attempted to transport food into the Acropolis. The attempt was unsuccessful, as fighters repelled them and killed two Muslims.
> In June, news of the encampment of Ottoman forces in Boeotia upset and sparked new plans on the besiegers' lines. The water tank of the Acropolis was targeted in their sights, so as to cause water shortages to the besieged. On July 2, despair from hunger and thirst caused the besieged to leave again. The rebels killed an African man of African descent, beheaded him, and placed his head in public. The Muslims responded with retaliation. They beheaded 10 Greeks who were held prisoner in the Acropolis and raised their heads against the revolutionaries. These two practices brought the corresponding results to the morale of both sides. The rebels rushed to the home of the Austrian consul, where 15 Muslim residents of Athens had taken refuge.[3]"

The descriptions of Spyridon Trikoupis reflect a version of the revolutionary period in which the Acropolis as a landmark delimits relations between Muslims and Christians within the same city. In the everyday reality of the revolutionary period the ancient monuments on the Acropolis stood more as a military fortress than as a monument and custodian of the ancient Greek past. Experiences of hunger and thirst determine the military tactics of those involved, who, to exert pressure, become increasingly violent towards the other side. The tactics of beheading and showing the heads to the other side reveal the uses of the body to enforce the power of each faction. Everyday life in the city seems to be very different and in conflict from what we know.

REVAthens aspires to bring such largely unknown, ignored or even hidden aspects to the fore through different narratives. For example, through the narration of a Greek soldier, an Ottoman resident, a Greek woman, a Muslim servant etc., which the visitor can choose at will, when he/she is in a place of historical reference around the rock of the Acropolis. Thus, according to visitors' choices, different approaches to the

---

[2] For a close look at the facts that preceded the siege of Athens, we may take into account the narration of Spyridon Trikoupis (1788–1873). He was a renowned politician of these times (he served at the post of Governor, of Foreign Affairs Minister and in his late years as the Greek Ambassador in London) who participated actively in the procedures that built the first Greek Kingdom.

[3] Translated by the authors.

historical experience emerge. The visitors will not only have the opportunity to listen to the narratives, but also watch what is happening on their screen through a series of three-dimensional and two-dimensional simulation scenes with gameplay elements (see below).

Finally, our project proposes a gamified approach to the field of history and heritage interpretation. Gamification is a relatively new term in the lexicon of game studies describing "the use of game design elements in non-game contexts" [41] with broad definition freely encompassing concepts of games and playfulness as fundamental elements of society and culture. While the term finds narrow use in contemporary discourse to describe participatory approaches in consumer marketing practices (eg: collecting frequent flyer reward points, liking and unliking in social media), we consider a more general understanding of gamification, informed by the work of the French sociologist Roger Caillois (1958) who proposed play (in the context of games) as activity that is: free, separate (within defined limits of space and time), uncertain, unproductive (creating neither goods or wealth), governed by rules, and make-believe (invoking the imagination). Caillois' work draws from the earlier ideas of Johan Huizinga (1949) who used diverse examples such as lawsuits, dancing, and the military battlefield to show how civilization arises and unfolds in and as play.

3 Methodology

Our research methodology has been structured as follows:

1. Research and application of modern historiographical and museological approaches to the processing of historical material.
2. Selection and shaping of subjective narratives with the methodology of museum theater.
3. Research and configuration of the digital application.
4. Pilot evaluation with members of the public.

Our approach is informed by contemporary research into the overall quality of the experience of visitors in museums and places of cultural reference; particular emphasis is placed on data confirming the dynamics of the personal involvement of visitors with the content of digital applications, as well as their ability to interact with this content in unusual ways. In addition, we exploit the possibilities offered by multisensory experiences to users of digital applications, especially when they are used in a natural environment [42–49].

The methodology for designing subjective narratives includes the following stages: primary and secondary research, role formation, configuration of the script. After gathering the historical material and data, some characters are selected, imaginary or real. The key criterion for the selection is the ability of these characters to illuminate different aspects of historical processes in a critical, reflective, and comprehensible way for different groups of people. "Imaginary" characters are defined as characters that did not exist but could have existed. Such an example is a female character named "Kyriaki" (see below), as, according to testimonies, in September 1826 about 500 women and children remained on the Acropolis [50, p. 153]. It should be noted here that "imaginary" characters are created by using the method of "documented hypotheses" [51]. Finally, the script is developed in three levels: dramaturgic, narrative, emotional.

The selection of characters, locations, scenes, and dialogs is followed by the development of the digital application. This includes shaping the digital environment and the digital characters, adding sounds, music and recorded dialogues, programming in the Unity game engine, programming for application on the android and iOS platforms, and integrating a geolocation system, which will allow the visitor to access the different scenes and subscenes of the application when he/she is at specific places around the rock of the Acropolis.

Finally, the pilot evaluation will employ both quantitative and qualitative methods and will use semi-structured interviews, focus groups and questionnaires with members of the public. In addition, quantitative data on the length of the users' engagement at specific points of interest, the degree of their interaction, etc., will be collected from within the application. Moreover, the website of the application will host a *forum* for exchanging comments among users, while an on-line questionnaire will also be available for their feedback.

4   The Digitization of Subjective Narratives

The digital form of historical narratives in our application is a series of three-dimensional and two-dimensional interactive simulation scenes with game elements, analogous to those found in modern historical video games[4]. As already explained, the narrative structures and the historical content will be based on the methodology of museum theater.

Unlike traditional historiographical narratives, historical games have become one of the most widespread and successful forms of public history. This, in combination with the choices of their historical content, may make them particularly influential as narratives, which are also experienced in informal settings [24]. Video games and similar playful applications are a new form of historical text, which changes the ways in which history is perceived by the general public [52]. They are more of a simulation and "modeling" of experience rather than representing it as text and image. Not only do they cultivate the imagination over alternatives, but they provide practical tools that may prove useful for their realization.

---

[4] Such as Assassin's Creed Valhalla (2020 Video Game), Ghost of Tsushima (2020 Video Game), Assassin's Creed: Odyssey (2018 Video Game), Call of Duty: WWII (2017 Video Game), Assassin's Creed II (2009 Video Game).

REVAthens' digital application will have two parts: First, a website, which will contain brief explanations of background research illustrating the new interpretive approach to the specific historical material derived from it and intended to be included in the digital simulation scenes of the application. Second, the simulation of historical *loci* and events that will form the main content of the application. The aim is for the player to interact with the elements of the game (game elements) without being disconnected from the narratives of historical events. In other words, the game simulations leave the player free to explore and understand the broader context of historical events.

The website will also host the game elements and code that will be created for the simulation. That is, the characters, objects, architecture, topography, and elements of the natural environment (fauna & flora), which correspond to the historical events that are simulated through the application. The data will be freely available with an appropriate license of Creative Commons in educational and cultural institutions so that they may be applied for possible extensions of the application model in other regions of Greece, or for other creative uses. Commercial use of the data could also be considered after consultation with the project stakeholders.

The application will be available on the website for download, storage and use on mobiles, tablets, and computers. When not in the physical space related to any of the historical events, the user will be able to use it with limited access to the content, either through partial access to the total content of some scenes, or through short animations related to the scenes, or a combination of both. The application will be activated, "unlocked" and fully accessible when the user directly visits the site, with geolocation data enabled.

5   The Structure of the Application

The game-space of the application will consist of two (or more) primary, independent, interactive scenes, and several subscenes related to them. All scenes and subscenes will be based on the approach of museum theater; they will relate to historical incidents as recorded in different descriptions; each incident having occurred at a specific location in the area around the Acropolis.

A primary scene defines the real-time experience by the user of the game scenario and will be located either at the North part of the Acropolis or the South part. The historical content of the narrative embedded in a primary scene will have taken place within these specific locations during the period of the third siege of the Acropolis in 1826–1827. It is at these physical locations where the primary scenes are set, that the geolocation tracking will be activated, and where the player will then be able to run the full section of the application related to that scene and its subscenes (Fig. 1).

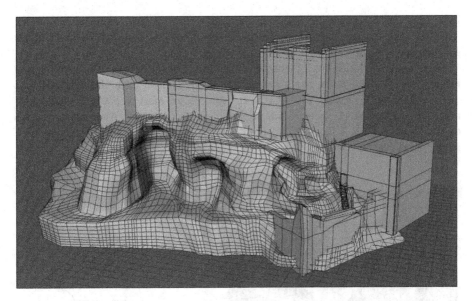

Fig. 1. North side of the Acropolis; game environment, low-detail early model.

A subscene will relate to a primary scene by extending its narrative scenario and gameplay. Subscenes may be situated around the Acropolis, but not necessarily. The potential of digital technology to topologically connect distant geographical areas allows the construction of scenes beyond those that took place at the specific location (of the Acropolis), but that are directly related to it. One such example is the meeting of Kioutachis, Karaiskakis and Derigny at the latter's flagship in the Faliron Bay. This can be named as a moment of great importance, if we acknowledge that most people deem that enemies always meet in fierce battles but never under the same roof. Georgios Karaiskakis was a Greek guerilla uplifted to a General at the time of the siege and represented the side of the revolutionaries. Kioutachis Pasa was a great General of the Ottoman army that claimed Athens in the name of the Sultan. Marie Henri Daniel Gauthier comte de Rigny (known by the Greeks as Derigny) was a brave General and later Admiral of the French Navy. He arrived at the time of the siege of Acropolis and in the battle of Navarino and proved a helpful friend of the revolutionaries. A subscene can be also frame a "leap in time" in which events can be simulated that took place at a different period, e.g. during the first or second siege of the Acropolis (1821–1823) when the Ottomans were besieged by the Greeks. Furthermore, a subscene may simulate other spaces, locations and time periods that are historically related to the social and cultural context of the revolutionary period, and which help to better understand the conditions of the 1826–1827 siege. For example, the visit and stay of François-

René de Chateaubriand in Eleusina around 1803, or the architecture of the Athens market bazaar and the social life of the inhabitants of Athens in the early 19th century.

A primary scene in development is situated around the Klepsydra, a well spring inside a cave located at the North part of the Acropolis near to the Propylaea. It was discovered under the leadership of Odysseus Androutsos most probably in 1822 and is related to various stories and events, e.g. the conflict between Androutsos and his deputy chief Yannis Gouras that led to the imprisoning and finally the death of Androutsos (Figs. 2 and 3).

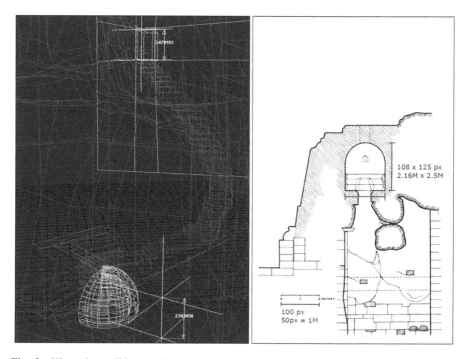

Fig. 2. Klepsydra well-house; development model with source schematic; based on Parsons (1942: 257).

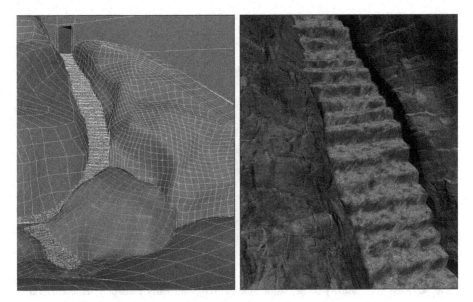

Fig. 3. Klepsydra scene; Stairway working model.

An actual example of narrative action being developed with the methodology of museum theater and taking place in the Klepsydra scene is composed of the following elements. Two main characters, Manolios and Kyriaki, meet inside the cave where Kyriaki is raising water from the well. It is December 1826 and the conditions for the besieged are very harsh. The dialogue that they have, which the player may follow, may be about:

- The development of the siege, and the battles and skirmishes.
- The months long epidemic among the besieged on the Acropolis.
- The doctor who is among them and tries his best.
- Androutsos and his role in the discovery and fortification of the well spring.
- The death of Gouraina (the wife of Gouras).
- The competition and conflict between Gouraina and Androutsaina (the wife of Androutsos).
- The presence of the French soldiers of Fabrier that are with the Greeks on the Acropolis.
- The torture and killing of the historical character Iousouf (Figs. 4 and 5).

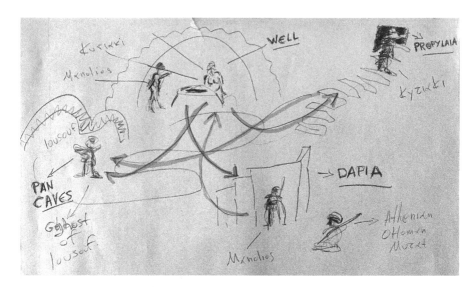

Fig. 4. Klepsydra primary scene, North side of Acropolis, early gameplay representation.

Fig. 5. Klepsydra scene; draft sketch of female figure ("Kyriaki") in the well.

The dialogues in the primary scene of Klepsydra (and generally within all scenes and subscenes) will not only narrate significant events occurring during the 1826–1827 siege: as a matter of gameplay, they will provide hints for the player to understand where to navigate within the simulated game-space, which character (avatar) to follow, and by doing so, to visit the totality of the simulated terrain. In other words, dialogues together with the simulated environment form an inter-relational network between primary scenes and subscenes that the player can explore, to understand the conditions of the specific momentum of the Revolution (Fig. 6).

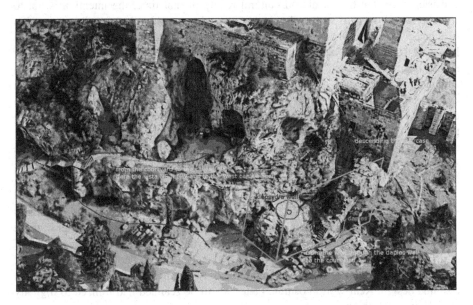

Fig. 6. Klepsydra scene; game play scenario, development map.

It should here be noted that while the creation of the application will utilize the same digital production tools employed by the commercial games and film industry, the development of the project differs from more commonplace approaches with a unique, non-linear methodology to its' workflow; this reflects the inter-disciplinarity of the core team of a historian, a museologist, a museum theater practitioner, and four video game developers. Each member of the team brings to the project their expertise as specialists in their particular areas of practice; however, the process of research and each stage of development is occurring in a collaborative space of ongoing conversational exchange.

6 Application Development and Workflow

Multiple references will be used as source material for simulating the physical environment with an attention to the visual accuracy of the representation. Contemporary maps, aerial photography and other resources will be utilized to model the geological topography of the space (Google Earth etc.). Late 18th and early 19th century drawings, etchings, and watercolors of traveler visitors to Athens together with contemporaneous written accounts and early Daguerreotypes will inform the location, form and accuracy of architectures, objects, and other constructions [53–56, etc.].

The artistic style of the graphics, and the audio-musical part which will create the interactive environment of the application, will play a key role in the user experience differing from corresponding simulations found in commercial historical video games. While the aim is to visualize the space with an informed concern for historical accuracy consistent with the historical and cultural reality of that time, the intention is not to simulate with hyperreal verisimilitude, but instead to consider the virtual space as akin to a theater stage and to digitally paint the environment with the aesthetic of a theatrical look and feel. We note here that the term "hyper-realistic" refers to a specific genre of modeling simulation used extensively in the videogame industry. These graphics aim to simulate the appearance of reality, often aiming to exceed it, showing details of the avatars and the simulated environment to a high degree. The scope of this effort is to captivate players via the verisimilitude of the graphics in the simulation, increasing their immersion in the game/world. Hyper-realistic graphics have been strongly criticized for interfering with the game play, distracting the player, and turning the gamespace of the video game into a mere spectacle [57]. We aim to simulate the historical reality of the period, but not to put the accent on its spectacularisation[5].

Motion capture techniques will be used to facilitate a naturalism with the movement, actions, and facial animation of the avatar characters. Ethnographic considerations will inform the development of the appearance, personality and character of these virtual actors who will be dressed in common everyday clothes reflecting the distress of ordinary people during a period of revolt and under siege. The creative process of clothing digital avatars is analogous to the use of two-dimensional patterns in theatrical costume design. Real-world costume patterns will be scanned and utilized to digitally model virtual clothing.

Application development with gameplay elements allows for non-linear scene sequencing. This means that a user can make choices regarding pathways and characters to follow. Scenes can be developed that reflect different points of view to simulated events. For example, a user can choose to follow an Ottoman and a narration of his/her account of an event, traversing the environment and encountering activities and spaces that reflect their lived experience; or otherwise to follow that of a Greek engaging with his/her particular perspective and experience, or to follow one after the other. In this way, the player can gain insight into the multifaceted and multimodal record and account of historical events.

A key opportunity for a user of the application is to see for themselves how different the space of historical events appears today from how the space appeared during the revolutionary period. Geolocation data and GPS compass tracking of the handheld device will permit a coordinated registration of the user's line of sight so that the virtual camera of the simulation frames the same point of view the user has of the real-world space they are situated within (Fig. 7).

---

[5] *Cf.* "If once we were able to view the Borges fable in which the cartographers of the Empire draw up a map so detailed that it ends up covering the territory exactly [...] this fable has now come full circle for us, and possesses nothing but the discrete charm of second-order simulacra. [...] It is the real, and not the map, whose vestiges subsist here and there, in the deserts which are no longer those of the Empire, but our own: The desert of the real itself..." [58, p. 1].

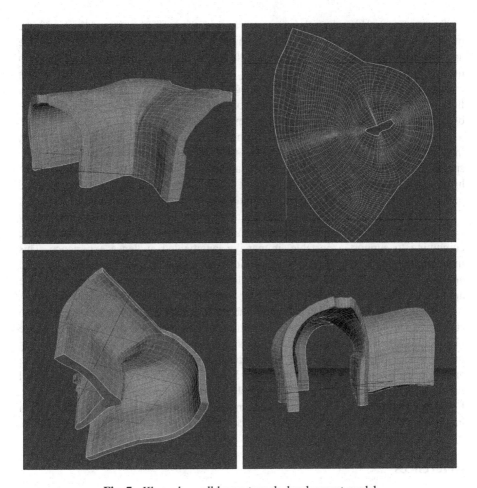

Fig. 7. Klepsydra well-house tunnel; development model.

7 Conclusion

REVAthens aims to fill a significant gap in the research, acquisition and dissemination of documentation related to the 1821 Greek Revolution. It also seeks to place historical episodes of the Revolution into the socio-economic environment of the time so that they are disconnected from the typical national narrative. The project's originality lies in the creation, for the first time at an international level, of a digital interpretive tool assisted by the methodology of museum theater to form new, differentiated views of historical events. These will be accessible to different groups of people and will integrate contemporary historiographical and museological approaches into subjective narratives in a playful and comprehensible way. Through this process an understanding of different aspects of the past and the critical engagement of the visitor with the historical narratives are encouraged.

The transfer of historical characters, narratives, the environment and the landscape of the time to the digitally played environment of the scenes that will structure the application, is an experiment of merging elements of environmental art and museum theatre in digital space and time. In this context, the historical and social events concerning Athens during the 1826-27 siege in combination with the landscape, the flora and the fauna, constitute the canvas for highlighting sensory experiences and for offering a multi-layered perception of the events and their effects.

The combination of the users' tour of the natural space of the action (for example, in places around the rock of the Acropolis) with the virtual simulation can connect the spectacle with the experience. Through the application, users can be "immersed" in the historical space-time of the action, without this preventing them from perceiving the present time and space at the same time, thus providing ground for a critical approach.

The potential of the project to realize a new digital genre of encounter with history leverages off emergent advances with the computational technologies of mobile computing to support a portable, immersive, augmented audience experience. This model can then be used by other organizations (e.g. municipalities, museums, cultural agencies, etc.) and/or cultural heritage professionals at relatively low cost, while the application may also be a valuable tool for the development of cultural tourism.

Overall, REVAthens concentrates on the transformation of historical research into subjective narratives, which employ the immediacy of theatrical discourse to give the historical content new perspectives.[6] It aims at developing a different way of capturing the historical narrative available to different groups of audiences by creating an engaging interpretive tool within the larger field of public history, seen broadly as "all the ways in which history is made available to a non-specialist public" [59, p. 192]. From this perspective, the project is an innovative application in this field and an interpretive "tool" that can be a model for communicating history to a wider audience.

References

1. Kirscheblatt-Gimblett, B.: Museum as a catalyst. In: Museums 2000: Confirmation or Challenge, organized by ICOM Sweden, the Swedish Museum Association and the Swedish Traveling Exhibition / Riksutställningar in Vadstena, 29 September 2000. http://www.michaelfehr.net/Museum/Texte/vadstena.pdf. Accessed 28 Feb 2021
2. Lee, P.: Historical literacy and transformative history. In: Perikleous, L., Shemilt, D. (eds.) The Future of the Past: Why History Education Matters, pp. 129–167. The Association for Historical Dialogue and Research, Nicosia (2011)
3. Nakou, I., Barca, I. (eds.): Contemporary Public Debates Over History Education. Information Age Publishing, Charlotte (2010)
4. Gallant, T.: Modern Greece. From the War of Independence to the Present. Bloomsbury Academic, London (2016)

---

[6] Thus far theatrical techniques in Greek museums and heritage sites have been limited to the dramatization of related literary texts. See, for example, "From the silence of the showcase to the theatrical speech" co-organized by the Benaki Museum and the National Theater: https://www.nt.gr/el/news/?nid=1955&st=160, last accessed 2020/11/9.

5. Gerontas, D.: Οι Αθηναίοι και η Αττική στην επανάσταση του 1821 [Athenians and Attica during the 1821 Revolution]. Library of the Association of Athenians, Athens (2018)
6. Kremmydas, B.: Η ελληνική επανάσταση του 1821. Τεκμήρια, αφηγήσεις, ερμηνείες [The Greek Revolution of 1821. Documents, Narratives, Interpretations], Gutenberg, Athens (2016)
7. Loukos, Ch., Dimitropoulos, D. (eds.): Όψεις της επανάστασης του 1821 [Aspects of the 1821 Revolution]. EMNE-Mnimon, Athens (2018)
8. Pizanias, P. (ed): Η ελληνική επανάσταση του 1821. Ένα ευρωπαϊκό γεγονός [The Greek revolution of 1821. A European Event]. Kedros, Athens (2008)
9. Stathis, P.: Ανανεώνοντας τη ματιά μας για το εικοσιένα. Με αφορμή το Μακρυγιάννη του Νίκου Θεοτοκά [Renewing our look for the 1821 Revolution. On the occasion of Makriyannis by Nikos Theotokas]. Mnimon 33 (2014). https://ejournals.epublishing.ekt.gr/index.php/mnimon/article/view/8555. Accessed 7 Nov 2020
10. Veremis, T.: 1821 Η δημιουργία ενός έθνους κράτους [1821 The Creation of a Nation State]. Metaixmio, Athens (2018)
11. Veremis, Th.: 1821 Τριπολιτσά - Μεσολόγγι. Πολιορκία και Άλωση [Tripolitsa – Messolonghi. Siege and Fall]. Metaixmio, Athens (2019)
12. Faroqhi, S.: Kultur und Alltag im Osmanischen Reich. CH Beck, Munich (1995)
13. Iggers, G.: Historiography in the 20th c Con. Wesleyan University Press, Middletown (1996)
14. Pinol, J.L.: Le monde des villes au XIX siècle. Hachette, Paris (1991)
15. Sugar, P.: Southeastern Europe under Ottoman Rule, 1354–1804. Washington University Press, Washington (1977)
16. Bhattacharya, S.: History from below. Soc. Scientist 11(4), 3–20 (1983)
17. Adamek, A., Gann, E.: Whose artifacts? Whose stories? Public history and representation of women at the Canada science and technology museum. Historia Critica 68, 47–66 (2018)
18. Liakos, A.: Πώς το παρελθόν γίνεται ιστορία [How the past becomes history]. Polis, Athens (2007)
19. Cauvin, T.: Public History. A Textbook of Practice. Routledge, London (2016)
20. Franco, B.: Public history and memory: a museum perspective. Public Historian 19(2), 65–67 (1997)
21. Liddington, J.: What is public history? Publics and their pasts, meanings and practices. Oral History 30(1), 83–93 (2002)
22. Lyon, Ch., Nix, E., Shrum, R. (eds.): Introduction to Public History. Interpreting the Past, Engaging Audiences. Rowman & Littlefield, Lanham (2017)
23. Nakou, I.: Μουσεία, ιστορίες και Ιστορία [Museums, Stories and History]. Nissos, Athens (2009)
24. Chapman, A.: Digital Games as History: How Videogames Represent the Past and Offer Access to Historical Practice. Routledge, London (2016)
25. Farthing, A.: Authenticity and metaphor: displaying intangible human remains in museum theater. In: Jackson, A., Kidd, J. (eds.) Performing Heritage: Research, Practice and Innovation in Museum Theater and Live Interpretation, pp. 94–106. Manchester University Press, Manchester (2011)
26. Smith, L.: The 'doing' of heritage: heritage as performance. In: Jackson, A., Kidd, J. (eds.) Performing Heritage: Research, Practice and Innovation in Museum Theater and Live Interpretation, pp. 69–81. Manchester University Press, Manchester (2011)
27. Alsford, St., Parry, D.: Interpretive theatre: a role in museums?. Museum Manage. Curatorship 10(1), 8–23 (1991)

28. Jackson, A., Kidd, J.: Performance, Learning, Heritage: Research Report, Center for Applied Theater Research, Manchester (2008). http://www.plh.manchester.ac.uk/documents/Performance,%20Learning%20&%20Heritage%20-%20Executive%20Summary.pdf. Accessed 7 Nov 2020
29. Munley, E.M.: Evaluation study of 'Buyin Freedom'. In: Hughes, C. (ed.) Perspectives on Museum Theater, pp. 69–94. American Association of Museums, Washington, DC (1993)
30. Maggelsen, S.: Living History Museums: Undoing History through Performance. The Scarecrow Press INC, Maryland (2007)
31. Maggelsen, S., Justice-Malloy, R. (eds.): Enacting History. The University of Alabama Press, Alabama (2011)
32. Janes, R., Conaty, G.: Looking Reality in the Eye: Museums and Social Responsibility. University of Calgary Press, Calgary (2005)
33. Mairesse, F.: La belle histoire, aux origines de la nouvelle muséologie. Publics et Musées **17–18**, 33–55 (2000)
34. Alexander, E.: Museums in Motion: An Introduction to the History and Functions of Museums. American Association for State and Local History, Nashville (1979)
35. Sandell, R.: Social inclusion, the museum and the dynamics of sectoral change. Museum Soc. **1**(1), 45–62 (2003)
36. Sandell, R. (ed.): Museums, Society, Inequality. Routledge, London (2002)
37. Schultz, L.: Collaborative museology and the visitor. Museum Anthropol. **34**, 1–12 (2011)
38. Smith, L.: Uses of Heritage. Routledge, London (2006)
39. ICOM: Statutes (2017). https://icom.museum/wp-content/uploads/2018/07/2017_ICOM_Statutes_EN.pdf. Accessed 28 Feb 2021
40. Trikoupis, S.: Ιστορία της Ελληνικής Επαναστάσεως [History of the Greek Revolution]. The Red Lion Typography of Taylor and Francis, London (1860). http://anemi.lib.uoc.gr/metadata/2/c/f/metadata-01-0000761.tkl. Accessed 17 Nov 2020
41. Deterding, S., Dixon, D., Khaled, R., Nacke, L.: From game design elements to gamefulness: defining 'gamification'. In: MindTrek 2011 Proceedings of the 15th International Academic MindTrek Conference: Envisioning Future Media Environments, pp. 9–15. ACM Press, New York (2011)
42. Ahern, S., et al.: ZoneTag: designing context-aware mobile media capture to increase participation. In: Proceedings of the Pervasive Image Capture and Sharing, 8th International Conference on Ubiquitous Computing. California (2006). http://web.mit.edu/21w.789/www/papers/Ahern_et_al_zonetag_pics06.pdf. Accessed 7 Nov 2020
43. Claisse, C., Petrelli, D., Dulake, N., Marshall, M., Ciolfi, L.: Multisensory interactive storytelling to augment the visit of a historical house museum. In: Proceedings of the 2018 Digital Heritage International Congress. IEEE (2018). http://shura.shu.ac.uk/22646/1/DH18-Paper-Multisensory%20Interactive%20Storytelling%20to%20Augment%20the%20Visit%20of%20a%20Historical%20House%20Museum-revised.pdf. Accessed 7 Nov 2020
44. Fernandes Vaz, R., Fernandes, P., Rocha Veiga, A.: Interactive technologies in museums: how digital installations and media are enhancing the visitors' experience. In: Rodrigues, J., et al. (eds.) Handbook of Research on Technological Developments for Cultural Heritage and eTourism Applications, pp. 30–53. IGI Global, Hershey (2018)
45. Heath, C., vom Lehn, D.: Interactivity and collaboration: new forms of participation in museums, galleries and science centres. In: Parry, R. (ed.) Museums in a Digital Age, pp. 266–280. Routledge, New York (2010)
46. Kidd, J.: Museums in the New Mediascape: Transmedia Participation. Ethics. Routledge, New York (2014)
47. Levent, N.S., Pascual-Leone, A.: The Multisensory Museum: Cross-Disciplinary Perspectives on Touch, Sound, Smell, Memory, and Space. Rowman & Littlefield, Plymouth (2014)

48. Mikalef, K., Chorianopoulos, K.: Game playing in the field: effects of interactivity on learning and museum experience. In: Proceedings of the DEG Workshop on Involving End Users and Domain Experts in the Design of Educational Games (2011). http://citeseerx.ist. psu.edu/viewdoc/download?doi=10.1.1.301.2217&rep=rep1&type=pdf. Accessed 7 Nov 2020

49. Simon, N.: The Participatory Museum. Museums 2.0 (2010)

50. Sourmelis, D.: Ιστορία των Αθηνών κατά τον υπέρ της ελευθερίας αγώνα [History of Athens during the struggle for freedom]. Tipografia Andreou Koromila, Athens (1834)

51. Pustz, J.: Voices from the Back Stairs: Interpreting Servants' Lives at Historic House Museums. Northern Illinois University Press, DeKalb (2010)

52. Dougherty, J., Nawrotzki, K. (eds.): Writing History in the Digital Age. Michigan University Press, Ann Arbor (2013)

53. Dodwell, E.: Views in Greece. Rodwell & Martin, London (1819)

54. Revett, N., Stuart, J.: The Antiquities of Athens Measured and Delineated by James Stuart F. R.S. and F.S.A. and Nicholas Revett Painters and Architects, vol. II. John Nichols, London (1787)

55. von Stackelberg, O.M.: La Grèce. Vues pittoresques et topographiques. Chez I. F. D'Ostervald, Paris (1854)

56. Stademann, F.: Panorama von Athen. Franz Wild'schen Buchdrueckerei, Mannheim (1841)

57. Bycer, J.: Risks of realism in game design. Why the pursuit of realism can hinder playability. https://medium.com/super-jump/the-risk-of-embracing-realism-4673a8bb724c. Accessed 20 Feb 2021

58. Baudrillard, J.: Simulacra and Simulation. University of Michigan Press, Ann Arbor (1994)

59. Tosch, J.: Public history, civic engagement and the historical profession in Britain. History 99(2) (335), 191–212 (2014)

60. Baudrillard, J.: Simulations. Semiotext(e), New York City (1983)

61. Caillois, R.: Man, Play, and Games. University of Illinois Press, Chicago (2001/1958)

62. Christidou, D., Pierroux, P.: Art, touch and meaning making: an analysis of multisensory interpretation in the museum. Museum Manage. Curatorsh. 34(1), 96–115 (2018)

63. Huizinga, J.: Homo Ludens: A Study of the Play Element in Culture. Beacon Press, Boston (1955/1938).

64. Parsons, A.W.: Klepsydra and the paved court of the Pythion. Hesperia 12(3), 191–267 (1942)

65. Venieri, F.: Μουσειακό θέατρο: Ιστορικές διαδρομές και σύγχρονες προσεγγίσεις [Museum Theater: Historical Routes and Contemporary Approaches]. Unpublished doctoral thesis, University of Thessaly, Greece (2017)

Emerging Technologies, Difficult Heritage and Affective Practices

Tangible and Embodied Interaction for Scaffolding Difficult Heritage Narratives

Areti Damala[1,2]([⊠])

[1] CNRS and Ecole Normale Supérieure, Paris, France
`areti.damala@ens.psl.eu, damala.areti@ac.eap.gr`
[2] Hellenic Open University, Patras, Greece

Abstract. "Atlantic Wall, War in the City of Peace" was a temporary exhibition on display in Museon, The Hague in 2015. The exhibition visited the story of the city of the Hague in World War 2, when a large part of the city had to be demolished, to make space for the Atlantic Wall. Hundreds of people were evicted from their houses. The exhibition had multiple, non-linear entry points, with exhibition sections corresponding to existing neighborhoods in the Hague. In each section, various objects on display served as entry points for different, first-person, narratives entwined around a particular neighborhood. In addition to seeing the exhibited objects, the visitors had the possibility to activate different audio narratives, corresponding to three different perspectives, using smart, 3D printed replicas: the perspective of the German soldier, the perspective of the Dutch civilian, or the perspective of the Dutch civil servant. This paper presents an overview of the key-findings from a survey that was filled in by 88 participants. The survey was part of a mixed methods evaluation study which occurred in Museon throughout a period of two weeks.

Keywords: Tangible and embodied interaction · 3D replicas · Evaluation · Visitor studies · Museum · Visiting experience · Emotions · Learning · Meaning-making

1 Tangible and Embodied Interaction for Difficult Heritage Narratives: The meSch Project

1.1 Introduction

Digitally mediated learning has grown to become a norm in museums of the 21st century [1, 2]. Despite the constant debate around the advantages and shortcomings of digital museum learning, education programs and outreach, the recent co-vid 19 crisis proved beyond any doubt the importance of digitally mediated learning not just as an accessory but as a seminal, fundamental tool for museum education, communication, and outreach [3]. Still, there is a lot of concern about whether these digital learning interpretive resources assist visitors in getting the best out of their visit or whether they compete with the real museum artefacts and objects on display, causing distraction and isolation: screen-based museum applications and interactives have often been characterized as attention grabbers [4, 5]. This raises the question of whether technology can

M. Shehade and T. Stylianou-Lambert (Eds.): RISE IMET 2021, CCIS 1432, pp. 187–198, 2021.
https://doi.org/10.1007/978-3-030-83647-4_13

be used in ways which -rather than digitally complementing or "augmenting" the physical object on display- bring back the attention of the visitor to the physical and tangible properties of heritage artefacts, ideally by engaging the visitor physically, emotionally, and cognitively [1, 6].

Material encounters with digital cultural heritage (meSch) was an FP7 EU funded project which sought to provide answers to the above question by exploring the potential of digitally enabled tangible, embodied and multisensory museum visiting experiences [7]. This was made possible through technologies of the internet of things (IOT), where different types of sensors, small computational devices and their wireless networks are interweaved with smart tangibles the museum visitor can interact with. To showcase the potential of tangible and embodied interaction, an important number of museum interactives and prototypes as well as specific case-studies were developed within the lifetime of the meSch project. Furthermore, three temporary exhibitions in three museums in Italy and the Netherlands, featured the meSch technology, allowing for a cross-border comparison among different museums, exhibitions, and heritage narratives [8–11].

1.2   meSch and the "Atlantic Wall: War in the City of Peace" Exhibition

The most extensive use of meSch technology was featured in the Atlantic Wall exhibition, hosted by Museon in the Netherlands. The exhibition opened its doors to the public between April and November 2015 and was visited by more than 20,000 visitors. Museon is a popular, eclectic, hands-on science museum with a large appeal to children of all ages and their families as well as among primary and secondary schools in the Netherlands and with a strong experience and track-record in participation in digital heritage EU funded research projects.

As in contrast with small and medium scale meSch technology experimentations, Museon took a bold step by hosting a temporary exhibition fully integrating the meSch technology. The exhibition would evolve around the story of the city of the Hague in World War 2 (WW2). The exhibition's name "The Hague and the Atlantic Wall: War in the City of Peace" acted as a dramatic reminiscence of the stark contrast between now and then: today, the city of the Hague is known as the city of peace and justice as it is home to the International Criminal Court, The Hague Institute for Global Justice, Europol, the International Court of Justice and the Organisation for the Prohibition of Chemical Weapons [12]. It is difficult for the "average" visitor to apprehend how different were things during WW2: then, a large part of the city had to be demolished to make space for the Atlantic Wall, an elaborate system of fortifications, fortresses and defense walls built by Nazi Germany between 1942 and 1944 to protect against an attack from the sea [13]. The Atlantic Wall stretched from Portugal and Spain to Scandinavia, with an overall length of over 6000 km. The city of the Hague changed forever during that period as within this context, a broad strip throughout the city was demolished to make room for the fortifications of the Atlantic Wall. Parts of the city became accessible only to those who had a special permission. To better link and connect for the visitor the now and then, the exhibition plan had -unlike what is used in most museum exhibitions- nothing linear.

Instead, the exhibition was divided in various sections with each section corresponding to a city neighborhood, clearly named, and labelled. The visitors could thus choose to visit the exhibition sections (i.e. neighborhoods) in any order they liked, on their own pace, guided by neighborhood and street names as well as representations of various buildings of the city of the Hague [14].

On top of this unconventional, non-linear system of wayfinding and navigation within the museum exhibition, voices of the past came to be added as an additional layer of information [15]: at the beginning of the exhibition, a check-in point and alternative museum display was available. It displayed a selection of six everyday objects used in the Hague in WW2: a teabag with surrogate tea, a box of surrogate sugar, a Delft beer mug offered as a Christmas gift to German soldiers, a Dutch German phrase book and an armband worn by civil servants acted as keys which unlocked additional audio content in each exhibition section (Fig. 1, right). At the side of the display, a box divided in six sections contained several replicas of each real, WW2 object featured in the main display (Fig. 1, left). The only replicas featured in a different size than the real objects, was the 3D printed beer mugs. Inside each replica, an RFID tag was integrated [16]. By selecting one or more of the replicas, the visitor also opted for getting one of the three perspectives in Dutch or English: The voice of the German soldier, the voice of the Dutch civilian and the voice of the Dutch civil servant. The latter had to comply with the German occupying forces. The replicas could thus activate the audio and multimedia contents available at each exhibition section. At each visiting section (or exhibition section), the objects on display served as entry points for different narratives, topics and exhibition themes (e.g. "How was it to be forced to leave your home? To enter or leave the fortress? To experience the launch of a V2 rocket? To live in the almost empty fortress?"), accessible through the audio activation that occurred using the replicas [8, 14, 15].

The Atlantic Wall exhibition was the most large-scale experimentation of meSch which seamlessly incorporated several components of the meSch technologies and accompanying authoring tool. More than 20,000 visitors of all ages visited the exhibition. Approximately 120 accepted to take part in the visitor study we set up through collaboration of project partners in 3 countries (UK, Ireland, Netherlands). Throughout a period of two weeks, a multidisciplinary team worked on site to gather data through videos, photos, observations, semi-structured interviews, and a survey.

At each exhibition section, each story could be narrated from three different perspectives: this of the Dutch civilian, the German soldier, or the Dutch civil servant who had to collaborate with the occupying forces. The narratives unlocked were specific to the neighborhoods and landmarks presented in the exhibition [17].

Fig. 1. Left: The check-in station with the original WW2 objects and the replicas. Right: the museum panel introducing the use of the replicas to the visitors.

2 Devising an Evaluation Plan for Tangible and Embodied Interaction

2.1 The Materiality, Multimodality and Multisensoriality of Tangible and Embodied Interaction

A mixed-methods summative evaluation was carried out using qualitative and quantitative research methodologies. The reasons and motivations underpinning the evaluation protocol retained for evaluating the museum visiting experience for the Atlantic Wall exhibition in Museon and the Illusion of Movement in Ancient Greek Art (hosted in Allard Pierson Museum in Amsterdam) have been exposed in a methodology related publication in a comparative manner juxtaposing the choices made for both exhibitions [8]. In the Museon evaluation study, approximately 120 visitors participated, 88 of whom filled in the survey distributed after the visit. In parallel, available and possible visitor studies and evaluation methods that might help apprehend and evaluate the museum visitor experience with the replicas and the different offered perspectives were also scrutinized. A major preoccupation was whether we should focus on the use of the replicas only or adopt a holistic approach which would evaluate several aspects of the visit. One way to figure out how to carry out evaluation for the Atlantic Wall exhibition was to focus on the main questions we wanted to answer, in an intensive collaboration with Hub Kockelkorn, the Museon curator who coordinated the complex work of the set-up of the exhibition for all analogue and digital contents and exhibits. Here is how the main research questions where eventually formulated:

- How are the different meSch and non-meSch exhibition components (real museum objects, replicas, audio narratives, slideshows, text labels and signs, multimedia stations, polling stations) used by the visitors?

- How do visitors use and share the smart replicas, and what is their impact on the museum visiting experience?
- Are the different perspectives appreciated by visitors?
- What is the role of emotions and memories for learning and meaning making?

This contribution aims at providing an overview of the key-findings of the results yielded by the survey. We anticipated that the qualitative data (logs and surveys) would allow us to understand the "what" as in contrast with the qualitative data (interviews and observations) which would assist us understand the "why". The survey assisted us in obtaining answers mainly for questions 1, 2 and 3, giving interesting insights for question 4, which would be answered principally using the results of the interviews.

Prior to carrying out the study, the exhibition plan and contents were thoroughly investigated to gain un a better understanding of the space and the optimal set-up of the team that would work on-site. A first version of the evaluation protocol was trialed and fine-tuned. In terms of resources committed, the evaluation occurred for a period of nine days (spread over two weeks) in Dutch and in English. The survey was filled in by 88 visitors. In addition to the completed surveys, 37 hours of video were also captured while 49 interviews occurred on-site immediately after the visit. It was also possible to talk to 17 visitors approximately 6 months after the visit. In addition, 14.853 logged sessions generated from 19.000 visitors became available thanks to the resources committed by the researchers of Sheffield Hallam University. In addition, the survey findings were triangulated with the findings of a shorter, Museon-led survey. Our own sample featured 120 active study participants, out of which 88 filled in the survey. Other visitors chose to only participate in the interview conducted just after the visit. This contribution presents an overview of the key-findings as they emerged from a preliminary analysis of the survey.

3 The Atlantic Wall Survey: Key Findings

3.1 Survey Overview

The survey contained 30 questions, was divided in four sections, and took approximately 15 to 20 min to fill in. Intensive trials and several iterations were needed to optimize the questions to avoid respondents' fatigue and acquiescence effect, taking under consideration that the survey had to be filled in just after the visit. Visitors were thus approached by one of the team members and offered a drink at the cafeteria of Museon and a book featuring some of the most representative objects exposed in Museon.

Section 1 of the survey gathered general -mainly demographic- information about visitors. Section 2 focused on questions related to if and how much the exhibition was enjoyed. Section 3 included knowledge and understanding self-perception evaluation questions with regards to the exhibition while Sect. 4 attempted to find out more about the moods, emotions and feelings experienced by the visitor during their visit.

88 visitors filled in the survey while more than 40 also accepted to give an interview as well. Follow up interviews approximately 6 months after the visit were also proposed and finally carried out with 17 visitors.

3.2   Visitor Demographics

In terms of demographics, men and women were equally well represented in our sample reflecting an overall balance in terms of visiting numbers and appeal of the exhibition. Most of our respondents lived in the Netherlands (97%) and had already visited Museon in the past, while roughly half were inhabitants of the city of the Hague (48%). 65% of the visitors indicated that they specifically planned to come to visit the exhibition. When asked more specifically what they were expecting, most of them said they wanted to get more information about the WW2 in the Netherlands, the Atlantic Wall and the city of the Hague. The tag cloud in Fig. 3. represents the main words used by the 43 visitors who answered this open-ended question regarding their motivations prior to visiting the visit. Most of the visitors talked about finding out more about the story of the city of the Hague during WW2 (e.g., "I came hear to learn", "find out", "get information about the story of the city", "WW2", etc.). In terms of visiting habits, 87% said they prefer visiting museums with others, confirming what is known from the literature, that museum visiting is a social activity [18].

The demographics in terms of age were also interesting. Traditionally, Museon proposes in its surveys the following age-groups: Under 12, 13–18, 19–64, over 65. For this exhibition, we chose to provide several additional age groups, as follows: Under 12, 13–18, 19–24, 25–34, 35–44, 45–54, 55–64, 65–74, 75–84, over 84. We were right to do so, as the Atlantic Wall exhibition attracted a quite different public as in comparison with most temporary exhibitions in Museon, targeting mainly families and schoolchildren and less an adult population. These additional age groups provided more granularity in museum visitors' profiles. The findings proved this approach was indeed well suited to the profile of the visitors which were attracted by this exhibition: almost 28% of the visitors were between 65–74 years old. Another 15% came from the categories 75 to 84 and over 85. Younger visitor (for example the 25–34) groups were less well represented (5,75%). We wanted to find out which are the main interpretive media visitors most often use when museum visiting. It was interesting to see that when it comes to museum visiting habits, text ranks first. This finding has appeared in other evaluation studies on museum learning through the digital carried out within [19] and outside meSch [20]. An important message here is that despite the use of digital technologies, the role of other more traditional interpretive media should not be underestimated. Most visitors spent mostly 30–60 min (45%) or 60 to 90 min (37%) in the exhibition. This finding is consistent with the visitor fatigue effect as discussed in the literature [21]. We asked all visitors to rank the activities in which they most engaged. Here once again reading text labels and information panels comes first (88,51%, 77 visitors), above even looking at the actual museum objects which came in the second place (87,36%, 76 visitors). An introductory video displayed at the entry of the exhibition proved to be one of the most attractive contents offered within the exhibition (81,61%, 71 visitors). The use of the replicas for listening to the audios (for one or more perspectives, using one or more replicas) came 4th but was globally well appreciated (68 visitors, 78,16%).

3.3   Findings on the Use and Appreciation of the Replicas

The use and appreciation of the replicas was one of the main topics we were interested in. 3 out of 4 visitors used them. We also asked the visitors which was the main reason that made them choose a replica: most visitors were primarily driven by the perspective (34%), though the visceral qualities of the replica as an object (touch, look and feel) also scored well (26%). The visitors who did not use a replica were asked why they did not: 1/3 of them said that they were not aware that they existed, so in reality they had missed the check-in station at the beginning of the exhibition proposing them to choose one or more replicas, to activate audio contents throughout the visit. Another 1 out of 5 (22%) said that they were not sure how to use them. The observations showed that when the exhibition space was full, visitors could grasp more easily how to use the replicas by "modelling" or imitating the interactions that other visitors had with their replicas. On the contrary, when the exhibition space was quiet with no other visitors in the same space, older visitors had more trouble figuring out how to use the replicas. We were also interested in finding out whether the visitors thought that using the replicas was easy and intuitive as in other studies of meSch prototypes, "easy" did not always rime with "intuitive". In this case, visitors had to use a 1 to 5 Likert scale, (with 5 being "I very much agree with the statement" and 1 "I completely disagree with the statement"). Unfortunately, though the use of the replicas was judged easy (with a mean of 4.46, using a scale from 1 to 5), it was not judged equally intuitive (mean 3.01). The videos and observations showed indeed some imaginative ways of trying to activate the contents. Some visitors would just pick up the handset, press the circle where the replica had to be placed or even would place other objects on the socles. Another important question was finding out which were the replicas (and thus also the perspectives) that were most preferred. For both English and Dutch narratives the classification is the same: The perspective of the civilian was the one most used, followed by this of the German soldier and then this of the Civil Servant. The curators' explanation since the beginning was that the civil servant perspective was either not that appealing or not so easy to grasp by the visitors. These findings are coherent with the meSch logging system of all active sessions which were recorded and logged [22]. The surrogate tea representing the perspective of the civilian comes first, then the beer mug and the travel pass for the Dutch language. The English version also follows the same tendency, the civilian comes first, followed by the German soldier and the civil servant perspective.

Fig. 2. Tag cloud with the main words which were given when visitors were asked what the main motivation was for visiting the exhibition.

3.4 Emotions and Feelings

The protocols set up privileged the use of semi-structured interviews immediately after the visit for gathering evidence and context on the emotions and feelings experienced while visiting. Though it was thought that interviews are indeed the most appropriate mean for discussing these aspects of the experience, it was decided to trial the use of a few closed and open-ended questions on emotions and feelings also within the survey. It was surprising to find out that a lot of interesting as well as quite unexpected data was gathered. For example, one of the questions the visitors were asked was "Has visiting the exhibition made you feel differently or strongly about the subject (something you saw, heard or talked about)?". Out of all visitors who answered, 66% percent said yes. What is more impressive is that all 55 visitors who answered yes, provided more information in an open-ended question that followed ("could you tell us more?"), encouraging them to give us more specific information about the things that touched them. Here are a few of the answers: "The prison door: my father-in-law went through this door as a prisoner". Another visitor answered "I realized that the dune hills of my youth are not natural but that under that hill is a bunker. We call the highest hill "Volcano". It is a nice place for birdwatching!". Another visitor wrote down "I have come to know how my neighbourhood in a different time period was.". Finding out shocking truths about the story of the city was also among the things that were mentioned. One of the visitors wrote: "I never realized that all of the people living near the beach had to be relocated.". Several visitors linked with their own, family experiences, memories and recollections: "The fear of the V2s coming down. My parents lived in the Hague and often talked about this."

Another question in the "Emotions and Feelings" section asked from the visitors to share something they learned or that was memorable while visiting the exhibition. After reading the answers, we came up with the idea of creating a tag-cloud, just like the one we saw at "the main motivation for visiting" question. The tag cloud visualisation is clear on the impact the visit had to the visitors (Fig. 3). Unlike the more generic terms used to describe the motivations before visiting the exhibition (Fig. 2), here we see appearing words that refer to specific things that came to be discovered through the visit: Specific city neighbourhoods appear in the tag cloud (Scheveningen, Waalsdorpervlakte), several nouns about the main actors of this period (family, inhabitants, children, people) or themes and terms that were presented in the exhibition (bunkers, evacuation, construction). Phrases such as "getting to know more about the stories of the people and the families" are in stark contrast with the more generic words and terms the visitors used to describe their visiting motivations.

4   Discussion, Conclusions and Directions for Future Work

Though tangible and embodied interaction has theoretically a lot of potential, it is extremely difficult to evaluate the tangibility, multimodality and multisensoriality a museum visiting experience can procure. It is for this reason that the evaluation planned for the Atlantic Wall exhibition featured the gathering of rich qualitative and quantitative data. This contribution provided an overview of the main findings we obtained through administering a survey at approximately 90 (N = 88) visitors and juxtaposed the findings with important elements that came to the surface using other qualitative (observations, interviews) and quantitative (logs) evidence. In terms of methodology, the adoption of a mixed methods evaluation protocol as well as our conviction that we needed to try to evaluate the experience holistically and not just focus on the use of the digital approach (in this case the replicas and the interaction of the visitors with them) paid off: it is indeed important to cater for all -digital and non-digital- components and aspects of the museum visiting experience. Indeed, some of the most successful components of the exhibition were the most traditional: reading the exhibition panels and text labels, watching the exhibits, and watching the introduction video came before the answer "using the replicas". The results we obtained in some of the questions also show the importance of providing different media, both analogue and digital as well as many narratives and different entry points for the visitors. The Atlantic Wall exhibition was possible to be visited both with and without using the replicas of everyday objects issued by the meSch project. This helps in catering for different visitor interests and needs. The replicas were well appreciated but the intuitiveness question revealed that new interaction metaphors and affordances may be challenging to grasp. This was particularly true for older visitors.

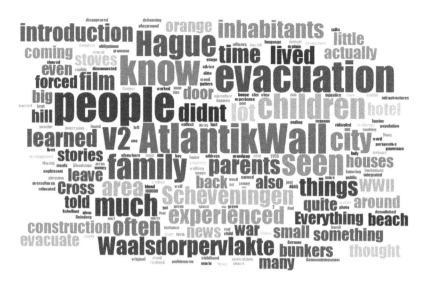

Fig. 3. Tag cloud with the main words which were given by visitors after visiting the exhibition when asked what the most memorable things were, they learned or found out.

Another interesting consideration regarding methodology, is that several open-ended questions, asking the visitors to talk about the feelings they experienced in the exhibition, performed well, providing interesting insights about feelings encountered, an aspect that we thought we would quasi-exclusively better understand through the interviews. The visitor study itself and the data analysis that followed confirmed our research design approach: it is important to first focus on the research questions before figuring out what the best way for is carrying out evaluation, as different methods have different strengths and weaknesses. The evaluation team was extremely meticulous in logging, structuring, and modelling our data on an everyday basis. Trialing and adopting onsite the evaluation protocol proved to be of paramount importance. Visiting and studying the exhibition space too. However, 3 years after the end of the project, the interviews (both the ones carried out immediately after the visit and over the phone, a few months later) are in the course of being analyzed. 37 hours of synchronized video footage from various cameras still waits to be coded. The detailed presentation of all survey findings is also underway. The main strength of the evaluation study, the gathering of rich qualitative and quantitative data, came to also became the main weakness, particularly in conjunction with the fact that the data came to be gathered round the end of the lifetime of the project. An open data approach which would render available datasets to the wider community, all by taking under account the appropriate ethical considerations might be the next most important thing to watch out for in the field of museum and visitor studies, particularly with regards to emerging technologies.

Acknowledgements. The research described in this paper was part of the meSch project, Material Encounters with Digital Cultural Heritage. meSch (2013–2017) received funding from the European Community's Seventh Framework Programme "ICT for access to cultural resources" (ICT Call 9: FP7-ICT-2011-9) under the Grant Agreement 600851. Partners in meSch were: Sheffield Hallam University, University of Limerick, University of Strathclyde, University Carlos 3 Madrid, DEN Foundation, MUSEON, University of Amsterdam and the Allard Pierson Museum, Museo Storico Italiano della Guerra, Fondazione Bruno Kessler, eCTRL, WAAG Society, University of Stuttgart. The gathering of the data of which an overview is presented in this paper occurred was coordinated by the University of Strathclyde, Glasgow, UK with the participation of colleagues from the University of Limerick and Museon, which provided all possible support for the onsite gathering of all data.

References

1. Perry, S., Economou, M., Young, H., Roussou, M., Pujol-Tost, L: Moving beyond the virtual museum: engaging visitors emotionally. In: Proceedings of the 23rd International Conference on Virtual System & Multimedia (VSMM), pp. 1–8. IEEE (2017). https://doi.org/10.1109/VSMM.2017.8346276

2. Pescarin, S.: Museums and virtual museums in Europe: reaching expectations. SCIRES-IT-SCIentific RESearch Inf. Technol. **4**(1), 131–140 (2014)

3. Samaroudi, M., Echavarria, K., Perry, L.: Heritage in lockdown: digital provision of memory institutions in the UK and US of America during the COVID-19 pandemic. Mus. Manag. Curatorship. **35**(4), 337–361 (2021)

4. Bradburne, J.: Foreword. Digital technologies and the museum experience: Handheld guides and other media. Rowman Altamira (2008)

5. Hornecker, E.: The To-and-Fro of sense making: supporting users' active indexing in museums. ACM Trans. Comput. Hum. Interaction (TOCHI) **23**(2), 1 (2016)

6. Petrelli, D., O'Brien, S.: Phone vs. tangible in museums: a comparative study. In: CHI 2018, p. 112 (2018)

7. Petrelli, D., Not, E., Damala, A., van Dijk, D., Lechner, M.: meSch – Material encounters with digital cultural heritage. In: Ioannides, M., Magnenat-Thalmann, N., Fink, E., Žarnić, R., Yen, A.-Y., Quak, E. (eds.) EuroMed 2014. LNCS, vol. 8740, pp. 536–545. Springer, Cham (2014). https://doi.org/10.1007/978-3-319-13695-0_53

8. Damala, A., et al.: Evaluating tangible and multisensory museum visiting experiences: lessons learned from the meSch project. In: Museums and the Web 2016, pp. 1–18 (2016). https://mw2016.museumsandtheweb.com/proposal/evaluating-tangible-and-multisensory-museum-visiting-experiences-lessons-learned-from-the-mesch-project/. Accessed 12 Dec 2020

9. Petrelli, D., Dulake, N., Marshall, M., Kockelcorn, H., Pisetti, A.: Do it together: the effect of curators, designers, and technologists sharing the making of new interactive visitors' experiences. In: Museums and the Web 2016, Proceedings (2016). https://mw2016.museumsandtheweb.com/paper/do-it-together-the-effect-of-curators-designers-and-technologists-sharing-the-making-of-new-interactive-visitors-experiences/

10. Marshall, M., Dulake, N., Ciolfi, L., Duranti, D., Kockelkorn, H., Petrelli, D.: Using tangible smart replicas as controls for an interactive museum exhibition. In: Proceedings of the TEI'16: Tenth International Conference on Tangible, Embedded, and Embodied Interaction 2016, pp. 159–167 (2016)

11. Not, E., Zancanaro, M., Marshall, M.T., Petrelli, D., Pisetti, A.: Writing postcards from the museum: composing personalised tangible souvenirs. In: Proceedings of the 12th Biannual Conference on Italian SIGCHI Chapter, pp. 1–9 (2017)

12. Hulleman, B.-A., Govers, R.: The Hague, international city of peace and justice. In: Dinnie, K. (ed.) City Branding, pp. 150–156. Palgrave Macmillan UK, London (2011). https://doi.org/10.1057/9780230294790_19
13. Zaloga, S.J.: The Atlantic Wall (2): Belgium, The Netherlands. Bloomsbury Publishing, Denmark and Norway (2011)
14. Kockelkorn, H.: Presenting hidden layers in an exhibition? blogpost, meSch EU project, 12 June 2015., https://www.mesch-project.eu/presenting-the-hidden-layers-of-an-exhibition/. Accessed 12 Dec 2020
15. Kockelkorn, H.: Why do we use smart replicas in the museum? blogpost, meSch EU project, 2 April 2015. https://www.mesch-project.eu/why-we-are-using-smart-replicas/. Accessed 12 Dec 2020
16. Risseeuw, M., et al.: An authoring environment for smart objects in museums: the meSch approach (2016)
17. Kockelkorn, H.: Connecting opposites? blogpost, meSch EU project, 12 December 2014. https://www.mesch-project.eu/connecting-opposites-mesch-technology-integrated-in-an-exhibition/. Accessed 12 Dec 2020
18. Packer, J., Ballantyne, R.: Solitary vs. shared: exploring the social dimension of museum learning. Curator Mus. J. 48(2), 177–192 (2005)
19. Van der Vaart, M., Damala, A.: Through the Loupe: visitor engagement with a primarily text-based handheld AR application. In: 2015 Digital Heritage Conference, vol. 2, pp. 565–572. IEEE (2015)
20. Damala A., Cubaud, P., Bationo, A., Houlier, P., Marchal, I.: Bridging the gap between the digital and the physical: design and evaluation of a mobile augmented reality guide for the museum visit. In: Proceedings of the 3rd International Conference on Digital Interactive Media in Entertainment and Arts, pp. 120–127. ACM, New York (2008)
21. Falk, J., Dierking, L.: The Museum Experience. Howells House, Washington (1992)
22. Marshall, M.T., et al.: Audio-based narratives for the trenches of World War I: intertwining stories, places and interaction for an evocative experience. Int. J. Hum. Comput. Stud. 85, 27–39 (2016)

The Atlas of Lost Rooms:

Digitally Reconstructing Dark Heritage Sites in Ireland

Chris Hamill[(✉)] [iD]

Queen's University, Belfast BT7 1NN, UK
chamill625@qub.ac.uk

Abstract. This paper explores the use of 3D digital reconstructions of dark heritage sites (defined as sites associated with death, injury, injustice, abuse and torture) for architectural investigations and public dissemination of difficult and emotionally challenging historic events.

The particular case study examined is the ongoing Atlas of Lost Rooms project (http://atlasoflostrooms.com/), a digital reconstruction of the Sean MacDermott St Magdalene Laundry in Dublin, one of Ireland's most poignant sites of institutional abuse. The project seeks to create a repository of oral histories from the now demolished laundry complex, using digital architectural modelling to situate survivor testimony within an online model of the former site.

The paper explores the theoretical justification for the use of digital technologies in examining dark heritage sites, and sets out a workflow for how 3D reconstructions can be created from limited and fragmentary sources. The paper concludes by suggesting future areas for further study to determine the usefulness of digital tools in the field of dark and contested heritage.

Keywords: Digital reconstruction · Dark heritage · Oral history in architecture

1 Introduction

This paper focuses on the ongoing Atlas of Lost Rooms project (http://atlasoflostrooms. com/), created as an exploration via digital reconstruction of the mostly-demolished Sean MacDermott Street Magdalene Laundry in Dublin. The project had two primary aims; firstly, to establish a digital reconstruction workflow which could be used where key source material is restricted or missing (a situation common when dealing with dark heritage sites), and to evaluate its potential as an architectural research method. Secondly, to explore the use of digital reconstructions as a means enhancing public engagement with dark heritage sites by employing a virtual architectural model through which survivor testimonies and other historic information could be accessed and viewed in their appropriate spatial contexts.

As the project is ongoing, this paper will primarily discuss the former objective. Section 2 sets out the historic and contemporary context of Ireland's Magdalene

© Springer Nature Switzerland AG 2021
M. Shehade and T. Stylianou-Lambert (Eds.): RISE IMET 2021, CCIS 1432, pp. 199–216, 2021.
https://doi.org/10.1007/978-3-030-83647-4_14

Laundries. In Sect. 3, a critical framing of how the process of digital reconstruction itself can become an investigative tool for architectural researchers is laid out. Section 4 details the workflow adopted for the creation of this digital reconstruction and web interface, and Sect. 5 discusses key initial findings. Finally, Sect. 6 looks at future developments within the project and suggests additional areas for further study.

2 Context

2.1 The Magdalene Laundries

Ireland's 'Magdalene Laundries' have become infamous in recent decades as Church-run and State-supported institutions deeply involved with the coercive confinement of the nation's female citizens [1]. Women deemed to have 'fallen' morally were often confined in these institutions, and put to work, unpaid, in difficult and often gruelling industrial laundries [2].

What constituted a 'fallen' woman varied according to time and place, but reasons for confinement within a Magdalene Institution could include repeating the 'offence' of becoming pregnant out of wedlock [3], becoming a victim of sexual assault [4], or those who were 'sexually aware' [Ibid]. Whilst it is important to stress that none of these 'offences' were criminal acts at the time, Titley also notes that imprisonment within a Magdalene Institution could be 'pre-emptive', meaning that girls and young women who, *'were pretty'* or were *'perceived to be in danger of losing their virginity'* could find themselves in a Magdalene Laundry without ever having a chance to 'fall' [5].

In 2013, *The Report of the Inter-Departmental Committee to establish the facts of State involvement with the Magdalen Laundries*, found that between 10,000 and 14,000 women had spent time in a Magdalene Institution since 1922 [6], although many groups have criticised this figure as a significant under-estimate [7].

Duration of confinement within a Magdalene Laundry varied greatly, with the Inter-Departmental Report stating the median length of stay to be 7 months [6]. Activist groups such as Justice for Magdalenes Research have criticised the use of the median as misleading, noting that the mean length of stay was in fact 3.22 years, and that data is only available on 42% of confirmed admissions to the laundries [8]. Furthermore, this use of averages masks the fact that for a significant number of women, confinement within a Magdalene Institution was for life [9]. It is also important to note that, regardless of the length of time spent in the laundries, many survivors report that they were given no indication as to when they might be released, further adding to the stress and anxiety of their situation [10].

Fig. 1. The former Magdalene Laundry and Convent on Sean MacDermott St (formerly Gloucester St) in Dublin (Source: Author's Own)

2.2   Sean MacDermott St Magdalene Laundry

The last laundry in operation was that on Sean MacDermott Street in north, inner-city Dublin (Fig. 1). An '*asylum*' for '*troubled and homeless*' women was present at this location as early as 1822 [6]. In 1873, the Order of the Sisters of Mercy took over the site and began its institutional and architectural development. This role was later taken on by the Sisters of Our Lady of Charity in 1887 [11], and continued under their stewardship until 1996 when the laundry closed.

The Sean MacDermott St site was one of the larger Magdalene Institutions, with a reported capacity for up to 150 women [6]. Whilst portions of the site still stand, all buildings connected with the operation of the industrial laundry were demolished following a fire in 2006. Thus, any physical connection to one of the key parts of the site's former purpose has been lost.

The site is currently owned by Dublin City Council, making it the only Magdalene Institution site in state ownership. As such it has become a focal point for advocacy groups as to how best to re-use the site and memorialise the story of the Magdalene Women.

2.3   Lack of Public Engagement with Ireland's Magdalene History

Those seeking to reappropriate the Sean MacDermott St site as a public memorial must also grapple with the significant public-engagement deficit which has been observed in relation to contemporary Ireland and Magdalene history. Yeager & Culleton note that, not only were Magdalene women '*hidden from society and written out of Irish history*' while the Magdalene Laundries were in operation, but also continue to be subject to social erasure through '*a collective "therapeutic voluntary amnesia*"' [12]. Even the official State report into the Magdalene Institutions was criticised for placing '*[l]ittle significance...on the survivors' testimony*' [13].

This lacuna of public engagement with the story of the Magdalene Laundries is further emphasised by the physical locations of sites such as Sean MacDermott St. These institutions were not located in remote, rural locations, far from the public gaze; but were centrally positioned in urban environments, visible to the inhabitants of cities such as Dublin, Cork and Limerick, and yet heterotopically outside the usual ordering of space and 'respectable' life [14].

2.4   Difficulties in Researching Magdalene Institutions

Since the closure of the Magdalene Institutions, the relative lack of public engagement has made it significantly easier for those in possession of these sites to demolish or aggressively redevelop the physical remnants of the laundries, resulting in limited amounts of surviving architectural fabric for contemporary researchers to examine and interpret.

This is further compounded by the relative lack of 'traditional' archival sources available to researchers. As the Magdalene Laundries were ostensibly private institutions (albeit operated with the support of the Irish State), records relating to the construction and running of these sites remain, for the most part, in the archives of the various religious orders. These orders have in recent years been notably unwilling to open their records to researchers (with very few exceptions [15]), believing that they have been unfairly maligned in recent retellings of Magdalene history [16].

This restriction on access to key primary and secondary sources has led to Prof. James Smith remarking that, '*the Magdalen laundry exists in the public mind chiefly at the level of **story** (cultural representation and survivor testimony) rather than history (archival records and documentation)*' [17]. This highlights the importance of oral history work (survivor testimony) in contemporary scholarship on the Magdalene Institutions. To date, two large oral history projects (along with numerous smaller-scale interviews and media appearances by survivors) have been carried out [18, 19].

Of particular interest to this project was the 2013 study carried out between University College Dublin and the Irish Research Council, which contains interview transcripts of five women who passed through the Sean MacDermott St Magdalene Laundry in the 1960s and 70s, and is therefore one of the key extant sources relating to the history of that site.

In summary, the Atlas project sought to address the lack of public engagement with one of Ireland's darkest heritages, for which there exists little in the way of 'traditional' source material or physical remnants, and where survivor testimonies remain some of the best evidence available to researchers.

3 Theory

3.1 Why Digital 3D Reconstruction for Dark Heritage Sites?

Each of Ireland's ten[1] Magdalene Laundries has been subject to significant dereliction, demolition or redevelopment (or some combination thereof). This lack of physical evidence and access to sites, coupled with the scarce and fragmentary nature of mediated source material such as architects' drawings and construction records mentioned previously, poses a challenge for contemporary architectural research. Indeed, this may explain why the architectural history of the Magdalene Institutions represents a significant gap in the literature at present.

However, digital 3D reconstruction of these sites allows for the combination of these limited extant sources in virtual space; allowing both for the visualisation of these sites as they *'might have been,'* but also representing a critical research methodology itself – what Webb & Brown refer to as *'digital forensic investigation'* [20].

Addison notes that there are 3 primary purposes to digital heritage, namely *'Documentation, Representation, and Dissemination'* [21] however, this paper would suggest the inclusion of an additional category of *'Investigation'*. As Mascio et al. note, *'The digital reconstruction...allows elaborating hypotheses and evaluating them through 3D modelling; hence it typically represents a moment of investigation'* [22].

In the literature to date, these investigative methods have been primarily focused on 'never-built' architectures [23], or those where available sources are limited by the passage of time [24], however, the Atlas project found these techniques equally applicable to instances of dark heritage where key sources are deliberately restricted, and sites are often unavailable to researchers either through gatekeeping processes, or outright demolition of remaining built fabric.

3.2 Oral Histories as Source Material for Digital Reconstruction

As discussed, restricted archival access has rendered oral history work some of best available evidence for researchers studying Ireland's Magdalene Laundries, including their physical architectures. Interviews with former Magdalene women often contain important details about the layout of particular sites, interior furnishings, smells and sounds now lost; as well as recounting events which revolve around, or were hosted within, specific parts of the buildings, making the resulting testimonies highly architectural [25].

The use of oral history in architectural research is relatively nascent, but with a growing amount of scholarship [26]. Gosseye, Stead and van der Plaat note that, *'...by giving a voice to those who have remained unheard, oral history can build accounts... that are currently absent from the historical record in architecture...by documenting*

---

[1] Donnybrook, Dublin (derelict); Sean MacDermott St, Dublin (derelict; partly demolished); High Park; Dublin (partly demolished; redeveloped); Dun Laoghaire (partly demolished; redeveloped); Galway (demolished); New Ross, (demolished); Limerick (redeveloped); Peacock Lane, Cork (redeveloped); Sundays Well, Cork (derelict; largely destroyed by fire); Waterford (redeveloped).

the experience of and interaction with buildings over time, oral history can give a dynamic fourth dimension to...static three-dimensional structures' [27].

One of the advantages of digital reconstruction methods when visualising oral histories is the ability to add this *'dynamic fourth dimension'* through the use of overlapping iterations of the model. The same techniques which have been used previously to represent changes to heritage sites over time [28] are also well suited to illustrating the ephemeral natural of spatial memory; allowing for the accommodation of multiple, occasionally contradictory recollections, or those which do not align with what is known of the physical site from other sources and extant buildings [29]. This in turn allows the digital reconstruction to be a vehicle for illustrating and conveying to an unfamiliar audience the lived realities of interviewees, rather than becoming a 'fact check' on the veracity of these memories, and in so doing, treating them as inherently less reliable than other, 'traditional' sources.

3.3   Public Engagement with Dark Heritage Through Digital Reconstructions

An emerging body of literature supports the hypothesis that, in addition to overcoming limitations of physical access to sites and artefacts, virtual models and digital reconstructions can present an engaging user experience and, as Boskovic et al. state, *'an entertaining way to engage users in exploring historical artefacts and to motivate them to learn more.'* [30].

In the field of dark and contested heritage, the literature on the role of digital reconstructions in public engagement is more limited, however there are several notable examples.

Of particular interest and relevance to the Atlas of Lost Rooms is a recent project using a VR/AR visitor-tour app at the site of the former Bergen Belsen concentration camp in Germany, which is built around a geo-located reconstruction of the now demolished camp buildings [31]. Preliminary studies on user engagement indicate that the ability to freely explore the reconstructed site in augmented 3D, coupled with the access to additional information provided via 'hotspots' within the model resulted in enhanced participation and interaction with the particularly sensitive material presented [32].

Furthermore, studies on user responses have found that an *emotional* engagement with the site (achieved for example by conveying survivor testimony to the user in the first person) enhanced engagement and boosted information retention [33]. These findings are supportive of the use of oral histories in digital heritage reconstructions, not only as source material as discussed previously, but also as overlays onto the model itself as a means of engaging users emotionally. As Perry et al. note, *'digital empathic stories can evoke narrative transportation, and in some cases, personal attachment and critical (self-)reflection...[and] might be pushed even further into the building of broader, collective social conscience'* [34].

This potential for telling engaging stories about sensitive topics was one of the key objectives of the Atlas of Lost Rooms project, which sought to bridge the engagement gap relating to Ireland's Magdalene history by creating a digital venue for dissemination and contemplation, overlaid with excerpts of survivor testimony.

4   Method

4.1   Construction of the Digital Model

The Atlas project centres around a detailed reconstruction of the former Magdalene Laundry on Sean MacDermott St, as it would have looked c.1960 (Fig. 2).

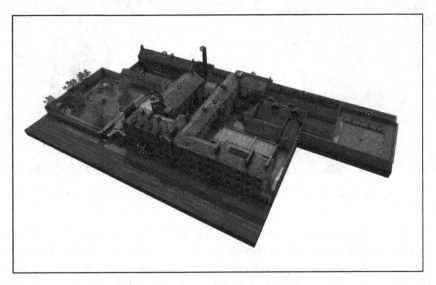

Fig. 2. Final version of the digital reconstruction of the site c.1960. (Source: Author's Own)

The digital modelling process was carried out in Blender, a free, open source modelling software. This programme is well suited to speculative architectural modelling as its extensive use of Boolean operations and modifiers allow for a 'non-destructive' workflow, enabling rapid prototyping and experimentation whilst retaining editability and reversibility for the modelling process.

Fortunately for this reconstruction project, the Sean MacDermott St laundry was better documented than many of its contemporaries in terms of the available architectural information and orthographic drawings. Of particular interest was a plan survey of the buildings on the site dated to 1954. Additionally, in the early 2000s, the Dublin City Corporation commissioned a survey of the site, providing several floorplans and elevations as .dxf files, which are an industry recognised CAD format. These were imported into Blender at real-world scale and used as reference for the reconstruction of the relevant portions of the site (Fig. 3).

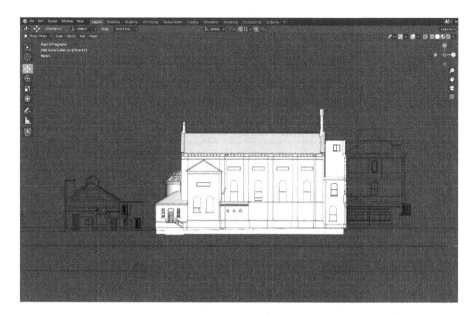

Fig. 3. Use of reference drawings for modelling. (Source: Author's Own)

However, there were large areas of the site, especially building elevations, which were not captured in any of the survey information. In order to reconstruct these areas, research revealed several photographs of the site prior to the 2006 fire. Blender allows for 'camera objects' to be positioned within a model as a means of mimicking a real-world camera.[2] This feature was coupled with the open-source software plugin, fSpy, which allows the 'reverse engineering' of existing photographs based off perspectival vanishing points to reveal key camera parameters. In terms of the reconstruction process, this means that 3D models can be reconstructed from a 2D photograph, and when combined with known references this allows for an accurately dimensioned[3] virtual model to be produced from very limited sources (Fig. 4).

---

[2] The user can for example adjust depth of field, focal length, sensor size, camera position and rotation, using similar settings to real world photography.

[3] Within a margin of error – it should be stressed that this method is not as accurate as traditional survey techniques.

Fig. 4. Use of photographic reference and 'digital cameras' for modelling. (Source: Author's Own)

Consideration was given to executing the project through the use of Heritage Building Information Modelling (H-BIM) software such as Autodesk Revit. As Pauwels et al. note [35] there are clear advantages to a H-BIM workflow in terms of the metadata and paradata which can be stored within the model, as well as the ability to quickly layer new information, or alter building components at a later date as and when new sources of information become available (indeed, the relative difficulty the non-H-BIM, Blender based approach would encounter when attempting future revisions is one of its major disadvantages). Ultimately however, the reason the Blender/fSpy approach outlined above was adopted was its ability to generate accurately scaled geometric data from a single photographic source, especially since significant parts of the reconstruction of the site were based largely or entirely on a scant number of historic photographs (this is also the reason a photogrammetry-based approach was not viable) [36]. Whilst H-BIM is capable of embedding and using photographic sources, and can make use of highly dimensionally accurate LiDAR scan data, the perspectival reconstruction the adopted approach allowed was deemed to offer greater utility and affordability for this particular project.

4.2 Level of Detail and Representing Uncertainty

The Level of Detail (LoD) and graphic fidelity of the digital reconstruction were given particular consideration. Whilst noting the concerns that Rahaman [37] and others have expressed, namely that perhaps too often in Digital Heritage project, photorealism is idealised as the 'ultimate' form of representational technique without due criticality or consideration for alternative options, for the Atlas of Lost Rooms it was ultimately decided to adopt a high level of graphical realism. This was resolved upon for two primary reasons. Firstly, the fact that some parts of the site remained extant, and the availability of (some) colour photography of demolished areas meant the materiality of the site *could* be determined and represented with a high degree of accuracy. Secondly, and perhaps more influential upon the final decision, was an attempt to use the perceived 'realism' of the reconstruction to counteract the enduring sense that the Magdalene Laundries, due to their lack of 'official' histories and 'legitimate' source material, were and are often seen, as Smith's notes, as '*story*' or '*myth*', and not as '*history.*' [17]. The intention was therefore to use a photoreal depiction of the site as a means of encouraging users to engage more seriously with the material, and to prevent its easy dismissal as something abstract, or 'unreal.'

However, this approach poses a difficulty in conveying uncertainty, quality of source material or other paradata to the user. The risk of misleading the audience was unacceptable, both in terms of good practice in digital reconstructions as set down in the London Charter [38], but also because of the importance of transparency when dealing with such emotive and sensitive material.

One option to communicate uncertainty is the use of localised variations in level of detail of the finished model [39], however this was deemed to run the risk of breaking user immersion and so an alternative approach was sought. Instead, a form of representation based on Apollonio's classification schema [40] was adopted. This saw the production of a retextured 'reference' version of the master model, colour-coded to refer to the sources/inferences used to inform its initial production (Fig. 5). Where regions of the model were the result of multiple, overlapping sources, this was represented by a banded hatch pattern. This resulted in two versions of each model, one realistically textured and one coloured and annotated with key references, both linked from the project website, as a form of digital graphic footnoting (Fig. 6).

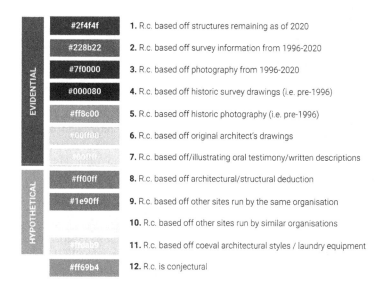

Fig. 5. Colour coding key for levels of uncertainty/quality of source material. (Source: Author's Own)

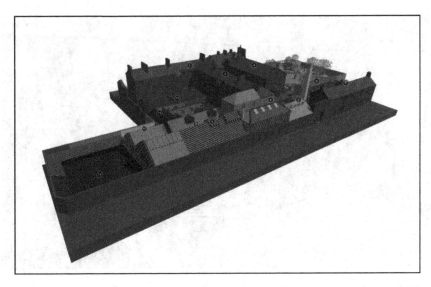

Fig. 6. Colour-coded 'uncertainty' model. Additional sources and information added via annotation 'hotspots.' (Source: Author's Own)

4.3 Design of the Web Interface

The production of the digital reconstruction of the former laundry was only part of the project, with public engagement and dissemination also being key objectives. To this end, the 3D reconstructions were uploaded to the web-hosting platform Sketchfab from where they could be embedded and made accessible via a custom website interface.

In addition to exploring and interacting with the model in digital 3D, Sketchfab also allows additional information to be overlaid on the model through the use of clickable hotspots with paired annotations. This feature was exploited as a means of overlaying excerpts of oral history transcripts onto the reconstruction (Fig. 7). Sections of transcripts were selected based on their relevance to a user's understanding of the site, as well as their ability to be confidently located within specific areas of the complex. This allowed for the survivor testimonies to be contextualised and illustrated by the digital model, whilst simultaneously creating a spatially distributed user interface for the oral history project, increasing the accessibility of the interview transcripts, several of which run to hundreds of pages of text.

Fig. 7. Oral testimony excerpts overlaid onto 3D reconstruction. (Source: Author's Own)

Using the architecture of the reconstructed Magdalene Laundry as the basis of a coherent and engaging User Interface was carried through to the design of the project website. This website not only prominently features the aforementioned digital model embeds, but is itself organised and structured spatially, with information such as photographs, historical material and oral histories grouped into various sub-pages according to their location within the Laundry complex. These are then accessed through a clickable map of the site (Fig. 8) located prominently on the home page, in a digital facsimile of an analogue road atlas. This allows the presentation of information to the viewer at various scales, and provides an easily modifiable and expandable framework for the website as additional data comes available in future.

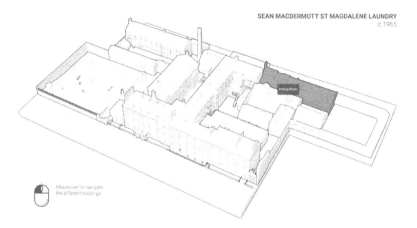

Fig. 8. Primary web interface using a representation of the Laundry Complex as an interactive site-map. (Source: Author's Own)

Another key feature of the website design was the inclusion of public feedback forms on every page of the site, soliciting comments or additional information from users. These are each keyed with a location ID related to the page on which they are located, so comments can also be used as spatially located data. This solicitation and implementation of public feedback was one of the recommendations of Pujol & Pastor with regards the Bergen Belsen VR app, and their rationale would seem equally applicable to the subject of Ireland's Magdalene Laundries:

'...because...survivors or descendants of people held at Bergen- Belsen are alive, the application may have chosen a more contributive approach so that information is not simply preserved and disseminated by experts, but open under control to visitors. Thus the database of historical knowledge is increased with oral memories, thus constituting a truly living archive, putting in contact past and present' [32].

5 Initial Findings

The use of photo-based reconstruction techniques in this project have opened new avenues for cross-comparative analysis of limited sources for lost heritage sites. Already, this approach has produced new information on the architectural design and chronology of several parts of the site.

For example, it was determined that a set of 3 window apertures on the site's south elevation which are still visible today (Fig. 9) were not original to the construction of the Ironing Room which once stood behind this wall. A perspective analysis of a postcard of the interior of this room dated c.1925, shows these windows should be clearly in view of the camera, but are not shown (Fig. 10). Therefore, they cannot have been installed by this date. An amateur film of the exterior of the site dating from the 1930s[4] does however show these windows in place, narrowing down their date of installation to c.1925–c.1939.

Similarly, upon reconstructing the glazed roof of the Ironing Room based on the 1930s film and geo-locating the model to its correct position, it proved impossible to recreate the shadows visible in the c.1925 interior postcard, even using digital solar modelling. Thus it was determined that this roof light had also been remodelled post-1925, a hypothesis supported by Prunty, who notes, '...re-roofing of the various workrooms...was a recurrent cost because of the steam and heat generated by the laundry work' [41].

As the project is ongoing, initial findings have been primarily limited to the use of digital reconstructions as an investigative aid when dealing with the architecture of dark heritage. A report on the public engagement aspect of the site will be forthcoming, although initial feedback has been positive, with several users remarking approvingly on the use and contextualisation of oral testimonies within the model, noting that this has been an engaging and accessible way of representing the voices of survivors.

---

[4] Fr Delaney Collection, Irish Film Institute. Gloucester St. https://ifiplayer.ie/father-delaney-collection-gloucester-street/ Relevant section begins at 6 min 15.

Fig. 9. Window in the southern external wall of the site as existing today. (Source: Author's Own)

Fig. 10. Interior of the Ironing Room matched with the perspective of the c.1925 postcard. The location the external window is outlined in blue, revealing that, had it been installed by the date this photograph was taken, it would have been visible. Therefore, it must have been installed after this date. (Source: Author's Own)

6 Future Developments

In order to test the effectiveness of the digital reconstruction and web interface in engaging the public with the difficult subject matter of the Magdalene Laundries, further assessment is required. This will take the form of a series of semi-structured interviews and questionnaires with members of the public and key stakeholders. It is hoped that feedback from these sessions will help to inform the future design iterations of the web interface as well as providing additional contextual information which can be overlaid onto the 3D reconstruction.

The existence of a digital reconstruction of the site also offers enticing possibilities as an aide-memoire in interviews with survivors. The benefits of hosting oral history interviews in the physical sites where these events originally occurred are documented in the literature [42], however recent examples suggest that where access to the original site is no longer possible (due to demolition, dereliction, distance, or lack of authorisation to visit), a digital facsimile of the site can have similarly positive effects on the ability of interviewees to recall and spatialise past events.

Eyal Weizman and the Forensic Architecture group at Goldsmiths University have coined the term 'situated testimony' to refer to this interview technique, defined as: '[the use of] *3D models of the scenes and environments in which traumatic events occurred, to aid in the process of interviewing and gathering testimony from witnesses to those events. Memories of traumatic or violent episodes can often be elusive, or distorted, but we have found that the use of digital architectural models has a productive effect on a witness's recollection*' [43].

Due to the limited nature of source material on Ireland's Magdalene Laundries, and the advanced age of many former Magdalene Women, the possibility of enhancing recall in oral history interviews with the use of digital modelling techniques presents itself as an exciting area for further study.

7 Conclusion

The Atlas of Lost Rooms project illustrates the potential of using 3D digital reconstructions as an architectural research methodology in cases where access to key sources and sites is restricted, due to its ability to combine multi-modal and fragmentary inputs. As this project remains a work in progress, the public engagement aspects remain to be fully tested, and further refinement of the model and the user interface will no doubt be required – again something the digital medium is well suited to accommodate.

As a final point of consideration, it may also be argued that the ability of the digital methods demonstrated in this project to use extremely limited source material in recovering a lost piece of dark architectural heritage might serve a broader conservative function. The potential to recover key evidence from such sites, despite a lack of physical remains, might give pause to those who seek to use demolition as a means of concealing or deliberately misremembering these difficult heritage sites in future, helping to preserve these important historic places for the benefit of society as a whole.

References

1. O'Sullivan, E., O'Donnell, I. (eds.): Chapter 24: Conclusions. In: Coercive Confinement in Ireland: Patients, Prisoners and Penitents, p. 250. Manchester University Press, Manchester (2012)
2. Cox, C.: Institutional space and the geography of confinement in Ireland, 1750– 2000. In: Bartlett, T. (ed.) The Cambridge History of Ireland, p. 701. Cambridge University Press, Cambridge (2018)
3. Fischer, C.: Gender, nation, and the politics of shame: Magdalen Laundries and the institutionalization of feminine transgression in modern Ireland. Signs 41(4), 831 (2016)
4. O'Mahoney, J.: Advocacy and the Magdalene Laundries: towards a psychology of social change. Qual. Res. Psychol. 15(4), 457 (2018)
5. Titley, B.: Heil Mary: Magdalen Asylums and moral regulation in Ireland. Hist. Educ. Rev. 35(2), 11 (2006)
6. Government of Ireland: Report of the Inter-Departmental Committee to establish the facts of State involvement with the Magdalen Laundries. Department of Justice and Equality, Dublin (2013)
7. O'Rourke, M., Smith, J.: Ireland's Magdalene Laundries: confronting a history not yet in the past. In: Hayes, A., Meager, M. (eds.) A Century of Progress? Irish Women Reflect, p. 4. Arlen House, Dublin (2016)
8. McGetrick, C., et al.: Death, Institutionalisation & Duration of Stay: A critique of Chapter 16 of the Report of the Inter-Departmental Committee to establish the facts of State involvement with the Magdalen Laundries and related issues, p. 57. JfMR, Dublin (2015)
9. Simpson, A., et al.: Doing compassion or doing discipline? Power relations and the Magdalene Laundries. J. Polit. Power, 257 (2014)
10. O'Donnell, K., Pembroke, S., McGettrick, C.: "Oral History of Mary May". Magdalene Institutions: Recording an Oral and Archival History, p. 19. Irish Research Council (2013)
11. Prunty, J.: The Monasteries, Magdalen Asylums and Reformatory Schools of Our Lady of Charity in Ireland 1853–1973, p. 269. Columba Press, Dublin (2017)
12. Yeager, J., Culleton, J.: Gendered violence and cultural forgetting: the case of the Irish Magdalenes. Radical History Rev. 135(140), 142 (2016)
13. O'Mahoney, J.: Advocacy and the Magdalene Laundries: towards a psychology of social change. Qual. Res. Psychol. 15(4), 460 (2018)
14. Focault, M.: Of other spaces: utopias and heterotopias. In: 'Architecture /Mouvement/ Continuité', October 1984
15. Prunty, J.: Documentary sources for Magdalen history and the challenges. Stud. Irish Q. Rev. 107(427), 267–292 (2018). The Nuns' Stories – Writing the Record
16. Pine, E.: Coming clean? Remembering the Magdalen Laundries. In: Memory Ireland: History and Modernity, vol. 1, p. 168. Syracuse University Press (2011)
17. Smith, J.: Ireland's Magdalen Laundries and the Nation's Architecture of Containment, p. Xvi. University of Notre Dame Press, Notre Dame (2007)
18. O'Donnell, K., Pembroke, S., McGettrick, C.: Magdalene Institutions: Recording an Oral and Archival History. Irish Research Council (2013). http://jfmresearch.com/home/oralhistoryproject/
19. Waterford Memories Project (led by Jennifer Yeager). https://www.waterfordmemories.com/oralhistories

20. Webb, N., Brown, A.: Digital forensics as a tool for augmenting historical architectural analysis: case study: the student work of James Stirling. In: Proceedings of the 16th International Conference on Computer-Aided Architectural Design Research in Asia, pp. 505–514 (2011)
21. Addison, A.C.: Emerging trends in virtual heritage. IEEE Multimedia **7**, 22–25 (2000)
22. Di Mascio, D., Chiuini, M., Fillwalk, J., Pauwels, P.: 3D digital reconstructions of lost buildings: a first critical framing. In: Herneoja, A., Österlund, T., Markkanen, P. (eds.) ECAADE 2016: COMPLEXITY & SIMPLICITY, vol. 2, pp. 511–20. University of Oulu, Oulu, Finland (2016)
23. Webb, N., Brown, A.: Augmenting critique of lost or unbuilt works of architecture using digitally mediated techniques. In: Zupancic, T., Juvancic, M., Verovsek, S., Jutraz, A. (eds.) Education in Computer Aided Architectural Design in Europe, pp. 942–950. eCAADe, Ljubljana (2011)
24. Münster, S.: Workflows and the role of images for a virtual 3D reconstruction of no longer extant historic objects. ISPRS Ann. Photogram. Remote Sens. Spatial Inf. Sci., 197–202 (2013)
25. Benjamin, M.: Oral history and the documentation of historic sites: recording sense of place. In: 16th ICOMOS General Assembly and International Symposium: 'Finding the spirit of place – between the tangible and the intangible', 29 September–4 October 2008, Quebec, Canada. [Conference or Workshop Item]
26. Jamrozik, J.: Growing up modern – oral history as architectural preservation. J. Archit. Educ. **72**(2), 284–289 (2018)
27. Gosseye, J., Stead, N., van der Plaat, D. (eds.) Speaking of Buildings: Oral History in Architectural Research, p. 26. Princeton Architectural Press, New York (2019)
28. Rodríguez-Gonzálvez, P., et al.: 4D reconstruction and visualization of cultural heritage: analyzing our legacy through time. ISPRS - International Archives of the Photogrammetry, Remote Sensing and Spatial Information Sciences, XLII-2/W3 (2017)
29. Weizman, E.: Forensic Architecture: Violence at the Threshold of Detectability, p. 93. Zone Books, New York (2008)
30. Boskovic, D., Rizvic, S., Okanovic, V., Sljivo, S., Sinanovic, N.: Measuring immersion and edutainment in multimedia cultural heritage applications. In: 2017 XXVI International Conference on Information, Communication and Automation Technologies (ICAT), Sarajevo, p. 5 (2017)
31. Pacheco, D., Wierenga, S., Omedas, P., Wilbricht, S., Knoch, H., Verschure, P.: Spatializing experience: a framework for the geolocalization, visualization and exploration of historical data using VR/AR technologies. In: Proceedings of Laval Virtual, VRIC 2014 (2014)
32. Pastor, Á., Pujol, L.: Analysis of the Bergen-Belsen VR/AR application by means of the Virtual Subjectiveness Model, pp. 6–7. ArXiv abs/2001.11571 (2020)
33. Oliva, L.S., Mura, A., Betella, A., Pacheco, E., Martinez, E., Verschure, P.: Recovering the history of Bergen Belsen using an interactive 3D reconstruction in a mixed reality space the role of pre-knowledge on memory recollection. In: 2015 Digital Heritage, Granada, p. 164 (2015)
34. Perry, S., Roussou, M., Mirashrafi, S.S., Katifori, A., McKinney, S.: Shared digital experiences supporting collaborative meaning-making at heritage sites. In: Lewi, H., Smith, W., vom Lehn, D., Cooke, S. (eds.) The Routledge International Handbook of New Digital Practices in Galleries, Libraries, Archives, Museums and Heritage Sites, p. 144. Routledge, London (2019)
35. Pauwels, P., Verstraeten, R., Meyer, R., Campenhout, J.: Architectural information modelling for virtual heritage application. In: Digital Heritage: Proceedings of the 14th International Conference on Virtual Systems and Multimedia, p. 2 (2008)

36. Kersten, T., Lindstaedt, M.: Potential of automatic 3D object reconstruction from multiple images for applications in architecture, cultural heritage and archaeology. Int. J. Herit. Digit. Era **1**, 399–420 (2012)
37. Rahaman, H., Das, R., Zahir, S.: Virtual Heritage: Exploring Photorealism, p. 193 (2012)
38. The London Charter for Computer Based Visualisation of Cultural Heritage. http://www.londoncharter.org/introduction.html. Accessed 19 Nov 2020
39. Schaefer, U.: Uncertainty Visualization and Digital 3D Modeling in Archaeology. A Brief Introduction (2018)
40. Apollonio, F.: Classification Schemes for Visualization of Uncertainty in Digital Hypothetical Reconstruction (2016)
41. Prunty, J.: The Monasteries, Magdalen Asylums and Reformatory Schools of Our Lady of Charity in Ireland 1853–1973, p. 506. Columba Press, Dublin (2017)
42. Fernyhough, C.: Pieces of Light: The New Science of Memory. Profile Books, London
43. Forensic Architecture. https://forensic-architecture.org/methodology/situated-testimony. Accessed 17 Nov 2020

Emerging Technologies and the Advent of the Holocaust "Hologram"

Cayo Gamber[✉]

The University Writing Program, The George Washington University,
2100 Foxhall Road, Ames 232, Washington, D.C. 20007, USA
cayol@gwu.edu

Abstract. Introduced in 2015, hologram-like recordings acquaint audiences with Holocaust survivors, survivors who soon no longer will be with us. Housed at various sites in the United States, from the United Nations to the Illinois Holocaust Museum and Education Center (IHME/Illionis), this emerging technology of Holocaust survivor "holograms" ensures survivors' histories will "live." What makes these recordings of Holocaust survivors innovative is that they are interactive. In response to visitors' queries, the recordings are prepared to answer 1,000 possible questions. In addition, over time, the survivor recordings refine "their" answers to those questions by learning to better understand what is being asked and providing the best answer in their repository. The analysis conducted and conclusions reached in this paper are guided by the research question: What are the ethical concerns related to the development of this technology and the relationships it engenders? To that end, this paper interrogates the role played by the visitors who engage with the recordings and help to determine, via algorithms, the narratives the recordings tell; the importance of the human and ethical alliance created between the interlocutors who ask and the recordings that respond; and, lastly, the significance of these recordings to the survivors themselves. In order to conduct this research, the author conducted interviews and consulted first-hand accounts from the creators of these survivor recordings, the museum staff who have introduced visitors to the recordings, and the survivors themselves offered in news stories, publicity announcements, conference proceedings, and journal articles.

Keywords: Holocaust · Survivors · Interactive video biography or recording · Holograms · Witnessing alliances · Digital humanities

1 The Holocaust and Technology: Here There Are Moments of Pause

Coupling the word *Holocaust* with the words *emerging technologies* is, initially, unsettling. Were it not for the advent of technology – the rail system that traversed all of Europe – millions would not have been brought to the ghettos and the camps. By the 1930s the rail system was 100 years old and well established throughout the continent. One of the greatest innovations of all time, it was the rail system, as Raul Hilberg argued, in "German Railroads/Jewish Souls," that made the Shoah possible [1]. To clarify, were it not for the technology that had honed and perfected the railroads, it

© Springer Nature Switzerland AG 2021
M. Shehade and T. Stylianou-Lambert (Eds.): RISE IMET 2021, CCIS 1432, pp. 217–231, 2021.
https://doi.org/10.1007/978-3-030-83647-4_15

would not have been possible to ensure the deaths of so many so efficiently. It also should be noted, this very same technology made it possible for office personnel and rail workers to divorce themselves from culpability. They believed the bureaucracy that surrounded their work and their fragmented involvement with the cattle cars themselves removed them, literally and figuratively, from responsibility and wrongdoing. During the Third Reich, the *Reichsbahn* employed over one million workers [1]. Any number of those employees could have unperturbedly claimed: "I am just a bureaucrat who signs papers and thus I am not ultimately responsible"; "I am just a cog in the machine; if I don't do this work, someone else will"; "My leaving won't change anything and thus I should just continue to do my job."

Coupling the words *Holocaust survivor* with *hologram* also is, initially, daunting. One's initial associations with holograms may evoke the worlds of science fiction and entertainment. For example, the "holograms" of *Star Trek* voyagers and of Princess Leia in *Star Wars* as well as the performances (using Pepper's Ghost technique) of celebrities who have died, such as Tupac and Michael Jackson, come to mind. As a result, creating a hologram of Holocaust survivors, at first, sounds as if one were trivializing both the Holocaust and the survivors. Heather Maio-Smith, CEO of StoryFile, who first pitched the idea, noted that people voiced their concern that "[y]ou're gonna Disney-fy the Holocaust" [2]. Stephen Smith, Executive Director of the Shoah Foundation, also confirmed that they initially encountered skepticism about this project: "We had a lot of pushback" [2]; that said, he discovered that "[e]veryone had questions except for one group of people, the survivors themselves, who said, 'Where do I sign up? I would like to participate in the project'" [2].

Thus, it isn't surprising that when speaking of emerging technologies and the transformation of Holocaust education, Holocaust Museums, and Holocaust Heritage Sites, there should be a moment of pause. However, ultimately, this pause is countered by the recognition that, while technology may fragment and dehumanize us, in Holocaust education and in Holocaust museums, today, emerging technologies facilitate visitors' knowledge of the Shoah. Museum visitors are able to participate in the vital act of bearing witness, now and into the future, because well-designed technologies – such as interactive digital recordings ("holograms") – augment visitors' abilities to become active, engaged witnesses to the personal, lived histories of survivors. In large part, that engagement comes from the fact that the visitors/interlocutors are able to direct their inquiry into the Holocaust by asking the video recording the questions they most want answered. In the process, visitors create an alliance with the survivors' individual biographical recordings.

In order to conduct this research, the author conducted interviews and consulted first-hand accounts from the creators of these survivor recordings, the museum staff who have introduced visitors to the recordings, and the survivors themselves offered in news stories, publicity announcements, conference proceedings, and journal articles. The analysis conducted and conclusions reached in this paper are guided by the research question: What are the ethical concerns related to the development of this technology and the relationships it engenders? To that end, this paper interrogates the role played by the visitors who engage with the recordings and help to determine, via algorithms, the narratives the recordings are prompted to tell; the importance of the human and ethical alliance created between the interlocutors who ask and the recordings that respond; and, lastly, the significance of these recordings to the survivors themselves.

2   Holograms?: Enabling the Future of Interacting with Holocaust Survivors

In recent newspaper articles and television programs, the Holocaust survivor recordings are referred to by a number of names: holograms, avatars, virtual recordings, personas, AI recordings, live recordings, virtual humans, interactive recordings [See: 2–13]. Stephen Smith argues: "[w]ords such as 'hologram' and 'avatar' fail to accurately describe Dimensions in Testimony. We avoid using these terms because to date the technology to display a hologram does not exist, and 'avatar' implies that the image is animated or is somehow unreal. *These are live recordings of living witnesses giving authentic answers*" [emphasis added; 14]. That said, while the term, hologram, may not apply now, during the process of filming survivors' responses to 1000 questions, the interviewees' recordings were "future proofed" [10] awaiting the day when their 2D digital projections can be adapted to 3D technology. As Kia Hays, the Program Manager for Immersive Innovations at the USC Shoah Foundation, explains, the future-proofing refers to volumetric capture. "We film most interviews in 360 degrees so that they are compatible with future display methods" [15], and, thus, one day these survivor recordings will become fully dimensional, interactive holograms. Currently, however, in their display within museum settings, the "virtual" survivors appear as 2D videos, on life-size computer monitors.

In their initial efforts to study interactions between visitors and recordings, the Shoah Foundation team discovered someone needed to demonstrate for visitors how to interact with the recordings. For example, the Illinois Holocaust Museum and Education Center (IHME/Illionis), the first museum to pilot a survivor recording in 2015, relied on docent-led interactions between visitors and the recordings. When testing out the first survivor recording – that of Pinchas Gutter – at the United States Holocaust Memorial Museum (USHMM) in 2016, "the Museum originally imagined the interaction as a stand-alone experience" [6]. However, during this pilot phase visitors often revealed they did not know how to engage with the life-size recording. As a result, "eventually the staff began to have a member of staff (paid or volunteer) in the space" [6]. The staff members would then model how to engage in conversation with Pinchas by "asking things they knew would have an interesting response: 'Tell a joke.' or 'Do you know any songs?'" [6]. As these initial interactions reveal, initially, visitors turned to a facilitator in order to engage with the video recordings.

With some modifications, however, and given the fact that a number of visitors were familiar with interactive platforms such as Skype and Facetime, over time, the installations of the survivor recordings felt familiar to many visitors. In 2016, Elissa Frankle argued, where the 2D technology is right now is exactly where it should be:

A number of people who came to the space where we displayed the system arrived in search of the "Holocaust survivor hologram." Which it wasn't: we displayed Pinchas on a 70" 2D flat monitor. Fortunately, *not* having a hologram is exactly the right technology right now. Today, the ubiquity of talking on Skype or Facetime means that the idea of asking questions of a face displayed on a flat screen, and having them answered in real time, is pretty natural for a number of our visitors [5].

This familiarity with the technology

meant that the technology faded into the background: rather than focusing on "whoa, this technology is so cool and futuristic!" our visitors were able to focus on learning from Pinchas' testimony. As 3D and hologram technology become more widely used, displaying New Dimensions in Testimony in the technological medium of the day will keep it feeling fresh, but until then, meeting our participants exactly where they are, with technology they know, is the perfect place to be [5].

Today, visitors may experience the recording in a stand-alone setting. That is to say, at some museum sites, the visitor walks up to a computer monitor and initiates a conversation with the recording. At other sites, visitors encounter the recording in a theatre along with other visitors and engage with the recording through a moderated experience. For example, at the Illinois Holocaust Museum and Education Center (IHMEC/Illinois), "[b]efore interacting with one of the survivors' holograms, there's a five-to-seven-minute video of that person relating their experience of survival through the Holocaust" [3]. The hologram then emerges from the film and interacts, as a hologram, with the visitors. Leaning forward, the survivor recording informs visitors: "But I have so much more to tell you. Now I'd like you to ask me questions." At this point, Shoshana Buchholz-Miller, Vice President of Education and Exhibitions at Illinois notes

there's usually an audible gasp when the survivor – the hologram appears. And then the first person asks a question, and the recording answers. And everyone seems to relax a little. And they're asking the questions. What did you feel like? What happened to your family? And I think the use of the word "you" is so important because they really think they're talking to this person. And the technology falls away, and it's about the story. And that's really what we want [11].

It is worth noting, here, that while Buchholz-Miller references the "first person" to ask a question, often in these group settings, "the docent will demonstrate a conversation with the survivor, and relay questions from the audience" [9].

Thus, the interaction between visitor and the virtual recording differs depending on how the survivor recording is housed. For example, if the recording is exhibited in such way that visitors approach the virtual survivor individually, on their own, then the experience is personalized in that audience members are able to ask their own, individual, questions. In this case, the visitor/interlocutor is directing the conversation and thus is empowered in terms of negotiating her/his/their own process. In their study of visitor interactions with Pichas Gutter's recording at USHMM, Bethany Lycan and Ron Artstein found that the visitors' interactions with the Gutter's recording were more interpersonal in nature. They observed that "[v]isitors introduce themselves (e.g., *My name is Sheila; I have three granddaughters with me*), apologize conversationally (*I'm so sorry to inter-rupt you*), and react emotionally to stories by the survivor (*I'm so sorry to hear that*)" [9]. In these one-on-one encounters, when visitors actually engage with Pinchas' recording, they become active participants in the story he tells because they not only listen to his narrative, they also personally respond to what they hear. And, given that they ask the questions, ultimately, they direct what parts of his story they want to hear.

Lycan and Artstein found that docents who were more familiar with conversing with the recording of Gutter, such as those in Illinois, "tailor their utterances to elicit survivor stories they know and like" [9]. Thus, in a theatre setting, unless they are able to offer a question they would like to ask, visitors may not be afforded the opportunity to feel they have entered into conversation with the recording on a personal level. As museums are able to observe visitor interactions, they may discover there need to be alterations in terms of how visitors encounter the survivor's recording. For example, it might be worthwhile to locate the recordings both in theatres where groups can gather and also in more personal spaces that invite one-on-one conversations. In addition, given our new fluency with interacting in multiple video conferencing/communication venues, employing the icons with which we now are so familiar – e.g., turning on the microphone by pressing Mute/Unmute under the microphone symbol – might aid in prompting individuals to converse with greater ease with the 2D recording.

Depending on the location, the recordings also, to some degree, may have been/may be personalized by housing specific live recordings that honour survivors who live/lived locally. The Illinois Holocaust Museum and Education Center (IHMEC) has hologram "recordings that kind of give the breadth of different survivor experiences," and "we have seven *survivors from the Chicagoland area* that tell their stories and answer questions" [emphasis added; 11].

On the other hand, the Los Angeles Museum of the Holocaust (LAMOTH) houses one recording – that of Renée Firestone. Firestone, who immigrated to the United States in 1948, settled in Los Angeles, CA where she worked as a fashion designer. For many years, Renée "did not speak about her experiences during the Holocaust; [s]he decided to start sharing her testimony after a Jewish cemetery and synagogue in the area were vandalized with swastikas" [16]. Now she is one of the thirty survivors who has been immortalized in this interactive witnessing project.

The significance of these testimonial interactions is not solely dependent on whether or not one encounters a survivor recording one-on-one or in a gallery, or whether or not the recording is someone who is/was local, it is the quality of the recording's ability to both answer a given question and to emote that determines how successful the interaction is. That is to say, while visitors note how well the recording responds, they also become acutely aware of the survivors' body language. They take note of their personal gestures and, of course, their facial expressions. For instance, they watch their mouths as they prepare to speak – is a smile forming, are their lips pursed, does the lower limp tremble? Each physical movement offers a clue into the recording's feelings about what they are going to say.

For example, the waiting stance of the survivor recording of Pinchas Gutter is revealing. He holds out both hands to us, beseeching us to join him. Seated in a red chair, looking directly at us, his posture is that of a storyteller. In his talk, "The Virtual Holocaust Survivor as Embodied Archive," Noah Shenker discussed his study of the pilot project with the Gutter recording at USHMM; he noted that it was the eye contact with Pinchas that kept drawing him into the ongoing conversations with the recording [12]. Stephen Smith credits Heather Maio-Smith for ensuring there is constant eye contact. As a result of her urging, the interviews are filmed in such a way that the survivor constantly is looking into the interviewer's face and is always aware "there is a human being on the other side of the lens" [14]. New Dimensions in Testimony should be credited for understanding how important it is that Pinchas appears inviting. In his waiting stance, he invites us to ask him questions; as he sits there, his eyes blinking, his mouthed pursed, almost in a smile, patient and yet attentive, he calls for us to interact with him.

Finally, it is worthwhile to revisit Frankle's claim, voiced in 2016, regarding visitors' familiarity with two-way video calls. Visitors' familiarity with video calls and, now video conferencing, carries even greater weight today in our "virtual world" during COVID-19. In fact, the everyday-ness of our 2D interactions may cause visitors who engage with these recordings to think they actually are engaged in the present time in a "Zoom interaction" with a living survivor. Given that technology now mediates most of our daily "face-to-face" interactions, technology need not fade "into the background." Visitors today no longer may be predisposed to recognize that they are listening to a pre-recorded virtual conversation with a survivor. Instead, they may need to be dissuaded from believing they are in a virtual, meeting, in real time, with a Holocaust survivor.

3   The Role of Interaction and Conversation: What Questions Will Be Asked and Answered?

Michael Haley Goldman, Director of Future Projects, at the United States Holocaust Memorial Museum (USHMM), explains that the interaction with these recordings was created by the Institute of Creative Technology (ICT), at the University of Southern California, using an algorithm-based technique for what the ICT staff call "Virtual Human" projects. These Virtual Humans were "developed with the military to create life-like interactions with pre-recorded, scripted dialogue. In general, the system takes the natural language questions from the audience and statistically matches that question with a response that is most likely to be a response related to the question" [6]. It also is important to note that while ICT should be credited, "[t]he project [initially] was envisioned by Heather Maio[-Smith]," who "specializes in exhibition design and interactive storytelling" [4].

From the outset, Goldman observes, "[t]here is a lot of human involvement in building this system – starting with the scripted answers themselves which are created to answer what the team expects to be the most common questions for the system. Then, there is a lot of human tweaking of the results to better fit the answers to the questions as understood by a human" [6]. During his observation of a young woman interacting with Pinchas Gutter, during the pilot study at USHMM, Goldman noted that the young woman kept reframing her question; she was doing so because the answer she received from Pinchas seemed to confound or surprise her. In fact, in "The Virtual Holocaust Survivor as Embodied Archive," Dan Leopard noted that he was unable to find the "right vocal pattern" to make Pinchas understand any of the questions he asked of the interactive recording [18]. In addition, regarding Pinchas Gutter's recording, Stephen Smith explains, he "does *not yet* have the ability to track the conversation," noting that this makes follow-up questions challenging [10]. As Smith clarifies, "[i]f you ask about 'them' – he doesn't necessarily know which 'them' it is" [18].

Nonetheless, given that the technology constantly is being updated, over time, the "fluency" of the virtual survivor will become more advanced; that is to say, the virtual human will be quicker to answer visitor questions and more accurate in its response. Human intervention ensures this fluency. All of the interactions with the survivor recordings are recorded and reviewed. Trained staff at the USC Shoah Foundation "periodically review the system logs to make sure the most appropriate answer was chosen for each question. When necessary, staff manually link to the more appropriate response" [19].

Moreover, recently, due to closing both Holocaust museums and schools as a result of the pandemic, IWitness and Dimensions in Testimony teamed up to create other opportunities for visitors to meet the survivor recordings. In November 2020, the USC Shoah Foundation launched an online teaching tool that enables students and educators to ask questions – from their own homes – that prompt real-time recorded responses from Pinchas Gutter. In the course of a one-hour activity, using their computers, students are introduced to Pinchas' interactive biography. Students also "learn the techniques for having a conversation with a survivor and how to construct questions appropriately to elicit personal, historical, and universal thematic responses. By the end of this activity, students choose a creative expression to share what they have learned from Pinchas Gutter" [20]. Similar to the encounter students would have (or would have had) with Pinchas in a museum setting, middle- and high-school students who engage with 83-year-old Pinchas "experience a learning environment in which he answers questions as if he was in the room with them. The technology uses new and emerging filming and display technologies, coupled with advanced natural language processing, to create the perception Pinchas is responding to questions conversationally with answers that are authentic and spontaneous" [20].

Furthermore, this cooperation between IWitness and Dimensions in Testimony will be able to make more recordings available to the public. According to Stephen Smith, given that each biography is "not linked to a platform, or a particular software or a particular gadget. It's going to emerge through all sorts of different ways as technology develops. What it means is, whether in a museum, or in an institution of learning, or at home, you're going to be able to interact with Holocaust survivors for generations to come" [20]. In responding to international exigencies related to the closing of museums world-wide due to the Coronavirus-19 pandemic, cooperations like the one between IWitness and Dimensions in Testimony, have made interacting with Holocaust history more interpersonal and more accessible, especially given that individuals can engage the Holocaust from the portals of their own computers. As a result, today, "[t]eaching with testimony is now more immediate and effective than ever before" [21].

For Stephen Smith, it is the interpersonal interactivity – the conversation between the visitor and the recording – that makes the interaction successful. As he explains, "It's about you. It's about what you want to know.... And that is where the deepest learning takes place" [14].

When I first spoke about this enterprise among colleagues who are educators, all of us wondered about visitors – especially teenagers – becoming invested in "gaming" the recording. We were concerned the recording would be treated as a game that could be manipulated, cheated, even broken. In my interview with Kia Hays, she noted that "[a]fter six years of various pilots and exhibits, we do not have many instances of anyone 'gaming' the system or being inappropriate" [15]. During a conference presentation when an audience member raised this very concern, Stephen Smith was both humorous and adamant in his answer to the audience member. He noted that in reviewing all of the interactions with the recordings, there was no evidence of fifteen year olds fooling around with the technology; he added that the ones the reviewers actually needed to watch out for were "Holocaust historians and techies" [22].

In addition, as a result of their study of individuals interacting with the recordings, analysts noted that some "audiences feel even more comfortable asking their questions to the hologram because they're not worried that they're going to hurt somebody's feelings or make them upset" [23]. They feel free to ask questions that might appear naïve or too sensitive. Moreover, Heather Maio-Smith believes that interacting with these recordings as holograms will be "somewhat normal in a hundred years time…; it won't seem so unnatural" because when the audience members are engaged in an interactive conversation they 'will lose sight that the person is not actually there'" [18].

Furthermore, as Martha Stroud, PhD, Associate Director and Senior Research officer, USC Shoah Foundation Center for Advanced Genocide Research, noted future research will be fueled by essential questions, such as,

In what ways might people feel inhibited or emboldened by the fact that they are interacting with a recording instead of a survivor sitting in front of them? In what ways might people feel inhibited or emboldened by the fact that *they* are asking the questions, as opposed to watching a traditional testimony where the questions are asked by an interviewer? What might people ask or learn in this engagement that they might not in a live interaction or through engaging with traditional testimony? [13]

Stroud observed that in their study of audience-recording interactions, "we have seen how quickly people fall into *normal patterns* of interaction" [emphasis added; 13]. This finding is evidenced in the *60 Minutes* episode between Lesley Stahl and Holocaust survivor, Eva Kor. In her televised interaction with the recording of Kor, Stahl engaged in the following dialogue:

"Hi, Eva. How are you today?" Stahl asked.
"I'm fine, and how are you?" Kor's digital image said back.
"I'm good," Stahl answered.
Stahl said it felt natural to answer Kor's question before posing her own [2].

This exchange also is reminiscent of the observations made by Lycan and Artstein regarding the interpersonal nature of one-on-one interactions with the digital recordings. In these one-on-one exchanges, it is natural to answer a survivor's question before posing one's own question. From that initial courtesy, one might surmise, other civilities and ethical responses may be engendered. In the end, the interaction between digital recording and human being not only will emulate a human interaction, but a human response to that interaction. Eva Kor no longer was living when Lesly Stahl interacted with her; Stahl was well aware of that fact; and yet Stahl interacted with Eva as if they were in an immediate, mutual dialogue with one another.

That said, while invoking normal patterns of conversation may be the desired result in these interactions, there also may be something to be gained from making the unsuccessful communications as well as the technology involved in creating these recordings more apparent. During her week-long interview session, Eva Geiringer Schloss was asked by a member of the interviewing team to repeat the following phrases:

- "Why don't you ask me a question about Auschwitz?";
- "I'm actually a recording, so I can't answer that question"; and
- "Maybe you should try to reboot." [18]

The interview team had pre-determined that each phrase would be useful to include in Schloss's repository of possible responses. Each pre-packaged response is revealing. The first response is meant both to incite the interlocutor's interest and, possibly, to give the interlocutor permission to ask a question that might be painful for the survivor to answer. The second response appears to be a ready-phrase for someone who might want to game the system (e.g., by asking, "Who won the Superbowl?"). The final phrase is meant to be helpful should the visitor encounter difficulties during the interaction. However, during her interview process, this final rote phrase – "Maybe you should try to reboot" – produced comical results because Schloss wasn't familiar with the computer term and kept replying, questioningly, "rebook?," as if she were contemplating changing a flight date. I found her confusion endearingly human. I don't imagine this quizzical response will come up in the queue of her voice-recognition-cued answers. It might be a point to consider. In all human interactions, there are moments of confusion and misdirection. Perhaps, rather than editing out those moments that cause confusion, by constantly perfecting the algorithm, it would be meaningful to keep some of these incongruous, discordant moments in the interactive space.

This algorithm of matching response to question not only might edit out the more human and unanticipated, it also may be cause for consternation. In the end, if frequency determines knowledge, as Noah Shenker queried, in their interactions with these recordings, in the end, will the user structure the knowledge that will be known? [12].

That is to say, will the most popular questions generate the most answers from the recording? The answer is, of course, yes. That said, it is important to note that often survivors themselves have curated their stories. Prior to working with Dimensions in Testimony in order to record their interviews, they already recognize which points in their personal narratives engender a response in audience members and, thus, they curate their narratives accordingly.

For example, Pinchas knows how important it is to explain what happened to his twin sister upon the family's arrival at Majdanek. He recalls this moment on the multiple occasions that he has offered testimony, whether in the film *The Last Goodbye* (2018), or in a recorded testimony for a Holocaust archive, or in daily encounters during an in-person "Q and A "with a Holocaust survivor. In all of these encounters, he remembers that his sister's first response, upon arrival at the concentration camp, was to find her mother and join her. In his various recollections of this moment, he focuses on the moment of seeing Sabina running, of seeing her long gold braid of hair as she moved into the distance, of seeing her finding their mother and hugging her. In his various recollections of this moment, he also pointedly and poignantly informs his audience members, this was the last time he saw either his sister or his mother.

And here we return to the question Noah Shenker asked: will the "user" of the recording structure the knowledge that is known about survivors of the Holocaust by virtue of determining what questions will be asked, and, thus, which answers will be given? [12]. For Holocaust scholars, survivor testimony serves as a primary source of knowledge about the Shoah. Working with an unedited oral history allows us to bear witness to an intimate effort. A solemn and sympathetic connection, based on trust and empathy, is established between the survivors who offer their stories and the interviewers who collect them. Furthermore, it is clear that those who interview Holocaust survivors not only take care in terms of how they craft specific questions, but also in terms of how they participate as supportive listeners. They know they are affirming the survivor's history in the very act of collecting the survivor's narrative. At their best, these oral history interviews are places of active listening and *active believing*. In the case of asking questions of a recording, however, the interlocutor isn't necessarily made aware of how delicate and complex collecting an oral history may be.

That said, returning to Lesley Stahl's interaction with a recording of Eva Kor, a recording of a survivor Stahl knew recently had passed away, is edifying. Stahl's response to Kor emulated a living human interaction. According to Martha Stroud, "[w]hen people are directing the questions themselves, they often express how shy they feel about asking intrusive or prying questions or diving into the difficult parts of the survivors' biographies, also suggesting *they are practicing an ethics similar to human interactions*" [emphasis added; 13]. Thus, while the visitor-interlocutors may not have have the training of interviewers who formally collect survivors' narratives, the visitor-interlocutors may practice an "ethics of human interactions" that calls upon them to listen sympathetically.

There also are concerns that in this dynamic – dictated in part by algorithms – the responses interlocutors will be overly-determined. Those of us who study oral histories, sometimes find, within an unedited given history, there are

> moments when it isn't always clear what the survivor wants to convey,
> digressions that may appear to be evasions,
> inconsistencies in terms of the time frame or point of view,
> memories that are perplexing rather than revelatory,
> narrative "jumps" that override the survivor's personal moments of cognition/recognition,
> interruptions from the interviewer or the videographer.

For the listener/researcher each of these unedited moments become places of contemplation and interrogation.

While the raw data of archived/daily recorded interviews always is vital to preserve and analyze, as an entry-point into Holocaust education, these interactive survivor recordings offer students and members of the general public an instructive and appealing place to engage with survivors. These personal and immediate interactions encourage the creation of a testimonial alliance between the visitor and the recording. Creating this type of alliance, potentially fosters a desire to learn more through encounters with other survivor testimony – testimony such as that offered in everything from unedited oral histories to published memoirs, from invited talks with students to interviews with journalists.

4   The Survivors' Experience of Creating These Recordings: "And, by Gosh, I Give the Answer"

As of November 2020, thirty interviews have been conducted with survivors, "in seven different languages (English, German, Hebrew, Mandarin, Russian, Spanish, and Swedish)" [15]. In the initial set of interviews, the theatre in Los Angeles employed 360-degree video, over 100 cameras, and cost 2.5 million dollars. In subsequent years, "they've shrunk the set-up required, so they can take a mobile rig on the road to record survivors close to where they live" [2]. Whether interviewed in Los Angeles or close to where they live, each interview requires a great deal of commitment on the part of the survivor. First off, there is a time commitment. For example, Aaron Elster recalls spending "a grueling week of interviews, [during] which he wore the same clothes every day and sat still in a chair for hours at a time under bright lights and cameras, answering difficult questions" [4]. Kia Hays confirms Elster's observation. She notes that when choosing among survivors to participate in this effort, "of the utmost importance to us is how comfortable the interviewee feels sitting for the interview and answering hundreds of questions over multiple days" [15].

In addition to a time commitment, as one would imagine, there is an emotional commitment. The survivors who were recorded clarify that engaging in a prolonged interview about the persecution and torment one both witnessed and experienced – both on a daily basis and over years – is harrowing and re-traumatizing. And yet, as Aaron Elster explains: "Why would you want to stand in front of hundreds of guests and open up your heart and bleed in front of them? Because it's important. This will exist longer than we will" [3]. While Elster was clear about his conviction in sharing his story, he also noted that while watching his introductory video, post-production, he wanted to cry. As he explains, the video recreated, for him, the reality of the event:

> I had a little sister, Sarah, who loved me so much. I created this terrible image of how she died, and that causes me such pain. Do you have any idea how long it takes to die in a gas chamber? It takes 15 to 20 min before your life is choked out. Think about it. A 6-year-old little girl, people climbing on top of her in order to reach out for any fresh air that still exists in the room. They lose control of all their bodily functions and they die in agony. This is what you carry with you. It's not a story. It's reality [3].

Sam Harris also found the interview experience lengthy and painful:

> They gave us a rest each hour. I had a T-shirt. I had to change my T-shirt. It was always wet. You see, to answer a question, I always put myself in the position to where the answer was, like watching somebody being hanged. And I'm really there watching it. And I see it. And I describe it. This goes on for five, six hours a day. And a lot of the questions are very intrusive [11].

Not only did Harris speak about witnessing someone being hanged, he confided: "I talk about my parents being killed and the crematorium, people being shot. You know, I was just a child, so when Hitler came to my town in Deblin, Poland, which [was in] the war zone, I was 4 years old. It's painful. And you begin to resent it" [11]. In spite of feeling resentful, Harris recalls feeling a sense of conviction similar to that of Elster, declaring that "what saves you is you do it for a purpose. You do it so that 50 years from now, a hundred years from now, people can look you in the face, ask a question. And by gosh, I give the answer" [11]. Renée Firestone echoes Harris' claim for engaging in this recording process: "It was very difficult, but the outcome is rewarding," she said. "I think it's amazing that this will be able to be seen a hundred years from now. That's why I'm doing it" [24].

While these survivors recognize the importance of the longevity of the digital recording, they also note that we cannot just invoke the watchword "never again." As Aaron Elster observes: "We're still killing one another" [3]. Eva Schloss was prompted to participate due to the current political climate. "Everybody said never again; after Auschwitz we have learned our lesson"; however, with sadness, she noted, "it looks bad again in the world" [18]. Thus, these recordings are not an assurance or a panacea.

Nonetheless, these survivors understand there is a pedagogical value in this effort given that these recordings represent a new platform for engaging the public. And they have hope for that engagement: "a whole new world of young people and adults will understand what people are capable of doing to one another, and that it just takes a little bit of goodness from each person to help change the world for the better" [3].

In response to the question – What do you want us to learn from your story? – the interactive-recording of Pinchas Gutter makes an eloquent appeal to his audience members to remember his story and to make the world a better place. With the kindly look of a grandfather, he intones:

> What I would like you to do now that you're actually part of me because I've handed over part of me to you. I've shared my life with you. I would like you, number one, to remember it. I'd like you to treasure it, but to use it as a vehicle to teach others to make the world a better place. And I would like you to start this kind of way of telling my story, trying to be tolerant, trying to teach other people acceptance of others, and change the world in this particular way [25].

In telling their stories, the survivors hope the testimonial alliance they create with their listeners not only will become a vehicle to teach others, but they will become a vehicle for change.

Another vital component of this effort is to establish that the history of the Shoah is deeply connected to each individual's life story. These recordings ensure that none of these thirty individuals will become one of a multitude, an anonymous individual among the six million who died. As Elster queried: "When we're gone, what happens next? Do we become one sentence in the history of World War II? They killed Jews and that's it?" [3]. Survivors who engage in this project recognize they have become part of the historical record by preserving historical and personal memory through a new interactive form of storytelling. Dimensions in Testimony, Elster notes, "have created something that's going to live on much after we're gone" [4].

Most importantly, perhaps, while the survivors achieve a type of immortality, Aaron Elster and Sam Harris point to one of the most pressing desires of those who survived: to speak on behalf of those who did not. There isn't only immortality; there is posterity – speaking to the generations who will come on behalf of those who were not able to do so. They want their "families to be remembered" [23]. Sam Harris poignantly observes, "I feel lucky to be picked to be that witness for the benefit of many of the survivors and those who died" [11]. From engaging with these recordings, we learn, for example, of the sisters of survivors who were murdered. We learn of Aaron's younger sister, Sarah's death. We are asked to contemplate the 15 to 20 min during which she was choking to death while also being crushed as a result of the frantic death struggle as neighbour climbed on top of neighbour, father upon child, in the gas chamber. We learn of Pinchas' twin sister, Sabina, who died in Majdanek along with their mother. From the moment he saw Sabina running towards his mother – her thick, long blonde braid the telling marker that it was her – Pinchas notes, "from that time on, my brain has shut off. Everything that I remember about my sister – I can't remember anything about my sister, and whenever I think of Sabina, my sister, all I remember is the braid" [25].

5   The Conclusion: "I've Handed Over Part of Me to You"

While Schloss, and other survivors involved in this project, may have been unfamiliar with the phrase "reboot," they understood that emerging technologies ensure that history lives. They trusted that their stories, and the stories of their dead, would live on. And, in living on that their stories not only will inspire others to change the world for the better, they also will ensure that Sarah, Sabina, and so many more of those who were murdered, are remembered as well.

Finally, it is important to note that in creating these recordings, neither the survivors or their stories are rehabilitated or improved upon. For example, "[d]uring the post-production phase, USC Shoah Foundation takes care to not edit, alter, manipulate, or censor any response the interviewee gave. The Dimensions in Testimony post-production methodology has been entirely created to preserve the integrity of the interviewee's voice, a promise made to the interviewees and their families" [19]. As a point of contrast, in 2020, the Anne Frank House released a YouTube series, *Anne Frank Video Diary,* in which both Anne and her story are re-imagined. In this series, Anne is transformed and her story is renovated. Over the course of fifteen episodes, Anne becomes a vlogger telling her story through a video camera. As the Anne Frank House explains: "The strength of the diary is that Anne speaks to you directly and gives you a personal and poignant glimpse into her life. We want to reach this group in the same personal and poignant way through [the] Anne Frank video diary. The video camera takes the place of the diary, yet the approach stays the same: Anne speaks to you directly and invites you into her world and her thoughts" [26]. In this process of retelling, Anne Frank the girl and her diary are transmuted in order to appeal to a new generation of audience members.

In their efforts to ensure that individual survivors' stories live on, the Dimensions in Testimony "do not edit, alter, manipulate, or censor" a given response, they also do not transform, renovate, or transmute how the survivors tell their stories. The thirty individuals always tell their stories as they would have during the course of the five days they were interviewed; *the survivors remain who they were during the telling.* Thus, Pinchas Gutter's claim, "I've handed over part of me to you. I've shared my life with you" is both accurate and inspirational.

The integrity of the Dimensions in Testimony's efforts in the design and capture of these interviews as well as their discerning "future-proofing" of the technology are awe-inspiring. As a result of those efforts, the integrity of the survivors themselves is – and will be – maintained and made manifest for generations to come. It is that integrity that will enable future generations to embrace the perceived intimacy, immediacy, and authenticity of these conversations with Holocaust survivors who have long since passed. As a result of their rigorous, ethical, shared efforts, these survivors and Dimensions in Testimony ensure that Holocaust history and individual survivors' crucial life stories will live on to educate and inspire generations to come.

References

1. Hilberg, R.: German railroads/Jewish souls. Society **35**(2), 162–174 (1998)
2. Stahl, L.: Artificial Intelligence is preserving our ability to converse with Holocaust survivors even after they die. 60 Minutes (2020). www.cbsnews.com/news/holocaust-stories-artificial-intelligence-60-minutes-2020-08-30/. Accessed 30 Aug 2020
3. Billock, J.: An exhibit in Illinois allows visitors to talk with holograms of 13 survivors. Smithsonian Mag. (2017). www.smithsonianmag.com/travel/chat-holographic-holocaust-survivor-180967085/. Accessed 23 Mar 2020
4. Braunstein, E.: At this Holocaust museum you can speak with holograms of survivors. The Times of Israel (2018). www.timesofisrael.com/at-this-holocaust-museum-you-can-speak-with-holograms-of-survivors/. Accessed 23 Mar 2020
5. Frankle, E.: A lesson in technology and humanity. USCE Shoah Foundation Institute for Visual History and Education (2016). sfi.usc.edu/news/2016/12/12689-lesson-technology-and-humanity. Accessed 26 Mar 2020
6. Goldman, M.: E-mail interview with author, 30 March 2020
7. Goode, L.: Are holograms the future of how we capture memories? The Verge (2017). www.theverge.com/2017/11/7/16613234/next-level-ar-vr-memories-holograms-8i-actress-shoah-foundation. Accessed 26 Mar 2020
8. Granberry, M.: For Holocaust survivor Max Glauben, the opening of Dallas' New Museum means, "now I have my closure." The Dallas Morning News (2019). www.dallasnews.com/arts-entertainment/visual-arts/2019/09/17/for-holocaust-survivor-max-glauben-the-opening-of-dallas-new-museum-means-now-i-have-my-closure/. Accessed 26 Mar 2020
9. Lycan, B., Artstein, R.: Direct and mediated interaction with a Holocaust survivor. Adv. Soc. Interac. Agents **510**, 161–167 (2019)
10. O'Brien, S.: Shoah Foundation is using technology to preserve Holocaust survivor stories. CNN (2017). money.cnn.com/2017/04/24/technology/shoah-foundation-holocaust-remembrance-day/index.html. Accessed 25 Mar 2020
11. Shapiro, A.: Illinois Holocaust Museum preserves survivors' stories – as holograms. NPR (2017). www.npr.org/transcripts/572068474. Accessed 23 Mar 2020
12. Shenker, N.: The virtual Holocaust survivor as embodied archive. In: International Conference: Digital Approaches to Genocide Studies, University of Southern California, Los Angeles, 23 October 2017
13. Stroud, M.: E-mail interview with author, 21 November 2020
14. Smith, S.: What Is Dimensions in Testimony: A Short Video Introduction to the Technology. sfi.usc.edu/dit. Accessed 25 Mar 2020
15. Hays, K.: E-mail interview with author, 21 November 2020

16. Firestone, R.: USC Shoah Foundation, Dimensions in Testimony. candlesholocaustmuseum. org/file_download/inline/25d72a3f-bb51-4c0c-9c72-ac1ed390e57e. Accessed 23 Sept 2020
17. Leopard, D.: The virtual Holocaust survivor as embodied archive. In: International Conference: Digital Approaches to Genocide Studies, University of Southern California, Los Angeles, 23 October 2017
18. Pardo, D.: Producer and Director. 116 Cameras (2017)
19. Dimensions in Testimony FAQ. sfi.usc.edu/dit/faq. Accessed 23 Nov 2020
20. Grossberg, J.: Initial evaluations (2016). sfi.usc.edu/pressroom/releases/new-dimensions-testimony-proven-be-valuable-educational-tool. Accessed 25 Nov 2020
21. USC Shoah Foundation Offers Dimensions in Testimony to Online Students and Educators in IWitness. USC Shoah Foundation, Dimensions in Testimony. sfi.usc.edu/news/2020/11/29561-usc-shoah-foundation-offers-dimensions-testimony-online-students-and-educators. Accessed 25 Nov 2020
22. Smith, S.: Interactive video biography: literacy, memory, and history in the Digital Age. In: International Conference: Digital Approaches to Genocide Studies, University of Southern California, Los Angeles, 23 October 2017
23. Safo, N.: U.S. debuts first 3-D holograms of Holocaust survivors. The Times of Israel. www. timesofisrael.com/us-museum-debuts-first-3-d-holograms-of-holocaust-survivors/. Accessed 23 Mar 2020 (2017)
24. Renée Firestone records interview for New Dimensions in Testimony. USC Shoah Foundation, Dimensions in Testimony (2015). sfi.usc.edu/news/2015/12/10485-renee-firestone-records-interview-new-dimensions-testimony. Accessed 25 Nov 2020
25. Gutter, P.: A conversation with Pinchas Gutter – Dimensions in Testimony. iwitness.usc. edu/sfi/Activity/DoActivity.aspx?stp=7701599e-0c67-4cd9-9f56-46c9983eda24.   Accessed 29 Nov 2020
26. Anne Frank House. New: Anne Frank Video Diary. www.annefrank.org/en/about-us/news-and-press/news/2020/3/30/new-anne-frank-video-diary/. Accessed 1 May 2020

Participatory Approaches,
Crowdsourcing and New Technologies

Storybase: Towards Cultural Transformation Driven by Design

Violeta Tsenova[(⊠)] [iD]

Newcastle University, Newcastle upon Tyne NE1 7RU, UK
v.tsenova2@newcastle.ac.uk

Abstract. Rising emphasis on the creation of participatory experiences in museum and heritage environments has resulted in the increasing implementation of technological and interactive interventions. For this participation to result in radical transformation of the interaction between audience and institution, there is a need to closely examine the way participatory interventions are designed and created, as well as the culture within which this "making" occurs. In this paper, I reflect on the process of introducing a new interaction and knowledge-generating paradigm within a traditional museum institution. I delve into the story of *Storybase* – an interactive system that explores new ways of "knowing" and "telling" by embracing audience contributions as accepted forms of expertise and incorporates them into the museum's visitors offer. By detailing *Storybase*'s conceptual direction and development, I offer lessons learned from embracing failed ideas within the design process as a means of making interactive cultural experiences polyvocal, dialogical, and an intrinsic part of the visitor experience long-term. Further, I propose that the inherent value of implementing a design cycle, such as the one exemplified by *Storybase*, is not only about the outcome, but rather frames the process itself as "the work" that contributes to institutional transformation.

Keywords: Design driven culture · Interactive design · Storytelling infrastructure · Participatory museum

1 Introduction

Digital design for museums and cultural organisations has undergone exciting developments. Since Bedford [1] declared that the real work of museums is storytelling, the design and museum research communities are witnessing a breadth of imaginative and engaging approaches to the presentation of stories (i.e. [2–5] among others). The notion of the participatory museum [6] emphasised that for participation to take place, museums' approach to storytelling and interactive exhibits requires a power shift – it is both visitors and institutions that are strengthening a common heritage mission. Moreover, adding discourses of polyvocality and plural heritages [7, 8] contributes insights into the multiplicity of heritage experiences which are missing from organisational settings. Brought together, storytelling, participation and plural heritages open up museum narratives and interpretation to communities and audiences and further the shared goal of decolonising museums and knowledges.

M. Shehade and T. Stylianou-Lambert (Eds.): RISE IMET 2021, CCIS 1432, pp. 235–253, 2021.
https://doi.org/10.1007/978-3-030-83647-4_16

Within these discourses, there are limited reports on how digital design interventions are ideated and prototyped, how these interventions nuance internal power-relations, and how interactive designs might contribute to achieving the shared aim of pluralising accepted knowledges. Additionally, many of the deployed interactive experiences are exhibited only temporarily. Indeed, short term interventions offer a safer approach for museums to explore how they might: meet the demands of the experience economy [9], challenge authorised voices [10], and transform themselves into audience-focused institutions. This paper offers another line of inquiry towards the consequences of introducing long-lasting transformative experiences for museum professionals and for the audiences they serve. Alongside established approaches to prevent perpetuating conventional understanding of authority and expertise in historical and object interpretation, a long-term approach to interactive design also calls for careful reflection. This kind of reflection allows design questions to explore how museums might embrace different ways of "knowing" beyond a hierarchical and patriarchal model of expertise. To this end, I offer the account of *Storybase*.

Storybase is an interaction system that embraces audience contributions as accepted forms of expertise and incorporates them into the visitor's museum experience. The *Storybase* design concept was developed within Cooper Hewitt, Smithsonian Design Museum's (henceforth, CH) Interaction Lab. The Lab is an embedded research and design program that focuses broadly on visitor experience across physical, digital, and human interactions. The Lab builds on the legacy of CH's existing interactive system, the Pen, designed around object collection. By accepting polyvocality that extends beyond the collections' record, one of the Lab's primary challenges is to imagine and manifest experiences that contribute to a dialogical museum [11].

Based on three months of ethnographic work, I investigate the process of developing the *Storybase* system as a Research through Design (RtD) [12] case study which illustrates what it means to introduce a new knowledge-generation paradigm in this traditional museum. Prior to telling *Storybase's* story, I begin with a background on storytelling and participation in museums followed by how design thinking has been applied to cultural institutions. My account then covers the influence of CH's existing interactive system on the implementation of new design approaches, the constraints hindering *Storybase's* development, and the need to facilitate a cultural shift which accepts the design process as a flexible site where ideas are allowed to fail. In the second half of this paper, I contribute a discussion on how imperfect designs can be used to create space for different epistemologies to co-exist in the museum space whilst maintaining criticality. I provide three lessons learned related to: 1) interactions towards polyphony; 2) restructuring interpretation; and 3) embracing design imperfection. As *Storybase* was conceived and developed within an industry context, I offer the lessons learned not because they are unprecedented but as check points when making interactive cultural experiences polyvocal, dialogical, and an intrinsic part of the visitor experience long-term.

2   Background

2.1   Storytelling and Participation

Storytelling is at the heart of contemporary museums' outlook on interpretation. Whereas storytelling was originally present implicitly, constitutive of an object's historical context and only accessible to expert interpretation, storytelling is now focused on presenting multiple points of view [13]. Yet much of storytelling design examples are limited in their approach to opening the interpretation experience to new ways of knowing and embracing different types of expertise. Interactions and designs of stories are largely tailored to the needs of heritage professionals and curators and offer a predetermined storyline, even when personalisation is factored in [14]. Ioannidis et al. [13] discuss opportunities for museums to engage with interactive technologies to facilitate a relation of 'one object – many stories', and introduce digital storytelling in cultural organisations. Roussou et al. [15] build on digital storytelling by emphasising the collaborative dimension of creating stories for heritage audiences. To this end, Vayanou et al. [16] developed a tool to support story authors (defined as curators, museum staff, script writers) to write interpretation around pre-selected museum themes. Petrelli [17] further reflects on smart objects' capacity to create interactive storytelling experiences in spaces with strong historical identity, supporting curators in piecing opposing perspective and prevalent themes together.

These examples exist in a context where the authority of museum institutions is rarely challenged by audiences. According to the American Association of Museums, museums are perceived as more trustworthy institutions in comparison to papers, nonprofit researchers, the U.S. government, and academic researchers [18]. Some interactive storylines have, however, questioned the trust people place in cultural institutions. *Traces* is one example of a guided audio exploration which asks participants to look at the environment in different ways, perform certain activities and engage with their presence at the space [10, 19]. *I Swear to Tell the Truth* similarly utilises voice narration to challenge visitors' perception and unsettle museums' truth claims [10].

Indeed, other existing projects address divergent publics' contribution to interpretation ranging from crowdsourcing [20, 21] to education [22] to accessibility [23, 24]. My focus here is on offering audiences' interpretations as meaningful aspects of other visitors' experiences. Ferris et al. [25] give visitors the opportunity to speculate and audio-record their interpretations of four "mystery" objects. These speculations are then shared with other visitors on site. Personalised interpretation is offered by the GIFT app [26], which leverages on the generative potential of combining the contexts of gifting and museum visits. An experience is created by a museum visitor who audio records their impressions of three museum objects and shares the interpretation to a predetermined gift-receiver [26]. Using text as interaction, Bødker [27] presents an interactive system that allows visitors, artists, curators, and staff to write and rewrite texts on digital panels. The system makes the interpretative role of visitors explicit whilst supporting participation in collaboratively interpreting artworks [27, 28], and offers a dialogue between heterogenous groups granted permission to take part in the process of cultural production.

Such dialogic possibilities of putting curators, visitors, and artists in continuous negotiation of their selves and others have been researched through temporary exhibitions and installations. The possibilities and challenges have not been discussed as part of designing larger interpretative storytelling systems in a cultural organisation. This paper offers one such account that uses RtD [12] methodology to shift the perspective from "the next digital tool" to the design process as a site to investigate museum and interpretation practices with the aim to create a more dialogical museum [11, 29] – one where different voices and perspectives are not presented as distinctly "othered" but on an equal plane [29]. I respond to calls for methodological shifts in heritage that rethink heritage practices in the current, and future, digital context rather than forecasting trends for digital tools [30]. With this I contribute a design-based perspective to discussions on more horizontal practices of heritage making and knowledge structures.

2.2 Design Thinking

Over the past decade, as design thinking has become ever more pervasive in the worlds of business and technology, there has been a dramatic increase in its adoption in museums. By definition, design thinking is a human-centred iterative process which seeks to understand a user or a situation, challenge assumptions, and redefine problems whilst devising strategies and solutions that may not be initially apparent [31]. Inherently solution-based, design thinking comprises five non-linear stages: empathise, define, ideate, prototype, and test. When approached iteratively, the five stages of design thinking support continuous results assessment, questioning of assumptions, and improving understanding. Because investing in digital experiences can be high-risk for commonly underfunded cultural organisations, it is no surprise that a process like design thinking can offer an important institutional safety net in the process of digital adoption based on its primary objective of surfacing and understanding audience desires through ongoing research, prototyping and evaluation.

Design thinking is praised for delivering tangible outcomes whilst challenging ingrained patters of thinking. Silvers et al. [32] adopt design thinking to 'tackle the big challenge' of engaging museum visitors. The authors reflect on a collaborative design process and the opportunity of 'scrappy' looking prototypes to shift museum professionals' perspective to a design concept rather than a design product [33]. Yet the impetus of doing design thinking is keeping pace, providing 'experiences, services, and products' which audiences are demanding from cultural institutions. In contrast, I investigate how the design-driven process drives a cultural shift towards accepting visitors' knowledge as generative of meaningful interpretations. This stems from an increased research commitment to a dialogical museum model being situated at the intersection of cultures, individuals, and experiences [29], and acknowledging that museums have adopted participatory rhetoric yet remain rooted in traditional knowledge structures [34].

Achieving audience and institutional transformation then requires looking beyond discussions on finalised design concepts and focusing on long-term processes instead. Investigating design process aimed at long-term digital intervention allows researchers and museum professionals to reflect on how different design activities engage museum staff and audiences in nuanced forms of meaning-making that provoke engagement with lived experiences different from one's own.

Nonetheless, museum professionals are not accustomed to working in a design paradigm where the process itself *is the work*. As Maris et al. [35] observe, the design thinking process used in museums is predominantly a top-down, linear approach with content decided on by curators and other experts. Recent publications such as *Systems Thinking in Museums* [36] assert the need for a paradigm-shift to "systems thinking" as an iterative practice better suited to create more vibrant museum institutions, grounded in self-reflective, outward-looking activities focused on achieving intentions rather than products [37]. French [38] turns to service design paradigms and cautions against adopting technology in cultural institutions as a product. If technology is seen as a product, the museum has control over how it is described and designed, how it functions and what purpose it serves [38]. French highlights the subtle change which occurs when we reimagine the technology as an experience – it invites visitors to enter a dialogue where both museums and visitors are in a dynamically negotiated space. Correspondingly, MacLeod et al. [39] emphasise the importance of research and design-led methods of 'inviting the process to happen'. The authors aim to translate design and design thinking into a systemic way of knowing that is also capable of generating new knowledge. This generative approach parallels the Interaction Lab's design philosophy.

Building on such research, my work with the Lab seeks to negotiate the distinction between product-driven design research and research and analysis of actual museum-making that facilitates cultural shifts. Thus, in this paper, I investigate what "trusting the design process" entails in a museum context. I then interpret this process by sharing lessons learned from applying design thinking as a process-centred rather than solution-focused approach. By engaging with iterative design activities my intention is to discover, exemplify and clarify the importance and effects of design artefacts' coming-into-being process, rather than solely privileging the artefacts themselves.

3   Research Context

This study forms an RtD [12, 40] inquiry into how a design-driven cultural shift within a museum institution might be facilitated. I worked alongside industry professionals with a goal of addressing a museum's interaction design challenges related to critical heritage themes of polyvocality and dialogue [11], plural heritages [41], and interpretation. My fieldwork took place over three months during which I was embedded as a member of the Interaction Lab. I worked closely with the Lab director in developing the *Storybase* system alongside my work investigating the museum's existing interactive experience. Informed by design ethnography [42] methods, I collected data through extensive observations of the museum's day-to-day operations, attending meetings, conducting semi-structured interviews, and design activities outlined below. Notes were collected, themed [43] and supplemented by writing analytic memos and carrying out documentation of the design process. The following is my analytical account. I begin by outlining the design and uptake of the current interactive experience – the Pen – and how it affects the design goals and processes for any new digital interventions. I then give background context on the Lab and its activities before outlining *Storybase*'s design development.

3.1 Background: Cooper Hewitt, Smithsonian Design Museum

CH is devoted to the collection and programming of historical and contemporary design. Housed in a Georgian style mansion, the museum underwent a substantial renovation in the early 2010s that offered significantly expanded gallery spaces, revised layout of the floors as well as a slew of interactive technology experiences. *Storybase* was, thus, not the first interaction paradigm to be introduced in the museum. This context added another layer of complexity in embracing new forms of knowledge-generation.

The Pen System
The Pen is currently the trademark of CH's visitor experience. At the core of the system is the exploration of the museum's collection. The Pen is a proprietary design tool that connects digital and physical museum experiences by allowing on site visitors to digitally "collect" objects as they move around the museum, by touching the back of the Pen to an object label. This interaction paradigm is categorised as collecting through bookmarking which essentially creates a shortcut to an object without having to manually search the museum's collection to find it.

Upon entry, each museumgoer receives a Pen – an oversized stylus containing a radio-frequency identification (RFID) reader and onboard memory – which the ticket seller then manually pairs with the paper ticket. Printed on the ticket is a URL and short code that allows visitors to access their collections from home. Staff members tell visitors how to use the Pen, which typically takes five to six minutes, providing little time for sharing other information in the onboarding process. Designed in-house, the bespoke system gave the then design team an opportunity to create an experience that encourages visitors to be fully present at the physical exhibitions, confident in their ability to access their saved objects on one of the touch tables around the museum, or later on from home. This individual object collection, though interesting, divorces the objects from the context in which audiences encountered them.

In addition to being related to the visitor offer, the Pen's data framework was developed alongside the collections digitisation process which took place during CH's physical renovation. Once introduced six months after reopening, the Pen and its related infrastructures impacted every layer of the museum's staff, physical plan, budgeting process and day-to-day operations in the first months of circulation [44]. After six years of use, the museum is better attuned to these demands. The Pen was a necessary stepping stone to paving the way for the next step – introducing the Inter-action Lab to explore the potential of different paradigms for visitor interaction, and introduce open innovation as a continuous workstream not driven by the development of one product or experience [45].

The Interaction Lab
The Interaction Lab is an R&D unit aiming to build CH's audiences by proposing new ways of interacting with them. The Lab leverages a variety of R&D processes including cycles of extensive research and testing, characterised by the frequent generation and

discarding of ideas – often with no specific goal or application in mind. The goal behind such agile processes is to drive innovation by growing ideas organically - and if they fail, they fail early. The Lab applies R&D cycles to a cultural institution without privileging 'engineering' ways of thinking. One major Interaction Lab priority is building on existing work in the museum to investigate possible futures of collecting from an interaction paradigm as opposed to the current technological infrastructure.

In-house, the Lab leads workshops with museum staff to prioritise the focus of prototyping activities, and to introduce new tools and methods to the regular work of the museum, across departments focused on public engagement. In addition, the Lab seeks ideas and concepts for a variety of interactive interventions by commissioning designers by invitation and through open calls and shares work process and outputs with the public through public programming. These collaborative interventions have generated ideas around topics like: adding digital intelligence to the historic mansion; on-boarding first-time visitors; and embedding storytelling capabilities in everything from information systems through in-gallery experiences. The goal is to capture socially-generated knowledge and index it, creating another set of pathways through the physical museum that also extend into online collections. The Lab strives to function as a vector of knowledge that provides meaningful experiences and interactions to staff, audiences, and the wider museum sector – proposing that museum experiences matter because they are connected to people. *Storybase* was the Lab's first design prototype to test these objectives.

3.2   *Storybase* Design Methodology

Storybase is a co-creative social storytelling platform that proposed a different way for visitors to think about and interact with objects at CH. Turning the conventional audio tour approach on its head, *Storybase* attached expert- and user-generated audio content to anything one might see, experience, or learn about in the museum, from the objects on display to the mansion itself.

Conceptual Direction
The design problem the Lab was looking to address was how to create more interpretive access points for visitors to learn about CH's collection beyond the data contained in its collections management system (necessarily designed with data integrity and security as the primary objectives). As an example of established knowledge infrastructure, collections management databases are traditionally maintained for the purpose of collections control and to serve experts with specific research objectives. Thus, the underlying design logic of a collection database has conventionally been structured to reflect a curatorial approach. However, since collections are now searchable online by wide audiences, museums have an opportunity to expand collections' relational data architecture into a rich interconnected reservoir of interpretative content that creates space for different lived experiences and brings forth the intangible values associated with objects and practices beyond questions of materiality and provenance.

Storybase, as a concept, presented one approach for restructuring the knowledge paradigm – for museum staff and for visitors. Its design was grounded in knowledge gathering activity whereby the system acquires rich metadata in the form of visitor contributions that might be used to create the connective tissues between objects, experiences, and platforms. *Storybase*'s paradigm was envisioned as co-creative, and social, focused on storytelling. It proposed a way for visitors to think about and interact with objects at CH by focusing on what other people's experiences bring to interpretation. The resulting four guiding principles were:

1. Introducing new types of expertise into the curatorial and internal interpretation system.
2. Building a generative system where people actively contribute content, and that content is used to build a more complex relational database.
3. Expanding the type of content which is interesting and valuable to audiences whilst challenging their preconceptions.
4. Building on a legacy interactive paradigm.

Initial Design Ideation

Storybase was initially ideated as expanding upon the conventional museum audio tour, making it co-creative and participatory, with a less formal tone and approach. Audio guides typically rely on the use of expert voices to provide spoken information about exhibits. Visitors can either use a mobile device offered by the museum upon purchasing entry or use their own devices to access audio guides hosted as webapps (i.e. as in MoMA and The Guggenheim Museum, New York, USA). The established interaction paradigm asks visitors to key a number associated with an exhibit to trigger pre-recorded content. Content is also provided as curated thematic routes in gallery spaces for audiences to follow. Museums, such as the ones above, have also leveraged on the podcast genre to improve engagement with audio tours and provide a conversational mode of information delivery. *Storybase*'s concept took the audio genre's conventions and developments and extended them. Users could interact with *Storybase* content in two ways, through "playback" and "capture". Playback resembled the audio tour experience, with a few key differences:

1. *Less scripting and formality* - snippets of audio were meant to accompany visitors as they explore the space, without feeling stilted, heavily designed, or overly didactic. Even if created by a curator or expert, audio was meant to be recorded as extemporaneously as possible, with an emphasis on story.
2. *Multiple options* - a number of different pieces of audio content attached to objects to create multiple access points for visitors with different interests.

The capture experience was where *Storybase* diverged from what audiences are accustomed to with an audio tour. The Lab had organised a series of brainstorm events, and this portion of the system took inspiration from participants seeking a more social museum experience, that allows visitors to engage more actively with the content inside of the museum. Another impetus was the hypothesis that involving visitors makes exhibits less "elitist" and more inclusive [28]. The vision for the capture functionality derived from common audio interfaces in messaging apps like iMessage and WhatsApp. This feature was meant to allow users to easily capture thoughts and ideas within the interface that they were working. Moreover, audio capture offered a heads-up interface that did not lock users into staring at their phones, created possibilities for equitable approaches to accessing information, and offered practically limitless options for transformations and analyses that could be performed on the content, thanks to a variety of widely available Application Programming Interfaces (APIs), such as speech to text, keyword analysis and more.

Storybase was ideated as a webapp that museum visitors could access on their devices when on and off site. On the webapp visitors would access existing content – that created by curators and that generated by fellow museumgoers. If a visitor wanted to record a message or their own interpretation, they would have been given the option to sign up. By registering, they would have been able to adjust their preferences as to whether to share their content with all other visitors (public), selected app users (semipublic), or not share (private). With the latter, the Lab envisioned an opportunity for visitors to record and note their own ideas, thoughts, and emotions in the form of voice memos. These could then become a record of visitors' on-site experience and integrate personal and shared interpretation, which builds upon the museum's existing collection paradigm.

Prototype Development
Prototyping began in-house and focused on object-by-object interpretation where each object in the museum was accompanied by a bank of recorded stories. Prior to beginning my fieldwork, the Lab had held four content-generating workshops in which 18 members of museum staff from five departments recorded their impressions on the objects in one of the museum galleries. These sessions were conducted in-gallery and during museum opening hours with visitors present in the spaces. The activity was met with enthusiasm, yet questions and concerns had arisen in connection to: what was the right length of a recording; what should be said in the recording; what is a "worthy" contribution. As the Lab's approach to design is open and non-prescriptive, the exercise was left intentionally open-ended. The Lab director reassured staff they could record anything that they saw fit regardless of length as long as they focused on a story they wanted to tell. My first task was to clean up these recordings and arrange them in playlists to constitute a low-fi prototype.

To test the concept, I devised an evaluation framework which reconciled methods from academia and museum practice. I adapted EMOTIVE's Evaluation Framework and Guidelines Deliverable [46] and combined it with the evaluation strategy of testing the audio tour in a prominent museum in Boston, MA which I had been granted access to. I held an evaluation event to test visitors' interest in the playback aspect of *Storybase* and their attitudes towards capturing and listening to visitor-generated content. The framework assessed the playback aspect around three objectives: 1) interest in listening to more than one perspective; 2) establishing attitudes towards different styles of content (formal vs informal; expert vs amateur); 3) comparing listening to audio individually vs socially. I measured these against indicators such as: keywords describing the experience and attitudes; what makes content important; comparative and attitudinal phrases.

Evaluation Findings
I approached 30 museumgoers of which 21 agreed to test the prototype. The majority of participants were North American, 13 were first time visitors to the museum, over

half (12) were in their 50s, 7 in the age range 16–30, and the remaining in the 31–50 range. Sessions lasted approximately 15 minutes. I gave participants a phone device with headphones and took them around the exhibition space playing content for objects they were interested in, followed by an informal discussion of their impressions. Notes were recorded on printed evaluation sheets and transcribed after each event. I coded and categorised data [43] synthesizing three themes around visitors' pre-conceptions of and reactions to audio guides in general, as well as their responses to the content of the prototype itself.

The Audio Experience Determines Interpretation

All visitors noted that audio guides are an individual experience which does the interpretation for them. Some described this aspect as a positive, providing them with more context and information. These visitors emphasised that audio guides should provide added value. For instance, there were positive views on thematic audio-tours as they factor in specific interests and visitors' existing expertise. In relation to multiplicity of recordings, some visitors found the idea of curating channels as an approach which could cater for different preferences and time constraints. However, three participants explicitly said they would not listen to more than one recording per object due to time limitations.

Visitors also pointed towards negative aspects of pre-determined interpretation – it *'turns you into a zombie'* (V4). The interpretation is done by someone else and structures the visitors' thinking too much. The act of listening was described as determined mode of engagement based on space and temporality. V6 specifically felt strongly that the audio guide bounds visitors physically in front of an object, limiting the experience: *'If you start listening, you feel like you have to commit to the whole recording and that might be too much for some visitors.'* This sentiment resonates with how participants approached listening to content – shifting their attention between the object on display, the object label, and piecing it together with the recording. For V6 there was a strong feeling of disconnect hearing the ambient sounds of the time when recordings were produced, negatively augmenting the space in the present, populating it with disassociated sounds.

Desired Knowledge

Visitors were divided in their responses to the stories provided. Whilst some of them found the personal narratives and associative stories engaging and stimulating, others deemed them "unacceptable". Personal connections to objects sound *'weird'*; information is meant to be a matter-of-fact and to the point. A common sentiment was that if it is in a museum, it has the stamp of knowledge authority and some of the recordings were not meeting that standard. One visitor (V1) described the content style as *'childish and immature'*, *'soft-spoken and hesitant'*. Other visitors (V2–3, V7, V12–16) also noted they would have preferred a more informative and authoritative content, whereas personal anecdotes are appropriate for a live tour.

Visitors said they thought this style of content would appeal to younger audiences and could be engaging for them, but not for academic and professional visitors. V4 envisioned it as a vlog-like content where the museum invites a vlogger to create such style of recordings to bring different audiences in.

Contributions is for Others

The overarching sentiment was that visitors were not interested in recording themselves, as they would have nothing to contribute to a *'pile'* of recordings. For instance, as visitors commented on the associative and descriptive nature of all recordings, they reflected that they do not see value in listening to and recording about something they can see and feel themselves. V3 elaborated that they might not want to share their recordings with everyone. However, they thought about doing it as a journal of the experience – recording their impressions, notes, and ideas and having access to them later on as attached to the objects they liked and collected. V2 found personal contribution an option if one could do it post-visit, allowing for time to create a 'script'. I interpret this in relation to asserting one's voice with more authority, producing content up to par with the museum-provided one.

Continuing the theme of intended audience, visitors associated co-creation with school groups and teenagers. Some speculated that leveraging paradigms of timed content (such as Snapchat and Instagram stories) would engage young adults and incite them to share their own experiences in the museum space.

Next Steps

Upon reflecting on the findings, within the Lab, we adjusted our approach to focus on developing the playback functionality and continued with producing an informal sounding but high-production quality content. This time we invited a curator to record in a dedicated space rather than in-gallery. I transcribed the audio and followed up with approving the text and sound quality with the curator to determine whether we needed to produce another recording. However, constraints piled up throughout the process including limited staff time to dedicate to *Storybase*'s development, the prototype's broad scope, coupled with requirements of the wider museum's operations. The apprehensive visitor attitudes towards an audio-guide experience influenced opinions of this particular prototype as a high-risk product – if developed, it might not be met with enough enthusiasm. In this climate the Lab director and I made the decision to step away from further prototyping *Storybase* and use its process to inform lessons for facilitating design-driven cultural transformation.

4 Discussion

Up to this point I have explored *Storybase* as a design case study by outlining the legacy interactions it built on, contextualising the introduction of the Interaction Lab, and the steps taken in developing *Storybase*. The design methodology prioritised how the design process helps to investigate what is entailed in introducing new knowledge-generative paradigms in a traditional institution. In the remainder of this paper, I split my discussion into three lessons learned. I position the Pen's paradigm as a stepping-stone to investigate interactions supporting polyphony. I reflect on how *Storybase* proposes a process for restructuring interpretative knowledge. Finally, I make a case for embracing imperfection as integral to facilitating a cultural shift. These lessons intertwine and overlap, reflecting on existing approaches to design practice and knowledge generation.

4.1   Interactions Towards Polyphony

The Pen is a significant technological experiment creating an integrated interactive experience [47] meant to transform CH into a 'museum of the future' [48] exemplifying 'how designers solve real-world problems' [49]. Despite positive responses, the system did not capture curatorial quirks present in the on-site experience [50]. Curators organise objects in themes, colours, shapes and sizes, creating imaginative juxtapositions when experienced in context. Using the Pen to "collect" content encourages visitors to focus on the exhibition arrangements, yet objects are saved individually. Visitors may review these objects post-visit, but the context in which they have "liked" them is missing, reducing the Pen's potential for interlinked interpretation.

Nonetheless, adopting the Pen was a crucial step in CH's digital transformation, which thus enables the museum to continue working to expand its interaction and knowledge building paradigms long term. First, this allowed investigating the potential of bookmarking. It works well for collecting but it does not add to the interpretation of an object, nor does it expand forms of accepted knowledge. In fact, the Pen system supports multiplicity of objects but not polyvocality of stories as neither objects, nor stories are connected on- or offline. Stories (and histories) are contextual and through bookmarking the opportunity to generate knowledge based on "one object-many stories" is suboptimal. Such consequences pose the question how visitors might reconstruct context and possible object-stories relationships if they wanted to.

This requires investigating how to challenge relational structures by incorporating other interaction paradigms. Museums are re-examining themselves and the need for multisensory, engaging and entertaining experiences [51], and designers are facing challenges how to remain critical in the interactions they provide. It is why *Storybase* was not attached to being strictly an 'audio-tour'. It was not set to 'reinvent the wheel' and innovate audio-based interactive experiences by finding solutions to their setbacks, albeit this is how it was perceived by the museum and its visitors upon pitching the idea. The audio-guide genre is well established in the museum world, and the Interaction Lab, as an R&D unit, was seen as developing a product which might build on thematic tours, allow for personalisation, follow standards and successful approaches to audio guides in other cultural institutions.

Instead of emphasising audio interactions, the system aimed to leverage ambiguity [52] in approaching its relationship with visitors and contributors. Drawing on examples of including younger people and marginalised groups to contribute ways of knowing [53], *Storybase* was an attempt to envision such possible future for CH. Similarly to Bødker [28], *Storybase* aimed to start a dialogue and open space for co-creation between visitors and curators. By co-interpreting stories, visitors are solicited to provide their experience in what is an institutionally controlled process; to see museums not as "elitist" but shared spaces of meaning making. To this end, *Storybase* as a project, recognised that visitor stories are more than anecdotal, and hold the potential for more authentic and democratised storytelling. By "gifting" personal interpretation to other audiences, the knowledge generated captures not only variety of perspectives but incites sharing divergent lived experiences. This corresponds to discussions of plural heritages [41, 54] which frame experiences, pasts, heritages and identities within society as heterogenous, dynamic, shaped by structural inequalities.

Polyphonic interactions then, should aim to capture this plurality and communicate it to those using the interactive system. As there are many means to achieve polyphonic interpretation, designers should remain flexible in their approach and willing to make sometimes difficult decisions to pivot or shelve a project based on whether the methods in question support a diversity of perspectives, and offer nuanced audience experiences.

4.2   Restructuring Interpretation

It is already challenging to employ methodologies that put the visitor as the force to diversify displays and exhibitions [55]. I further emphasise the methodological renewal needed to achieve a cultural shift. Cultural transformation is grounded in opening new forms of interpretation within frameworks of existing institutional practices [56]. New paradigmatic thinking is achieved by investigating the knowledge infrastructuring of institutions [56]. In this climate, a design process scaffolds the examination of existing attitudes and attachments and develops possible approaches to pluralising knowledge. By doing so, the emphasis is on *the process being the work* – the process becomes of greater value than the output.

To that end, the process of prototyping *Storybase* provoked conversations within the museum that revealed connections to 'how things happen'. As Stuedahl et al. note 'transformative knowledge infrastructuring involves re-thinking and re-conceptualizing existing factual knowledge and situated knowledges that have strong relations to the past.' [56]. As technology is undoubtedly a fundamental way in which we organise society, the Pen and *Storybase* offer different paradigms of agency in contributing interpretation. The former "collects" objects which are interpreted based on an expert lens validated by the museum, while the latter attempts to represent even a small number of the many intersecting stories which collectively form a more compelling and holistic context. In evaluating *Storybase*, however, I discovered that presenting more than one story with an object, relegated non-curatorial voices to be "alternative" or ancillary to a dominant or default [curatorial] narrative held up as the "truth" about a work. This aligns with conventional understandings of interpreting exhibitions, art-works and interactive paradigms based on audiences' experiences and expectations. Similarly to Bødker's [28] report, visitors to CH were confused about who recorded the messages, what their own contributions might be, were they saying something that was "smart enough". Within this our own design response in the Lab may have perpetuated expectations – too colloquial recordings are dismissed as uninformative whilst strong authoritative voices are not inviting to create a community of different contributors.

The practice of inclusion in museum storytelling is inherently one of space-making. The need to make space for more individuals and communities to control and deliver the narrative is in tension with traditional methods of display which privileges a single point-of-view. *Storybase*'s paradigm attempted to create space where all objects might be interpreted through any and all individual or collective lens(es) on an equal plane. This larger objective clearly cannot be achieved through short-term testing of one prototype. The intention of *Storybase*, had it been implemented to production, was to build, regularly update and respond to challenges over the medium- and long-term. This would have allowed the museum to study the contributed content as data in its own right, as well as robust metadata connected to objects and exhibitions capable of creating interpretative connections based on societal perceptions and dynamic values over time.

Some audiences would inevitably have felt more comfortable contributing content than others which would have been taken into account in assessing the data collected. This is where *Storybase*'s goal of less scripting and formality served to provide more freedom. By doing so, it was the Lab's intention to explore generative interest in learning and more just ways of distributing power over who writes heritage and interpretation. With such data, the system could be updated to incite diverging contributions which enter in meaningful dialogue, recognising that there is an element of the other in one's self [29, 57]. In validating visitor stories as part of the object record, designers and museum professionals can glean deeper meaning to how objects are understood by specific individuals – different stories are realised differently depending on who is participating [58]. In this way *the process as the work* carves space around the curatorial point of view, interrogating its position as a singular truth for the museum and its visitors. Insofar as contemporary museology strives to decolonise stories, voices and structures of interpretation, and to communicate the need to do so, the need to counteract the belief in one singular truth remains a pertinent and critical challenge.

4.3   Embracing Imperfection

Design objects are most often the result of privileged outbursts of collaboration driven by the need 'to be successful' based on the pressure of funding. Instead, aligning with Gaver [59], accepting that interpretative systems are allowed to fail is reassuring. Creating a culture which embraces failed examples is a culture where imperfection can be used to reimagine core interpretation structures.

In this project, the existence of *Storybase* reflected the present state of design culture in museums which requires testing 'tangible' outcomes. Following five months of brainstorms and workshops, and as my work in the Lab commenced, we could not have known whether *Storybase* was the "right" approach to replace the existing system or not, but we had to proceed as if it were. The activities taken to develop and work on the concept followed the trajectory of design-thinking processes. The Lab understood that there was an opportunity to change the approach and the mandate of aging technology; the problem identified was needing more than a bookmarking interaction to support polyphony; we ideated during workshops and brainstorms; created a low-fi prototype; tested it in-gallery; and revised ways of content creation.

In order to evaluate design as successful or not, it is necessary to choose the dimensions relevant for success. Gaver et al. [59] provide an 'anatomy of a failure' depending on how people achieve a meaningful relationship with a given design. The authors conclude that: 'even the most mundane tool will be valued not only to the degree that it solves a problem, but for its ability to evoke enthusiastic engagement, to be understood as congruent with other valued experiences, to fit with ongoing activities, and to suggest surprising new possibilities' [59].

Following that logic, *Storybase* met the 'failure' condition - it did not provide the experience desired by the museum or visitors. *Storybase* wanted to extend the audio tour but during evaluation, visitors noted that the genre's conventions force them to expect specific content style and mode of interaction. There was limited enthusiasm about the prototype. For example, during the prototyping activity, non-curatorial staff members were unsure of the value of their contribution to interpretation whereas others expressed mixed feelings towards the "success" of such an open approach. Museum-goers who tested the prototype voiced similar apprehensions, expressing concerns about the value and relevance of their contributions, speculating that the system might be appealing to younger audiences. This further points to a design assumption that interactive experiences bring about hesitancy in older visitors who might be less comfortable with digitally mediated play. The challenge is to facilitate shared responsibility and value in both institutions and audiences to create meaningful interpretation.

Museums should embrace imperfection. It is a common goal of academia and cultural organisations to explore paradigms which enable polyvocality and decolonise storytelling. Driving a cultural shift through design means placing emphasis on the process of *doing design* as constituting *the work*. A culture unafraid of testing, failing, and discarding ideas early in the process can drive a cultural shift. To this end, the lessons of design thinking go beyond the familiar outlook that design cycles solve existing issues by producing finalised designs. Even when the value of a final design is emphasized, allowing designers and museum professionals to embed failure into the museum making cycle helps to better leverage the knowledge produced during process-centred activities. What I suggest here is that designers pay attention to the peripheral conversations that the design process provokes within the organisation. Then, if designs fail, research and industry benefit from their anatomy as a failure. An agile design methodology responds to these conversations by updating designs, nuancing existing challenges, prioritising them and contributing to efficient strategizing.

Nonetheless, implementing a cultural change is a long process which requires work on many levels. Many institutions will not have the capacity to develop design artefacts in-house and discard of ideas easily. This means designers and museum professionals have to 'play it safe'. The Lab faces the same challenges and drives cultural change by utilising established tools such as bringing external consultants, commissioning work, and leading public facing programmes. Those activities contribute to an open-door approach to cultural transformation that carves opportunities for introducing and discussing imperfect ideas which illustrate that institutions have actually been doing the work all along.

5 Conclusions

In exploring ways of bridging differences and opening up to audiences, museum and heritage institutions have turned to design thinking as a solutionist approach to designing objects and interactive experiences. Audiences want to engage in certain types of experiences and museums work towards providing them in a drive to satisfy audiences as customers. Meanwhile, museums' hierarchical structure hinders positive attitudes to openness and co-created knowledge. Subsequently, physical designs and interactive experiences have consequences which need be acknowledged. Hence, in this paper, I discussed how 'failed' designs could be used to continue valuable work of allowing different epistemologies to co-exist in the museum space. I did so by exploring the process of working on and introducing *Storybase* as a system paradigm which opens space for new forms of knowledge within a traditional museum.

I offer three lessons learned that discuss how design drives meaningful cultural transformation. First, learning from existing paradigms leads us towards being more malleable in testing interactions that support polyphony. Secondly, doing so requires reflecting on how interpretative knowledge is structured and how we might address existing authoring dynamics to better legitimise the inclusion of a plurality of heritages. Finally, though nobody personally enjoys failure, embracing imperfection teaches us that the *process is itself the valuable work* required to achieve a cultural transformation. *Storybase* system provoked museum staff to think about the process as "the work" rather than focusing on a final design. To this end, the design principles of *Storybase* continue to underpin the work done by the Interaction Lab.

Practical opportunities of adopting the lessons learned lie in permitting low-fidelity prototypes to exist long term, to allow for incremental improvements to their system, and to systematically collect data over time to influence an ongoing trajectory. This data will support designers and museum professionals to make critical decisions, further the shared mission of decolonising knowledge structures, and – depending on the approach – create a sense of ownership for those who contribute their lived experience, stories, and interpretations.

Acknowledgements. I wish to thank staff at Cooper Hewitt, Smithsonian Design Museum for their time and contributions, and Carolyn Royston and Rachel Ginsberg in their cooperation and support throughout my research. This project is supported by the Northern Bridge Consortium, funded by the AHRC NPIF grant number AH/R504701/1 and undertaken as part of the AHRC International Placement Scheme, grant number AH/T000651/1.

References

1. Bedford, L.: Storytelling: the real work of museums. Curator Museum J. **44**, 27–34 (2001). https://doi.org/10.1111/j.2151-6952.2001.tb00027.x
2. Lewi, H., et al.: Shared digital experiences supporting collaborative meaning-making at heritage sites. In: Lewi, H., Smith, W., vom Lehn, D., Cooke, S. (eds.) The Routledge International Handbook of New Digital Practices in Galleries, Libraries, Archives, Museums and Heritage Sites, pp. 143–156. Rout (2019). https://doi.org/10.4324/9780429506765-13
3. Claisse, C., Petrelli, D., Ciolfi, L., Dulake, N., Marshall, M.T., Durrant, A.C.: Crafting critical heritage discourses into interactive exhibition design. In: Proceedings of the 2020 CHI Conference on Human Factors in Computing Systems, pp. 1–13 (2020). https://doi.org/10.1145/3313831.3376689
4. Galani, A., Durrant, A., Chating, D., Farley, R.: Designing for intersubjectivity and dialogicality in museum interactive installations about migration. Digit. Creat. **0**, 1–18 (2020). https://doi.org/10.1080/14626268.2020.1848873
5. Perry, S., Economou, M., Young, H., Roussou, M., Pujol, L.: Moving beyond the virtual museum: engaging visitors emotionally. In: Proceedings of the 2017 23rd International Conference on Virtual System & Multimedia, VSMM 2017, January 2018, pp. 1–8 (2018). https://doi.org/10.1109/VSMM.2017.8346276
6. Simon, N.: The Participatory Museum. Museum 2.0, Santa Cruz (2010)

7. Schofield, T., Foster-Smith, D., Bozoğlu, G., Whitehead, C.: Co-producing collections: re-imagining a polyvocal past with cultural probes. Open Libr. Humanit. **4**, 1–23 (2018). https://doi.org/10.16995/olh.296
8. Ashworth, G.J., Graham, B., Tunbridge, J.E.: Pluralising Pasts: Heritage, Identity and Place in Multicultural Societies. Pluto Press (2007). https://doi.org/10.5860/choice.46-1625
9. Pine, J., Gilmore, J.: The experience economy: work is theatre & every business a stage (1999). https://doi.org/10.5860/choice.37-2254
10. Kidd, J.: "Immersive" heritage encoutners. Museum Rev. **3** (2018)
11. Galani, A., Mason, R., Rex, B.: Dialogues and heritages in the digital public sphere (2019). https://doi.org/10.4324/9780429053511-9
12. Durrant, A.C., Vines, J., Wallace, J., Yee, J.S.R.: Research through design: Twenty-first century makers and materialities (2017). https://doi.org/10.1162/DESI_a_00447
13. Ioannidis, Y., Raheb, K.El., Toli, E., Katifori, A., Boile, M., Mazura, M.: One object many stories: Introducing ICT in museums and collections through digital storytelling. In: Proceedings of the DigitalHeritage 2013 - Federating the 19th Int'l VSMM, 10th Eurographics GCH, and 2nd UNESCO Memory of the World Conferences, Plus Special Sessions fromCAA, Arqueologica 2.0 et al., pp. 421–424 (2013). https://doi.org/10.1109/DigitalHeritage.2013.6743772
14. Pujol, L., Roussou, M., Poulou, S., Balet, O., Vayanou, M., Ioannidis, Y.: Personalizing interactive digital storytelling in archaeological museums: the CHESS project. In: Archaeology in the Digital Era. Papers from the 40th Annual Conference of Computer Applications and Quantitative Methods in Archaeology (CAA), pp. 77–90 (2013)
15. Roussou, M., Pujol, L., Katifori, A., Perry, S., Vayanou, M.: Collaborative participatory creation of interactive digital experiences. In: Museums and the Web 2015 (2015)
16. Vayanou, M., Karvounis, M., Katifori, A., Kyriakidi, M., Roussou, M., Ioannidis, Y.: The CHESS project: adaptive personalized storytelling experiences in museums. In: CEUR Workshop Proceedings, pp. 15–18 (2014)
17. Petrelli, D.: Tangible interaction meets material culture: reflections on the meSch project. Interactions **2**(26), 34–39 (2019). https://doi.org/10.1145/3349268.
18. American Alience of Museums: Museum Facts & Data. https://www.aam-us.org/programs/about-museums/museum-facts-data/#_ednref23. Accessed 23 Feb 2021
19. Huws, S., John, A., Kidd, J.: Traces — Olion National Museum Wales. In: Lewi, H., Smith, W., vom Lehn, D., Cooke, S. (eds.) The Routledge International Handbook of New Digital Practices in Galleries, Libraries, Archives, Museums and Heritage Sites, pp. 441–449. Routledge (2019)
20. Oomen, J., Aroyo, L.: Crowdsourcing in the cultural heritage domain: Opportunities and challenges. In: C T 2011 - 5th International Conference on Communities Technology Conference Proceedings, pp. 138–149 (2011). https://doi.org/10.1145/2103354.2103373
21. Ridge, M.: From tagging to theorizing: deepening engagement with cultural heritage through crowdsourcing. Curator Museum J. **56**, 435–450 (2013). https://doi.org/10.1111/cura.12046
22. Roussou, M., Kavalieratou, E., Doulgeridis, M.: Children designers in the museum: applying participatory design for the development of an art education program. In: Proceedings of the 6th International Conference on Interaction Design and Children, IDC 2007, pp. 77–80 (2007). https://doi.org/10.1145/1297277.1297292
23. Jamieson, K., Discepoli, M.: Exploring Deaf heritage futures through critical design and 'Public Things.' Int. J. Herit. Stud. **00**, 1–17 (2020). https://doi.org/10.1080/13527258.2020.1771750
24. Seale, J., Garcia Carrizosa, H., Rix, J., Sheehy, K., Hayhoe, S.: A participatory approach to the evaluation of participatory museum research projects. Int. J. Res. Method Educ. **44**, 20–40 (2021). https://doi.org/10.1080/1743727X.2019.1706468

25. Ferris, K., Bannon, L., Ciolfi, L., Gallagher, P., Hall, T., Lennon, M.: Shaping experiences in the Hunt Museum: a design case study. In: DIS 2004 - Designing Interactive Systems: Processes, Practices, Methods, and Techniques, pp. 205–214 (2004)

26. Spence, J., et al.: Seeing with new eyes: designing for in-the-wild museum gifting. In: Conference on Human Factors in Computing Systems – Proceedings, pp. 1–13. Association for Computing Machinery (ACM) (2019). https://doi.org/10.1145/3290605.3300235

27. Bødker, S.: Third-wave HCI, 10 years later—participation and sharing. Interactions **22**, 24–31 (2015). https://doi.org/10.1145/2804405

28. Bødker, S., Klokmose, C.N., Korn, M., Polli, A.M.: Participatory IT in semi-public spaces. In: Proceedings of the 2014 8th Nordic Conference on Human-Computer Interaction: Fun, Fast, Foundational, pp. 765–774 (2014). https://doi.org/10.1145/2639189.2639212

29. Tchen, J.K.W., Ševčenko, L.: The "dialogic museum" revisited. a collaborative reflection. In: Adair, B., Filene, B., Koloski, L. (eds.) Letting go?: Sharing Historical Authority in a User-Generated World, pp. 80–97. Pew Center for Arts, Philadelphia (2011)

30. Galani, A., Arrigoni, G.: Heritage futurescaping: developing critical digital heritage practice through participatory speculative design. In: 5th Association for Critical Heritage Studies Biannual Conference (2020)

31. Friis Dam, R., Siang, T.Y.: What is Design Thinking and Why Is It So Popular?. https://www.interaction-design.org/literature/article/what-is-design-thinking-and-why-is-it-so-popular. Accessed 11 Nov 2020

32. Silvers, D.M., Wilson, M., Rogers, M.: Design thinking for visitor engagement: tackling one museum's big challenge through human-centered design. In: MW2013: Museums and the Web 2013, Portland, OR, USA (2013)

33. Silvers, D.M., Lytle-Painter, E., Lee, A., Ludden, J., Hamley, B., Trinh, Y.: From post-its to processes: using prototypes to find solutions. In: MW2014: Museums and the Web 2014, Baltimore, MD, USA (2014)

34. Coghlan, R.: 'My voice counts because I'm handsome.' Democratising the museum: the power of museum participation. Int. J. Herit. Stud. **24**, 795–809 (2018). https://doi.org/10.1080/13527258.2017.1320772

35. Maris, I., Huizing, A., Bouman, W., Oosterbroek, M.: The curious case of design thinking in museums. In: Electronic Visualisation and the Arts (EVA 2013), pp. 250–257 (2013)

36. Jung, Y., Love, A.R.: Systems Thinking in Museums: Theory and Practice. Rowman & Littlefield, Lanham (2017)

37. Sutton, S.: Systems thinking in museums – theory and practice. Museum Manag. Curatorsh. **33**, 297–300 (2018). https://doi.org/10.1080/09647775.2018.1464547

38. French, A.: Service design thinking for museums: technology in contexts. In: Museums and the Web 2016, Los Angeles, CA, USA (2016)

39. MacLeod, S., Dodd, J., Duncan, T.: New museum design cultures: harnessing the potential of design and 'design thinking' in museums. Museum Manag. Curatorsh. **30**, 314–341 (2015). https://doi.org/10.1080/09647775.2015.1042513

40. Frayling, C.: Research in Art and Design (1993)

41. Schofield, T., Foster-Smith, D., Bozoğlu, G., Whitehead, C.: Design and plural heritages composing critical futures. In: Conference on Human Factors in Computing Systems - Proceedings (2019). https://doi.org/10.1145/3290605.3300236

42. Van Dijk, G.: Design ethnography: taking inspiration from everyday life. This is Service Design Thinking, pp. 1–3 (2010)

43. Saldaña, J.: Coding Manual : Constitutions (2013). https://doi.org/10.1017/CBO9781107415324.004

44. Chan, S., Cope, A.: Strategies against architecture: interactive media and transformative technology at the Cooper Hewitt, Smithsonian Design Museum. In: Museums and the Web 2015 (2015)
45. Ginsberg, R.: The Interaction Lab: New Approaches for an Emergent Landscape. https://www.cooperhewitt.org/2019/11/22/introducing-the-interaction-lab/. Accessed 30 Sept 2020
46. Economou, M., Perry, S., Young, H., Katifori, A., Roussou, M.: Deliverable 9.1 –Evaluation Framework and Guidelines, EMOTIVE project, pp. 1–50 (2017)
47. Hornecker, E., Ciolfi, L.: Human-computer interactions in museums. Synth. Lect. Human-Centered Inform. **12**, i–153 (2019). https://doi.org/10.2200/S00901ED1V01Y201902 HCI042
48. Meyer, R.: The Museum of the Future Is Here. https://www.theatlantic.com/technology/archive/2015/01/how-to-build-the-museum-of-the-future/384646/. Accessed 05 Mar 2021
49. Murphy, A.: Cooper Hewitt Smithsonian Design Museum: reinventing the pen. https://advisor.museumsandheritage.com/features/cooper-hewitt-the-major-renovation-and-reinventing-the-pen/. Accessed 05 Mar 2021
50. Sadokierski, Z.: Reinventing old technology: Cooper Hewitt's interactive pen. https://theconversation.com/reinventing-old-technology-cooper-hewitts-interactive-pen-44009. Accessed 05 Mar 2021
51. Golding, V., Modest, W.: Museums and Communities: Curators, Collections and Collaboration. Bloomsbury Academic, London (2013)
52. Gaver, W., Beaver, J., Benford, S.: Ambiguity as a resource for design. In: Proceedings of the Conference on Human Factors in Computing Systems - CHI 2003 (2003). https://doi.org/10.1145/642651.642653
53. Stuedahl, D., Skåtun, T., Lefkaditou, A., Messenbrink, T.: Participation and dialogue: curatorial reflexivity in participatory processes. In: Galani, A., Mason, R., and Arrigoni, G. (eds.) European Heritage, Dialogue and Digital Practices, pp. 62–85. Routledge (2019)
54. Ashworth, G.J., Isaac, R.K.: Have we illuminated the dark? Shifting perspectives on 'dark' tourism. Tour. Recreat. Res. **40**, 316–325 (2015). https://doi.org/10.1080/02508281.2015.1075726
55. Villaespesa, E., Álvarez, A.: Visitor journey mapping at the Museo Nacional Thyssen-Bornemisza: bringing cross-departmental collaboration to build a holistic and integrated visitor experience. Museum Manag. Curatorsh. **35**, 125–142 (2020). https://doi.org/10.1080/09647775.2019.1638821
56. Stuedahl, D., Runardotter, M., Mörtberg, C.: Attachments to participatory digital infrastructures in the cultural heritage sector. Sci. Technol. Stud. **29**, 50–69 (2016)
57. Bakhtin, M.: The Bakhtin Reader: Selected Writings of Bakhtin, Medvedev, Voloshinov (1994). https://doi.org/10.2307/3734307
58. Boje, D.M.: Stories of the storytelling organization: a postmodern analysis of disney as "Tamara -Land." Acad. Manag. J. **38**, 997–1035 (1995). https://doi.org/10.5465/256618
59. Gaver, W., Bowers, J., Kerridge, T., Boucher, A., Jarvis, N.: Anatomy of a failure. In: CHI 2009, pp. 2213–2222 (2009)

The Collection is Dead; Long Live the Collective: Rethinking the Role of Content and Collections in the Museum's Purpose Post-pandemic

Nancy Proctor[✉]

The Peale, Baltimore, MD, USA
CSO@ThePealeCenter.org

Abstract. Originally titled, "From Treasure House to Production House: Community-driven storytelling and the 'born digital' collection in the museum as distributed network," this paper began as an attempt to share the storytelling and "digital first" strategies being developed at the Peale in Baltimore, Maryland. Inspired by the "new citizenship" approach to organizational participation developed in the UK [1] and leading work in the cultural sector presented at the international MuseWeb conferences among others, the Peale is an experiment in dismantling museum hierarchies, from the primacy of the object to the curatorial process, with the aim of transforming the 21st century museum from treasure house into a production house of culture. After the RISE-IMET conference at which this paper was to be presented was postponed due to the pandemic, this thesis had to be expanded to take into account the impact of 2020's quarantines on museums. The closure of physical institutions globally, and the corresponding pivot to online content and audiences, compels us to redefine "collection" in the post-pandemic museum as more than content, be it digital or analog, and instead put the expanded concept of "collective," including content and its connections with creators and audiences – i.e. stories – at the heart of the museum's purpose and economy.

Keywords: Museums · Collections · Content · Community · Digital · Peale · Baltimroe · MuseWeb · Pandemic · COVID-19

1 Digital Inversions

When the pandemic struck in the United States and museums across the country closed their doors, there was a rush to put more content online. From re-purposed to new, digitized collections and virtual programs were suddenly given pride of place in many museums' online offerings. There was a sense of urgency as debates raged on "museum Twitter" about what online audiences wanted and digital teams raced to find new approaches to content and programs that would engage the large audiences now locked down at home. It seemed that even museums that had been reluctant to digitize and put collections online in the past, or had gotten into digital primarily because of FOMA ("fear of missing out") and/or the hope that an app or "going viral" would solve

© Springer Nature Switzerland AG 2021
M. Shehade and T. Stylianou-Lambert (Eds.): RISE IMET 2021, CCIS 1432, pp. 254–268, 2021.
https://doi.org/10.1007/978-3-030-83647-4_17

institutional problems, would now invest seriously in online content for fear of losing their audiences entirely.

As a long-term member of an international community of technologists and innovators in the cultural field and former co-chair of the MuseWeb conferences (founded in 1997 as Museums and the Web), I welcomed the rising visibility of the "digital museum" as a thin silver lining in the global tragedy of COVID-19. The 2020 MW conference, scheduled to open in Los Angeles on March 31, 2020, had only a couple of weeks to move entirely online after California's governor prohibited large gatherings on March 11. Our community rose to the occasion, however, and MW20 was the first of the major international conferences on technology in the cultural sector to be held entirely online during the pandemic, demonstrating the power and value of digital content and skills to sustaining organizations and activities in the sector [2].

The emphasis on digital content generation in the first months of the pandemic also seemed to signal that museums were grasping the nature of their role as "content businesses." This is a fundamental concept that has informed the relaunch of the Peale in Baltimore, of which I am founding director and now Chief Strategy Officer, as a "production house" for authentic Baltimore stories, and platform for storytellers in all media (Fig. 1).

Fig. 1. The Peale in Baltimore, Maryland USA. Photo by the author, 2018.

Other than our historic building and garden, the Peale's "collection" currently includes over 1,650 stories of the city – the largest digital collection of Baltimore stories in the world [3]. Most of these are location-based audio recordings, and are available on a wide range of free and open platforms, from Soundcloud and social media to the Be Here Stories app. But the Peale is also a platform for creators to present their exhibitions, performances, conversations, research, and expertise in live encounters with diverse audiences from across Baltimore. The storytelling and other programming at the Peale comes from Baltimore's communities, grassroots-up, rather than through a top-down process led by myself, a curator, or other "authority." This is perhaps a risky, and is certainly a counter-intuitive approach, but pretty much all the programs and exhibitions we offer at the Peale have come to us – with many of their creators literally walking in off the street – rather than as a result of staff planning and seeking out programs ourselves. As a result, relevance is baked into everything we do. Our audiences are the creators of our programs. This approach goes beyond crowd-sourcing; it is community-led programming. I was inspired to try this approach partly because of lack of time and resources to operate any other way – we are, after all, a small museum! – but also by "Joy's Law," as explained by Chris Anderson, editor of *Wired* Magazine, in a talk he gave as part of the "Smithsonian 2.0" convening in 2009 [4]. Bill Joy, the founder of Sun Microsystems, said the smartest and best person to do any given job in your organization does not work for you [5]. Moreover, you cannot find that person; however, they can find you – if you are putting out the right signals and messages to attract them. I see my job at the Peale as this: ensuring that we are sending out signals and messaging that invite people to participate in and use the Peale as their platform. My colleagues and I simply open the door and strive to provide the support and resources necessary to enable them to tell the stories that they perhaps would rarely if ever have an opportunity to present elsewhere.

The Peale Museum building itself does a fair share of this work attracting creators and audiences alike. Although never a home for its founder, the Peale was constructed in the style of Federal townhouses of the period, with enlarged rooms and a large gallery with skylight on the back to facilitate the display of paintings. Its proportions therefore retain a sense of "hominess" and human scale, providing people space to create rather than dwarfing them in grand architecture. And to be fair, the state of decay of the Peale Museum after 20 years of abandonment gave the building a certain charm that also made it less intimidating. Pre-renovation the Peale has been a space where artists could enjoy greater freedom than in a typical museum or white cube gallery because there was little they could do to the rooms that would be more damaging than the water stains and crumbling plaster.

Rather than putting the object at the center of the museum experience, at the Peale the participant is at the center of the design process (this is also called audience-centric design), and the objects are often props and multiples that can be handled and used by participants during productions, enabling multi-sensory experiences and greater access and inclusion for people who learn in diverse ways. Today's popular immersive theater and transmedia games are key sources of best practices and learnings about how to re-introduce context and user-led engagement at the Peale. But this is nothing new: Charles Willson Peale built dioramas and natural environments for the birds and other exhibits on display in his museum, precisely to immerse the visitor in the place and time of the stories his museum was telling. As the Peale's Chief Experience Officer, David London, has noted, in any given age, the most popular entertainment is that which is most different from daily life.[1] In the 19th century, for example, when most people lived in small, homogeneous communities, vaudeville and the circuses emerged with their eclectic array of acts and performers from exotic backgrounds with diverse and often unheard-of skills and talents. Today, we are connected with more people than ever, but those interactions are largely mediated by screens and other technology interfaces. As a result, a huge appetite is emerging for in-person experiences that immerse people in the here and now, and get them interacting "with the real world." Across all platforms, we see new forms of engagement today coming from immersive experience design, with the participant as a co-creator – not just a consumer – of the experience. The question of how to translate these experiential qualities into online environments and encounters gained a new urgency at the Peale and beyond as lock-downs began during the pandemic.

2   The Pandemic Pivot

In many ways the peale was optimally positioned to pivot to an entirely online presence when the pandemic struck, with a largely "born digital" collection and deep in-house expertise in online publishing and community engagement. As calls and demonstrations for social justice and centering black experiences grew in the United States, the Peale doubled-down on the work it had been doing since its re-inception in 2017: amplifying the voices and preserving the authentic stories of the majority African American city of Baltimore. Nonetheless, COVID-19 forced the peale like so many others to confront a number of blind spots and lacunae in our operations and practices. We had to figure out how to bridge the digital divide when we were suddenly cut off from easy access to communities that had no internet access under quarantine, and how to continue to provide Baltimore's creators with access to platforms and resources when their means of support, like ours, were drying up. This led us to re-consider what being a community-driven platform really meant post-pandemic, and to re-evaluate our understanding and the role of the Peale's collection of digital stories in the organization's mission and Baltimore's cultural eco-system.

The activities of museums from their beginnings through the 20th century have largely been around collections: acquiring, preserving, and interpreting objects, be they physical or digital media. But as my colleague, Selwyn Ramp from the Smithsonian's Museum on Main Street Program has argued, the stories that grow up around objects and give them meaning and relevance are just as important as the objects themselves, and deserve just as much care, attention, and resources (see Footnote 1). The principal focus of our work at the Peale, therefore, is gathering, stewarding, and sharing the authentic stories of Baltimore in an effort to ensure that the city's cultural record is truly inclusive of its full history and diverse communities. At the Peale, the museum's role has been less about caring for a collection and more about supporting the creation of

---

[1] Personal communications with the author.

content by our communities and collaborators. This is not new or unique to the Peale – museums have served as ateliers for professional artists and amateur creators from their earliest days, not to mention for researchers and subject-matter experts who use their collections to create new knowledge and understandings in all media that support humans' greater understanding of the world around them. Today, we might describe the Peale's business model as that of a "content business." Our mission is not *just* to be a "treasure house" that preserves cultural objects, born-digital or otherwise, but also to be a production house for the ongoing creation of culture by and with the communities we serve.

The challenge in 2020 was to achieve this objective in a world in which physical public spaces had become potentially deadly in new ways, and strangers could kill you without meaning to. "Going viral" gained a new, sinister meaning, and fear of infection now extended beyond malware. Most museum income sources had been profoundly disrupted if not eliminated. The Peale was not alone in struggling to fulfill its mission online. But the "pandemic pivot" we saw from museums who were waking up to the value of digital and content in general to their missions was short lived. Relatively soon after the lock-downs began, museum staff were furloughed and laid off as directors and financial officers tried to find ways of coping with reduced income from box office sales and on-site visitors. All kinds of teams suffered staff cuts, including digital specialists and the very people in charge of creating engaging content and experiences for museum audiences, from educators to interpreters. Faced with tough choices, many museums seemed to choose financing care for their collections and physical plants at the expense of content and the people who produce it. From one perspective, collections that had long defined museums and their value now threatened to be their undoing.

It is fair to ask if this was simply a reactionary move on the part of museums who still don't appreciate the value of digital and content to their missions, or a long-term view that defends the core value of the museum's collection, from which, after all, so much content and programming – online or off – stems. It can also be argued that relatively little museum content is "evergreen," and digital content in particular is subject to the rapid obsolescence of platforms and media in the online world. When forced to economize, it is arguably not unreasonable to invest in that which promises to hold its value the longest, including after the pandemic.

But the Peale was not alone in seeing its audiences more than double as the demand for online content exploded under quarantine. And this phenomenon was not confined to museums: online content businesses of all sorts grew exponentially in 2020. A survey by JCA Arts found that 43% of the online audiences surveyed had never attended an in-person production by the theater companies they patronized online during the pandemic, [6] as time spent consuming content online daily doubled in 2020 [7]. Clearly serving that demand was not just an important way of fulfilling the museum's mission during the pandemic, it was also a sound investment in expanding audiences and impact in measurable ways.

Ultimately both extremes – cutting out digital and all who produce it to fund the preservation of the physical collection, and throwing money and resources at digital teams in an attempt to "win the pandemic" online – miss the mark and pervert the museum's mission. Both fall into what Bharat Narendra Anand would call, "the content trap" [8]. Written for capitalist enterprises and a neoliberal economy, Anand's observations nonetheless have relevance for the non-profit sector and cultural organizations: "Success comes not just from creating content, or the 'best content', but from creating content that connects users. In other words, success comes from recognizing user connections" [9]. Content for content's sake is unlikely to connect with users, let alone forge connections among them. This applies to physical collections as well as to online presentations.

3   The Redefine/ABLE Exhibition at the Peale: A Case Study

"Redefine/ABLE: challenging Inaccessibility" was an international collaboration that began with the goals of sharing the challenges, successes and stories of people living with disabilities in Baltimore and Maryland at large; interrogating the idea of "ability" within historical, cultural and ethical contexts; and creating a model for the ways exhibits and other information delivery can be more accessible. During the 2019–2020 academic year, the 2020 University of Maryland, College Park graphic design cohort conducted research and worked with disabled stakeholders to create the *Redefine/ABLE* exhibition under the leadership of Professor Audra Buck-Coleman. The project was presented in partnership with cultural sites in the UK: the De La Warr Pavilion, the Royal Pavilion and Museums Brighton, and the University of Brighton, and developed in Second Life by Linden Lab and Virtual Ability, Inc. Halsey Burgund built the open source platform and app, including a new mobile web site, used by the project.

We intended this project to manifest as a cross-platform or "transmedia" exhibition in two different physical spaces—the Carroll mansion in Baltimore and the Herman Maril gallery on the university of Maryland, college park campus—and in an online space, all planned to open in march 2020. When covid-19 hit, we initially thought the project would have to be limited to being just an exhibition microsite [10] and social media presence where we could at least still share stories by people living with disabilities and publish essays on the topic (Fig. 2). But we knew that something critical would be missing if we simply dropped *Redefine/ABLE's* physical exhibitions from the project. These stories also needed a sense of place, a space for community, live conversations, and serendipitous encounters in order to forge the connections that would bring this project's content to life.

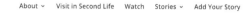

Fig. 2. Home page of the Redefine/ABLE website at www.Redefine-ABLE.ThePealeCenter.org.

We turned to our partners at Virtual Ability, Inc., who had worked with Linden Lab to build virtual meeting spaces in the virtual world, Second Life, for MuseWeb's 2020 conference when the MW20 conference had to move online due to the outbreak of the COVID-19 pandemic. Second Life afforded the conference attendees a digital space where they could run into and casually mingle with other participants in a digital format that goes far beyond the flat talking heads of video conference platforms. In partnership with Linden Lab, the Virtual Ability Team was able to install a re-imagined version of the physical exhibition in a virtual Peale in Second Life, the largest and oldest of the virtual world platforms [11]. The "virtual Peale" is a 3D recreation of the historic Peale Museum building in second life, built by Linden Lab's "moles" based on a model created by UMBC's Image Research Center for the 3D map of Baltimore ca. 1815, EarlyBaltimore.org (Fig. 3) [12].

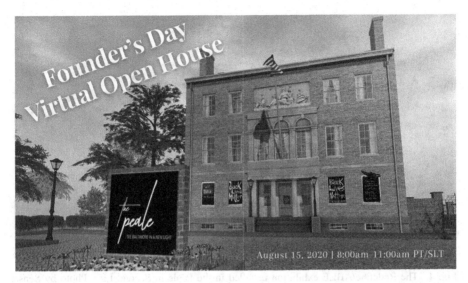

Fig. 3. The Peale in Second Life, exterior view, shown in a graphic promoting the opening of the virtual museum on August 15, 2020. https://secondlife.com/destination/peale?d=peale

The 3D digital gallery for *Redefine/ABLE* was modeled on the physical Peale's "Picture Gallery," the room that makes the historic museum building architecturally unique. Like the *Redefine/ABLE* website and social media posts, the exhibition in Second Life is accessible to online audiences 24/7 and engages an entirely new global public for the Peale. Opened August 15, 2020, the virtual Peale already receives more visits than the Peale in Baltimore, even when it is open (the Peale has been closed since September 2019 for renovations). The reach of the online exhibition was further extended by a robust program of online workshops and panel discussions hosted in Second Life, Zoom, the Peale's website, and YouTube as part of Strawberry Linden's "Lab Gab" live-streamed variety show, tripling the Peale's audience engagement numbers in 2020 from preceding years. The project's Second Life presence attracted groups and bloggers to visit and report on RedefineABLE and the virtual Peale, including Novata, who voluntarily created a comprehensive video for their YouTube Channel and generously created a shortened version of it for this GLAMi award submission (Fig. 4).

Fig. 4. The Redefine/ABLE exhibition installed in the Peale in Second Life. Photo by Sensei Maximus, Founder, Builder's Brewery.

The pandemic both altered *Redefine/ABLE's* installation plans and heightened the pertinence of the project's mission. By restricting us to online interactions, covid-19 showed us how ill-prepared we were at the Peale to use technology to its full potential, and where our digital blind spots lay. Even with a technologically-savvy team and a born-digital collection, we found ourselves in April 2020 wondering why we hadn't been doing more online pre-quarantine, given the extraordinary increase in our global reach and audiences as we took all of our programs online for the duration of the pandemic. For example, the Peale now has a growing audience of Deaf participants thanks to adding captioning and ASL interpretation as standard in all online programs – an inclusive design development that was inspired by the Redefine/ABLE exhibition's move online and will continue into the Peale's programming in the physical world as well. what took us so long?

As "the oldest new museum in Baltimore," the Peale has embraced its unparalleled opportunity to question and reinvent the very concept of the museum for the 21st century, while building on two centuries of cultural, technological, and educational innovation within its own historic walls. Opened in 1814 by artist Rembrandt Peale, Peale's Baltimore Museum and Gallery of the Fine Art Arts was housed in the first purpose-built museum in the United States. Rembrandt's museum was inspired by his father, Charles Willson Peale, who had opened the first American museum in Philadelphia in 1786. Rembrandt also introduced gas lighting to the city of Baltimore. By 1816 his Baltimore Gas Light Company was installing the country's first gas streetlight network, giving Baltimore its nickname, "Light City."

Peale sold his building to the city to become Baltimore's first City Hall in 1829, and in 1878 the City located Male and Female Colored School No. 1 in the Peale Museum building: the first of the city's public schools to offer black students a secondary school education. After the school moved onto bigger and newer premises, the building was used for manufacturing and finally became a museum again in 1930 – the city's first Municipal Museum. Part of the City Life Museums, the Peale Museum was known in the 20th century as the go-to place for those wanting to learn about Baltimore, from students to out-of-town visitors, and along with an impressive collection presented ground-breaking and critically-acclaimed exhibitions that focused on the social history and fabric of the city. Unfortunately, the Peale Museum was shuttered in 1997, along with a number of other city-owned museums. Its collection was transferred to the Maryland Historical Society, and the vacant historic building was left to decay for 20 years.

In 2017, we began bringing the Peale back to life as a home for Baltimore stories and a laboratory for museum practice. today the Peale is the only museum dedicated to the intangible cultural heritage of the city, and stewards the largest digital collection of Baltimore stories in the world. Our aim is to preserve and share the **whole** story of the city to help people see Baltimore in a new light. At the same time, we are reimagining the 21st century museum as much more than a treasure house: it is a production house of culture, and a laboratory in which we can experiment and share new models for accessibility, sustainability, and relevance while helping create a more inclusive cultural record of the city. The Peale is a platform where local creators – storytellers, griots, performers, artists, architects, historians, students, educators, and other culture-keepers – can produce and present authentic narratives of the city, its places, and diverse communities. In the Peale Museum building, Baltimore's stories and voices have a showcase that honors their contributions to the city's cultural heritage.

Redefine/able served this mission by specifically addressing the needs of and inviting people living with disabilities to amplify their voices and share their stories through the peale's web-based story recording tools, the free Be Here Stories iOS app, a new web app version of the same, which was made possible thanks to funding for this project, and a free "storytelling hotline" that can be accessed without a smart phone, as well as in-person and online story recording events. All of the exhibition's events happened online with live professional captioning and ASL interpretation. The recordings of these events and their transcripts remain a free online resource after the end of the project.

Nonetheless, as a panel discussed during the exhibition's opening event in Second Life, there are barriers to accessibility even in the internet's oldest and most developed virtual world: sign language interpretation is not yet possible due to the limitations of rendering for avatars, and some find the need to build and navigate the world via an avatar too onerous, either for their technical skills or their computers' processing power. Even as virtual worlds have enabled access for people of many differing needs and abilities to a wide range of experiences and communities, they are not a panacea for inclusion. With no single platform or solution for universal accessibility, inclusion must be approached, as Debbie Staigerwald from the Arc Baltimore commented during a Redefine/ABLE online event, "one person at a time."

Spanning multiple physical and digital platforms, the structure of the Redefine/ABLE exhibition reflects the emergent nature of the museum as distributed network even as we address each platform's affordances and limitations 'one technology at a time.' Perhaps more now than even in its original dual-site format, the Redefine/ABLE exhibition represents an important initiative for testing and exploring

ways of creating spaces that are not just more accessible but, especially when connected, also more inclusive. The project has transformed the way we approach presenting online exhibitions and events at the Peale, helping us make important advances
in the accessibility of our programming, as well as delivering on our mission to be a
laboratory for developing more accessible and inclusive cultural spaces.

In a sense, the Peale has never been more accessible than since the pandemic
began. The Redefine/ABLE exhibition exemplifies this pivot in the wake of the Covid-
19 outbreak as well as the Peale's commitment to inclusion. But is the Peale more
inclusive as a result? As the Peale's focus on online programming since the pandemic
started has demonstrated, there are limits to the reach and accommodations afforded by
digital technologies. Like the historic Peale Museum building, currently under renovation to add accessible facilities and an elevator among other improvements, the tools
and techniques needed to bridge the "digital divide" today are incomplete, in development, and in some cases completely absent. How can we "dismantle the master's
house" using the digital tools currently at our disposal?

Speaking in a panel discussion on this topic as part of the Redefine/ABLE exhibition project, Dr. Nettrice Gaskins, digital artist and educator, argued that we can only
be fully inclusive when those who have been excluded by the systems of power and
oppression build and control the platforms and tools necessary to create a new cultural
discourse. This is an important inflection on the 1980s rallying cry of disability rights
activists, "nothing about us without us," suggesting the need to rethink not only the
Peale's commitment to accessibility, but also its strategy for inclusion. It requires the
Peale and cultural organizations of all kinds to commit to capacity-building and
enabling access to the means of cultural production for constituents. *Redefine/ABLE*
took us some way toward this goal by funding the further development of the open
source platform on which the Peale's Be Here Stories app and mobile website are built.
Developed by the artist Halsey Burgund, the Roundware framework has been adopted
by a number of other institutions and initiatives around the world, including heritage
sites in the UK as a result of the RedefineABLE project. The experience of reimagining
the Peale in a virtual world and reconceiving an exhibition on "redefining ability"
during a pandemic helped the Peale develop new tools, resources, and strategies for
bridging the physical and the digital to become a truly global distributed network. At
the same time, it opened our eyes to the deep structural re-engineering that we must still
undertake in order to facilitate the writing of a soundtrack of the city that, by including
all its voices, helps people everywhere see Baltimore in a new light.

4   Stories = Content + Collections

If museums are fundamentally content businesses, then they are not immune from the
content trap, and by the same token we need to understand what it means to be a
content business. "So many businesses fail … simply because they have failed to
correctly define themselves," wrote John Hendricks, founder of Discovery Communications, one of the first cable businesses built on educational content [13]. Museums'
misrecognizing their business and doubling down on "content" alone – be that digital
or physical collection objects – in times of crisis will not save them. Content without

connections to users of that content is like collection objects that never see the light of day: expensive to maintain, and of dubious impact or relevance to the communities the museum is intended to serve. Such tunnel vision can just as easily lead to demise by irrelevance even in "good" years. Relevance, as Nina Simon has written, starts with audience: for and by whom is the content being produced? [14]. In other words, with whom is the content connecting? As we learned in our experience of installing the *Redefine/ABLE* exhibition in Second Life, connections are also about place. Meeting people "where they are" is not just about offering relevant content in an accessible language and format: it also entails being present on the platforms where people meet, from social media platforms, to Second Life, to their physical neighborhoods. The context added by "place" is what gives location-based storytelling its immersive power.

Collections, traditionally seen as the essence and lifeblood of the museum, can quickly become an albatross potentially lethal to its existence if they do not also forge connections that make the museum's well-being and survival important to its communities. Avoiding "death-by-collection" is not just a question of what content and experiences to create, what objects to preserve and which to de-accession, or even how to monetize the museum's content, digital or analog. Rather, the collection's purpose should be understood as one of connecting people, communities, and their places. As I have written elsewhere, in a networked world, the value of content comes not from its production values, but from its ability to connect (with) people [15]. This is why even low-cost, user-generated content with poor production values amplified by the connections possible on social media platforms can make such an impact in a world where Hollywood and other broadcast media budgets continue to reach stratospheric proportions.

During the pandemic, the museum field and others saw an explosion of content and even businesses focused on offering workshops, webinars, conferences and the like, and many found large and eager audiences. Some of this demand may have been an understandable desire on the part of professionals to address any weaknesses they perceived in their skills as the world pivoted around them. Some may have used such convenings to stay connected to their field even after being furloughed or laid off. Some may have even tuned in because they had nothing better to do under quarantine. But I would argue that it was as much if not more the communities that attracted participants to this content. As participants in the MW20 Online conference confirmed, the value of that convening in the early days of the pandemic lay not just in the papers and knowledge shared by presenters, but in the connections forged among participants and the renewal of community ties. As one attendee remarked, particularly in the early weeks of the pandemic, "it meant a lot, to many people, to be able to connect as peers, colleagues, and friends, and be able to concentrate our attention back towards the topics we care so much about" [16].

Content may be king, but it is dead without the connections it inspires. In order not to become zombie institutions, museums must therefore go beyond being "content businesses" to become platforms for stories, in which stories are defined as content PLUS connections between and among its creators and audiences. It is impossible to conceive of a story as content in isolation from a storyteller and an audience. A story is not just "about" something, or a narrative that follows a particular arc and includes defined literary elements. Nor is it just the content that grows up around the object – the other side of the coin of the collection, be it digital, physical, or even conceptual. The museum's stories, the "sticky" content of its collections, is the glue that connects the object with the museum's communities. To be sure, these communities include scholars and experts as well as citizens and even non-participants whom the museum is seeking to engage. In each case, the value the museum accords a community is reflected in the connections it has with that community through the stories the museum facilitates, preserves, and shares.

As a center for community storytelling with a "digital first" approach to its collection, the pandemic forced the Peale to rethink the concept of "story" and therefore come to understand the purpose of the collection in a new way: as a collective of content, creative participants, audiences, and platforms [17]. Along with these, we are in the process of reconceiving key principals behind our core activities:

1. **Stories are as important as objects** – not because content is more important than collections, but because through stories we create connections with the communities we serve. This expanded understanding of "stories" leads us to redefine the collection in a post-digital age [18] as a "collective" of stories – content + connections – where connections include the content's creators, their audiences, and the museum as a platform for their co-emergence [19].
2. **The museum is not just a treasure house; it should also be a production house of culture,** a platform where participants find opportunities for co-creation and connecting with each other's communities. But as the digital divide grew into a chasm during the pandemic, new partnerships and the museum's investment of resources in new ways to bridge that gap became even more essential to ensure the audiences, voices, and stories that don't have access to the internet are not excluded from cultural production and discourse.
3. **Relevance comes from inverting the curatorial process.** Again, the museum as production house is powered by its communities and the creators who use it as a platform for their storytelling – not by "top-down" narratives that stem from curators and other subject-matter experts with privileged access to the museum's cultural resources. How can the Peale and others attract creators in a digital environment that may be alien if not inaccessible to them? What new strategies and tactics are necessary to overcome online "threshold fear" and ensure that the museum's continues to be driven by its participants, grassroots-up?
4. **Innovation comes from inclusion.** From ramps to captioning to telling the whole history of a place or people, a more inclusive design is simply a better design for everyone. Related to the imperative to overcome the digital divide, the pivot of the Peale's programming online made it glaringly apparent that live captioning and ASL were no longer "nice to have" but essential for inclusion and therefore innovating our programming as well as expanding audiences during the pandemic. Elaine Gurian's reminder is as valid for museums' online activities as in-person ones, "If a museum accepts that it owns public space, then it also owns the impediments to it and should go about erasing them" [20].
5. **Location, location, location.** With the advent of quarantine, even digitally-active museums like the Peale found they hadn't been doing enough to "meet audiences where they were" online. Henceforth, it will be difficult for museums to justify not

digitally recording and sharing their in-person events with online audiences, as well as continuing to produce "born digital" programming to meet remote audiences where they are, be they in a virtual world like Second Life, or in popular social media platforms: the decrease in their total audience numbers, an important if regrettable metric against which museums are measured, will simply be too great. At the same time, the sense of place and location-based storytelling have never been more valued for giving people a sense of travel and "being there" in a time when we have too few options for either. Moreover, there is a profound ethical dimension to ensuring that local cultural context is not stripped from content when collections are presented in new digital or physical spaces [21].

5   Conclusion: The Collection as Collective

Stories are content that makes connections. Location-based storytelling grounds those connections in communities, be they in the physical or virtual worlds. By making collection objects available as raw ingredients for stories, museums enable connections with people and communities. When those stories are created by and with the communities they address, they are fundamentally relevant and compelling to those audiences. This deeper understanding of what role content plays in the museum's business leads us to reconsider what the museum collection is post-pandemic. With its "distributed" nature [22] and expanded online audiences, the museum must now put the "collective" of collection plus connections – stories – at the heart of its purpose.

Although this pivot centers communities in museum practice, it does not turn museums into community centers. Indeed, the collection in this expanded sphere and the creators who forge its connections through their storytelling is one of the key features that distinguishes a museum from a community center. But as Dr. Lonny Bunch, Secretary of the Smithsonian, affirmed: "I believe very strongly that museums have a social justice role to play, that museums have an opportunity to not become community centers, but to be at the center of their community, to help the community grapple with the challenges they face, to use history, to use science, to use education, to give the public tools to grapple with this" [23]. This vision takes the museum far beyond the role of destination to serve as platform in both the digital and the physical worlds. "Museums always take a point of view by what they choose to exhibit and what they decide not to exhibit," Sec. Bunch observes. By passing the microphone to their communities' creators, museums can find a new purpose and impact as community creators.

References

1. New Citizenship Project website https://www.newcitizenship.org.uk/ and in particular The Citizen Shift report https://www.citizenshift.info/. Accessed 20 Dec 2020
2. Proctor, N.: MW20 Online Conference Learnings and Feedback. MuseWeb News blog, 28 May 2020. https://www.museweb.net/mw20-online-conference-learnings-and-feedback/. Accessed 20 Dec 2020

3. The digitally-recorded stories that the Peale stewards are not a collection in the traditional sense, insofar as the Peale intentionally claims no copyright or other intellectual property ownership in the stories it helps preserve and share. The storytellers retain all rights in their stories, and provide the Peale with a free, non-exclusive, perpetual license to distribute their work

4. Unfortunately the video recording of this paper is no longer available online, so I am relying on earlier citations for this reference, e.g. Proctor, N. "Digital: Museum as Platform, Curator as Champion, in the Age of Social Media," *Curator* 53:1, January 2010, and Edson, M., "Fast, Open, and Transparent: Developing the Smithsonian's Web and New Media Strategy." In J. Trant and D. Bearman (eds). *Museums and the Web 2010: Proceedings*. Toronto: Archives & Museum Informatics. Published 31 March 2010. Consulted 27 March 2021. http://www.archimuse.com/mw2010/papers/edson/edson.html. Accessed 27 Mar 2021

5. Wikipedia contributors, Joy's law (management). Wikipedia, The Free Encyclopedia. https://en.wikipedia.org/w/index.php?title=Joy%27s_law_(management)&oldid=10066766 16. Accessed 27 Mar 2021

6. Gordon, C.: All Arts Organizations Are Media Companies Now': How the Pandemic Is Transforming Theater, Variety, 24 November 2020. https://variety.com/2020/legit/news/digital-theater-pandemic-broadway-1234836759/. Accessed 20 Dec 2020

7. WARC: Global online content consumption doubles in wake of COVID, 24 September 2020. https://www.warc.com/newsandopinion/news/global-online-content-consumption-doubles-in-wake-of-covid/44130. Accessed 20 Dec 2020

8. Anand, B.: The Content Trap. https://www.thecontenttrap.com/. Accessed 20 Dec 2020

9. Ibid. https://www.thecontenttrap.com/user-connections/. Accessed 20 Dec 2020

10. https://redefine-able.thepealecenter.org/

11. https://secondlife.com/destination/peale?sourceid=dgw1

12. https://earlybaltimore.org/

13. Hendricks, J.: A Curious Discovery, p. 222. Harper Business. Kindle Edition.

14. Simon, N.: The Art of Relevance. http://www.artofrelevance.org/

15. Proctor, N.: Museum as platform, curator as champion, in the age of social media. Curator J. (2010). https://onlinelibrary.wiley.com/doi/full/10.1111/j.2151-6952.2009.00006.x. Consulted 13 Dec 2020

16. Proctor, N. op. cit. 2020

17. Collective was also helpfully defined as a combination of people, skills and resources by Scott Burkholder, email correspondence with the author, 13 December 2020

18. Dziekan, V., Proctor, N.: From elsewhere to everywhere: evolving the distributed museum into the pervasive museum. In: Drotner, K., Dziekan, V., Parry, R., Schroder, K.C. (eds.) The Routledge Handbook of Museums, Media and Communication, 1st edn., pp. 177–192. Routledge, Oxon (2019). 16 p.

19. The concept of "co-emergence" used here references the work of Bracha Lichtenberg-Ettinger, as cited in Proctor, N. "The Virtuality of the Feminine: 'New' Media, Feminism and the Art Museum," Politics in a Glass Case: Exhibiting Women's and Feminist Art, eds. Angela Dimitrakaki and Lara Perry, Liverpool University Press (2013)

20. Gurian, E.H.: Public spaces for strangers: the foundation for peacebuilding and implications for heritage institutions. In: Walters, D., Laven, D., Davis, P. (eds.) Heritage and Peacebuilding. The Boydell Press, Woodbridge (2017)

21. See, for example, Williams, P.: A Breach on the beach: Te Papa and the fraying of biculturalism. Museum Society **3**(2), 90. Cited in Gurian, E. H. op. cit.

22. Dziekan, V., op. cit.

23. Gelles, D.: Smithsonian's Leader Says 'Museums Have a Social Justice Role to Play'. New York Times, 22 July 2020. https://www.nytimes.com/2020/07/02/business/smithsonian-lonnie-bunch-corner-office.html. Accessed 20 Dec 2020

Participation in Cultural Heritage Hackathons: 'Carsharing' Between 'Meaningful Nonsense' and 'Unromantic' Networking

Franziska Mucha^(✉)

University of Glasgow, Glasgow G12 8QQ, Scotland
franziska.mucha@glasgow.ac.uk

Abstract. This paper addresses the question why hackers participate in cultural heritage hackathons and argues for a participant-centered shift in qualitative research of digitally-enabled participation in the cultural sector. It is based on an ethnographic study of the Coding da Vinci West hackathon, including participant observation and semi-structured interviews. Three interrelated motivational factors of hackers were identified: the role in which they join, the hackathon characteristics they build on, and the connection with culture they strive for. Two groups of hackers formed around these factors: one hobby-oriented group interested in creative doing and one work-oriented group driven by professional networking. Their relations with cultural heritage institutions were either outcome-oriented or process-oriented. While the social aspect of hackathons was important for all hackers, the relevance of learning and doing were unequally distributed. However, the study also found that mostly cultural digital experts participated in the hackathon. Building on previous research, a stronger emphasis on mediating skillful practices and an invitation process based on 'areas of curiosity' instead of predefined skilled roles would potentially speak to a wider group of participants and thus support the goals of opening up collections through digitization more effectively.

Keywords: Cultural heritage hackathon · Open GLAM · Participation · Motivation

1 Introduction

In the last ten years, galleries, libraries, archives, and museums (GLAMs) have embarked on a new journey to hack their digitized collections [1]. Inspired by tech events called hackathons – a neologism combining 'to hack' and 'marathon' – the GLAM sector seized the opportunity to bring their cultural heritage data to life. Hackathons originated in engineering and computing as time-limited events in which people come together to solve a challenge using hands-on collaboration [2]. For GLAMs, and particularly the Open GLAM movement, the hackathon trend around 2010 [3] offered a welcome public platform to draw attention to their openly licensed collections and thereby demonstrate their creative potential for reuse. Hence, cultural heritage hackathons were promoted as innovative events for enthusiastic volunteer hackers to use digitized collections [4–6].

© Springer Nature Switzerland AG 2021
M. Shehade and T. Stylianou-Lambert (Eds.): RISE IMET 2021, CCIS 1432, pp. 269–281, 2021.
https://doi.org/10.1007/978-3-030-83647-4_18

However, while the benefits and practicalities for GLAM institutions have been described by both hackathon organizers and researchers [7, 8], the central stakeholders of a collaborative event, the participants, are missing in most publications. Thus, the people who join hackathons and participate in hacking cultural heritage, in this paper subsequently called hackers, have received only collateral attention and their voices have been neglected.

In the broader field of digital and participatory approaches in GLAMs, researchers have pointed to different gaps in understanding user and participants' perspectives, of which three aspects are most important for this paper: 1) users' general interests in openly licensed digitized cultural heritage collections are understudied [9–11]; 2) Web 2.0 promises and buzzwords around co-creation and crowdsourcing fueled unrealistic expectations about creative user communities that have not been validated empirically [12, 13]; 3) the motivations of those who actually join GLAM crowdsourcing projects or hackathons have yet to be examined adequately [14–16]. Taken together, there is a desideratum in research and practice which is not only impacting the success of projects on the level of usability but rather challenging the basic values and credibility of participation in GLAMs. When the logic and benefit of the institution remains the dominating vantage point for organizing digital and participatory projects, the core values of participation – power sharing, opening up, and a caring relationship – are undermined [17].

Within this context, this paper contributes a new perspective by examining why hackers participate in cultural heritage hackathons, focusing on two interrelated topics: motivations to join and benefits of taking part. It is centered on qualitative research of the hackathon Coding da Vinci West (CDV West) which took place between October and December 2019 in Germany. Based on participant observation, semi-structured interviews and online surveys it explores the perspective of hackers in this event. This text will first give a brief introduction to the background of cultural heritage hackathons and literature on motivations of cultural heritage participants. Then it will outline the methodology and context of the research project, followed by a presentation and discussion of the findings, and a conclusion.

2 Definitions and Literature

2.1 Cultural Heritage Hackathons

Cultural heritage hackathons emerged around 2010 in Europe and North America and usually address the accessibility, usability and relevance of digitized cultural heritage collections within the Open GLAM framework [4, 6]. Taylor et al. [18] see the effective advantages of hackathons in three characteristics: bringing people together, emphasizing doing (instead of talking), and peer-learning. Building on these common traits the participatory modes of hackathons have been further described by practitioners and researchers as participatory design method [19], material participation in speculative design [20] and co-creation with collections [6].

The legal framework of Creative Commons (CC) licenses and the Open GLAM movement are deeply entangled with the spread of cultural heritage hackathons, as this format seemed advantageous for staging the potential of reusing collections [6]. To do so, and to convince other cultural institutions to share their collections with user-friendly licenses, hackathons were launched. Following an open call, people are invited to form teams, hack content and create prototypes. In their research of issue-oriented hackathons Lodato and DiSalvo call this process a "collective imagination of how future users could themselves participate" [20, p. 554]. Based on the concept of speculative material participation they conclude that issue-oriented hackathons are less about the output but more about "contribut[ing] to our social imaginaries" [20, p. 554]. This echoes the key drivers of Open GLAM hackathon organizers, who want to show the possibilities of reusing cultural heritage data. Their perspective highlights the creative and imaginative potential, but also the emergent and fragile operation mode of hackathons. Critiques see the unsustainable and unreliable nature of hackathon outputs as one of the format's main shortcomings [21].

Within this paper, cultural heritage hackathons are understood as collaborative events in which people come together to creatively explore and interpret the potential of digital collections within Open GLAM conditions. They work together throughout a predefined amount of time and the aim is to develop a tangible output to showcase their idea. This process of fast and focused ideation and prototyping follows ideas of design methodologies and agile project structures. The invitation to these events applies an open call principle – everyone who feels addressed as hacker or intrigued to create something with digital collections can join. Participation is voluntary but needs to follow the time schedule of the event. Cultural hackathons are a form of digitally-enabled participation, such as crowdsourcing projects. Both facilitate engagement with digital collections but while crowdsourcing projects often ask participants to do concrete tasks, the hackathon brief leaves the use of the collections open to the participants and employs co-creation methods.

2.2 Participants' Motivations to Join and Engage in Digital and Participatory GLAM Projects

At the present time, there is almost no research on the specific topic of hackers' motivations to join and participate in cultural heritage hackathons. One exception is Moura de Araújo's doctoral thesis which touches upon motivations of hackers [1], referring to Falk's museum visitor experience type coined 'professional/hobbyist' [22]. This group is characterized by the alignment of their passion or career with the institution's content and their engagement is described as focused and goal-oriented. In an online survey with 108 respondents Moura de Araújo further examined the profile of cultural hackers and found that they often show a professional maturity and sometimes work within the cultural heritage sector.

Looking at the wider context of community- and technology-oriented hackathons the topic of motivation and participation has gained more attention in recent years, leading to more quantitative research. Briscoe and Mulligan [23] refer to the results of a commercial survey which found that learning and networking were the main motivations for hackers in context of US tech-hackathons. And Ferreira and Farias' quantitative exploratory study identified "recognition, learning, financial rewards and fun" as main motivators [24, p. 2]. Conducting quantitative analysis, they also conclude that more research involving citizens would be needed "to identify what lies beyond motivation" [24, p. 19].

Building on the above definition of hackathons and their close neighborhood with crowdsourcing as digitally-enabled forms of participation in GLAMs, this paper also draws on studies of participation in crowdsourcing. Here, Mia Ridge [25] differentiates between three types of crowdsourcing motivations: altruistic, intrinsic, and extrinsic. The distinction between intrinsic and extrinsic motivation is a classic dichotomy in psychology and the self-determination theory shaped by Richard Ryan and Edward Deci. They discriminate intrinsic motivation as focused on the "inherently interesting or enjoyable" process of doing something, and extrinsic motivation as oriented towards a "separable outcome" [26, p. 55]. Internal or intrinsic motivations are often associated with positive emotions, such as enjoyment, fun, and curiosity, while external motivations are rather negatively connotated as control or punishment, but can also stand for money or other rewards. External motivators are often opposed in Open GLAM and Open Source contexts while ideas of passion and enthusiasm are foregrounded [27]. Usually, people are motivated by a combination of both, internal and external reasons and some scholars argue that the binary does not suit the complexity and entanglement of motivational factors, e.g., when it comes to internalized external reasons [14].

In the context of cultural projects researchers found that the relation between participants and cultural institution is a relevant component as well. In this vein, Russo and Peacock's study of tagging and Web 2.0 participation suggested that institutional affiliation was one of the main motivators, which interacts with both intrinsic and extrinsic aspects [14]. This special institutional attraction that museums seem to have on some participants is also identified by psychologists Csikszentmihalyi and Hermanson [28]. Defining curiosity and interest as hooks for intrinsic motivation, museums would offer various opportunities for involvement, flow, and learning. They also recommended that "the link between the museum and the visitor's life needs to be made clear" [28, p. 73].

Building on this short literature review, the hacker stereotype 'professional/hobbyist' seems to pose a contradiction of intrinsic motivations (e.g., passion and fun in doing something) and extrinsic motivations (e.g., goal-orientation and career development) which needs further exploration. These motivations also need to be put in relation to hackathon characteristics and the special connection between hackers and cultural institution. In the light of the work other people have done, it becomes clear that hackathons have been mostly studied as participatory tools useful for GLAMs and well described in their methodology, while the motivation and benefit of hackers have received only lateral attention. This paper addresses this research gap and aims to contribute a richer qualitative insight into the perspective of hackers to the discussion.

3   Methodology and Context

This paper builds on qualitative research in form of an ethnographic study of the cultural heritage hackathon Coding da Vinci West (CDV West) as this approach is best suited to generate the much-needed empathetic insights and further understanding of cultural hackers [29]. Based on participant observation [30], semi-structured interviews [31], and online surveys the enquiry followed two questions: why do hackers join and what do they gain throughout the process of participation?

3.1   Coding da Vinci West Hackathon

The hackathon CDV West took place in Germany (Dortmund) between October and December 2019 and it was the eighth event organized under the umbrella of Coding da Vinci (CDV) – a well-known series of cultural hackathons in the German GLAM sector. Based on its experience and impact on the sector, CDV received major federal funding in 2019 and has become the dominant organizer of Open GLAM hackathons in Germany. A set of values and arrangements which are applied to all events, including this case of CDV West, define this hackathon: values of the Open GLAM movement are essential; GLAM institutions have to provide data with CC licenses; hackers use these data to create prototypes. The underlying assumption is that culture and digital are two separated worlds and thus the hackathon timeframe is expanded to give both sides more time to get to know each other. A whole weekend is dedicated to the kick-off and exchange of cultural practitioners and hackers, which is followed by a self-organized sprint phase of six to eight weeks and concluded with an award ceremony.

While CDV sees an increase in interest by GLAMs, the communication with hackers is more instable and changes with every regional context. At CDV West the number of attendees changed over time but was estimated to be around 70 in total, of which 20 were registered as hackers by the organizers. During the eight weeks of the hackathon their numbers ranged between 13 who pitched ideas at the kick-off and 17 who presented prototypes at the award ceremony – although it has to be noted that some hackers were joining only remotely.

3.2   Methods and Analysis

As participant observer the researcher joined CDV West and followed several hacking teams throughout the kick-off weekend, sprint phase and award ceremony. Participant observation was based on well-established ethical guidelines for conducting ethnographic research [32–34] and informed consent by all hackathon attendees was sought in two steps: an email informed everyone previous to the hackathon and the researcher presented herself to the hackathon audience during the observed face-to-face events. Everyone at these events was provided with an information sheet and a consent form. Research was conducted in context-sensitive and reflexive way after gaining the approval by the ethics committee of the University of Glasgow.

Before and after the hackathon event an anonymous online survey on JISC was distributed to all hackathon attendees. Survey participants could choose between four functions at the event, of which the category 'participants' represented the hackers. Within this group, participation in the survey was low: four participants in the pre-survey and eight participants in the post-survey answered the open question: "What motivates/motivated you to participate?". A total of twelve free-text qualitative answers were gathered as preliminary information and gave first thinking points for the following steps of qualitative interviewing and coding.

Interviews were designed in the form of semi-structured interviews [31] following an interview guide with themed questions which covered creative practice, team collaboration and motivation to participate. Seven team interviews with 13 individual hackers were conducted after the hackathon, five in person and two via the video call apps Skype and Zoom. Interviewees had to have an active hacking role at the CDV West event using the provided data. All interviews were audio recorded by the researcher.

The software MAXQDA was used for the analysis of all generated data. Interview recordings were transcribed with the embedded transcription tool and coded following Rädiker and Kuckartz' guide on focused analysis of qualitative interviews with MAXQDA [35]. Grounded on a cyclical process for qualitative coding proposed by Saldaña [36], a rough category system was used as starting point for the basic coding which was then refined and extended through the coding process. For the topic of this paper, hackathon participation was structured following the categories deduced from previous studies: hobby, professional (as hacker stereotype); learning, people, doing (as hackathon characteristics); and institution, data (as cultural dimension). All direct quotes taken from interviews and fieldnotes are referred to by an anonymous numbering system ranging from Participant 1 (P1) to Participant 10 (P10) throughout this paper.

4 Findings

Using the survey data to get a first impression what hackers said about their reasons for joining, three motivational tendencies became visible: reasons concerning the outcome (e.g., building networks and connections between culture and technology), reasons concerning the process (e.g., collaboration with a team and cultural data), and reasons concerning the event format (e.g., interesting project).

In the further analysis of interview data and fieldnotes traces of the professional/hobbyist motivations were visible, but rather diverged in two groups: two teams highlighted their professional identity, while three teams foregrounded their hobbyist approach. Two teams did not fall into either category as they had mixed motivations and backgrounds. However, in line with Moura de Araújo's findings [1], CDV West mostly attracted cultural digital experts, who work as computer linguists, game/graphic/UX designers, media artists, data scientists, library computer scientists and developers. Thus, their orientations represented their role in the hackathon rather than their professional expertise. The next sections will introduce hackers of each group to follow their narrations and illustrate the interplay of motivations with other aspects of the hackathon and the cultural sector.

4.1 The Reality of 'unromantic' Networking

Two interviewed teams develop digital services as freelancers or start-ups and highlighted this professional role. In the interview with one of these teams, consisting of four young game designers specialized in 3D modelling, they expressed their frustration with the cultural sector. Prior to the hackathon they had experienced disappointing collaborations with museums that seemed to have a rather conservative stance towards technology. In turn, they hoped a hackathon would attract more technology-interested institutions and provide a fruitful environment to pave the way for paid contracts in the future. One team member commented with a sarcastic undertone: "Sounds unromantic, but that's just how it is." (P1). Framing their approach as 'unromantic' the participant marked a difference between their pragmatism and what they perceived as romantic Open GLAM ideals.

While their strategic reasons might not be the ones promoted first by the CDV framework, they were shared by other hackathon teams that wanted to "build a project portfolio" (P2) and thought the event "a good networking opportunity" (P3). Networking, strategic partnerships and building a project portfolio subsequently functioned as crucial factors for choosing a dataset and institution to work with during the hackathon. A regional museum with two very engaged young professionals was selected and addressed as potential customer. Besides the obvious local connection one hacker explained this choice referring to their technical expertise which matched the dataset so they could create an added value (P4). By choosing a dataset which helped them to showcase their skills and services, they could position themselves as professional agents in the field. The output was meant to be of high quality and function as portfolio project. This awareness about professional resources and expertise was shared by another agency-based hacker team who chose not to use one dataset because they simply lacked the skills to process it. This professional aspiration also became tangible in the way how these teams described their working process: a design-thinking approach with iterative cycles.

The outlook of work-related networking and the creation of portfolio projects can be assessed as extrinsic motivations focusing on the output and what participation in the hackathon leads to. This ties in with output-oriented reasons for joining found in the survey and the understanding of hackathons in computing and engineering, which have a stronger emphasis on competition, networking, and value-creation business models [23, 37].

4.2 The Joy of Doing 'meaningful Nonsense'

Three teams foregrounded their hobbyist approach to participation, although most of them also have a professional relation with the topic and work in GLAM institutions. However, to them the hackathon was a balance to and diversion from the job and the creative practice of coding was seen as inherently rewarding activity. This approach is rooted in the joy of doing something which is not following the rules of a paid contract but instead serves as hobby – signposting to intrinsic motivations. Three interviewed teams described their individual fun and enjoyment during the hackathon as a motivation to join. Comparing coding to baking, one interviewee explained the different aspects which made coding a fun activity:

"To engage with this data allows me to bring together different interests. At the same time, you can perceive this data again and again, you look at them, you work with the pictures or with the sounds. On the other hand, you have this constructive effect and the creative effect – i.e., constructive in the sense of programming, creative in the sense of interface and how to put these data into new contexts. It's simply a whole complex of activities that all come together and the mixture is actually what makes it fun." (P5).

Listening to and looking at cultural heritage data, using them to construct and program something new, designing and creating a new context, and spending time with programming are listed as ingredients of this hobby. At a hackathon this hobby can be shared with others and the event offered a reason to spend time together and do something together, which would not be possible during their working life (P6).

Another participant described hackathon projects as relaxing because they could let their creativity flow and produce anything that came to mind. In contrast to their daily job the output would not need to be overly serious but could be rather whacky. In this vein, the opportunity to produce "meaningful nonsense" (P7), to play around without any constraints using interesting and valuable content, would be their main motivation to participate. While at the same time they felt the freedom to follow their own interests and ideas, the production of new meaning with old cultural content was seen as a way to enhance their hobby.

Csikszentmihalyi [38] developed the concept of flow as one state of deep involvement in an activity which can be reached when challenges and skills are well matched, and goals, interest and feedback are aligned. In this group of hackers, immersion in the activity led to 'meaningful experiences' which played a major role in their hackathon participation. These insights add context to the process-oriented reasons for joining initially found in the survey and explain how they relate to increased interest in using cultural data, but not necessarily cultural partnerships. Their projects did, in fact, more often conflict with expectations of GLAM data providers because they chose their own interpretations of culture.

4.3 'Carsharing Phenomenon'

Hackathons were defined as being about people, learning, and doing. But which of these aspects are important to hackers and how do they interpret them? 'Doing' was mostly valued and mentioned by hobbyists in describing their creative practices in great detail. In this group, the immersion in the activity and combination of their skillful practice with culturally interesting content led to 'meaningful experiences' which played a major role in their hackathon participation. Their practices illustrate a form of active and creative engagement which many institutions hope for when opening up and digitizing their collections. All three teams had participated in CDV hackathons before and emphasized these positive experiences as motivation to join again.

Learning for these hackers was less prominent as motivator in advance, but was seen as a side effect of the hackathon: two teams mentioned technologies they wanted to try out, such as 3D modelling software and stop-motion animation. Their interest in acquiring new technical skills was balanced with an interest in learning something about the cultural content they chose. Within the professional group, learning was mostly intended as outcome for end-users of their projects, while their own learning was rather seen as contribution to general knowledge production. This ties in with the future imagination work which Lodato and DiSalvo [20] see in hacking.

In contrast, learning was the main motivator for two hackers who did not identify with either of the described hacker groups: one student and one cultural data provider. The student joined the hackathon to learn how to build a web crawler. They chose CDV West because the timing suited and they were looking for any kind of hackathon, culture was not important. Within the tech-hackathon community, they explained, the motto "more learning than doing" (P8) would be the prevalent way of using hackathons. The other learner initially joined in the role of cultural data provider and was hoping to see others play around with their data. When no hacker chose their dataset, they just decided to hack their data themselves and used the hackathon context to learn the front-end programming language Java Script with the help of the wider CDV community. They were very thankful for this engagement and support, which allowed them "to build their idea on the code of someone else" (P9).

The effect of hackathons to bring different people together played a major role for all hackers and one interviewee coined this as "carsharing phenomenon" (P7): a situation in which you spend a limited amount of time with a surprising mix of people you would not have met otherwise. While professionals used this situation mostly to extend their network, hobbyists enjoyed the interdisciplinary collaboration and exchange with other perspectives. In the context of a cultural hackathon this social experience is defined by the individual relationships between hackers, organizers, and cultural practitioners. Hackers had varied experiences with cultural institutions and organizers, ranging from collaboration and support to disinterest and misunderstanding. For most hackers it was important to gain recognition for their work either directly by the cultural institution or through the award ceremony of the hackathon. The excitement of working towards the award ceremony, having a stage for creativity, and receiving positive feedback, motivated hackers throughout the hackathon.

In particular one team who had joined three CDV hackathons before described how other typical characteristics of a hackathon – time-limit and the focus on tangible outputs – increased their positive experience: "to do your own project from A-Z" and to see a result in the end would be a great feeling because "you would really reach a goal" (P10). The process was perceived as wholesome and concise, because the project has a beginning and an end. However, these impressions were counterbalanced with negative emotions they had experienced after hackathons – something they called "post-CDV depression" (P6) – when all their work was without effect and GLAM institutions were not interested in following-up on their collaboration.

5   Discussion

The qualitative analysis has looked behind motivational types, such as 'professional/hobbyist' to show how hackers link motivation and participation. Rich interview data and fieldnotes from the hackathon helped to outline two differently motivated groups of hackers who use hackathons in different ways. However, both share a digital cultural expertise and thus form a specialized user group which differs from the majority of GLAM visitors and users. Broader audience groups did not participate in CDV West which raises the question how hackathons might become more inclusive events for creative engagement with digitized collections. This matches the evaluations of other cultural hackathons, such as Museomix. Here, Rey observed difficulties of inviting participants based on the predefinition of roles. She concludes the call for digitally skilled experts would exclude "the 'classical' visitors, the very user at the centre of the participative design methodology" [19, p. 5]. In order to make hackathons more inclusive she recommends to bring in additional volunteers with the needed technical skills and in turn open the invitation for other types of expertise. Taylor et al.'s work on 'Community Inventor Days' illustrates how such an adapted hackathon version for a wider community, supported by expert practitioners, could look like. However, they also found that motivating skilled experts was more difficult than expected and would need more attention in future projects [18, p. 1202].

The findings in this paper suggest that what participants had gained from hackathons motivated them to join again: the possibility of a social experience, networking, learning, and creative doing. Emphasizing these aspects in the process of inviting might address a wider group of participants and would imply an important shift of perspectives from needed skills to participants' benefits. Following Lindström and Ståhl [39] these benefits could be further developed into shared 'areas of curiosity' to provide a bridge between GLAMs and participants. The findings show that this connection between hackers and GLAM institutions is important and needs more attention throughout the whole hackathon. Within CDV cultural heritage practitioners have a rather passive role in providing cultural data for hackers. Thus, a shift to more engagement and collaboration based on a shared interest could help to mitigate the 'post-CDV depression', increase the recognition of hackers' contributions, and make the collaboration more sustainable. While the scope of this paper only consists of one case study, more qualitative research of other cultural heritage hackathons is needed to compare participants' profiles and motivations across cases. Furthermore, participatory research projects might increase the collaboration between GLAMs and hackers and explore new ways of inviting and motivating people to hack cultural heritage.

6 Conclusion

This paper addresses the question of why hackers participate in cultural heritage hackathons. It did so by presenting and discussing data generated in an ethnographic study of the CDV West hackathon. Based on qualitative analysis of online surveys, fieldnotes and seven team interviews with 13 hackers, different interrelated motivational factors were identified: the role in which they join, the hackathon characteristics they build on, and the connection with culture they strive for. Two groups of hackers formed around these factors: one hobby-oriented group interested in creative doing and one work-oriented group driven by professional networking. Their relations with cultural heritage institutions were either outcome-oriented, as in building useful connections for the future, or process-oriented, as in collaboration and recognition throughout the hackathon. The social aspect of the event which was coined as 'carsharing phenomenon' creates the main attraction for participants – this and the hackathon potential of meaningful practices, networking, and learning could be further developed to share the possibility of interpretation, learning, and imagination based on open collections with a wider group of people.

Acknowledgements. The researcher is thankful to participants and organizers of Coding da Vinci West for sharing their knowledge and expertise, helping to create research data, as well as providing ideas and feedback.

References

1. Moura de Araújo, L.: Hacking cultural heritage - the hackathon as a method for heritage interpretation. Ph.D. Universität Bremen (2018)
2. Richterich, A.: Hacking events: project development practices and technology use at hackathons. Converg. Int. J. Res. New Media Technol. **30**(5), 1–27 (2017). https://doi.org/10.1177/1354856517709405
3. Leckart, S.: The Hackathon is on: pitching and programming the next killer app. Wired (2012). https://www.wired.com/2012/02/ff-hackathons/. Accessed 20 Jul 2021
4. Terras, M.: Opening access to collections: the making and using of open digitised cultural content. Online Inf. Rev. **39**(5), 733–752 (2015). https://doi.org/10.1108/OIR-06-2015-0193
5. Bartholmei, S., Mucha, F.: Wir wollen in die Köpfe. Interview mit Stephan Bartholmei über den Kultur-Hackathon Coding da Vinci (2019). https://bkw.hypotheses.org/1573. Accessed 11 Nov 2020
6. Schmidt, A.: Voraussetzungen für und Herausforderungen von Co-Creation mit digitalen Museumssammlungen. In: Holst, C. (ed.) Kultur in Interaktion, pp. 51–62. Springer, Wiesbaden (2020). https://doi.org/10.1007/978-3-658-27260-9_4
7. Davis, R.C.: Hackathons for Libraries and Librarians. Behav. Soc. Sci. Libr. **35**(2), 87–91 (2016). https://doi.org/10.1080/01639269.2016.1208561
8. Clark, H-L., et al.: Global History Hackathon Playbook Version 1.1: Practical Guidance for Hosting a Hackathon for the Arts, Humanities, and Social Sciences. Research Report, University of Glasgow (2019)
9. Terras, M.: So you want to reuse digital heritage content in a creative context? Good luck with that. Art Libr. J. **40**(4), 33–37 (2015). https://doi.org/10.1017/S0307472200020502
10. Clough, P., Hill, T., Paramita, M.L., Goodale, P.: Europeana: what users search for and why. In: Kamps, J., Tsakonas, G., Manolopoulos, Y., Iliadis, L., Karydis, I. (eds.) TPDL 2017. LNCS, vol. 10450, pp. 207–219. Springer, Cham (2017). https://doi.org/10.1007/978-3-319-67008-9_17
11. Valeonti, F., Terras, M., Hudson-Smith, A.: How open is OpenGLAM? Identifying barriers to commercial and non-commercial reuse of digitised art images. Journal of Documentation **76**(1), 1–26 (2019). https://doi.org/10.1108/JD-06-2019-0109
12. van Dijck, J., Nieborg, D.: Wikinomics and its discontents: a critical analysis of Web 2.0 business manifestos. New Media Soc. **11**(5), 855–874 (2009). https://doi.org/10.1177/1461444809105356
13. Kidd, J.: Public heritage and the promise of the digital. In: Labrador, A.M., Silberman, N.A. (eds.) The Oxford Handbook of Public Heritage Theory and Practice, pp. 197–208. Oxford University Press, New York (2018). https://doi.org/10.1093/oxfordhb/9780190676315.013.9
14. Russo, A., Peacock, D.: Great expectations: sustaining participation in social media spaces. In: Proceedings of Museums and the Web 2009. https://www.archimuse.com/mw2009/papers/russo/russo.html. Accessed 30 Nov 2020
15. Aljas, A.: Motivations for participating in museums' interventions. Media Transform. **11**, 84–105 (2015). https://doi.org/10.7220/2029-8668.11.05

16. Eveleigh, A.M.M.: Crowding Out the Archivist? Implications of Online User Participation for Archival Theory and Practice. University College London, University of London, Ph.D (2015)
17. Morse, N.: The Museum as a Space of Social Care. Routledge, Oxon (2021)
18. Taylor, N., Clarke, L. Gorkovenko, K.: Community inventor days. In: Mival, O., Smyth, M., Dalsgaard, P. (eds.) DIS' 2017: Proceedings of the 2017 ACM Conference on Designing Interactive Systems, Edinburgh, UK, pp. 1201–1212. The Association for Computing Machinery, New York (2017). https://doi.org/10.1145/3064663.3064723
19. Rey, S.: Museomix: lessons learned from an open creative hackathon in museums. In: Anastasiou, D., Maquil, V. (eds.) CEUR Workshop Proceedings - Proceedings of the 3rd European Tangible Interaction Studio, ETIS 2017, pp. 1–6 (2017)
20. Lodato, T.J., DiSalvo, C.: Issue-oriented hackathons as material participation. New Media Soc. **18**(4), 539–557 (2016). https://doi.org/10.1177/1461444816629467
21. Arrigoni, G., Schofield, T., Trujillo Pisanty, D.: Framing collaborative processes of digital transformation in cultural organisations: from literary archives to augmented reality. Museum Manag. Curator. **35**(4), 424–445 (2020). https://doi.org/10.1080/09647775.2019. 1683880
22. Falk, J.H.: Identity and the Museum Visitor Experience. Routledge, London (2016). https:// doi.org/10.4324/9781315427058
23. Briscoe, G., Mulligan, C.: Digital Innovation: The Hackathon Phenomenon: Creativeworks London, Working Paper No. 6. (2014)
24. Ferreira, G.d.D., Farias, J.S.: The motivation to participate in citizen-sourcing and Hackathons in the public sector. Braz. Administr. Rev. **15**(3), 2–23 (2018). https://doi.org/ 10.1590/1807-7692bar2018180006
25. Ridge, M.: From tagging to theorizing: deepening engagement with cultural heritage through crowdsourcing. Curator: Mus. J. **56**(4), 435–450 (2013). https://doi.org/10.1111/cura.12046
26. Ryan, R.M., Deci, E.L.: Intrinsic and extrinsic motivations: classic definitions and new directions. Contemp. Educ. Psychol. **25**(1), 54–67 (2000). https://doi.org/10.1006/ceps.1999. 1020
27. Estellés-Arolas, E., González-Ladrón-de-Guevara, F.: Towards an integrated crowdsourcing definition. J. Inf. Sci. **38**(2), 189–200 (2012). https://doi.org/10.1177/0165551512437638
28. Csikszentmihalyi, M., Hermanson, K.: Intrinsic motivation in museums: why does one want to learn? In: Falk, J.H., Dierking, L.D. (eds.) Public Institutions for Personal Learning: Establishing a Research Agenda, pp. 67–77. American Association of Museums, Washington (1995)
29. Mason, J.: Qualitative Researching, 3rd edn. Sage, London (2017)
30. O'Reilly, K.: Key Concepts in Ethnography. SAGE, Los Angeles (2012). https://doi.org/10. 4135/9781446268308.n26
31. Olsen, W.K.: Data Collection: Key Debates and Methods in Social Research. SAGE, London (2012). https://doi.org/10.4135/9781473914230
32. Yang, K., Kurian, A., Barankin, B.: Ethics. In: Nasir, A. (ed.) Clinical Dermatology Trials 101, pp. 143–159. Springer, Cham (2015). https://doi.org/10.1007/978-3-319-09027-6_8
33. Guest, G., Namey, E.E., Mitchell, M.L.: Collecting Qualitative Data: A Field Manual for Applied Research. SAGE, London (2013). https://doi.org/10.4135/9781506374680
34. American Association of Anthropology Statement on Ethics. https://www.americananthro. org/LearnAndTeach/Content.aspx?ItemNumber=22869. Accessed 2 Mar 2021
35. Rädiker, S., Kuckartz, U.: Focused Analysis of Qualitative Interviews with MAXQDA, 1st edn, MAXQDA Press (2020). https://doi.org/10.36192/978-3-948768072
36. Saldaña, J.: The Coding Manual for Qualitative Researchers, 2nd edn, SAGE, Los Angeles (2013)

37. Trainer, E.H., Kalyanasundaram, A., Chaihirunkarn, C., Herbsleb, J.D.: How to hackathon. In: CSCW'16: Proceedings & Companion of the ACM Conference on Computer-Supported Cooperative Work and Social Computing: February 27–March 2, 2016, San Francisco, CA, USA, pp. 1118–1130. Association for Computing Machinery, New York (2016). https://doi.org/10.1145/2818048.2819946
38. Csikszentmihalyi, M.: Applications of Flow in Human Development and Education: the Collected Works of Mihaly Csikszentmihalyi. Springer, Dordrecht (2014)
39. Lindström, K., Ståhl, Å.: Politics of inviting: co-articulations of issues in designerly public engagement. In: Smith, R.C., Vangkilde, K.T., Kjaersgaard, M.G., Otto, T., Halse, J., Binder, T. (eds.) Design Anthropological Futures: Exploring Emergence, Intervention and Formation, pp. 183–197. Bloomsbury, London (2016)

Museum Social Media Practices: In Need of Repair?

Cassandra Kist[(⊠)] ⓘ

University of Glasgow, Glasgow G12 8QQ, UK
Cassandra.kist@glasgow.ac.uk

Abstract. Within the museum sector, research and associated theories on technology can often lead to rhetoric on progression that results in the idealization of the new or the emergent. However, if we approach technologies with a sensitivity towards their fragility, we see it is not always progression that is most interesting, but processes of repair. Social media, it can be argued, is an outdated technology which has lost its excitement and like the larger ideals associated with digital in the cultural heritage sector, is perceived with skepticism. Yet, with the rise of the museum's social role, museums have an ethical responsibility to understand the factors that shape how social media practices are enacted. In this paper I take on perspective of repair to explore the intersection between social media and organizational structures through an in-depth ethnographic case study of Glasgow Museums Services (Glasgow, UK). The analysis provides essential insights into the (dis)-connections between museum social media practices and museum infrastructure. It suggests that the desire for more participatory social media practices overlooks the underpinning and incompatible elements of the museum institution.

Keywords: Museum · Social media · Infrastructure · Repair

1 Introduction

Museum literature often emphasizes the potential of social media for democratizing heritage, increasing access, enabling new social connections and for allowing new voices to be heard [1, 2]. Thus, it might seem odd to apply a framework of 'repair' to the use of these platforms. However, it is the critics in opposition to this idealization, who argue museums on social media often fail to fulfill their participatory promise which calls for a lens of repair [3]. Instances of discrepancy between the espoused potential of social media and museum practice are apparent by the surmounting evidence that many institutions prioritize marketing and broadcasting motivations for social media use over engagement, participation and associated social goals [4–6]. The reason for these critiques has been investigated in different ways, often through surveys of museum staff and interviews [4–6]. Few researchers have studied the intersection between context and staff's social media practices through an in-depth ethnographic case study, with notable exceptions [7]. To further nuance existing knowledge of museum social media work, I take on a perspective of repair grounded in Science and Technology Studies, to understand the use of social media as a fragile practice – which

© Springer Nature Switzerland AG 2021
M. Shehade and T. Stylianou-Lambert (Eds.): RISE IMET 2021, CCIS 1432, pp. 282–293, 2021.
https://doi.org/10.1007/978-3-030-83647-4_19

could be heavily impacted by the structures of museum institutions and social platforms.

Repair according to Nemer and Chirumamilla [8] is a process of "sustained engagement", it is making do with what one has and contending with states of "neglect" or "decay" (p. 221). Previous research has investigated the repair of physical components of technology such as ships [9], but this paper pays attention to practice and its intersection with museum infrastructure building off previous researchers that use this analytical lens [10, 11]. To do so, this paper draws on a wide range of data from an in-depth case study of Glasgow Museums, which is complimented by seven interviews with external social media professionals, from diverse cultural heritage institutions in Scotland. The paper argues that staff's practices of repair at Glasgow Museums exposes tensions between social media use and elements of museum infrastructure. In doing so, it also highlights the structures and spaces that may support staff's social media work.

2 Literature Review

According to a recent tweet from a MuseWeb conference "[s]ocial media is a dead topic...". This sentiment closely aligns with several publications that accuse museums of focusing on marketing, overlooking the participatory potential of social media and associated social intentions [5, 7, 12, 13]. Yet, social media is recognised as a medium through which museums amongst other institutions can increase accessibility, reach broader audiences and perhaps in a small way fulfill social goals [2]. This is partly due to the definition of social media as encompassing both a "culture and subset of networked digital media", which carries "connotations of democratizing the media landscape and societies in various ways" ([2], p. 282). Indeed, there are increasing examples of museums using social media for social goals by sparking discussions across staff and organization, on contemporary issues through hashtags such as, #MuseumWorkersSpeak and through associations such as Museum Detox [14]. Museums can also use social media to advocate for social justice by providing an alternative perspective on historical events and thus, the present [15]. Further, there is recognition of the potential for users to feedback into the institution and change practices [16] and to hold institutions accountable by calling publicly for change [17]. Together, these publications suggest that the museum field is not ready to accept social media as a dead topic.

However, due to persisting critiques of museum social media as prioritizing marketing over social initiatives, many academics have been quick to investigate musesocial[1]. Previous investigations considered the 'success' of museums' online activity by correlating the genre or frame of museum social media posts to such things as user likes, reposts, inspiration or popularity [18, 19]. Other researchers point to elements of museum structures and culture as impacting and shaping social media work. For example,

---

[1] 'Musesocial' is a term commonly used in the cultural heritage sector to refer to museum social media work and is frequently used as a hashtag on Twitter to enable discussions in the field.

some have taken a closer look at social media practices in terms of motivation and barriers through staff surveys and interview, noting that institutions lack strategies, goals, resources, and digital literacies [5]. Further, that social media engagement raises critical questions about sustainability, values, and ethics [20]. Museum staff have also published on their personal experiences, calling for change in the sector to recognize the under-valued skillset of musesocial professionals which often leads to burnout [21, 22]. Such calls for investment may be connected to long-standing concerns regarding the adoption of social media for its impacts on the authenticity of objects, control of its use and context, authorship or copyright concerns, and institutional image [23]. These factors which may shape and limit social media speaks to the concept of infrastructures.

Infrastructures are often considered to be invisible systems – the "substrate" from which "substance" takes place ([24], p. 5). Infrastructure enables life to continue normally and includes not only the tangible material or brick and mortar of vital structures such as roadways but also existing values and norms. Infrastructure connects people and things and draws attention to the "ways in which technical systems connect to other structures and social practices across different sites" ([25], p. 215). The museum here is acknowledged to operate on infrastructures composed of the organi-zation of staff and work, institutional priorities, and norms [25] which are directly connected to practice [26]. In other words, infrastructure serves as the foundation or base from which activities and practices can occur. The above-mentioned concerns regarding social media in the museum field might suggest in part, infrastructural limitations to social media practices. Understanding infrastructure's relation to mus-esocial practices could be extended beyond previous research through greater attention to its operation within a specific context.

In particular, the concept of repair is used in this study to draw closer attention to the impact of infrastructure on museum social media practices. As Graziano and Trogal [10] suggest, repair draws attention to the "interaction between humans, machines and materials", but also "refers to the necessity of maintaining systems of social relations in institutional practices" ([10], p. 203). When we think of repair, it can suggest the fixing of broken things, but as a concept, repair has been applied in various ways to materials, objects, organizations, and even activist movements. Building on organizational studies, Henke [27] describes repair practices as "negotiating order in contexts where heterogeneous elements come together to create complex social and technical systems" (p. 257). While repair can relate to achieving a fix, it can also be perceived as main-tenance. Maintenance encompasses both staff practices and micro-frustrations that consistently contend and engage with breakdown which could provide insight into the infrastructural elements that cause disjuncture in social media practices [8]. In doing so, repair could also enable future organizational change by pointing to the spaces, structures, or skills that support staff's social media work. Therefore, to further understand the relation between museum infrastructure and social media work, this paper takes a unique approach by being embedded in Glasgow Museums.

3   Methodology

This research takes on the form of an in-depth case study which aims to understand a phenomenon in relation to context. In this case, the phenomenon is the frequently critiqued marketing frame of social media use in comparison to its potentials for inclusivity and social goals. The research questions investigated in this paper which stem from a portion of my larger thesis research include: What are the infrastructural factors that intersect with and shape staff's social media practices? What can staff's micro-frustrations and acts of maintenance tell us about how staff contend with infrastructure? As part of this case study, I undertook a year-long social media ethnography (Sept. 2019–Sept. 2020) of and within Glasgow Museums Service (GM)[2], based at the Open Museum (OM), an outreach team and one of the 11 institutions under the branch of GM. Glasgow Museums is known for its long history of social inclusion policy statements and strategy documents [28], which is reflected in co-created community projects and exhibitions, often led by the Open Museum staff [29].

Postill and Pink [30] define social media ethnography as focused on the intersection of online and offline contexts and practices. As such, it could be conceptualized as an internet-based ethnography rather than an internet ethnography. Due to social media ethnography's focus on the relations between social media practices and context, it aligns with central research questions by pointing to its intersection with local histories, political structures or in this paper, institutional infrastructures. The social media ethnography involved attending several staff meetings and volunteering for OM activities which enabled my understanding of the relation between staff practices and museum infrastructure. I also immersed myself in social media practices by cocreating a social media strategy with OM staff and helping to create and coordinate Instagram posts. In this process I tried to maintain an active reflexivity in my involvement with staff and the institution. As a result, the research relied on a variety of data sources including, Glasgow Museums' social media meeting notes, ethnographic notes and 23 semi-structured interviews with staff who contribute to the social media channels across the institutions. These forms of data were stored and analyzed on the software MAXQDA using a thematic analysis following an iterative approach to data collection and analysis [31]. Due to some comments being sensitive, all staff here are anonymous and cited as 'GM staff'. The field work at Glasgow Museums was further complimented by seven semi-structured interviews with external social media professionals, from diverse cultural heritage institutions in Scotland.

---

[2] Glasgow Museums is the largest museum service in the UK outside London, consisting of 11 venues which is managed by the charity Glasgow Life - an institution that supports activities related to culture, sports, and learning.

4 Analysis and Results

As proposed by Nemer and Chirumamilla [8] repair can be conceptualized as "sustained encounters" in which infrastructural conditions are contended with, placing emphasis on "making do" over progression (p. 221). However, processes of making do can also reveal the reasons for a perceived disconnection in media practices [8]. During my placement, Glasgow Museum staff frequently suggested a negative perception of their social media practices, describing it as "haphazard" (GM Staff B), "dis-jointed" (GM staff D), "patch-work" (GM staff M) and "not very organized..." (GM Staff V). They also often referred to the social media of the institution as "boring" (GM Staff X) and "needing some work" (GM Staff H). Such descriptors imply a lack of consistency across social media work and therefore might suggest a perception of practices as 'broken'.

When probed further, staff cite a variety of evidence such as a tendency to "broadcast messages", "relay essential information" or simply "putting things out there" as proof of their inadequate practices (GM Staff A; GM Staff X; GM Staff H) and they explicitly and implicitly state that this is due to digital and institutional infrastructures. This holds meaningful lessons in relation to the connection between the museum's infrastructure and its impact on staff's social media practices. By putting social media practices forward into the ongoing entanglements of agency, daily work, and interests, the relations of value and order that structures the social media work within Glasgow Museums began to become apparent [9]. Specifically, these infrastructural elements include the division of responsibilities and associated content, hierarchal control, and risk aversion.

4.1 Balancing Responsibilities

It is increasingly acknowledged in museum literature that there tends to be an over-use of social media for marketing or broadcasting rather than engagement, let alone engagement aimed towards social change [5, 12, 13]. According to a digital staff member at a Scottish museum (personal communication, 2019) and a marketing staff member at a Scottish library (personal communication, 2019) social media is its own thing that encompasses cross departmental content and concerns, including: customer service, marketing, curatorial, research and engagement. As a result, these social media professionals suggest that social media work requires an active effort to continuously balance content and forms of use. The process of finding that balance may take years, as the Scottish library staff member suggests when they started at their institution social media was a "poor man's marketing channel" and today its privileged for how it can enable engagement. Further, the staff member explains in their experiences, no institution has social media in the same place/department or approaches it in the same way.

As evident in the discussion below, this balancing process of social media responsibilities and expectations at Glasgow Museums, manifests as an ongoing tension between staff responsibilities, priorities, and content. At Glasgow Museums there is no clear agreement on where social media should sit in the larger institution and by whom or how it should be run. There are three main Glasgow Museums digital staff members: One staff member, a Digital and New Media Manager leads digital initiatives across 10 Glasgow Museum venues in conjunction with a Digital Curator, while a second Digital Media Manager manages digital interpretation for the Burrell Renaissance big capital project. Both the Digital and New Media Manager and Digital Curator always have their hands full with high demand for their work and input across the 10 institutions. As a result, the upkeep of the institution's social media channels (over 28 accounts encompassing Facebook, Instagram and Twitter amongst others) is often passed between the digital team, the other museum staff members and Glasgow Life's marketing department[3]. Due to these shared responsibilities, staff comment that it is unclear who is leading social media, critically asking "who is the person who is really in charge of public messaging and who do you listen to?" (GM staff V).

Others have observed that "no one has really taken the reigns of social media…" (GM Staff G). In discussing other institutions one staff member reflected, "I feel like here, they don't even know themselves where it goes, you know is it marketing, is it something else – what is it?" (GM Staff V). In addition to this uncertainty, staff critique the channels as being filled with too much marketing content which drowns out staff voices and engagement. As one staff member reflected, "[f]rom a personal perspective, when you lose that identity of engagement within a social media channel - kind of what's the point?" (GM Staff F). As a result, some staff referenced pushing marketing to "let up" for their voices to be heard and not lost amongst the marketing stream (GM staff G). Such critical observations regarding the shared nature of social media work are also coupled by staff being occasionally referred to as digital "representatives" and a "team against marketing", encouraging a sort of staff alliance in trying to expand the balance of social media responsibilities (GM staff I; GM staff G).

The uncertainty of where social media goes and tension between a shared social media responsibility may also be caused by a lack of standards or guidelines for best practice. Compared to other digital positions, social media at Glasgow Museums has been described as "oddly structured" due to gaps in guidance (GM Staff R) and an absence of clear standards (GM Staff W). External social media professionals suggested in finding that 'balance' between content and responsibilities, social media guidelines and institutional direction could be empowering (Social media staff member, personal communication, 2020; Marketing staff member, personal communications, 2019). In comparison, several staff at Glasgow Museums, when queried if strategies or goals exist for the social media platforms stated, they simply "do the best they can" (GM Staff M; GM Staff F; GM Staff G). These common reflections of doing their best within constraints speaks to the idea of staff practices of repair as an ongoing maintenance.

4.2   Working Around Hierarchal Control

Frequent references to making do or doing their best suggests a continuous effort on the part of GM staff regarding the maintenance of social media use within an infrastructural backdrop of neglect. Staff's maintenance practices and micro-frustrations point to not only the reason for breakages but also factors that support staff's ability to carry-on. For instance, around 2012 digital staff members set up a monthly meeting for staff who

---

[3] Glasgow Life's marketing team is responsible for Glasgow Museum's marketing capacities.

contribute to social media to address any concerns, discuss upcoming events, and talk about things that worked or failed at their respective institution. During these meetings staff shared and reflected with their colleagues on content and forms of engagement they had experimented with, from mystery objects at the Riverside Museum to April Fool's Day across the institutions. The monthly meetings exemplified that experimenting with content and approaches is possible and desired by staff on the ground, taking place to different extents even amid uncertainty.

However, it was clear these meetings were also a space to express concerns or even fears regarding ideas for content, campaigns, or projects. For instance, staff reflected on their lack of participation in museum meme day due to fear of being inappropriate or taking it too far (Social media meeting) and in making suggestions for April Fool's Day questioned if management and marketing would be "onboard" (Social media meeting). These reflections and hesitancies on the part of staff may be related to social media restrictions and censorship by the marketing team. Although staff's expressions of uncertainty highlight the institutional restrictions, they also expose the importance of staff support and spaces for sharing their fears and triumphs. As one staff member emphasized, the social media meetings were useful for discussion and felt it provided a "network of support", insinuating the importance of colleagues for social media work within constraints (GM Staff C).

Indeed, during my placement the actions of marketing appeared to be based on uncertainty in the use of these publicly visible channels for institutional identity. Restrictions were mainly evident in staff's expressions of disappointment in relation to not having direct access to social media profiles, complaints about being told a change in passwords for Sprout Social at the last minute or being audited for the content they post, as was expressed in interviews (GM Staff M; GM Staff D; GM staff R; GM staff N) but also several social media meetings. Sprout Social is a collaborative social media scheduling tool through which staff members can create and schedule posts and is a central source of stress and complaints. Sprout allows upper management and marketing to schedule and oversee social media content. As a result of these controls, some staff find workarounds by not using Sprout or relying on personal mobile devices to work with the platform more easily. On the other hand, several staff prefer to use their own accounts even when associated with their work and museum related content. Similar experiences were also recounted in external interviews, with musesocial staff stating that responding to critiques or comments required getting approval from a long chain of command, which was at odds with the on-demand nature of social media.

4.3 Rebelling or Exerting Caution in Response to Risk Aversion

While infrastructural restrictions were evident though everyday GM staff work, several disruptive events also caused these restrictions to increase exponentially impacting staff's practices. For instance, during the challenging period of Covid-19, marketing was put in control of gatekeeping the social media posts due to a fear of insensitive messaging. Frustration during this period was tangible as staff expressed more desire than usual to test out different forms of engagement on social media. Several channels were initially cut, and differential access was created as prioritization was placed on keeping up the main channels or those of the larger institutions. One GM staff member speaking from a smaller institution critically suggested that "the lack of access to social media, in the early days of lockdown showed us in a very poor light" (GM Staff L). As a result, several staff resorted to using personal social media accounts, even creating new ones to keep in touch with community groups, until controls on the institution's channels were loosened.

Due to these reactions GM staff express a certain antagonism towards marketing and upper management associated with a lack of personal agency or empowerment in using their institution's social media accounts. In fact, projects associated with social media were also occasionally referred to as being "rebellious", "subversive" or "going rogue" (GM Staff F; GM Staff G; GM staff K; GM Staff X). However, I noticed that these projects were often supported and celebrated by other colleagues in informal conversations and meetings - creating a feeling of congeniality amongst conspirators. On the other hand, in comparison to instances of rebelling or experimenting many Glasgow Museum staff members are also in a precarious position within which they may be averse to altering the status quo or taking part in risky behavior. This is due to several staff working on a contract basis, as institutional funding is not guaranteed over the next several years; Glasgow Museums is currently in a major deficit due to the financial status of Glasgow Life, which is predicted to be short 38 million pounds [32].

Therefore, staff who are not guaranteed permanent work, may feel limited in their ability to experiment with content, tone of voice and personality, especially since the museums operate at arms-length to the city council. As one staff member explained, they feel restricted in their experimentation stating, "there is a certain level of reputation to uphold" (GM Staff M). Another staff member expressed a need to exert caution in their practices and avoid "stepping on toes and pushing the boundaries" (GM Staff X). According to a previous study on social media use by memory institutions in New Zealand, Liew et al. [33] similarly found that museum staff felt "obliged to monitor their use of social media to prevent the broadcast of opinions or content that council communications teams would deem unpalatable" (p. 100). As a result, GM staff check in with their colleagues to look over their posts: "[t]here's no guidance really, we just try to negotiate responses together – like does this look okay?" and or as discussed above, share their ideas within social media meetings for feedback. Thus, staff's precarious positions are further propagated by restrictions such as those imposed by Sprout Social, resulting in staff having to exert caution.

In turn, staff believe that upper management attributes less value to the use of social media as an engagement tool. Such a position is evident by staff who suggest management sees it as a secondary activity or an "after-thought" (GM staff G). This lack of value is in part ascribed to a paucity of resources and investment into the social media use of staff. For example, one staff member complained, echoing many others, that "there is no time or budget" (GM Staff P), and this according to another colleague, forces staff to choose between "community engagement or social media work" (GM Staff C). To work around time limitations some staff try to schedule months ahead, but in doing so, may negate the reactionary nature of social media. Thus, staff argue that the institution has yet to attribute a realistic value to digital media in general, in comparison to other museum institutions (GM Staff F). A lack of investment in social media for staff may thus, insinuate that management does not attribute value to social media work and propels staff's disregard over acts of maintenance.

5 Discussion: Maintenance Work and Future Infrastructures

Nemer and Chirumamilla [8] argue that "it is this small-scale frustration...that provides us with a more poignant and meaningful window into thinking about what technology does to us, and what we can do with it" (p. 237). In this study, GM staff's everyday frustrations and acts of maintenance highlights contradictions between the use of social media which demands an ongoing reflexivity [34] with elements of museum infrastructure. Social media practices can cause tension with a hierarchical organization, an institution's risk aversion and the balancing of cross-departmental content and responsibilities. The instances of GM staff's micro-frustrations, expressions of disappointment, "doing the best they can" and perceived subversions, not only highlight the existing tensions but also the spaces and factors that enable ongoing social media work.

Certainly, the infrastructural factors discussed in this paper are not necessarily new, as research on social and digital media adoption already in the early 2000s pointed to associated barriers of resources, institutional image, and the relinquishing of control [35]. However, this study by taking an ethnographic approach highlights not only the persistency of these factors, years after social media adoption, but also how staff contend with these limitations. GM staff employed a variety of tactics to ensure the maintenance of social media, including the subversion of hierarchical controls by using their own social media accounts or mobile devices and mitigating a lack of time by using opportune moments to schedule content in advance. Further, some staff maintained their social media practices by exerting caution while others pushed forward with projects in perceived acts of rebellion. Cutting across the limitations posed by museum infrastructure was also staff's reliance on colleague support, this was offered through the social media meetings and everyday work encounters which enabled staff to keep-up social media work. This suggest that investing in additional mediums to create spaces for informal staff sharing and support such as online chat groups could be beneficial. An online chat or Slack group that bridges staff who contribute to social media across institutions could assist staff in balancing social responsibilities and accessing peer support on a frequent basis[4].

While cultivating staff networks of support are important factors in the maintenance of social media, a critical question looms regarding infrastructural change. What is likely needed considering the tensions discussed, is a shared social media mission with clear responsibilities to allow a balance of content to form including and beyond marketing. This is supported by Culture24 a social and digital media consultancy charity, who suggests social and digital media practices must be underpinned by a clear mission with actionable social values [36]. However, both upper management and marketing must also emphasize their trust and confidence in staff's social media practices and embrace the ambiguity of social media and potential failures or foolery. Finally, the institution's investment into social media is important for staff to allocate time and resources into its continued use.

---

[4] During Covid-19 this was implemented by some individual institutions in the form of online platforms such as Whatsapp, however their usefulness has yet to be assessed.

While the persistency of infrastructural factors in hindering social media use within museum literature may seem discouraging, staff's acts of maintenance may lead to future infrastructures. Acts of repair in terms of maintenance can sometimes seem stationary, but some have suggested that they are also sites of alteration [37]. Through continuous repair incremental changes may take place not only in terms of social media work but also the institution's underpinning infrastructure. When asked about future visions of social media use, staff had enthusiastic ideas that relate to social initiatives such as: platforming visitor voices, challenging normative discourse and as a way for staff to learn from communities' expert knowledge. What this study underlines is that the discourse around museum staff's idealization of social media for social goals and its use in practice is complex reflecting larger issues regarding the organization of responsibilities, institutional neutrality, risk, and perceived value.

6 Conclusion

To conclude, persisting critiques of museums "signaling openness" on social media which condemn staff's social media practice as passive due to reliance on utopian discourses ([6], p. 240), must recognize systemic issues that go beyond a lack of staff agency to be nuanced by continuing tensions between social media and museum infrastructure. While this study focused on museum infrastructure, the structures of social media platforms must also be contended with and closer attention to how platforms intersect with museum practices could provide further insight into its potential for social initiatives. According to Graziano and Trogal [10] repair can manifest as "counter-conducts that demand an active and persistent engagement of practitioners with the systemic contradictions and power struggles shaping our material world" (p. 221). Contrary to an idealistic approach to social media, the study forefronts the agency of staff working with social media within the confines of contradictory museum structures and uncertain social media terrain, exemplifying the need for respect of its professionalization and recognition of the legitimacy of burn-out.

Acknowledgements. This work is part of the POEM (Participatory Memory Practices) project and has received funding from the European Union's Horizon 2020 research and innovation program under the Marie Skłodowska-Curie grant agreement No. 764859. I would like to thank Gareth Beale, Angeliki Tzouganatou, and the reviewers for their useful comments on different versions of this paper, and to Glasgow Museums and Open Museum staff for their time and for welcoming me into their workspaces.

References

1. Drotner, K., Schroder, K.C. (eds.): Museum Communication and Social Media: The Connected Museum. Routledge, London (2013)
2. Wong, A.: Social media towards social change: potential and challenges for museums. In: Museums, Equality and Social Justice, pp. 329–341. Routledge (2013). https://doi.org/10.4324/9780203120057-31

3. Labrador, A.M., Silberman, N.A., Kidd, J.: The Oxford Handbook of Public Heritage Theory and Practice, vol. 1. Oxford University Press, Oxford (2018). https://doi.org/10.1093/oxfordhb/9780190676315.013.9

4. Fletcher, A., Lee, M.J.: Current social media uses and evaluations in American museums. Mus. Manag. Curatorship **27**(5), 505–521 (2012)

5. Iwasaki, S.T.: Social Media and Museums: Reframing Audience Engagement in the Digital Communication Age. San Francisco State University, San Francisco (2017). http://sfsu-dspace.calstate.edu/bitstream/10211.3/196383/1/AS362017MUSSTI937.pdf

6. Walker, D.: Towards the collaborative museum? Social media, participation, disciplinary experts and the public in the contemporary museum. Apollo, University of Cambridge Repository (2013). https://doi.org/10.17863/CAM.7082

7. Hartley, J.A.: Museums and the digital public space: researching digital engagement practice at the Whitworth Art Gallery. Ph.D. University of Manchester (2015)

8. Nemer, D., Chirumamilla, P.: Living in the broken city: infrastructural inequity, uncertainty, and the materiality of the digital in Brazil. In: Vertesi, J., et al. (eds.) DigitalSTS: A Field Guide for Science & Technology Studies, pp. 221–239. Princeton University Press, Princeton (2019)

9. Jackson, S.J.: Rethinking repair. In: Gillespie, P., Boczkowski, J., Foot, K.A. (eds.) Media Technologies, pp. 221–240. The MIT Press, Cambridge (2014)

10. Graziano, V., Trogal, K.: Repair matters. Ephemera Theor. Polit. Organ. **19**(2), 1–25, (2019).

11. Rosner, D.K., Ames, M.: Designing for repair? In: Fussell, W., Lutters, S., Morris, M.R., Reddy, M. (eds.) CSCW"14: Compilation publication of CSCW'14 Proceedings & CSCW'14 Companion: February 15–19, 2014, Baltimore, MD, USA, pp. 319–331. ACM, New York (2014). https://doi.org/10.1145/2531602.2531692

12. Baggesen, R.H.: Augmenting the agora: media and civic engagement in museums. MedieKultur J. Media Commun. Res. **30**(56), 15 (2014)

13. Kidd, J.: Enacting engagement online: framing social media use for the museum. Inf. Technol. People **24**(1), 64–77 (2011)

14. Schellenbacher, J.C.: Museums, activism and social media (or, how Twitter challenges and changes museum practice). In: Janes, R.R., Sandell, R. (eds.) Museum Activism. Routledge, New York (2019). https://doi.org/10.4324/9781351251044-36

15. Spruce, L., Leaf, K.: Social media for social justice. J. Mus. Educ. **42**(1), 41–53 (2017)

16. Schlagwein, D., Hu, M.: How and why organisations use social media: five use types and their relation to absorptive capacity. J. Inf. Technol. **32**(2), 194–209 (2017)

17. Scottish Social Media Heritage Group Social Media and Decolonising Scottish Heritage. (2020). https://scottishheritagesocialmediagroup.com/2020/10/08/social-media-and-decolonising-scottish-heritage/

18. Camarero, C., Garrido, M.-J., San Jose, R.: What works in facebook content versus relational communication: a study of their effectiveness in the context of museums. Int. J. Hum. Comput. Interact. **34**(12), 1119–1134 (2018)

19. Lessard, B.d., Whiffin, A.L., Wild, A.L.: A guide to public engagement for entomological collections and natural history museums in the age of social media. Ann. Entomol. Soc. Am. **110**(5), 467–479 (2017)

20. Laws, A.S.: Museum Websites and Social Media: Issues of Participation, Sustainability, Trust and Diversity, Museums and Collection, vol. 8, 1st edn. s.n., New York (2015)

21. Byrd-mcdevitt, L.: Museum social media: burnout or moral injury? (2019). https://medium.com/@LoriLeeByrd/museum-social-media-burnout-or-moral-injury-b05c211b3a9

22. Dornan, R.: Social Media Burnout (2019). https://medium.com/@RussellDornan/social-media-burn-out-be31286a4d59

23. Wellington, S., Oliver, G.: Reviewing the digital heritage landscape: the intersection of digital media and museum practice. In: Macdonald, S., Leahy, H.R. (eds.) The International andbooks of Museum Studies, pp. 577–598. John Wiley & Sons Ltd., Chichester (2015)

24. Simonsen, J., Karasti, H., Hertzum, M.: Infrastructuring and participatory design: exploring infrastructural inversion as analytic, empirical and generative. Comput. Supp. Cooper. Work 29(1–2), 115–151 (2019). https://doi.org/10.1007/s10606-019-09365-w

25. Dindler, C.: Designing infrastructures for creative engagement. Digit. Creat. 25(3), 212–223 (2014)

26. Huvila, I.: Learning to work between information infrastructures. Inf. Res. 24(2) (2019). paper 819. http://InformationR.net/ir/24-2/paper819.html (Archived by WebCite® at http://www.webcitation.org/78mnTEFK7)

27. Henke, C.: Negotiating repair: the infrastructural contexts of practice and power. In: Strebel, I., Bovet, A., Sormani, P. (eds.) Repair Work Ethnographies: Revisiting Breakdown, Relocating Materiality. Springer Singapore, Singapore (2019). https://doi.org/10.1007/978-981-13-2110-8_9

28. Beel, D.: Reinterpreting the museum: social inclusion, citizenship and urban regeneration of Glasgow. Doctor of Philosophy, University of Glasgow (2011). http://theses.gla.ac.uk/2668/

29. Macleod, F. (ed.): Out There: The Open Museum: Pushing the Boundaries Of Museums' Potential. Culture and Sport Glasgow, Glasgow (2010)

30. Postill, J., Pink, S.: Social media ethnography: the digital researcher in a messy web. Media Int. Aust. 145, 123–134 (2012)

31. Vaismoradi, M., Jones, J., Turunen, H., Snelgrove, S.: Theme development in qualitative content analysis and thematic analysis. J. Nurs. Educ. Pract. 6(5), 100 (2016)

32. Leask, D.: Glasgow life sends begging letter to ministers over cash shortage. Glasgow Times, 26 July 2020. https://www.glasgowtimes.co.uk/news/18608707.glasgow-life-sends-begging-letter-ministers-cash-shortage/

33. Liew, C., Oliver, G., Watkins, M.: Insight from social media use by memory institutions in New Zealand. Online Inf. Rev. 42(1), 93–106 (2018)

34. Kidd, J.: Digital media ethics and museum communication. In: Drotner, K., Dziekan, V., Parry, R., Schrøder, K.C. (eds.) The Routledge Handbook of Museums, Media and Communication. Taylor & Francis, New York (2018)

35. Ellis, M., Kelly, B.: Web 2.0: how to stop thinking and start doing: addressing organisational barriers. In: Trant, J., Bearman, D. (eds.) Museums and the Web 2007: Proceedings, Toronto Archives & Museum Informatics (2007)

36. Malde, S., Kennedy, A.: Let's get real 6 report - connecting digital practice with social purpose (2018). https://www.keepandshare.com/doc/8229093/let-s-get-real-6-culture-24-bw-singlepage-for-web-pdf-3-0-meg?da=y

37. Strebel, I., Bovet, A., Sormani, P. (eds.): Repair Work Ethnographies: Revisiting Breakdown, Relocating Materiality. Springer Singapore, Singapore (2019)

Digitization, Documentation and Digital Representation of Cultural Heritage

Mixing Visual Media for Cultural Heritage

Roberto Scopigno[(✉)] [iD]

CNR-ISTI, Pisa, Italy
r.scopigno@isti.cnr.it

Abstract. The Cultural Heritage (CH) domain is a field where many different visual media are constituent elements of the main activities: study, conservation, dissemination, and presentation to the public (museum visitors, tourists, practitioners). Those media are usually used in isolation, adopting specific visualization tools. This paper aims to present several experiences where multiple visual media have been used in a coordinated manner by fusing or presenting them in the same visualization context. These approaches experimented with new interaction and visualization methodologies to use different media in a synergic way. CH domain is an ideal field of experimentation of the potential of media integration/fusion/ cross-analysis. According to our understanding, using multiple media can improve insight capability. We guide the reader in the analysis of some pioneering experiences and approaches and try to deduce, for each of them, the potential improvement granted in terms of data communication or analysis. A final discussion tries to highlight the work needed for a wider acceptance and increased impact of those approaches.

Keywords: Cultural Heritage · Visual media · Interactive visualization · Media integration

1 Introduction

Visual media play a foundational role in communication concerning art and Cultural Heritage (CH). In our era, visual media are de facto mandatory ingredients in communication and dissemination actions [1, 2]. Indeed, the presentation of visual media is not straightforward as text or speech, mostly when more sophisticated media or presentation modes are adopted (requiring user training and specific devices). For example, impaired people deserve proper support in the fruition of visual media. Thus, several methods have been proposed to translate images into other stimuli easier to perceive by impaired people, such as the conversion of paintings into a tactile surface [3]. Anyway, communication is enforced or simplified when it is based on visual stimuli. This work's scope is not to make a historical essay of the use of visual media for CH communication, but conversely to present some flashes on how they are used. The digital domain introduced new visual media modalities that go beyond the usual picture used as an illustration. These new approaches employ dynamic and interactive fruition (interactive navigation, visual comparison, interactive lighting, etc.).

A CH content producer can choose his preferred media type and visualize it with modern display/interaction tools. But CH practice has also shown that in several

© Springer Nature Switzerland AG 2021
M. Shehade and T. Stylianou-Lambert (Eds.): RISE IMET 2021, CCIS 1432, pp. 297–315, 2021.
https://doi.org/10.1007/978-3-030-83647-4_20

applications, a single type of media is not sufficient anymore because an adequate representation and analysis is possible only by merging and integrating multiple media and datasets. Therefore, canonical digitization and visualization technologies require being augmented by software technologies, fusing or creating relations between different visual datasets or media.

This work's primary focus is to discuss a specific opportunity: different visual media can be used in a synergic manner, removing the constraints of accessing a single media at a time. We can experiment with several different ways to integrate, fuse, or cross-compare different media. To enable this, we need technical instruments and methodologies: while single media management is nowadays relatively straightforward from a technical point of view, the integration, fusion, cross-navigation of those media still present some issues and potential for further research (data management, user interfaces, interaction metaphors, new approaches in visual presentation and storytelling). Therefore, this paper aims to present a few previous experiences concerning media integration, showing how to manage those data and which benefits we gather in terms of understanding and communication.

This paper's application context is primarily public fruition and communication of CH to the public and the related and partially intersecting domain of the communication to more advanced and expert communities (such as art historians, conservators, and restorers).

The paper will cover this open subject, endorsing a practical approach. The first step is defining the different media types (Sect. 2). We mention the case of visualization tools and how they could focus on multiple data types (Sect. 3). Then, we review available experiences where visualization technologies allow users to browse and analyze different media in the same shared space, intermixing data content in a single visualization context (Sect. 4). Digital systems supporting conservation and restoration also need similar features (Sect. 5). We conclude with some final remarks (Sect. 6).

2 Data Types in CH Applications

The technological status is mature if we consider the enabling technologies for building visual assets (either accurate digital samplings of reality or recreation of lost or dismantled artworks/architectures) and presenting them using interactive displays or VR/AR devices [4]. The excellent communication potential of these technologies for museums and the CH community is quite clear.

Digital representations come with different data types and data sources—whether 2D, 3D, 4D [5], or beyond, digitized or modeled. Multiple data types are also used to produce digital representations (e.g., 3D models [6]). We introduce here those different media.

2.1 High-Resolution Images

Images are the more common visual media. They have been part of art history and archaeology from the very beginning, initially employing the analogic, printed version and, more recently, digital supports (either digitally native images or scanned from old prints/slides).

While images are fully integrated with the web and HTML since the *Wold Wide Web* birth, few aspects lack a standard solution for archival and visualization purposes. Most of the images produced nowadays are very high-resolution. High-resolution images are now a commodity resource, given the impressive evolution of digital photography (just to mention a single example, recent off-the-shelf smartphones provide 20–80 M pixel cameras). Moreover, the availability of tools that allow aligning and stitching image patchworks supports users in reaching huge image resolutions.

Visualization on the web of high- or huge-resolution images can be tricky but doable, using specific methodologies (data compression, efficient progressive data transmission). Examples are the multiresolution approaches based on tiling and hierarchical image representations [7, 8]. Another important and critical issue could be protecting the data (image watermark technologies [9]).

2.2 Multispectral Images

Images depicting the image reflected by a surface while sampling only a specific wavelength are quite common in CH, especially for investigation and conservation purposes. Some examples are *infrared images* (allowing the detection of under-drawings) or *ultra-violet images* (which disclose the presence of patinas or layers of biologic substances, as well as faded or modern paints).

2.3 Reflection Transformation Images (RTI)

Re-lightable images (usually named *Reflection Transformation Images - RTI*) are becoming an increasingly used technology to acquire detailed and interactive documentation on quasi-planar objects [10, 11]. This is particularly useful for artifacts characterized by complex light reflection attributes. The advantage of this representation is the possibility of changing the direction of the light incident over the image in real-time (i.e., at visualization time) and using enhanced visualization modes to inspect fine details of the objects' surface. The visual quality and fidelity supported by this media are impressive, in many cases, superior to what we can simulate with 3D models.

RTI images' acquisition is quite simple, requiring a calibrated lighting system and shooting multiple photos for a stationary camera position under variable lighting. Those input images are then processed to produce a single RTI image. The images' lighting information is mathematically synthesized to generate a mathematical surface reflection model for each specific parcel of the surface reflection, enabling users to re-light the RTI image interactively and in real-time. The RTI image encodes, for each pixel image, nor the RGB value but a *function* able to return the surface's color given a specific direction of the incoming light incidence.

2.4 Video

Video is another medium that is extremely easy to produce (a mobile phone is enough for many application cases) and present to the public (the commercial platform

YouTube is an immediate example). But we need more professional grabbing devices and a solid knowledge of the cinematographic language if the goal is to produce high-quality videos.

Moreover, videos are not just grabbed but also synthetically produced with computer animation tools. This latter source of data is becoming common in CH.

2.5 Panoramic/360 Images and Videos

Panoramic or 360 degrees images[1] or videos are a quite new media which adds an *interactive* opportunity, allowing users to navigate and interact with these visual assets. Acquisition easiness and speed, together with the richness of details granted by the high-resolution supported, makes panoramic images an ideal medium for CH[2].

The acquisition of panoramic videos is straightforward, either from multiple poses taken by a camera positioned over a tripod or using specific devices (based on multiple cameras).

2.6 Terrains Models

Terrain models are commonly termed as 2.5-dimensional data. They are quite common in geographic or land representations and are often used to represent the context of CH discoveries visually. These data are managed with GIS approaches or as standard 3D data.

2.7 3D Models

3D representations also become quite common in CH. Two classes of models are used:

- *Sampled models*, usually produced with active 3D scanning (laser-based systems or systems using structured light) or with photogrammetry approaches (production of 3D models from set of 2D images);
- *Modelled representations,* produced using the user-driven modeling systems designed for 3D modeling and computer animation applications (e.g., Blender, Maya, etc.).

Sampled models give much more control on the accuracy of the representation than modeled representations. Conversely, the latter are more common for broad public applications (e.g., to produce videos or virtual reconstructions).

There is a pressing need for platforms supporting easy and free publication on the web of 3D models. SketchFab [12] is a recent commercial solution, supporting automatic web publishing and a nice and easy to use interface.

Animated/deformable 3D models are used in CH to present and add an interactive behavior to the artifact. They are complex models which allow encoding both the shape

---

[1] https://en.wikipedia.org/wiki/360_photography.

[2] For an example of panoramic images adopted to enable the virtual visit to museum see: http://www.youvisit.com/tour/louvremuseum (accessed on 26 November 2020).

and the functioning of an artifact. Therefore, not just how it looks but also how one could operate/manipulate/act.

Depth images (or *depth maps*) are another type of visual data with a predominant 3D interpretation. These are usually the raw result of 3D sampling performed with an active scanning device: an image where each pixel encodes a point sampled in the 3D space. We can render a depth map as an image (thus, rendering in false color the distance from the observer), or we can convert it into a cloud of points.

2.8   Beyond Visual – Sound

Sound is another essential component for the simulation or representation of virtual spaces. A silent 3D scene is not realistic nor sufficiently immersive in a virtual reality context. Thus, the sound should be taken into account while producing sophisticated visual products, as computer games that pair visual and sound contents. Anyway, the scope of this work is limited, and we cannot cover here also the case of sound and its use in CH applications.

3   Data Integration at the Level of the Generalist Visualization Tool

The primary task with visual media is to provide proper visualization tools. Visual media are usually complex data and thus, we need efficient visualization processes, taking care of several technical issues (data simplification, multi-resolution encoding, compression, progressive transmission, GPU-enabled rendering). All those themes have been the subject of intense research. Nowadays, we dispose of an arsenal of efficient technical solutions for the implementation of effective visualization tools.

Visualization tools are available for each different media (e.g., RTI images [13], 3D models [14–16, 21], videos [17]). An issue perceived by the CH community is that each tool has a different interface and its specific design; moreover, many of them have been designed for technical communities and expose to the user a very complex set of features and parameters. Not all those features are of interest for the average CH user, and more are the features more complex is usually to master the tool. Moreover, since those tools have different interfaces, the synchronous analysis of different media becomes a rather cumbersome process.

Workflows requiring the contemporary analysis of multiple media are common in the CH domain. Therefore, a comprehensive approach has been endorsed by Yale University while designing the CHER-Ob system [18]. Their starting point was to provide support for the many different media types and formats needed in CH through a single tool. The goal is to offer a single and congruent GUI (an example is the manipulation modality, implemented frequently in graphics systems with different interpretations of the trackball concept), unified terminology, and the usual basic visual analysis functionalities. CHER-Ob is an open-source software tool, having a single intuitive interface consistent with CH needs. The system handles various types of 2D and 3D data and preserves user-generated metadata and annotations (see Fig. 1).

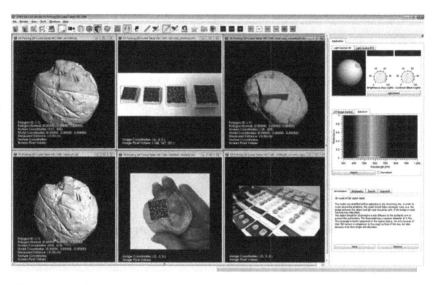

Fig. 1. A snapshot from the CHER-O system (YALEUniversity, https://graphics.cs.yale.edu/soft ware-packages/cher-ob-open-source-platform-shared-analysis-and-video-dissemination-cultural)

According to our experience, this is the first complex open-source tool focusing on data visualization of CH digital assets rather than on generic geometry processing tasks. It provides tools for the integrated visualization of various types of visual data (2D images, hyperspectral images, volume data encoded using the DICOM standard and triangulated 3D models, with or w/out textures). But in this system each data resides in its specific visualization window, i.e., data are not fused or integrated.

4 Towards Data Integration in Interactive Visualization

A step beyond is providing methodologies and tools for integrating and fusing different data types in the framework of a single visual presentation context. The following subsections present some related experiences. In each of these subsections we present a representative example(s) and describe which research questions could be more easily answered, the lessons learned, or the potential impact of this approach for the CH community.

4.1   2D Images and 3D Models

The study of artworks, the visual or narrative presentation provided to a generalist user (museum visitor, tourist), often requires both 2D and 3D media. In our vision, there is not a predominant medium, since each one has specific advantages (visual quality, resolution, completeness, easy of manipulation or analysis, etc.). Thus, we should offer access to both media, possibly in a coordinated manner.

Fig. 2. The light table component of the Cenobium system, supporting side-by-side analysis of a selected group of 2D/3D representations.

This requirement was at the basis of the design of the Cenobium[3] system on 2006 [19]. We designed this system to support art scholars and students in studying medieval sculptures (in this specific case, decorated capitols) through multiple visual representations. From the very beginning, the Cenobium system provided what we called the *light table*, i.e., a facility to support the side-by-side visual analysis of different media. The Cenobium system provides several high-resolution images and a 3D model for each capitol; the user can select any image or 3D model (belonging to the same or different capitols) and selectively activate their visualization in a common interactive space (see Fig. 2).

---

[3] Cenobium project: http://cenobium.isti.cnr.it/.

A much more sophisticated approach for the joint management of 2D images and 3D models was introduced by the seminal paper PhotoTourism [20]. This paper presents a single working space where the user can navigate a 3D scene and, in a synchronous manner, a large set of geo-located 2D images. The availability of geo-location information for each 2D image (position and orientation of the camera at shooting time) allows locating them precisely in the 3D space and navigating and visualizing all data with a unified interface.

This kind of joint dataset (a high-resolution 3D model plus an extensive collection of pictures), describing a real-world object or a scene, can be generated by multiple sources and is becoming increasingly common due to the advent of photogrammetric methodologies for 3D acquisition [21, 22].

This approach has been later on refined for CH use by the PhotoCloud[4] system [23]. It extended the PhotoTourism approach by: redesigning the GUI with a more flexible management of the image thumbnail-bar [24]; adding increased 3D data flexibility (allowing the use of high-res triangulated 3D models and not just pointsets); proposing a methodology for computing image cameras over unregistered image dataset; and improved visualization and navigation features that fully exploit the underlying 3D dataset.

The potential of this new visualization paradigm is of high interest for CH applications. There are several CH conservation or monitoring activities where the capability of managing in a unified context a 3D representation and multiple sets of images (taken at different times and, maybe, also by other people) could be a crucial asset. Another example is the added value of presenting historical photos of an urban context to tourists, by immersing the old photographs in the 3D scene and enabling an easy navigation and selection of the images.

One major innovation introduced by this approach is the new methodology introduced for browsing a large set of images, solved with the adoption of a *space navigation* approach: while I navigate the space, the system presents in real-time the subset of 2D images nearer to my current view. That seems to be a major innovation with respect to previous image archives supporting a query-based interface.

Thus, one could wonder why we have not seen a real impact in CH applications of this innovative approach. It might be due to the increased implementation complexity of a system such as PhotoCloud compared with a standard image browsing system or a 3D viz tool. Since CH is an under-funded domain, unfortunately, complex approaches (either to implement or to use) often do not pay.

---

[4] PhotoCloud system: http://vcg.isti.cnr.it/photocloud/ and https://www.youtube.com/watch?v=-Bb9k2Gy2Yg.

Fig. 3. Two examples of use of PhotoCloud: over a statue dataset and in an urban context (one of the 2D images is projected on the 3D scene); the third image (on the bottom) presents the thumbnail-based interface provided to browse the image set.

Research questions/Lesson learned/Impact:

Presenting 2D and 3D data in a unified rendering context allows:

- To simplify the search of images in an extensive database (replacing search queries based on text or codes with virtual navigation);
- To enable easy comparison of images taken at different times and covering the same physical space (e.g., monitoring of changes in urban contexts);
- To use images to increase the visual quality of 3D models (e.g., mapping high-resolution 2D content over a low-resolution 3D model; adding effects depending on illumination, weather condition, time of the day);
- Requires sophisticated solutions able to geo-locate precisely the input images over the 3D scene (now possible in an automatic manner with AI-based solutions).

4.2   Textual Data and 3D Models

The integration of textual descriptions and visual model is another potential subject of work in the fusion of different media. One early attempt was the inclusion of 3D models in pdf files pioneered by Adobe[5], thus evolving the usual static figures into interactive 3D illustrations.

An ideal testbed to experiment a tighter integration of 3D models and text was a project concerning the interactive presentation of a peculiar artwork, very complex in size and decorative apparatus. The Ruthwell Cross is a big (5 m tall) medieval stone cross whose surface contains carved figures, symbols, and runic inscriptions related to an ancient poetic text. It is an artwork that cannot be presented by just a visual representation, as well as we cannot describe it using only text. We verified that those media do a much better work jointly.

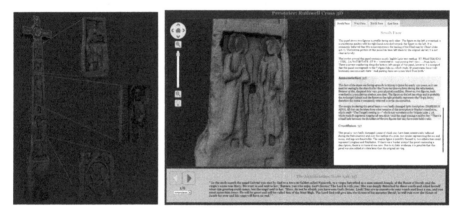

Fig. 4. The Ruthwell cross (left); (right) the snapshot presents the system used in Lecture mode, the text description has induced the system to open a view over the 3D model which poses in foreground the related carved panel.

We designed a web-based presentation platform [25] to provide full integration of 3D content with heterogeneous multimedia data; it allows to easily encode and visualize interlinked modules, covering different types of data (i.e., text, 3D models, and digital editions of the poetic text). Users can select the navigation over the 3D model, discovering the minutes geometric and iconographic details (automatically, he will also receive indication by the system on the specific text section(s) which describe the region under visual focus). Conversely, the user can read the descriptive text (in this case, the system will highlight the region over the 3D model associated with the specific text section and automatically pose the user in the ideal view to visually analyze that region).

---

[5] 3D pdf: https://helpx.adobe.com/it/acrobat/using/displaying-3d-models-pdfs.html (accessed on 26 November 2020).

The Ruthwell cross is an ideal testbed for this approach since the artwork is very dense of figurative carvings and carved inscriptions; decoding and understanding those elements is quite complicated and requires a dense, descriptive apparatus.

Since the Ruthwell cross project was directed towards the CH community (specifically, to provide didactical support for teaching), great attention was given to the design of an intuitive and easy to use GUI[6]. Navigation over the cross was implemented to facilitate interaction (an example is the support for constrained view selection).

Research Questions/Lesson learned/Impact:

- Complex artworks require sophisticated descriptions (text) and long interactive visualization sessions. The availability of a common data presentation context (3D & text) allows to structure the access to those data channels in a coordinated manner;
- Testing this approach with students produced very encouraging results;
- A system which allows both *free navigation/inspection* and *guided navigation* is also convenient. Guided navigation is provided through a sequence of pre-defined "lectures" (these are similar to the slides of a Power Point presentation, they allow to disclose knowledge on the artwork by presenting to the student several starting points to both the text and the 3D model);
- Structuring the content is a time-consuming process (writing text, structuring it in sections, creating the links with the visual content, designing the "lectures"); it requires a motivated tutor, but it could also be an ideal cooperative task for a course project, involving the teacher and some students.

4.3   Panoramic Images and 3D Models

Panoramic or 360 images are an excellent type of media. Even if they are based on 2D content, they provide a visual experience that emulates 3D navigation, offering some advantages (the visual quality offered by 360 images is often much better than the one of 3D models, while data encoding complexity is smaller) and disadvantage (they are usually sampled sparsely and limit the interaction of the user to just a rotation of the view direction).

Integration with a 3D representation could be an excellent solution to solve the inherent sparsity of 360 images. This approach has been endorsed and experimented by the Zamani Project[7] [26]. The Zamani Project is an excellent example of a wide-scope digitization project taking place in entire Africa. It undertakes data collection and analysis, heritage communication, training, and capacity building for experts and the public. It provides access to high-quality spatial heritage data (most of them related to endangered African heritage sites in complex-to-reach locations). It aims at fostering public capability to learn from, preserve, and protect cultural heritage.

---

[6] A video of the system presenting the Ruthwell cross is at: https://www.youtube.com/watch?v=Wov-2ik4ibY (accessed on 26 November 2020).

[7] Zamani Project: https://zamaniproject.org/.

Fig. 5. A clip from a video of the Zamani Project, showing the use of 3D navigation enriched by the presence of interactive 360 images (represented with *glass spheres* immersed in the 3D scene).

The Zamani staff proposed an excellent example of media integration: the navigation of 3D scenes enriched by panoramic images, as it is exemplified in one of their videos[8]. Here, the approach is to immerse several 360 images inside a 3D scene, marking their position in the scene with a *glass sphere* depicting the related 360 image's visual content. The idea of using the *glass sphere metaphor* to present visually the presence of a panoramic image in a specific location is space is brilliant: very easy to understand and to interact with. Once the user is navigating the 3D scene, as soon as he passes in the proximity of a 360 image, he is trapped by the sphere. The visualization context switches from the 3D navigation to the 360-image navigation. The user can then escape from the sphere/panoramic image and continue navigation over the 3D scene. This is shown at the suggested link by a pre-recorded video (see Fig. 5), but can be implemented in interactive browsers as well.

A similar approach is also endorsed in [27]. The authors propose the integration of high-resolution spherical panoramas, a variety of maps, GNSS, sound, video, and text information for representation of numerous cultural heritage objects. The focus is to include other media (for example maps) inside the navigation of the panoramic images; thus, maps and other data are rendered inside each single panoramic image.

---

[8] Zamani – Use of 3D & Panoramic images in the video "3D Heritage Documentation of African Heritage Sites" (accessed on 26 November 2020):
    https://www.youtube.com/watch?v=8jTlKjUAzn8&list=PLlWdPQN2XnmR4lj19bRRCkT0FEQ W1E9b8.

Research Questions/Lesson Learned/Impact:

- It is an ideal way to solve the limitations of the two media: the scene contains only a few spherical images, but the visual quality provided by each of them is very high; the 3D model is by definition continuous and complete, covering all the visible scene, but we know it is not easy to sample at full resolution and high-fidelity (color and surface reflectance) large scenes. Joining the two media allows summing the respective advantages.
- It is relatively easy to integrate spherical images and 3D into an interactive visualizer. Switching among media is also quite intuitive.

5   Data Integration While Supporting Conservation and Restoration

CH conservation and restoration are important professional domains, where media integration is also required.

5.1   Integration of Different Media for Conservation Condition Analysis

Multiple scientific investigation technologies are commonly used to assess the conservation conditions of artworks. In many cases, the diagnostic results produced are visual data (RGB or hyperspectral images, 3D models, discrete volumetric representations, etc.). The clear comprehension of a phenomenon often requires to analyze all those investigation data, not in isolation but jointly.

A very recent example is the study of a painting (the Ecce Homo by Antonello da Messina, oil on wood). This very fragile artwork has been subject to a complex scientific investigation project [28]. One of the conservator's research queries was to get insight into the relations linking several areas on danger visible over the surface (cracks and lifting of the painted surface) to possible woodworm galleries existing in the underlying wood substrate.

The investigations executed to gather data on this phenomenon were: the high-resolution 3D scanning of the surface, aimed at producing a very detailed sampling of the status of the painted surface; the CT scan, aimed at sampling the conditions of the wooden table in its internal volume. The data produced can be analyzed, using standard 3D visualization tools (for the 3D scanned geometry) and tools for the segmentation and visualization of volumetric data (for the CT scanning data). Nevertheless, the conservator's analysis would have been simplified by a system able to render both datasets in a joint context. Therefore, one of the tasks in the Ecce Homo conservation project was to segment the CT data, detect all the worm galleries, produce the related 3D geometries, and design a visualization and analysis tool able to render both geometries (panted surface and worm galleries). The goal was to enable the interactive search of correspondences of color detachments and underlying worm galleries, to assess potential critical areas over the painted surface.

The resulting system, implemented as a web application on top of 3DHOP [15] allows using transparency and cut-through/sections to discover these potential pairs and to compute metric distances between locations over the painted surface and the underneath wood cavity. An example is presented in Fig. 6 or, better, in a video[9].

Fig. 6. Analysis of the status of the Ecce Homo painting: the painted table is tilted, only part of its panted surface is rendered using interactive sections, the underlying worm's cavities are rendered. The depth of the nearer worm gallery to the point selected by the user (green point, on the right-bottom of the Ecce Homo mouth) is computed and shown in the left panel (4.42 mm).

Research questions/Lesson learned/Impact:

- We can visualize and interrogate data on the painted surface (optical 3D scan) and the interior (radiographic CT scan). This allows easily to create correspondences and to compute measures (e.g., distances) to give numeric evidence to the conservator's queries.
- The same approach can be extended to multi-spectral images to add other data to be cross-related with the 3D data.

5.2   Integration of Different Media in Restoration Documentation

A major focus in CH restoration and the related digital documentation is: (a) to allow storing data and documents by means of the geo-referenced interconnection of those sources of informations over the digital 3D representation and (b) to annotate the 3D model to encode information or insight gathered. An example is the documentation system developed for the Nettuno Fountain restoration [29]. This system enriches a high-quality 3D model with hot-spot links to other media (pdf text, images, drawings)

---

[9] The EcceHomo project is presented at: http://vcg.isti.cnr.it/activities/eccehomo/ and a video is at: https://www.youtube.com/embed/_cG0uR_h8VM (accessed on 26 November 2020).

and with annotated regions, defined over the 3D surface and associated with textual descriptions. It was implemented as a web-based system using 3DHOP technology [15]. In this information system (based on an underlying relational data base) the 3D model acts as a spatial index to the information contained and referred (i.e., to several other types of data) and as a canvas where the restores can draw and select spatially-defined annotations.

The AIOLI[10] restoration documentation system developed by CNRS adopts also a similar approach. It manages 3D representations (based on pointset), RGB images and RTI images in the same visualization space [30]. This system also supports creating and visualizing annotations, defined on a single media (in this case, 2D images) and projected automatically on all other media depicting the same spatial area. Automatically inheriting annotations on any media supported is an essential plus of this system.

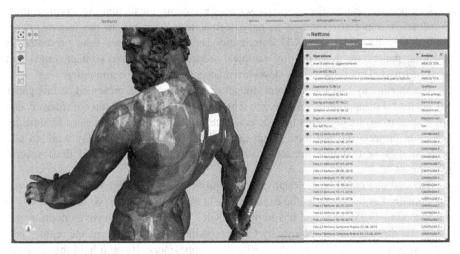

Fig. 7. The interface of the Neptune information system: a portion of the monument is rendered in forefront, some annotated regions and the related subset of data linked to this statue are presented with the list on the right and can be interactively accessed with a mouse click.

Research questions/Lesson learned/Impact:

- Restoration documentation is an application domain where multiple media types have to be stored, interconnected, and consulted.
- The 3D media could be the ideal index to available information, either augmenting the 3D model with geo-referenced links to other media, or mapping information on its surface through spatial annotations.
- The restoration of Neptune fountain demonstrated that this approach is doable, can be quickly learned by restorers and curators, and it can support cooperative and on-site work.

---

[10] The AIOLI system is presented at http://www.aioli.cloud/ (accessed on 26 November 2020).

6 Discussion and Concluding Remarks

The paper has presented some examples of interactive systems where a single interactive visualization context manages different media. The aim has been to show that we should not just select a single medium and restrict our analysis capabilities. Still, we could use as many media are needed/useful for a given communication or study task. We tried to show that using multiple media in a single application framework may increase the information we can communicate, grasp, and learn. The examples shown demonstrate that several innovative approaches have been presented and evaluated; the required enabling technology is available (even if not yet at the level of ready-to-use commercial tools).

Concerning the potential *impact* of digital solutions for CH data, we often miss proper assessment of the approaches presented in literature since only a minority of the works report the results of structured user tests involving substantial user communities. In effect, it is not so common to have formal user tests run in the framework of applications directed to the CH community (or, often, the user tests presented in scientific papers are done on tiny samples, reducing the analysis's effectiveness and level of trust). This issue might slow-down acceptance by the community.

We should say that the apparent impact of the approaches presented in this paper has been a bit disappointing. Moving to a broader discussion level and considering also other similar works, it seems that several nice methods presented in the literature by academic projects did not have a substantial impact on the day-by-day work of CH professionals or that this impact is very slow to emerge. We could draft several hypotheses.

The first one could be the relatively *slow* process of *technology endorsement* in the CH domain. Let me consider the example of 3D digitization: the basic technology was introduced in 1995–2000 and has improved since then. But the effective adoption and use of 3D digitization technology by CH professionals became a concrete reality only very recently, at least 15 years after technology appearance. It could hold the same for sophisticated visualization systems, such as those presented here and proposed in the literature in 2005–2020. Should we patiently wait the year 2030?

Let us move to another debate, concerning *complex/sophisticated methods vs. easy/straightforward approaches*. We could consider just a subset of the CH&ICT related literature: the papers authored by influential users (e.g., museum curators who implemented digital content for their expositions, teachers developing digital resources for their courses, art historians or archaeologists reporting use of digital media in their work) but NOT co-authored by academics. Those papers could be considered a report of what the CH community is doing autonomously and independently. Unfortunately, this literature subset mostly describes the adoption of simple or basic visualization approaches. An example of the tools reported is Sketchfab, a success story due to the simple approach provided for publishing 3D models on the web and making them available to colleagues or the public. Many of the latter papers report the selection of Sketchfab as the chosen viz platform. Let me move to another example concerning a more flexible visualization platform, 3DHOP. 3DHOP was designed to support: (a) easy and standardized viz tasks with a basic viewer, analogous to the Sketchfab approach; and (b) more complex communication and presentation functions, enabled by its configurable and extendable design. The analysis of what external users have done with 3DHOP [31] shows that many have just used the basic viewer. CH users very often ignore the potential of the configurability and the extended features.

These examples and our experience with CH professionals lead us to think that the technology adoption process is very slow and that *easy and basic solutions win*. Moreover, one could believe that most of the more sophisticated approaches proposed in the literature are just the result of technology geeks. An open query is if the real CH user community does require that level of sophistication. Thus, concerning the issue of who is driving innovation, we are back to the usual technology- or user-driven debate.

We still need a strong effort in *disseminating* innovative technologies and sophisticated solutions to the community of users. Since the CH domain is still characterized mainly by personnel having a human-science background, we need intense training and consulting. A related problem is the perduring *hiring policy* in museums and CH institutions. Since digital communication cannot be implemented on the shoulders of just art historians and curators, we need real multidisciplinary teams established in CH institutions.

Finally, the role of *private companies* is critical in any digital domain. In many CH experiences, open-source resources and academic prototypes are common solutions, while in other application domains, this role is taken by commercial software tools. This is a weakness for the CH domain, justified by the limited financial resources dedicated to digitization and digital communication, which is not attracting enough the private sector. The CH domain's economic growth could be beneficial for attracting companies who could deliver more sophisticated and easier to use software solutions.

To summarizing, we envision some *actions* which might have an impact on some of the issues mentioned:

- CH institutions need financial resources to enable a concrete and tangible jump in the digital era, but these resources should be bound for a significant share to *permanent hiring* of staff with ICT background, and only the rest should finance projects;
- The availability of funds dedicated to digitization and creation of digital content (for example, as part of the EU Recovery Plan) should include the CH domain and could be crucial for implementing the point above and for attracting private companies towards the CH domain;
- Academia should still pair research efforts with dissemination and training actions directed to CH professionals.

References

1. Scopigno, R., et al.: 3D models for cultural heritage: beyond plain visualization. IEEE Comput. **44**(7), 48–55 (2011). http://ieeexplore.ieee.org/xpl/articleDetails.jsp?reload=true&arnumber=5958706

2. Adamopoulos, E., Rinaudo, F.: 3D interpretation and fusion of multidisciplinary data for heritage science: a review. Int. Arch. Photogram. Remote Sens. Spatial Inf. Sci. **XLII-2/W15**, 17–24 (2019)

3. Reichinger, A., Maierhoffer, S., Purgathofer, W.: High-quality tactile paintings. J. Comput. Cult. Herit. **4**, 2 (2011)

4. Bekele, M., Pierdicca, R., Frontoni, E., Malinverni, E.S., Gain, J.E.: A survey of augmented, virtual, and mixed reality for cultural heritage. ACM J. Comput. Cult. Herit. **2018** (March) 7 (2018). https://doi.org/10.1145/3145534

5. Rodríguez-Gonzálvez, P., et al.: 4D reconstructionnand visualization of cultural heritage: analyzing our legacy through time. Int. Arch. Photogram. Remote Sens. Spatial Inf. Sci. **XLII-2/W3**, 609–616 (2017)

6. Remondino, F., Rizzi, A.: Reality-based 3D documentation of natural and culturalheritage sites—techniques, problems, and examples. Appl. Geomat. **2**, 85–100 (2010)

7. Hussain, A.J., Al-Fayadh, A., Radi, N.: Image compression techniques: a survey in lossless and lossy algorithms. Neurocomputing **300,** 44–69 (2018). https://doi.org/10.1016/j.neucom.2018.02.094. ISSN:0925-2312

8. Google Maps. (http://maps.google.com) and Google Earth (https://www.google.it/intl/it/earth/)

9. Potdar, V. M., Han, S., Chang, E.: A survey of digital image watermarking techniques. In: 2005 3rd IEEE International Conference on Industrial Informatics (INDIN 2005), Perth, WA, Australia, pp. 709–716 (2005). https://doi.org/10.1109/INDIN.2005.1560462

10. Malzbender, T., Gelb, D., Wolters, H.: Polynomial texture maps. In: Proceedings of the 28th ACM SIGGRAPH Conference, pp. 519–528. ACM (2001)

11. Palma, G., Corsini, M., Cignoni, P., Scopigno, R., Mudge, M.: Dynamic shading enhancement for reflectance transformation imaging, ACM J. Comput. Cult. Herit. **3**(2) (2010)

12. Sketchfab, a 3D web viewer. https://sketchfab.com/

13. Palma, G., et al.: Telling the story of ancient coins by means of interactive RTI images visualization. In: CAA 2012 Conference Proceeding, pp. 177—185 (2012)

14. Cignoni, P., Callieri, M., Corsini, M., Dellepiane, M., Ganovelli, F., Ranzuglia, G.: MeshLab: an open-source mesh processing tool. In: Sixth Eurographics Italian Chapter Conference, pp. 129–136, Eurographics (2008)

15. Potenziani, M., Callieri, M., Dellepiane, M., Ponchio, F., Scopigno, R.: 3DHOP: 3D heritage online presenter. Comput. Graph. **51**(Nov), 129–141 (2015)

16. Ponchio, F., Potenziani, M., Dellepiane, M., Callieri, M., Scopigno, R.: ARIADNE visual media service: easy web publishing of advanced visual media. CAA 2015, **1,** 433–442 (2016). https://visual.ariadne-infrastructure.eu/

17. YouTube: video sharing platform. https://www.youtube.com/

18. Wang, Z., et al.: CHER-Ob: a tool for shared analysis and video dissemination. ACM J. Comput. Cult. Herit. **11**(4) (2018)

19. Dercks, U., Ponchio, F., Scopigno, R.: CENOBIUM 10 years after: an evolving platform for digital humanities. Archeol. Calcolat. **10**, 123–141 (2018)

20. Snavely, N., Seitz, S.M., Szeliski, R.: Photo tourism: exploring photo collections in 3D. ACM Trans. Graph. **25**, 835–846 (2006)

21. Remondino, F., Spera, M.G., Nocerino, E., Menna, F., Nex, F.: State of the art in high density image matching. Photogram. Rec. **29**(146), 144–166 (2014)

22. Aicardi, I., Chiabrando, F., Lingua, A.M., Noardo, F.: Recent trends in cultural heritage 3D survey: the photogrammetric computer vision approach, J. Cult. Herit. **32**, 257–266 (2018). ISSN: 1296-2074

23. Brivio, P., Benedetti, L., Tarini, M., Ponchio, F., Cignoni, P., Scopigno, R.: PhotoCloud: interactive remote exploration of large 2D–3D datasets. IEEE Comput. Graph. Appl. **33**(2), 86–96 (2013)
24. Brivio, P., Tarini, M., Cignoni, P.: Browsing large image datasets through Voronoi diagrams. IEEE Trans.Visual. Comput. Graph. (Proc. Visual. 2010) **16**(10), 1261–1270 (2010)
25. Leoni, C., et al.: The dream and the cross: a 3D scanning project to bring 3D content in a digital edition. ACM J. Comput. Cult. Herit. **8**(1), 5 (2015)
26. Rüther, H., et al.: From point cloud to textured model, the Zamani laser scanning pipeline in Heritage documentation. South Afr. J. Geomat. **1**(1), 44–59 (2012)
27. Koeva, M., Luleva, M., Maldjanski, P.: Integrating spherical panoramas and maps for visualization of cultural heritage objects using virtual reality technology. Sensors **17**, 829 (2017)
28. Albertin, F., et al.: "Ecce Homo" by Antonello da Messina, from non-invasive investigations to data fusion and dissemination, Nature - Scientific Reports (2021, in press). Accepted for publication
29. Apollonio, F.I., et al.: A 3D-centered information system for the documentation of a complex restoration intervention. J. Cult. Herit. **29**, 89–99 (2017)
30. Messaudi, T., Veron, P., Halin, G., De Luca, L.: An ontological model for the reality-based 3D annotation of heritage building conservation state. J. Cult. Herit. **29**, 100–112 (2018).
31. Potenziani, M., Callieri, M., Scopigno, R.: Developing and maintaining a web 3D viewer for the CH community: an evaluation of the 3DHOP framework. In: 16th Eurographics Workshop on Graphics and Cultural Heritage, pp. 169–178 (2018)

Formalization of the "Immaterial Features" Conveyed by the Iconographic Cultural Heritage Entities

Gian Piero Zarri[✉]

STIH Laboratory, Sorbonne University, 75005 Paris, France
zarri@noos.fr

Abstract. The "digitization practices" used up-to-now to produce digital counterparts of the iconographic Cultural Heritage entities – paintings, drawings, sculptures, frescoes, mosaics, murals etc. – have mainly focused on the "physical" (dimensions, materials, supports, painting etc. techniques …) aspects of these entities. This means that all the "immaterial features" that characterize these items – from the stories/narratives they tell to all sort of feelings, memories, evocations and aesthetic experiences they can evoke in their end-users – are largely neglected. We argue that, to take correctly these immaterial aspects into account, we must use particularly powerful and expressive knowledge representation systems. In this context, the paper presents and discusses then in some detail the formal representations, obtained using the NKRL's (Narrative Knowledge Representation Language) tools, of complex iconographic situations that characterize two masterpieces of the Renaissance period. The results obtained, even if very preliminary, show that NKRL should be borne in mind as a useful tool for properly representing in digital format the "immaterial features" above.

Keywords: Iconographic items · Narratives · Knowledge representation · Inferences

1 Introduction

We can define the "Iconographic Cultural Heritage Entities" as those works of art whose aim is *to tell, explicitly or implicitly, a "story" under visual form* – they are also called in short "Iconographic Narratives"[1] and we will use this wording in the

---

[1] An age-old controversy that still raises debate among the narratology's specialists concerns the possibility of speaking of "*narratives*" in the case of "*iconographic narratives*". Some people note that, e.g., a picture, is deprived of any temporal/dynamic quality and represents only a static situation, not a narrative. Others say that a representation of any sort of mythological or hagiographic scene does not convey any real narrative but only refers the observer to a particular "story" he knows well; see [1] for a survey of these topics. Note, however, that any user/observer will always be able to create some sort of "*description*" of the "*visible content*" of any possible iconographic item. This even if this last is a Mondrian's work; in this case, the resulting description (the story/narrative) will probably be represented by a mix of feelings, memories, evocations of all sort of aesthetic experiences, leading eventually to produce a sort of "*concrete*" *representation* of what, normally, is deemed *not to be representable*.

© Springer Nature Switzerland AG 2021
M. Shehade and T. Stylianou-Lambert (Eds.): RISE IMET 2021, CCIS 1432, pp. 316–330, 2021.
https://doi.org/10.1007/978-3-030-83647-4_21

following. A story (more exactly, a specific instant of the story) is *explicitly* told in a picture like Géricault's "The raft of the Medusa", whilst several possible stories are *implicitly* suggested when regarding the Gioconda or any possible still life. The range of the possible visual story's supports is very large. In a Cultural Heritage context, they correspond to paintings, drawings, frescoes, sculptures, bas-/high-reliefs, tapestries, mosaics, murals… but we could continue by mentioning photographs, comics, posters, advertising artworks, cartoons, movies, etc.

The "digitization practices" used to produce *the digital counterparts* of the Iconographic Cultural Heritage entities have mainly focused, up to now, on the encoding of the *"physical" characteristics* of these entities. For the sake of simplicity, we englobe under the term "physical" all those usual features/properties, easy to collect and represent, that correspond to dimensions, supports, execution techniques, styles, name of the artists, information about the owner, places and collections the item is or was in the past, etc. The problem of producing an *accurate formal description* of the "story" carried on by a particular iconographic entity is, in general, *carefully avoided*, and the same happens with respect to the modelling of the *"message"* these entities would like to convey along with their historic, social and cultural background. This situation that leads to neglecting what we could call the *"immaterial features"* of the Iconographic Cultural Heritage entities has been recently acknowledged by the European Commission that, in the description of a recent Call, says, "So far, digitization focused mainly on capturing the visual appearance of individual objects, collections or sites. There is a real need to establish a comprehensive picture of the studied assets, capturing and re-creating not only visual and structural information, but also stories and experiences (stored in language data), together with their cultural and socio-historical context, as well as their evolution over time" [2: 41].

Satisfying the above requirements – i.e., *representing in digital form* also the "immaterial" (as opposed to "physical") information – means, however, to have available *very high-level knowledge representation tools*. These should be able, in fact, to correctly represent in digital form those *"structured/dynamic" situations* corresponding to complex events, actions, behaviors, attitudes and to their mutual relationships that can be found within *advanced conceptual structures like scripts, scenarios, narratives etc.* This is very difficult – and in some cases impossible – to obtain making use of the so-called "standard" knowledge representation proposals corresponding, e.g., to the Semantic Web tools. These are all based on the use of RDF, Resource Description Framework [3] triples, which correspond in practice to *"binary" relationships* characterized by an "individual1-property-individual2/value" format. This means that, whenever an RDF concept is instantiated into a concrete individual, *each associated property can only link this individual to another individual or a value* – a trivial example is denoted by the property "phone number" linking people's names to numeric strings. Binary relationships are particularly simple to deal with from a formal point of view; it is then easy to understand why, e.g., "standard" ontologies are basically built up using a binary approach for the definition of their concepts. Unfortunately, *the real world is far from being reducible to sets of binary relationships*, and more and more voices are presently asking for *"going beyond triples"* – see [4] to give only a very recent example.

In this context, the paper presents and discusses in some detail some preliminary experiments concerning the formal representations, obtained using the NKRL's

(Narrative Knowledge Representation Language) *n*-ary tools, of complex, "*immaterial*" iconographic narratives situations proper to two masterpieces of the Renaissance period. Thanks to its advanced knowledge representation and inferential characteristics, NKRL has been recently used, in fact, in several application domains implying the formal representation and the concrete use of *high-level "narrative" information in the widest meaning of these words*. This ranges from news about "terrorism in the Philippines" and "War in Afghanistan" [5] to high-level IoT/WoT applications [6], passing through the investigation of accident messages in an industrial context [7], sentiment analysis at conceptual level [8], etc.

In the following, Sect. 2 proposes a short state of the art intended mainly to confirm the present unsatisfactory situation with respect to the digitization techniques used in the Iconographic Cultural Heritage domain. In Sect. 3, we introduce those particularly innovative characteristics of NKRL that could bring significant changes in the way of representing at least some of the "*immaterial features*" that characterize the iconographic entities. Section 4 supplies some concrete examples by referring in case the reader, because of the space limitations, to previous publications about NKRL. Section 5 is a short "Conclusion".

2   Short State of the Art

The "digitation" procedures in the Cultural Heritage (CH) domain in general and in the iconographic narrative domain in particular have a long tradition of work that goes back to the sixties. They were limited, initially, to some elementary descriptions of the CH entities boiling down to standard annotation operations using keywords extracted from thesauri as AAT [9], ICONCLASS [10] or ULAN [11]. The use of (relatively simple) data models very popular in the eighties-nineties as the original Dublin Core proposal [12] or of more sophisticated models like VRA (Visual Resources Association) Core 4 Schema [13] has contributed to improve the efficacy and generality of these annotation procedures. Moreover, the conversion of these models into RDF-compatible tools under the influence of the Semantic Web initiative – see the DCMI (Dublin Core Metadata Initiative) Abstract Model [14] or the RDF(S) version of the CIDOC CRM tool[2] – has further increased their *interoperability/standardization potentials*.

The introduction of a Semantic Web/RDF approach in the CH domain has indubitably produced important beneficial effects, but it does not seem to have introduced *real progresses* with respect to the search for concrete solutions to represent the immaterial features of the iconographic narratives. A canonical example is represented by the RDF-based description of Claude Monet's "Garden at Sainte-Addressee" painting included in the Image Annotation on the Semantic Web W3C Incubator Group Report [16]. This description supplies in fact *an impressive number of details about the "physical" (dimensions etc.) characteristics of the painting*. However, with respect to

---

[2] CIDOC CRM (Conceptual Reference Model) – see [15] for the version 6.2.6 – is a powerful tool that provides definitions and a *formal, ontological-oriented structure* for describing the main implicit and explicit concepts and relationships used in the CH documentation.

the proper content/deep meaning and to the "message" the painting could transmit to the observer, the representation is reduced to *three xml-like statements* relating the presence on the picture of three persons (three Claude Monet's relatives). No information is given about the *real semantic content* expressed by the painting, for example, the mode of sitting of the personages facing of the sea, their mutual relationships, their attitude about the peaceful and bright landscape, the impressive number of flowers, etc.[3]

The Incubator Group Report goes back to 2007, but, apparently, few real progresses with respect to a really complete "semantic" description of the iconographic narratives have been made in recent years. We can see in this context, e.g., the flat statements in the style of "the subject of the painting is a woman" included in the very complex and convoluted formalization of the Mona Lisa painting carried out in 2013 in an Europeana context [18]. Another, more recent example, can be found in the formal description of a Giambologna's sculpture [19] denoting the kidnapping of a Sabin woman by a Roman warrior, on display at the Capodimonte museum in Naples. This description is restricted to *purely documentary-oriented statements* telling us that this sculpture is part of the "Collezione Farnese", without any attempt to model the frightened woman, the kidnapper, the man who tries to prevent the kidnapping, the reciprocal attitudes of the different protagonists of the scene, etc. Several additional examples in the same style can be found, e.g., in Sect. 1.1 of [20][4].

---

[3] From a *"semantic description"* point of view, the significance of this sort of (manual) descriptions is even less than what we could get making use of the most recent Deep Learning approaches about the use of *NLP techniques for image captioning* – i.e., the activity of automatically producing a natural language description of the (*surface*) contents of an image. See, to give only an example, a recent paper [17] produced in the context of Yahoo Research, which introduces significant progresses in the way of taking into account the *spatial relationships between the detected objects*, like the relative position and size.

[4] We can conclude this short State of the Art by noticing that the Natural Language Processing (NLP) community has developed for many years knowledge representation systems that, *superficially*, could be equated to that used by NKRL, see the examples in the next Sections. This corresponds to the fact that both the AI-oriented knowledge representation systems like NKRL (and Knowledge Graphs, Conceptual Dependencies, Topic Maps etc.) and those NLP-oriented like FrameNet [21] or PropBank [22] have, in practice, the same origin, i.e., the publication of Charles Fillmore's ground-breaking paper about the Case Grammars theory [23]. A discussion about this topic can be found in [24: 551–554]. However, *the NLP-oriented and AI-oriented systems deeply diverge about their final aims.* NLP scholars – like Fillmore, by the way – are linguists and, as such, mainly interested in the description of the syntactic/semantic relationships proper to the *surface aspects* of any sort of linguistic utterance, i.e., of the relationships between natural language (NL) words in a specific language. AI researchers, on the contrary, are interested in the *formal representation of the deep meanings* underlying the surface expression of events, situations, states, actions. While, as in the NKRL case, they make use of "roles/cases" still labelled with terms in the Fillmore's style, these are now *"deep cases"* that link together *conceptual entities* (concepts, concept instances, semantic predicates, spatio-temporal abstractions etc.) *instead of words*, and are independent from a particular natural language even if they are often drafted in a sort of Basic English for human understanding. Pure surface phenomena like the idiosyncrasies in the lexical choices, the active/passive alternation, the morphology, *are disregard at deep level*. Very significantly, the standard AI-oriented *inference procedures* intended to automatically discover, e.g., new relationships between characters, events, situations etc. are normally not taken into account in an NLP context.

3   Key Notions about the NKRL Language

From an ontological point of view, the most striking characteristic of NKRL concerns the addition of an *"ontology of elementary events"* to the usual *"ontology of concepts"*. This last – called "HClass", hierarchy of classes, in NKRL – presents some interesting aspects, with respect in particular to the modelling of difficult notions like color and substance [25: 123–137]. However, its architecture is a relatively traditional one, and the HClass concepts are represented, in practice, according to the usual "binary" model that, as already stated, is the basis of the whole Semantic Web approach.

A (relatively limited) binary-based approach experiences, however, major difficulties when the entities to be represented are not simple plain notions/concepts that can be defined a priori and inserted then in a graph-shaped "static" ontology, but denote at the contrary *dynamic states/situations/actions/episodes/experiences etc.* characterized by the presence of *spatio-temporal information* and of *complex, mutual relationships among their constituent elements* – including, e.g., intentions and behaviors. The "stories/narratives" of any possible type (including then the "iconographic" one) pertain, of course, to this second type of entities. In designing then the ontology of elementary events of NKRL, an *"augmented n-ary approach"* has been chosen. *"n-ary* approach" means to make use of a sort of formal representation where *a given predicate can be associated with multiple arguments* – using a standard example, representing the *n*-ary "purchase" relation implies associating with the purchase predicate several arguments as a seller, a buyer, a good, a price, a timestamp, etc. *"Augmented"* means that – following a suggestion that goes back to the "What's in a Link" paper by William Woods [26] – in the context of *n*-ary representations, the logico-semantics links between the predicate and its arguments are *explicitly represented* making use of the notion of *"functional role"* [24]. The *n*-ary representation of a narrative like "Peter has given a book of art to Mary" should also include, then, the indication that "Peter" plays the role of "subject/agent" with respect to the action of giving, "book" is the "object" of this action and "Mary" the "beneficiary", see below.

Returning now to the ontology of elementary events, its nodes are represented by augmented *n*-ary knowledge patterns called *"templates"* in an NKRL context – this second ontology is then called HTemp, the hierarchy of templates. Templates denote formally *general classes of elementary states/situations/actions/episodes etc.* (for the sake of simplicity, designated collectively as "elementary events"). Examples of these general classes can be "be present in a place", "experience a given situation", "have a specific attitude towards someone/something", "send/receive messages", "be characterized by a given property", etc. The instances of these templates – called *"predicative occurrences"* in an NKRL context – describe then formally the *"meaning/inner content" of specific elementary events pertaining to one of these classes.* The basic, general representation of a template, i.e., of a node of the HTemp hierarchy, is given by Eq. (1).

$$\big(L_i\big(P_j(R_1a_1)(R_2a_2)\ldots(R_na_n)\big)\big). \tag{1}$$

In Eq. (1), L_i is the *symbolic label* identifying (reifying) the particular augmented *n*-ary structure corresponding to a specific template. P_j is a conceptual predicate. R_k is a *generic functional role*, see above. It is then used to identify the *specific logico-semantic function* performed by its "filler" a_k, a generic predicate argument, with respect to the predicate P_j. When a template denoted as Move:TransferMaterial ThingsToSomeone in NKRL is instantiated to provide the representation of the quite simple elementary event above, "Bill gives an art book to Mary", the predicate P_j (MOVE) will introduce its three arguments a_k, JOHN_, MARY_ and ART_BOOK_1 ("*individuals*", i.e., instances of HClass' entities, where HClass is the NKRL binary ontology of concepts) via, respectively, the three functional relationships (R_k roles) SUBJ(ect), BEN(e)F(iciary) and OBJ(ect). These last specify, then, the function/task/role of each of the three individuals with respect to the predicate and, as a consequence, with respect to the global meaning of the (formalized) elementary event. The full *n*-ary construction is then *reified* through the symbolic label L_j. This label is particularly important in the context of the global Eq. 1's symbolism. It has, in fact, the function of *unique internal handle* proposed by Woods in the 1975 paper already mentioned to allow us to manage all the constituents of the formal representation of an elementary event as a *single and coherent block*. This block can, then, be associated with similar blocks within (potentially very large) consistent conceptual structures, see the examples in the next Section.

4   Examples in a Narrative/Iconographic Context

This Section supplies some concrete examples of formalization in NKRL terms of specific "*immaterial features*" proper to the iconographic cultural heritage entities and, at the same time, to provide additional details about the general NKRL's modeling techniques. The examples are derived from *two recent experiments*, described in detail in [27] and [20], which concern the NKRL formal description of two iconographic narratives pertaining to the "universal masterpieces" category. The first concerns the central scene of Diego Velazquez's painting about "The Surrender of Breda", which represents Ambrosio Spinola, Commander in Chief of the Spanish Army during the Eighty Years' War, receiving, on June 5, 1625, the keys to the city by Justinus van Nassau, governor of Breda. The main interest of this scene resides in the *benevolent attitude* of the winner, Spinola, towards the loser, van Nassau, a not so common behavior at that time. The second concerns Leonardo Da Vinci's The Mona Lisa ("La Gioconda") painting, which certainly does not require any particular presentation note.

4.1   Templates and Their Instances

Table 1 shows the creation of *an instance* (a "*predicative occurrence*") of the Receive: TangibleThing template; this occurrence is identified by the symbolic label breda.c8. This predicative occurrence corresponds to the elementary event "Ambrosio Spinola receives the keys to the city from Justinus van Nassau in the context of particular celebrations" and is part of the global NKRL narrative that encodes the content of the Velazquez's picture, see [27].

The formalism utilized to draw up the template of Table 1 corresponds to the syntax of Eq. 1. We can note that, to avoid the ambiguities of natural language and any possible combinatorial explosion problem, see [25: 56–61], both the conceptual predicate of Eq. 1 and the associated functional roles are *"primitives"*. Predicates P_j belong then to the set {BEHAVE, EXIST, EXPERIENCE, MOVE, OWN, PRODUCE, RECEIVE}, and the roles R_k to the set {SUBJ(ect), OBJ(ect), SOURCE, BEN(e)F(iciary), MODAL(ity), TOPIC, CONTEXT}. The HTemp hierarchy is structured into *seven branches*, where each of them includes only the templates created – see Eq. 1 – around *one* of the seven allowed predicates P_j. HTemp includes presently (February 2021) more than 150 templates, very easy to specialize and customize, see [25: 137–177].

Table 1. Deriving a predicative occurrence from a template.

```
name:  Receive:TangibleThing
father:  Receive:
position:  7.1
natural language description: "Receive Some Tangible Thing from Someone"

RECEIVE    SUBJ          var1: [var2]
           OBJ           var3
           SOURCE        var4: [var5]
           [BENF         var6: [var7]]
           [MODAL        var8]
           [TOPIC        var9]
           [CONTEXT      var10]
           { [modulators], ≠abs }

var1   =   human_being_or_social_body
var3   =   artefact_, economic/financial_entity
var4   =   human_being_or_social_body
var6   =   human_being_or_social_body
var8   =   activity_, process_, symbolic_label, temporal_sequence
var9   =   sortal_concept
var10  =   situation_, symbolic_label
var2, var5, var7 = location_


breda.c6)   RECEIVE    SUBJ       AMBROSIO_SPINOLA: (BREDA_)
                       OBJ        (SPECIF key_to_the_city BREDA_)
                       SOURCE     JUSTINUS_VAN_NASSAU : (BREDA_)
                       CONTEXT    CELEBRATION_1
                       date-1:    05/06/1625
                       date-2:

Receive:TangibleThing (7.1)
```
Ambrosio Spinola receives the keys to the city from van Nassau in the context of particular celebrations.

As we can see from Table 1, in a template the arguments of the predicate (the a_k terms in Eq. (1)) are actually represented by *variables (var$_i$) with associated constraints*. These last are expressed as *concepts or combinations of concepts* (structured concepts or expansions, see next sub-section), i.e., using HClass terms – this confirms that the two NKRL's ontologies work in a *strictly connected way*. When creating a predicative occurrence as an instance of a given template, the constraints linked to the variables are used to specify the legal sets of HClass terms, *concepts or individuals*, that can be *substituted* for these variables within the occurrence – note that, in the "external" version of the NKRL metalanguage used to represent the examples of this paper, the *"concepts"* are in lower case characters and the *"individuals"* in upper case. For example, in the context of Table 1, we must verify that the *individuals* AMBROSIO_SPINOLA and JUSTINUS_VAN_NASSAU are really HClass instances of individual_person, a specific term in HClass of human_being_or_social_body, see the constraints on the SUBJ and BENF roles of the Table 1 template. The generic HClass *concept* key_-to_the_city is a specific term, through intermediate elements, of artefact_, see the constraint associated with OBJ in Table 1. CELEBRATION_1 is an instance, through intermediate steps – e.g., official_cerimony – of the reified_event concept, a specific term of situation_ in the HClass hierarchy.

4.2   Structured Arguments (Expansions)

The example of Table 1 allows us to introduce an important feature of NKRL, "structured arguments" or "expansions" [25: 68–70], which contributes strongly to the high level of *"expressiveness"* of this language.

Structured arguments/expansions concern the possibility of building up the predicate arguments a_k associated with the roles R_k in Eq. 1 as a set of *recursive lists*; these lists are introduced by the four *AECS operators*. These are the disjunctive operator ALTERN(ative) = A, the distributive operator ENUM(eration) = E, the collective operator COORD(ination) = C and the attributive operator SPECIF(ication) = S. An example of "expansion" is (SPECIF key_to_the_city BREDA_) – the filler of the OBJ(ject) role in the predicative occurrence of Table 1 – denoting, via the use of the operator SPECIF, that the "keys to the city" we are speaking of are *more exactly "specified"* through the addition of the property BREDA_.

As a more complex example, we can now look at the NKRL encoding of the Mona Lisa painting, more precisely to the part concerning the problem of the identification of the woman represented in the *"hidden painting"*, i.e., the portrait, visible to us only in x-rays, indubitably painted by Leonardo and that lies beneath Mona Lisa on the same poplar panel, see also [28]. Table 2 shows the NKRL formalism associated with the predicative occurrence gio2.c4 (an instance of the Own:CompoundProperty template) that is part of this encoding. In NKRL, the instances of the Own:Property and Own:CompoundProperty templates are systematically used to introduce the properties of *inanimate entities*; the templates of the type Behave:HumanProperty introduce, on the contrary, the properties of *human (animate) entities* see in this context, e.g., [8]. The formal difference between the Own:Property and Own:CompoundProperty's instances concerns the way of representing concretely the property *via the filler of the TOPIC role*. This filler is simply a HClass term, concept or individual, in the Own:Property instances, while it is a structured argument (expansion) in the instances of Own:CompoundProperty. In the gio2.c4 occurrence, PAINTING_2 is the hidden painting. Its properties, represented by the TOPIC's filler, are denoted by a COORD(ination) list including two arguments, both represented by SPECIF(ication) lists. The first states that the execution of PAINTING_2, painted_on, is characterized by two features, i) it as been realized on the same POPLAR_PLANK_1 introduced earlier in the global NKRL encoding of the Mona Lisa' portrait as the support of this last portrait (the PAINTING_1) and ii) it is located under PAINTING_1 – this second feature is expressed making use of an additional **SPECIF** list. The second argument tells us that **PAINTING_2** is known as the **HIDDEN_PAINTING**.

Note that the interweaving of the AECS operators is controlled by a *"priority rule"*, mnemonically formulated as **(ALTERN (ENUM (COORD (SPECIF))))** that forbids, e.g., the use of **COORD** lists within the scope of lists **SPECIF** – the inverse is allowed see, e.g., the above **TOPIC** filler[5].

Table 2. Representing the properties of the "hidden painting".

```
gio2.c4)  OWN    SUBJ    PAINTING_2
                 OBJ     property_
                 TOPIC   (COORD
                            (SPECIF painted_on POPLAR_PLANK_1 (SPECIF under_ PAINTING_1))
                            (SPECIF labelled_as HIDDEN_PAINTING))
                 { obs }
                 date-1:  today_
                 date-2:

Own:CompoundProperty (5.42)

PAINTING_2 has been painted under the plank of PAINTING_1, and is known as the HIDDEN_PAINTING.
```

4.3   Determiners (Attributes)

The semantic predicate P_j, the seven functional roles R_k and the (simple or structured) arguments a_k of the predicate introduced by Eq. 1 are the *three basic building blocks* (the *"basic core"*) strictly necessary to give rise to a *meaningful representation*, in the digital world, of narrative entities under the form of elementary events or of classes of elementary events (templates). The three blocks of the basic core *cannot* receive separately an interpretation in terms of the above narrative entities: a valid interpretation will only arise after their (*mandatory*) assembling through a L_j label.

When the addition of further information-carrying elements is required to better specify the "meaning" expressed by the basic core, these elements (basically *locations, modalities and temporal information*) are dealt with simply as *determiners/attributes*.

In Table 1, for example, the variables *var2*, *var5* and *var7* associated with the template denote determiners/attributes of the *location* type that are then represented, in the corresponding predicative occurrences, by specific terms of the HClass concept location_ or by individuals derived from these terms – BREDA_ in the case of Table 1. We can note that the determiners of this particular type can only be associated with *specific role fillers*, e.g., with the fillers AMBROSIO_SPINOLA (SUBJ functional role) and JUSTINUS_VAN_NASSAU (SOURCE) in the occurrence breda.c6 of Table 1.

---

[5] Given its logical clarity, expressiveness and readability properties, the NKRL "structured arguments" tool compares favourably with other solutions proposed in an *annotation of non-textual data context* see, e.g., [29] – this last proposal is based on the much-discussed TimeML system [30].

Modulators (modalities) represent an important category of determiners/attributes that *apply on the contrary to a full, well-formed template or predicative occurrence* to particularize its *full meaning*. They are classed into three categories, *temporal* (begin, end, obs(erve)), *deontic* (oblig(ation), fac(ulty), interd(iction), perm(ission)) and *modal* (abs(olute), against, for, main, ment(al), wish, etc.) modulators, see [25: 71–75]. An example of use of the temporal modulator obs(erve) is reproduced in Table 2: we can see, as of today, that PAINTING_2 is…; today_ is a concept, specific term of time_period in HClass through intermediary steps. A last category of attribute/determiners concerns the two operators date-1 and date-2. They can only be associated with *full predicative occurrences* (e.g., the two occurrences in Table 1 and 2) and are used to materialize the temporal interval (or a specific date, as in the case of these two occurrences) that was originally linked to the elementary event corresponding to the occurrence. A recent description of the formal system used in NKRL for the representation and management of temporal information can be found, e.g., in [31].

To highlight the importance, from an *"expressiveness"* point of view, of the attribute/determiners in NKRL, we reproduce in Table 3 another fragment of the global formalization of the Mona Lisa painting, the occurrence gio2.c6 that represents a typical example of NKRL modelling of the notion of *"negation"*. This consists in adding to a complete and well-formed predicative occurrence a specific *"modal modulator"*, negv (*"negated event"*) to point out that the corresponding elementary event did not take place. In our example, WOMAN_53, the woman represented in the "hidden painting", has not been recognized (see Table 5 below) as WOMAN_52, where this last individual corresponds to Mona Lisa in the NKRL coding – WOMAN_53 is probably Isabella d'Aragona, the wife of the Duke of Milan Ludovico il Moro, one of the Leonardo's employers, see [28]. The association of the temporal modulator obs(erve) with today_ has the usual "as of today" meaning.

Table 3. An example of "negated event".

```
gio2.c6)   BEHAVE  SUBJ    (SPECIF WOMAN_53 (SPECIF identified_with WOMAN_52))
                   { obs, negv }
                   date-1: today_
                   date-2:

Behave:HumanProperty (1.1)
```

We can remark (modulator obs) that the elementary event represented by gio2.c6 is a "negated event" (modulator negv), i.e., WOMAN_53 is not WOMAN_52.

4.4   Second Order Events

What described until now concerns mainly the NKRL solutions to the problem of representing *single elementary events*. In the context of digitally representing *real iconographic situations*, several predicative occurrences corresponding to multiple elementary events must be associated. An evident and easy way of representing these links concerns the possibility of making use of a *co-reference mechanism* that allow us to logically associate two or more predicative occurrences *where the same individual(s) appear(s)*. Returning then to the predicative occurrence breda.c6 of Table 1, we can note that, thanks to the presence of the filler (individual) CELEBRATION_1 in the CONTEXT functional role, the ceremony of handing over the keys occurs in the context of more general "festivities". Occurrence breda.c8 tells us now that CELE-BRATION_1 appears also as the SUBJ of an Own:CompoundProperty predicative occurrence, see Sect. 4.2 above, where the filler of the TOPIC role is an AECS structure corresponding to (SPECIF surrender_ BREDA_). The festivities that come with the handing over the keys are then associated with the surrender of the city.

The most general and interesting way of logically associating single predicative occurrences is, however, to make use of *second order structures* created through the *reification* of single occurrences. These structures reflect, at the digital level, "*surface connectivity phenomena*" like causality, goal or indirect speech. *Reification* is intended here as the possibility of creating new objects ("*first class citizens*") out of already existing entities and to *say something* about them without making reference to the original entities. In NKRL, it is implemented using the *symbolic labels* (the L_i terms of Eq. (1) of the predicative occurrences according to *two different conceptual mechanisms*.

The first concerns the possibility of referring to an elementary (or complex) event *as an argument* of another (elementary) event – a "complex event" corresponds to a *coherent set of elementary events*. The (surface) connectivity phenomenon involved here is the "indirect speech". An example can be that of an elementary event *X* describing someone who speaks about *Y*, where *Y* is itself an elementary/complex event. In NKRL, this mechanism is called "*completive construction*" see [25: 87–91]. It is illustrated, e.g., by the association of the occurrences breda.c5/breda.c6 in Table 4, where breda.c6 is introduced by breda.c5 as *filler* of its CONTEXT role. The full encoding of breda.c6 is reproduced in Table 1; the # prefix in breda.c5 indicates that the associated term is not a HClass item but introduces the label of an occurrence. breda.c5 and breda.c6 represent then, together, a *coherent entity* that supplies the formalization of the most important narrative element of the scene: while he receives the keys (breda.c6), Ambrosio Spinola *prevents* (PRODUCE activity_blockage) a Justinus' attempt to genuflect in front of him (breda.c5). activity_blockage is a specific term of activity_ in HClass, genuflecting_ is a specific term of negative_relationship and then of relationship_.

Table 4. An example of completive construction.

```
breda.c5)  PRODUCE   SUBJ      AMBROSIO_SPINOLA: (BREDA_)
                     OBJ       activity_blockage
                     MODAL     (SPECIF moral_suasion hand_gesture)
                     TOPIC     (SPECIF GENUFLECTING_1 JUSTINUS_VAN_NASSAU)
                     CONTEXT   #breda.c6
                     date-1:   05/06/1625
                     date-2:

Produce:CreateCondition/Result (6.4)

(Within the breda.c6 framework), Spinola stops van Nassau to genuflect.

breda.c6)  RECEIVE   SUBJ  AMBROSIO_SPINOLA...
Ambrosio Spinola receives the keys...
```

Note that the genuflecting_ concept has been instantiated in breda.c5 into a GENUFLECTING_1 individual to allow us to *reference unambiguously this term within several occurrences* (*co-reference*, see above). It appears, e.g., in the occurrence breda.c7 of the full "Surrender of Breda" NKRL representation, where it is specified that the genuflecting gesture is both (COORD) sketched_ (specific term of qualifier_) and in_front_of (specific term of binary_relational_property) Ambrosio Spinola.

The second (more general) process allows us to associate together, through several types of *connectivity operators*, elementary (or complex) events that, to the contrary of the previous case, can still be regarded as *fully independent entities*. This mechanism is called "*binding occurrences*", see [25: 91–98], and it is implemented under the form of lists formed of a binding operator Bn_i and its L_j arguments. The general expression of a binding occurrence is then:

$$(Lb_k \ (Bn_i \ L_1 \ L_2 \ \dots \ L_n)), \tag{2}$$

where Lb_k is the symbolic label identifying the global binding structure. The Bn_i operators are: ALTERN(ative), COORD(ination), ENUM(eration), CAUSE, REFER (ence), the weak causality operator, GOAL, MOTIV(ation), the weak intentionality operator, COND(ition). These binding structures are particularly important in an NKRL context given that, in particular, the *top-level formal structure* introducing the whole NKRL representation of any kind of narrative necessarily has the general form of a *binding occurrence* (Eq. 2) – see, e.g., in an iconographic narrative context, [20, 27]. An example of binding occurrence is given in Table 5.

Table 5. An example of binding occurrence.

gio2.c5)   (CAUSE gio2.c6 gio2.c7)
The elementary event modelized by gio2.c6 has been caused by what is collectively described in the completive construction involving occurrences gio2.c7 and gio2.c8.
gio2.c6)   BEHAVE SUBJ   (SPECIF WOMAN_53 … { obs, negv }
The elementary event represented by gio2.c7 is a "negated event"…
gio2.c7) MOVE   SUBJ   LILLIAN_FELDMANN_SCHWARTZ OBJ   #gio2.c8 MODAL (SPECIF SCIENTIFIC_PAPER_2 (SPECIF published_on THE_VISUAL_COMPUTER_JOURNAL)) date-1:   1/1/1988, 31/1/1988 date-2: Move:StructuredInformation (4.42)
Lillian Feldmann Schwartz has circulated what described in gio2.c8 by means of a paper in "The Visual Computer" Journal.

This Table explains that the CAUSE of what is related in gio2.c6 concerns the publication – see gio2.c7, an instance of the Move:StructuredInformation template – of a paper of Lillian Feldman Schwartz. In this, she had listed all the incoherencies preventing us from identifying the hidden painting woman with Mona Lisa. The formal description of these incoherencies is represented by a set of predicative occurrences collected within the binding occurrence #gio2.c8, which is introduced in gio2.c7 in a completive construction mode.

4.5   Inference Procedures

Space limitations do not allow us to deal with this topic in some detail – the interested reader is then referred to [25: 183–243] for a complete description of the NKRL inference procedures, and to [20, 27] for their use in an iconographic narrative context.

We will only remark here two important points. The first is that the quite detailed and rich modeling of the original information allowed by the use of NKRL enables the implementation of particularly interesting inference procedures see, e.g., in [20], the possibility of *automatically associating* the clear imbalance between the two parts of the background landscape in the Leonardo's masterpiece – chaotic mountains and flooding river on the right, peaceful flatland on the left – with some "odd" particularities of the proper Mona Lisa's portrait. The second is particularly interesting from a Computer Science point of view, and concerns the fact that the use of a rich augmented *n*-ary approach in the NKRL style appears to be particularly important for creating *highly expressive inference rules* whose "atoms" can represent *directly* complex situations and events, actions, scenarios, narratives etc. without being reduced to the use of the (inexpressive) usual binary clauses.

5   Conclusion

In this paper, we have utilized some examples of an *advanced formal treatment of complex iconographic cultural heritage situations* to highlight the interest of using in this context the *n-ary approach* of NKRL. As we have already noticed above, there is actually, in fact, a widespread consensus about the difficulty/impossibility of using, because of *their weaknesses from an "expressiveness" point of view*, the traditional, binary knowledge representation tools to deal with this sort of high level, structured, dynamic entities. These are characterized, in fact, by the presence of *"immaterial features"* as feelings, memories, evocations, aesthetic experiences etc. that, to be accurately dealt with, require the use of *advanced tools in the NKRL's style* allowing an easily modelling of complex conceptual structures like recursive predicate arguments, modalities, spatio-temporal information, indirect speech, coordination, alternative, causal/purpose and conditional clauses, advanced inference techniques, etc.

We can note that the above features do not denote specific characteristics of the Iconographic Cultural Heritage domain, but represent in general *distinguishing qualities of Human Sciences in their entirety*. NKRL could be borne in mind, then, as an *attractive possibility* for implementing really accurate digitization activities, and interesting applications of the corresponding results, for the whole Human Sciences field.

References

1. Speidel, K.: What narrative is. Front. Narrat. Stud. **4**(S1), s76–s104 (2018)
2. European Commission: Horizon 2020: Work Programme 2018–2020: 13. Europe in a Changing World – Inclusive, Innovative and Reflective Societies, pp. 41–43. Publication Office of the EU, Luxembourg (2020)
3. Cyganiak, R., Wood, D., Lanthaler, M. (eds.): RDF 1.1 Concepts and abstract syntax – W3C Recommendation 25 February 2014. W3C. https://www.w3.org/TR/rdf11-concepts/. Accessed 27 Feb 2021
4. Suchanek, F.: The need to move beyond triples. In: Proceedings of Text2Story, Third Workshop on Narrative Extraction from Texts Co-located with 42nd European Conference on Information Retrieval (ECIR 2020) – CEUR Workshop Proceedings, vol. 2593, pp. 95–104. CEUR-WS.org, Aachen (2020)
5. Zarri, G.P.: A conceptual methodology for dealing with terrorism "narratives." Int. J. Digit. Crime Foren. (IJDCF) **2**(2), 47–63 (2010)
6. Zarri, G.P.: High-level knowledge representation and reasoning in a cognitive IoT/WoT context. In: Sangaiah, A.K., Thangavelu, A., Sundaram, V.M. (eds.) Cognitive Computing for Big Data Systems Over IoT. LNDECT, vol. 14, pp. 223–262. Springer, Cham (2018). https://doi.org/10.1007/978-3-319-70688-7_10
7. Zarri, G.P.: Knowledge representation and inference techniques to improve the management of gas and oil facilities. Knowl-Based Syst. **24**(7), 989–1003 (2011)
8. Zarri, G.P.: Sentiments analysis at conceptual level making use of the narrative knowledge representation language. Neural Netw. **58**(1), 82–97 (2014)
9. ATT Homepage. http://www.getty.edu/research/tools/vocabularies/aat/index.html. Accessed 27 Feb 2021
10. ICONCLASS Homepage. http://www.iconclass.nl/home. Accessed 27 Feb 2021
11. ULAN Homepage. http://www.getty.edu/research/tools/vocabularies/ulan/index.html. Accessed 27 Feb 2021
12. Dublin Core Homepage. http://dublincore.org/. Accessed 27 Feb 2021
13. VRA Core Schema Homepage. https://www.loc.gov/standards/vracore/schemas.html. Accessed 27 Feb 2021
14. DCMI Abstract Model Homepage. https://www.dublincore.org/specifications/dublin-core/abstract-model/. Accessed 27 Feb 2021
15. Le Boeuf, P., Doerr, M., Ore, C.E., Stead, S.: Definition of the CIDOC Conceptual Reference Model (version 6.2.6, June 2019). ICOM/CIDOC Documentation Standard Group, Heraklion (2019)
16. Troncy, R., van Ossenbruggen, J., Pan, J.Z., Stamou, G. (eds.): Image Annotation on the Semantic Web, W3C Incubator Group Report 14 August 2007. W3C (2007). https://www.w3.org/2005/Incubator/mmsem/XGR-image-annotation/. Accessed 27 Feb 2021
17. Herdade, S., Kappeler, A., Boake, K., Soares, J.: Image captioning: transforming objects into words. In: Proceedings of the 32nd Conference on Neural Information Processing Systems (NeurIPS 2019), vol. 14, pp. 11105–11115. Neural Information Processing Systems Foundation Inc., San Diego (2019)
18. Isaac, A. (ed.): Europeana Data Model Primer (14/07/2013). Europeana Foundation (2013). http://travesia.mcu.es/portalnb/jspui/bitstream/10421/5981/1/EDM_primer.pdf. Accessed 27 Feb 2021
19. Lodi, G., et al.: Semantic web for cultural heritage valorisation. In: Hai-Jew, S. (ed.) Data Analytics in Digital Humanities, pp. 3–37. Springer, Cham (2017). https://doi.org/10.1007/978-3-319-54499-1_1

20. Amelio, A., Zarri, G.P.: Conceptual encoding and advanced management of Leonardo da Vinci's Mona Lisa: preliminary results. Inf. MDPI **10**(10), 321 (2019)
21. Fillmore, C.J., Johnson, C.R., Petruck, M.R.L.: Background to FrameNet. Int. J. Lexicogr. **16**(3), 235–250 (2002)
22. Palmer, M., Gildea, D., Kingsbury, P.: The proposition bank: an annotated corpus of semantic roles. Comput. Linguist. **31**(1), 71–106 (2005)
23. Fillmore, C.J.: The case for case. In: Bach, E., Harms, R.T. (eds.) Universals in Linguistic Theory, pp. 1–88. Holt Rinehart and Winston, New York (1968)
24. Zarri, G.P.: Functional and semantic roles in a high-level knowledge representation language. Artif. Intell. Rev. **51**(4), 537–575 (2019)
25. Zarri, G.P.: Representation and Management of Narrative Information – Theoretical Principles and Implementation. Springer, London (2009)
26. Woods, W.A.: What's in a link: foundations for semantic networks. In: Bobrow, D., Collins, A. (eds.) Representation and Understanding – Studies in Cognitive Sciences, pp. 35–82. Academic Press, New York (1975)
27. Zarri, G.P.: Use of a knowledge patterns-based tool for dealing with the "narrative meaning" of complex iconographic cultural heritage Items. In: Proceedings of the 1st International Workshop on Visual Pattern Extraction and Recognition for Cultural Heritage Understanding (VIPERC 2019) – CEUR Publications, vol. 2320, pp. 25–38. CEUR-WS.org, Aachen (2019)
28. Amelio, A.: Exploring Leonardo da Vinci's Monalisa by visual computing: a review. In: Proceedings of the 1st International Workshop on Visual Pattern Extraction and Recognition for Cultural Heritage Understanding (VIPERC 2019) – CEUR Publications, vol. 2320, pp. 74–85. CEUR-WS.org, Aachen (2019)
29. Lee, K.: Multi-layered annotation of non-textual data for spatial information. In: Proceedings of ACL-2013, pp. 15–23. Association for Computational Linguistics (ACL), Stroudsburg (2013)
30. Mani, I., Pustejovsky, J., Gaizauskas, R. (eds.): The Language of Time: A Reader. University Press, Oxford (2005)
31. Zarri, G.P.: Modelling and exploiting the temporal information associated with complex "narrative" documents. Int. J. Knowl. Eng. Data Mining **6**(2), 135–167 (2019)

Ethical Considerations and Methods for Diversifying Representations of Cultural Heritage: A Case Example of the Swayambhu UNESCO World Heritage Site in Nepal

Bhikshuni L. Trinlae[(✉)] [iD]

Tartu University, Ülikooli 18, 50090 Tartu, Estonia
bhikshuni.trinlae@ut.ee

Abstract. The Swayambhu (Svayambhū) UNESCO heritage site in Nepal has recently recovered from extensive earthquake damage. It serves as a social locus of ethnic and religious cultural heritage and identity for diverse local residents as well as domestic and international pilgrims and tourists. Here an applied case will be used to demonstrate processes necessary for producing an empirically authentic multimedia representation of an immersive experience related to a daily community devotional singing event with its own unique grassroots heritage. This case will illustrate how systematic phenomenological, ethnographic, and text-based methods are used as data inputs for representing the authenticity of experiences by way of diverse forms of verbatim interview data and recorded primary sources. Technical attention to the design phases of applications of digital technologies for heritage sites will be addressed. Ethical considerations and methods for diversifying enfranchisement of voices and perspectives employed in representing living cultural heritage will be discussed. Benefits of using VR/AR-supported immersive experiences of heritage to enable cultural literacy, appreciation of alterity, civic harmony, and local economic vitality will also be detailed.

Keywords: Heritage representation ethics · Representation methodology · Religious heritage · Swayambhu · UNESCO

1 Providing a Practical Ethics Reference Convenient for Technical Professionals

The contribution here is intended to be a convenient, practical, quick-reference resource especially for technical professionals and others working with cultural heritage for heritage sites or museums who are not themselves directly from humanities disciplines. Architects, data and software engineers, coders, graphics designers, and all such persons working with cultural heritage sites might benefit from this practical paper. Similarly, humanities researchers such as historians and anthropologists should find this paper of hermeneutical methods useful for leading multi- and intra-disciplinary

© Springer Nature Switzerland AG 2021
M. Shehade and T. Stylianou-Lambert (Eds.): RISE IMET 2021, CCIS 1432, pp. 331–346, 2021.
https://doi.org/10.1007/978-3-030-83647-4_22

heritage research teams. After reviewing some ethics and methods fundamentals, these will be demonstrated through an application to a technology-enhanced immersive experience of a daily community devotional singing event having a unique local heritage at the Swayambhu (Svayambhū[1]) UNESCO heritage site in Kathmandu, Nepal, and conclude with a practical procedural summary.

In traditional Himālayan Buddhist and Vedic community contexts, contemplative ritual practices are used to engage in activities for psychospiritual edification, and to continue an ancient tradition of oral transmission of historical cultural heritage and traditional Buddhist and Vedic contemplative themes such as compassion, wisdom, and appreciation of cultural heritage to new generations of visitors and residents [1–3] Buddhist contemplative practices, while doctrinally grounded in canonical literature, are principally experienced through meditation, opaque to outside observers. The Buddhist traditions of the Himalayas in particular extensively use artistically expressive imagery and sound media in contemplative liturgy to convey religious meaning complementary to ritual texts [4].

Religious ceremonies, if viewed or represented superficially, might nevertheless be received generously by the end user in a lucky scenario. There is a risk, however, that more skeptical observers, not seeing or knowing about the meditation behaviors corresponding to the externally-observed behaviors, might suspiciously presume such ritual behaviors to merely be irrational forms of naive idol-worship, thereby obscuring their elaborately elucidated meaning for meditation and well-being [5]. Especially for cultural events occurring in lesser-known international languages such as Nepali or Tibetan, international audiences of media representations of cultural heritage would likely be at even *further* risk of incomplete knowledge due to language barriers to alternate informative sources. Therefore, application of multimedia, AR/VR, and gamification modes of representation at religious cultural heritage sites requires meticulous, exacting care.

Religious symbols in particular can be radically misinterpreted and misappropriated. Perhaps the most notorious historical case is when the Vedic Hindu and Buddhist symbol of "well-being" or "auspiciousness," ("*svasti*" in Sanskrit), is mis-appropriated for a nefarious and lethal political agenda, as illustrated in Figs. 1 [6] and 2 [7].

Religious symbols are not always merely descriptive metaphors; especially in Vedic and Buddhist contemplative traditions, they can represent behavioral *processes* and not merely objective *content* [5]. Yet this deeper significance will be opaque to naïve observers. The late hermeneutic philosopher Paul Ricoeur defined a 'symbol' as "any structure of signification in which a direct, primary, literal meaning designates, in addition, another meaning which is indirect, secondary, and figurative and which can

---

[1] For interdisciplinary ease, the Nepali name of the UNESCO monument site "Svayambhū" is represented herein by the common English spelling of "Swayambhu" without diacritics.

Fig. 2. The ancient Vedic and Buddhist symbol was appropriated from Asian religious contexts and corrupted for political ideological purposes, as shown in this historical photo "Indian soldiers with Swastika Flag after Re-occupation of Benghazi, 1941;" Wikimedia Commons/National Army Museum.

Fig. 1. Vedic symbol of auspiciousness and "well-being" ("*svasti*"), drawn with colored powder in Nepal; Janak Bhatta, Wikimedia Commons.

be apprehended only through the first" [8]. As Ricoeur commentator Alexis Itao states, "Whereas mere signs hold only manifest meanings, symbols on the contrary carry much deeper, latent meanings behind the patent ones. This is why opacity characterizes all symbols because their latent meaning is not directly manifested and hence, not immediately discernible" [9].

1.1 Definitions

Accordingly, in this paper, *authentic representation refers to a validity established from diverse empirical, data-based sourcing for cultural descriptions*. It implies a correspondence of reliability between the respective descriptions and interpretations of cultural heritage made by outside observers (such as an AI technologist) and indigenous, *emic* cultural stakeholders and sources [10]. It can also include the disclosure of possible depth, breadth, and roles of meanings to which a surface-level media object might signify, but which might not be apparent or described in any given AR/VR representation. Therefore, such information will need to be asked about in interviews and/or researched in credible documents. Attention to such detail, or at least merely disclosing that it exists, without further immediate elaboration, will, I propose, provide a much richer and more gratifying immersive experience for the end user.

Salient processes for accurate representation are therefore essential for conflict-free, ethical engagement with religious cultural heritage. Immersive technologies such as

Augmented Reality (AR) can preserve and convey well-sourced, authenticated direct experiences of intangible culture at heritage sites while transmitting a 1st-person sense of presence. Poorly-sourced, un-authenticated representations and related potential for resulting conflicts need to be avoided as a matter of *systematic* and *routine* project design. Religious activities (experiences) at heritage sites can be methodically represented through *authentic transfer of meaning* expressed through a complex of diverse, indigenous site participants. These range from direct 1st-person religious contemplative experiences to 2nd-person values reflecting cultural self-identity and individual senses of belonging, shared meaning reflecting connections to place and language, social coherence, economic (financial) values, and history. Ethical representation therefore is an essential component of authentic, conflict-free transfer of cultural meaning.

1.2   Formal Ethics Standards

Formal ethical principles for working with cultural heritage derive from general ethics developed for working with living beings, or "human subjects research" [11]. Here these principles and norms will be presented in general, and thereafter will be applied to a particular heritage site cultural representation from Nepal as a case example. In general, before making an AR replica of a heritage site, the narrative descriptions and interpretations that will accompany that replica must be sourced and constructed ethically. Ethical norms are used when collecting interview data, conducting surveys, collecting metadata of participants, and engaging in environmental alterations. The US National Institutes of Health ethics training materials summarize as follows:

> *Investigators may perceive the outcomes of their studies to be more important than providing protections for individual participants in the research. Although it is understandable to focus on goals, our society values the rights and welfare of individuals. It is not considered ethical behavior to use individuals solely a means to an end. . . the relationship between investigators and human subjects is critical and should be based on honesty, trust, and respect* [11].

The need for ethics in research does not merely reflect the noble sentiments of humanitarians, but rather develops from the direst chapters of human history. The Nuremburg Code of 1947 was a response to Nazi medical war crimes. The USA Health and Human Services Policy for the Protection of Human Subjects and the US National Research Act of 1974 were belated responses to the unethical 1930s Syphilis study undertaken by the Tuskegee US Public Health Service, as well as to the human radiation experiments that took place during the 1944–1974 Cold War era [11].

Vital ethics principles developed for human subjects research must also guide heritage site cultural research: respect for persons, beneficence, and justice. These key ethical principles and related considerations are presented in Table 1. These principles are stated in the abstract, and a working understanding of them is usually tested and certified before researchers are approved for field research in the humanities, psychology, and clinical sciences. Later we will return to these general principles in the form of a checklist suitable for designing and checking the quality of projects representing culture at particular heritage sites.

Table 1. General ethical principles for working with cultural heritage [11].

Ethical principle	Normative directive Action/Non-Action	Details to consider
Respect for persons	Treat as autonomous agents	Provide protections/inclusions for minors, those with impaired faculties, vulnerable persons, etc.
Beneficence	Do no harm	Gain informed consent, protect privacy, confidentiality, respect cultural norms, ensure data security
Justice	Fair inclusion/exclusion criteria; fair procedures & outcomes	Employ authentic reasons for including participants other than mere expediency

Practical considerations such as gaining informed consent of interview participants, getting parental consent for any interactions with minors, using encrypted file storage with participant initials or pseudonyms instead of names for any interview or narrative data sources recorded must be established as a working culture from the beginning of project design phases and persist through to follow-up evaluation at project completion. The key ethical principles focused on in this paper are the *beneficence* principle related to *respecting cultural norms* and the *justice* principle of ensuring *diverse, authentic participation and principal enfranchisement of diverse cultural stakeholders*.

The question considered here in the case of the Swayambhu UNESCO world heritage site and others like it is how to *ethically* represent religious cultural heritage to unfamiliar others such as non-Buddhists and international visitors. Ethical representation here presumes the general ethics principles above, and furthermore indicates (1) an open-minded and non-suspicious[2] approach to *descriptions and interpretations* that are agreeable and do not contradict those expressed in the primary cultural resources of a heritage site such as written texts and oral histories; and (2) an authenticity indicating a concordant alignment between the representation media and primary cultural resources of qualitative data sourced from emic participant-observers. It furthermore (3) specifically appreciates interview participants and their expressed interactions with culture as "living [human] document sources" [12]; (4) includes "historically marginalized voices" across age, gender, class, etc. [13]; and (5) examines "actual practice versus doctrinal belief" alone [13]. These ethical criteria are detailed in Table 2.

---

[2] "There is in hermeneutics this double possibility: the possibility to interpret symbols with suspicion on one hand, and the possibility to interpret the same with faith on the other," Itao remarks, referencing Ricoeur [9].

Table 2. Checklist of elaborated ethical principles for use with specific cases of representing religious cultural heritage [5].

Ethical *principle* (elaborated)	Project *design consideration*	Quality control *action checklist*
Concordance of cultural values	Heritage media treats cultural information respectfully and with generosity vs. suspicion	Check for values contradictions between representations and sources: When in doubt, check it out
Authenticity of representation	Heritage media aligns and authentically represents primary cultural resources sourced from *emic* (indigenous) participant-observers	*Authenticate* and correct representations with indigenous participant feedback *before publishing;* use iterative project management processes
Living human document sources represented	Heritage media represents human participants and their interactions with culture	Indigenous (*emic*) sources such as verbatim interviews and primary cultural documents inform narrative representation media
Diversity of cultural voices represented	Heritage media cultural resources represents broad diversity of sources	Human sources representing diverse ages, genders, classes, education are interviewed
Lived experience of religion represented	Heritage media represents practical behaviors and not only doctrinal beliefs	Identify and represent religious behaviors along with their connections to beliefs and doctrines

Fortunately, authentic representation of religious cultural heritage can be accomplished by applying these ethical principles systematically. Ideally, a diversity of well-tested methods would be used in a complementary manner to develop a holistic, rich, and coherent representation of the cultural heritage. An example of this will be seen after discussing appropriate methods for scientifically representing cultural heritage.

2 Methods for Ethically Representing Religious Cultural Heritage

2.1 Relationship Between Perceptual and Expressive Modes

Modes of perceptions and expressions of meaning vary, and this is one reason why authentic sources must be maintained throughout the representation process. Paul Ricoeur developed thorough philosophical foundations of hermeneutic phenomenology [14]. This has been applied in research on representing and understanding the dynamics of contemplative ritual experiences in Vajrayāna Buddhism, which is the primary religious cultural context of the Swayambhu UNESCO heritage site [5]. The relations between perception and understanding can be seen from the schematic diagram of Ricoeur's affective synthesis model shown in Fig. 3. Any AR or VR representation of religious cultural behavior would ideally capture the relationship between sensate feelings and affective (emotional) feelings and the roles of sense objects in mediating meaning. For example, a votive lamp may have multiple roles, such as eliciting emotions and symbolizing religious meanings. This diversity of meaning related to a single sign or symbol is known as polysemy [14].

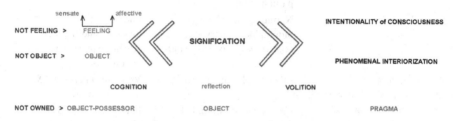

Fig. 3. Affective synthesis [5] (Figs. 3 and 4 used with permission of LIT-Verlag).

The varieties of experiential meaning and respective expressions can and should be captured by immersive media representations of religious cultural heritage (see Fig. 4). Which method is used will depend on the nature of the experience being represented with immersive media, such as audio, visual, symbolic, etc. [15].

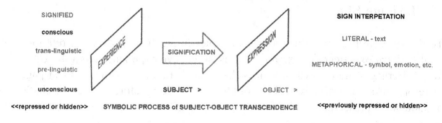

Fig. 4. Diagram of Ricoeur's hermeneutic phenomenology dialectic [5]

Thus, to virtually replicate a direct, 1st-person experience using VR or AR, such as lighting a votive lamp, a *phenomenological* description could be used to methodically and ethically reconstruct how such an act feels experientially using empirical interview data sourced from persons who have directly experienced the original experience. To recreate holistic experiences informed by narrations of social, historical, economic, and environmental dynamical factors, for example, group singing of hymns, diverse methods such as ethnography, review of historical records, and hymn textual description could root data empirically in authentic sources. The number of methods used are a function of the cultural heritage to be represented and interdisciplinary expertise and resources available to accomplish it, but phenomenology is the principal methodology for empirically representing 1st-person direct experience. The various methods [15] for empirically constructing descriptions of experiences and contexts can be seen in Table 3.

Table 3. Heritage representation scopes, methods, and related data sources [15].

Heritage representation *scope*	Methodologies used to obtain data	Data-source
1st-person subjective experience (verbatim report or multi-media expressions)	Phenomenological qualitative interviews following experience participation	Verbatim phenomenological interviews
1st & 3rd person narration	Narrative interview; biographical interview; content analysis; case study	Interviews; narrative journals; audio-visual artistic expressions; documents
3rd-person contextual information (social, historical, political, artistic, musical)	Ethnographic interviews	Verbatim interviews & observation notes
	Case studies; Grounded theory interviews	Interviews; records; observation notes; stone inscriptions
	Literature review	Peer-reviewed journals & scholarly monographs; documents

3   Example Case of the Swayambhu UNESCO World Heritage Site

To demonstrate the above-mentioned principles in practice, a particular religious cultural heritage experience is examined. This immersive experience from the UNESCO World Heritage Site of Swayambhu is described here on the 2-dimensional page and therefore lacks the qualitative texture of the original. It therefore mirrors the challenges of authentic representation, a bit like describing the taste of sugar to one who has never tasted it.

3.1   Using AR and VR at Religious Heritage Sites and Related Technical Linguistic Requirements

Most of the world's major religious traditions have been around for thousands of years. Here "religion" is used in the broad sense to include oral, non-literature-based spiritual traditions such as indigenous shamanic cultures. Therefore, while VR *could* be used effectively to represent religious cultural experiences, a greater priority is usually *preservation* of religious cultural heritage sites that are endangered due to various risks. In this case, AR can better capture and preserve existing heritage sites by creating truly historical visual records, and then render them as 3-dimensional immersive sets and settings for reproducing subjective experiential contexts. These contexts could later be fully virtualized with VR to provide exhibits of how sites might have looked in the past, or might look in the future. In other words, indigenous religious cultural heritage stakeholders will expect to see an *original* heritage site's contextual characteristics resembling how they had once seen them directly, especially when viewed through an immersive experience remotely. Especially for endangered sites, AR reproduction will become part of the historical archive for the site. Therefore, *an AR immersive experience will be preferable to VR for primary rendering*. Once the AR representation is thoroughly and ethically well-established and authenticated, then historical site virtualization according to timelines and prospective gamification might be feasible, appropriate objectives.

A secondary project design consideration is a technical linguistic requirement: immersive experience must be informed by primary empirical data, and the chain-of-custody of authenticity needs to be preserved in order to prove authenticity and hence compliance with ethical standards when later challenged to do so. All descriptive narrative data such as what might appear in user interfaces (UIs) must first be recorded with *primary sources* in *original* languages, with phonetic renderings for non-native audiences (users) available with diacritics that enable recovery of the original. Luckily for designers, over the past 20 years much work has been done to make this technically feasible and convenient: not only are Unicode fonts available for most languages, phonetic renderings have also become automated [16]. Aside from designing UIs to accommodate non-Western Unicode and diacritic font sets (such as Times Extended Roman), especially in the case of browser-based UIs, tables or other layout schemes can be used for narrative linguistic materials to be presented simultaneously with primary languages, phonetic diacritic renderings, and any other translations. See the example in Fig. 5.

रथ गज रत्न सालया धनी, सुरेन्द्र वीर विक्रम शाह देव ।५।

Ratha gaja ratna sālayā dhanī, Surendra Vīr Vikram Śāha deva |5|

Surendra [Vir] Vikrama Śāha is the Lord of the year "sentiment-elephant-jewel [985 N.E.=1864 A.D.] (English translation by Siegfried 1974, 135-36)

Fig. 5. Example of heritage material having extremely high historical significance, suggesting the origins of the hymn verse it follows dating to the mid-1800s. The authenticity of the linguistic data is preserved by using an interlinear table for presenting the original Nepali in Devanagari font, the phonetic rendering in Romanized diacritics font, and the English translation.

3.2 Swayambhu Monument Zone: A UNESCO World Heritage Site

Here the reader will initially have a limited exposure that will progressively become expanded. This will mimic the ways in which an immersive media experience would be informed using the methods discussed previously. This information will be used to understand representation of the heritage site context. Thereafter, representation of the hymn experience itself will be examined. First, view the three images in Figs. 6, 7 and 8:

Fig. 6. Frame from a video clip recording at the beginning of a typical evening Buddhist *bhajan* hymn experience, with a woman shown in the foreground. The clip is from the author's private video collection.

Fig. 7. Frame from the same video clip a few moments later during the same Buddhist *bhajan* hymn experience, wherein a monkey appears in the frame. The clip is from the author's private video collection.

Fig. 8. Frame from a video clip recording toward the end of the same Buddhist *bhajan* hymn experience, showing a young man delivering a notebook during the hymn performance. Video excerpt from the author's private video collection.

From a participant-observer perspective, a user reviewing the video representation of the direct experience would hear singing and musical instruments, and see a white mound in the background with an ornate golden *toraṇa* (arched doorway) in front of it. The viewer would see a woman sitting in the immediate foreground next to carved wooden columns and a glass box with an object inside between the columns, and a couple of statue-like objects to the left in the space beyond. While listening and viewing, they would see a young man appearing to the left, and seemingly take a few camera snapshots of a spot beyond. They would then see a dog trot by, and a couple of monument visitors walk by. They would then see a man walking toward the hymn singers with what looks like a candle-stick holder who then grabs a wooden box, see a few more visitors walk by, hear the woman sitting in front converse with someone unseen, see the earlier man lean over to lift a bag of lamp oil, see the woman passing him a cloth, see more pedestrians and then a monkey trot by. As the hymn proceeds, the viewer would also see a few more persons walk by, and a young man in a baseball cap with a similarly-dressed companion walk toward the hymn singers and step into the seating area to deliver a notebook and then walk away, and then finally see two young guys posing for camera shots.

For an AR immersive *direct*-experience of the hymn-performance, the perspectives to record must be decided. The perspective of the hymn-performers is distinct from the experiential perspectives of the casual visitors. A third perspective could also be established, recording those who appear to be supporting the hymn-singers *indirectly*, such as the woman, the man with the candle-stick holder, and the young man delivering the notebook. These second and third possible perspectives are perfectly valid in their own right, especially for a full 3-d rendering providing multiple viewing perspectives. For the purposes here, the media was deliberately designed to represent the hymn-singing experience directly from the 1st-person participant-observer perspective. This deliberately subjective *epoché* bracketing delineates the set from the setting, and the text from the context.

Even with the focus restricted to the hymn-singing experience, it is clear that it occurs in an extremely diverse social context and in an environment open enough to include dogs and monkeys! Reproducing an *authentic* experience of the hymn performance from an authentic *participant-observer perspective* is different than a film-maker, who might decide to exclude this incidental activity in order to focus "purely" on the hymn alone. However, for someone with life-long familiarity with the monument and hymn-culture of Swayambhu, seeing the dog and the monkey would likely *enrich the experience of authenticity* and therefore the realistic replication value of the immersion experience.

Applied Methodical Procedures. A phenomenological description helps define what an experience *is*, as an entity. This act of naming alone will both inform and comprise the language choices by which the experience will be further known and discussed.

1st-person Direct Experience Replication Using Phenomenological Methods A phenomenological description of the hymn-singing experience authentically narrates the subjective experience from the point of view of the indigenous (Buddhist) participant observers. This entails two components: (1) authentically representing the *hymn performers' experience* and (2) representing the *hymns* themselves. Regarding the hymns, as seen in Fig. 6, it can be seen that in the video the original hymn verses are shown in Devanāgarī font subtitles as they appeared in the hymn book, with accompanying phonetic transliteration in Latin (Roman) diacritic font. A third line with English translation will also be added, and translations into other languages such as Tibetan or Russian and so forth could also be made. More can be discerned from the hymn texts suggesting the historical significance of the experience, and, by extension, the Swayambhu monument itself, as evidenced in Fig. 5.

There are a number of varieties of phenomenological research methods that can be applied to construct the phenomenological description. Here I will outline the procedures of Moustakas's Transcendental Phenomenological Method [17] based on Husserl [18], because it clearly illustrates the data-based *empirical processes* by which the ethical principles of diverse enfranchisement are accomplished.

1. Devise interview questions relevant to the religious heritage site experience of interest, recruit reliable participants, and obtain informed consent and subsequent publication permissions for approximately 10 or more participant observers.
2. Accompany participants in observing the experience and/or at least interview participants soon after the experience.
3. Prepare textural phenomenological descriptions for each interview participant.
4. Prepare structural phenomenological descriptions for each interview participant.
5. Prepare a composite *textural* description from methodically combining the individual descriptions.
6. Prepare a composite *structural* description from methodically combining the individual descriptions.
7. Prepare a final *synthetic* phenomenological description by combining the respective composite textural and structural descriptions obtained in steps 5 and 6.

This final synthetic phenomenological description of the essential experience of the hymn singing is thereby empirically sourced from the verbatim interview data. By diversifying the participant reports as much as is feasible, for example to include youth, middle aged, and elder participants from male and female (or alternative gender[3]) reports, then an intersectional generalized phenomenological description will have been produced that meets the ethical principle of providing diverse enfranchisement and authenticity in the cultural representation.

Given a generous enough budget to fund the laborious field work involved and a sufficient number of participants to include 7–10 participants from any one diverse sector, say, for example, of elderly women, then another phenomenology could be created that represents the experience of distinct groups such as elderly women, young men, and so on. Repeated across multiple groups, the resulting description data could then become the fertile grounds for populating educational gamification and a full yet granular recording of a time slice of history.

1st-person direct reports derived from narrative interviews, biographical interviews, content analysis of multi-media expressions, and individual case studies. These methods can situate the subjective phenomenological descriptions within a broader

---

[3] Monastics, for example, could be regarded as an androgynous third gender, or could be offered as a self-reported choice in interview metadata. To avoid obtaining parental consent, which can be problematic if parents are not available, then the younger participants mentioned could be required to meet a minimum age of legal majority (typically 18 years).

context by using data sourced from stories, historical materials, and case descriptions. The reporting on these sources is typically made in the form of 3rd-person statements. It can be regarded as supplemental to the 1st-person subjective voice of the phenomenological descriptions.

3rd-person contextual information using ethnography, case studies, grounded theory, and literature review sources. From reliable ethnographic and literary sources such as those illustrated in Figs. 9 and 10, we have information about the history of the Swayambhu monument and can understand that it is a *stūpa* or Buddhist reliquary with a symbolic architecture and an ancient legendary history [1, 3, 19, 20]

Fig. 9. Drawing of the Swayambhu *stūpa* monument published in 1811 in a book on Nepal by Colonel Kirkpatrick: *An Account of the Kingdom of Nepaul. Being the Substance of Observations Made During A Mission to that Country in the Year 1793*; public domain [19].

Fig. 10. Aerial view of the Swayambhu *stūpa* included in a mapping by architects of the 2015 earthquake damage. The point of view of the scenes shown in Figs. 6, 7 and 8 is located in the area to the south of the *stūpa*, because the usual shelter normally used at the west of the *stūpa* was damaged. Photo courtesy of UNESCO.org/Public Domain [21].

From ethnographic and literature review sources we can also know that the Swayambhu monument zone was entered into the UNESCO World Heritage site listing of properties of "outstanding universal value" at the Third Session of the Convention Concerning the Protection of the World Cultural and Natural Heritage in Egypt in October, 1979 [22], that a stone inscription at the site records a 1098 renovation by King Śaṁkaradeva [23], and that an 18th century renovation was undertaken by Tibetans [20].

From further literature materials, the Buddhist doctrinal meaning of the monument as a symbol of Mahāyāna Buddhist Prajñāpāramitā (Perfection of Wisdom) and respective Madhyamaka Buddhist philosophical views can be discerned, and therefore that these Buddhist characteristics are celebrated by devotees and pilgrims in general [3]. These sources provide a rational religious doctrine other than blind faith or superstition alone. Particular reasons for celebration would be known empirically through phenomenological and other verbatim self-report data.

More relevant to this case of the hymn-singing experience, from the published literature sources we could learn that this tradition of singing the Buddhist *Jñānamālā Bhajan* hymns at Swayambhu was established in the 1930s and later officially persecuted [2]. We would learn how, in the 1940s under autocratic rule, devotees were arrested for singing the Buddhist hymns in the local Newāḥ dialect, and had their public singing gatherings banned. We would learn that the hymn groups nevertheless persisted until the King overturned the police superintendent's criminalization of the hymn singing in 1947, and that the hymn committees expanded and eventually developed into grassroots social welfare organizations and an accompanying social culture that persists into our present era [2].

It should therefore be apparent how the meaningfulness of the hymn experience to local descendants of the founders of the *bhajan* culture would be opaque and unknown to visitors who were not educated otherwise, and that such information would not necessarily be discovered through phenomenological methods alone. It is therefore the contention of this author that immersive technologies will function best to represent religious culture when constructed using diverse methods to produce an integral, holistic portrayal of 1st and 3rd person perspectives based on empirical data from systematic, ethical processes. These methodologies are summarized in Table 3.

4   Conclusion

In this paper, we have seen that there are long-established ethical norms to consider for projects developed for representing cultural heritage. There are general principles, specific design considerations, and action tasks needed for successfully applying ethical standards. Diverse sources can be considered when studying the epistemology of various modes of expression that comprise primary (raw) data sources. Contemplative behaviors and internal experiences of culture are not directly observed and therefore must be elicited methodically using interviews. Distinct methodologies empirically represent diverse contexts of experience, from direct subjective experiences to broader historical and social factors integral to a heritage site. How much an immersive technology will actually yield a gratifying end-user immersive experience will largely depend on the effort taken to consider and implement these ethical standards.

Augmented reality and virtual reality representations of cultural heritage sites will only empirically represent *reality* events when sourced using authentic data. Such authenticity and diversity of representation comprises necessary *but not sufficient* ethical practice. To be sufficient there must also be adequate verification. Therefore, after heritage site representations are created using one or more of the empirical methods mentioned above, beta versions must be presented for review and possible correction by indigenous participants of the experience (ideally, the original interview participants). No cultural heritage materials should be published until co-creators are satisfied with the adequate authenticity and coherence of the representations. Moreover, ethics of justice must extend to enabling open-access privileges to indigenous stakeholders through creative commons license protocols established for final heritage representation products.

All of these considerations, components, and scientific processes cannot be achieved by mere chance, but have to be planned, designed, and funded from the earliest proposal phases of project management. At the same time, cultural heritage is a reliable, time-proven economic engine that can humanize projects while bringing interdisciplinary professionals, culture stake-holders, and experts together. Humanities experts can learn more technical skills, while technical engineers can learn more humanities methods. Especially in the case of religious cultural heritage, the culture and its consumers continue to persist over millennia and exhibit a robust resilience to the fickle turbulence associated with political and environmental perturbations. Each living religious heritage site typically has a dynamic micro-economy of artisanry, psychospiritual wellness, hospitality, religious education and praxis, art, as well as expressive media and leisure associated with it.

Careless and reckless representation of religious heritage sites could inadvertently create divisive and contentious sources of conflict. Projects without conflicts run smoothly with minimal stress. Ethical, well-designed, and carefully executed projects applying immersive technologies to represent and preserve cultural heritage can provide enduring sources of intercultural literacy, social harmony, prosperity, and delight.

Acknowledgements. The present work has been made possible with humanitarian assistance from Mr. Trevor Stockinger, Ms. Angela Lai, and the gracious hospitality of the Jñānamālā Bhajan Khalaḥ community of Swayambhu, Kathmandu, Nepal.

References

1. Kivelä, S.: The Sacred Hilltop: A Hermeneutical Case Study on the Svayambhū Site of Kathmandu. MA, University of Helsinki, Helsinki (2005)
2. Pradhan, B.L., Khalah, J.B.: A movement for building up the Newar society. Newāh Vijñāna J. Newar Stud. **1**(1), 1–5 (1997)
3. Rospatt, A.V.: The sacred origins of the Svayambhūcaitya and the Nepal Valley: foreign speculation and local myth. J. Nepal Res. Centre XIII, 33–89 (2009)
4. Kohn, R.J.: Lord of the Dance: The Mani Rimdu Festival in Tibet and Nepal (SUNY Series in Buddhist Studies), pp. viii–ix. State University of New York Press (2001)
5. Trinlae, B.L.: Kun-mkhyen Pad-ma dKar-po's Amitāyus tradition of Vajrayāna Buddhist Transformative Care. Contemplative Text, Phenomenological Experience, and Epistemological Process, pp. 153; 212. Lit Verlag, Vienna (2018)

6. Bhatta, J.: Swastika, Symbol. Photo from Nepal; Creative Commons Share Alike 4.0 license (2019). https://commons.wikimedia.org/wiki/File:Swastika,_symbol.jpg. Accessed 3 Mar 2021

7. Birdwood, C.R.: Indian Soldiers with Swastika Flag after Re-occupation of Benghazi 1941: Jemadar Ali Musa Khan and men of 'A' Squadron, Central India Horse, Cyrenaica, December 1941. [Public Domain; original at National Army Museum, UK] [1940] (2020). https://commons.wikimedia.org/wiki/File:Indian_soldiers_with_swastika_flag_after_re-occupation_of_Benghazi_1941.jpg. Accessed 3 Mar 2021

8. Ricoeur, P.: Existence and hermeneutics. In: Ihde, D. (ed.) The Conflict of Interpretations: Essays in Hermeneutics, 13. Northwestern Univ. Pr., Evanston (1974)

9. Itao, A.D.: Paul Ricoeur's hermeneutics of symbols: a critical dialectic of suspicion and faith. Kritike **2**(4), 1–17 (2010)

10. Trinlae, B.L.: How to Communicate Complex Spiritual Care Practices of Religious Minorities Using Empirical, Clinical Language: "Proof of Principle" Field Research from Vajrayāna Buddhism. In: Taher, M. (ed.) Multifaith Perspectives in Spiritual & Religious Care. Canadian Multifaith Federation, North York (2020)

11. NIH Office of Extramural Research. Protecting Human Research Participants. https://grants.nih.gov/policy/humansubjects/training-and-resources.htm. Accessed 12 Sept 2019

12. Boisen, A.T.: Cooperative inquiry in religion. Relig. Educ. **40**, 290–297 (1945)

13. Graham, E..: Transforming Practice. Pastoral Theology in an Age of Uncertainty. Wipf & Stock, Eugene, OR (2002)

14. Ihde, D.: Hermeneutic Phenomenology: The Philosophy of Paul Ricoeur. Northwestern University Press, Evanston (1971)

15. Creswell, J.W.: Qualitative Inquiry and Research Design. Choosing Among Five Traditions. Sage Publications, Thousand Oaks (1998)

16. Lexilogos: Multilingual Keyboard: Sanskrit Devanagari to Latin Conversion (2020). https://www.lexilogos.com/keyboard/sanskrit_conversion.htm. Accessed 30 Nov 2020

17. Moustakas, C.: Phenomenological Research Methods. Sage Publications, Thousand Oaks (1994)

18. Kamppinen, M.: Cognitive study of religion and Husserlian phenomenology: making better tools for the analysis of cultural systems. In: Andresen, J. (ed.) Religion in Mind: Cognitive Perspectives on Religious Belief, Ritual, and Experience, pp. 193–207. Cambridge University Press, Cambridge (2001)

19. Kirkpatrick, C.: An Account of the Kingdom of Nepaul. Being the Substance of Observations Made During A Mission to that Country in the Year 1793. Illustrated with a Map, and other Engravings. East India Company, London (1811)

20. Ehrhard, F.K.: A Renovation of Svayambhunath-Stupa in the 18th Century and its History (According to Tibetan Sources). Ancient Nepal 114 (1989)

21. Bendele, P.G., Dusuzeau, L., Maharjan, A.:. 2015 Earthquake Damage Mapping [of] Swayambhu Monument Zone. Kathmandu Valley World Heritage Property Kathmandu (2015)

22. Report of the Rapporteur on the Third Session of the World Heritage Committee [XII. Consideration of Nominations to the World Heritage List: 46. Entered in the World Heritage List: No. 120 Sagarmatha National Park, Nepal and No. 121 Kathmandu Valley, Nepal; 30 November 1979]: CC-79/CONF.003/13. In UNESCO World Heritage Center, 5–17 (1979)

23. Shrestha, S.S.: Conservation of Swayambhu Mahachaitya. Ancient Nepal. 5–17 (2010)

Pioneering Advanced Recording Technologies for Post-earthquake Damage Assessment and Re-construction in Chilean Heritage Areas

Bernadette Devilat[✉] [iD]

Centre for Architecture, Urbanism and Global Heritage,
Nottingham Trent University (NTU), Nottingham NG1 4FQ, UK
bernadette.devilat@ntu.ac.uk

Abstract. The physical conservation of historic buildings is a challenge worldwide, but it is even more difficult in earthquake-prone areas. To avoid potential damage, mitigation strategies are required, such as periodic maintenance, repair and strengthening, usually not implemented at the scale of dwellings in heritage areas. Funding is generally available for monumental buildings—such as churches—leaving houses vulnerable to the effects of future earthquakes.

After earthquakes, damaged dwellings cannot be immediately reinforced to continue habitation; generating disruption. If buildings are repairable, the costs are high due to the difficulty of working with the existing remains, resulting in a preference for new constructions on-site and elsewhere. Large numbers of affected constructions make damage assessment difficult, impacting in slow and sometimes out-of-context responses.

This paper proposes an alternative to tackle these issues by using 3D-laser-scanning to document the as-built condition of houses after the 2010 earthquake in Lolol, a heritage village in Chile that was in progress of reconstruction and repair via the newly created Heritage Reconstruction Programme post-earthquake. The data obtained was used as a basis for designing alternative architectural interventions, with the potential of speeding up emergency responses and retrofits, leading to the re-use of the remaining built heritage. From this, the paper argues for the introduction of technology institutionally at a governmental level, to inform emergency strategies and a more sustainable, affordable and inclusive method for risk mitigation, repair and re-construction of domestic heritage in seismic-prone areas of Chile, which is also relevant for similar cases worldwide.

Keywords: Re-construction · Damage assessment · 3D-laser-scanning · Earthquakes · Heritage intervention · Reconstruction · Chile

1 Chile as a Case Study

1.1 Earthquakes as a Regular Agent of Risk

Depending on the magnitude, area, type of construction and context, earthquakes produce a specific type of destruction in Chile, since they usually damage buildings but do not

© Springer Nature Switzerland AG 2021
M. Shehade and T. Stylianou-Lambert (Eds.): RISE IMET 2021, CCIS 1432, pp. 347–369, 2021.
https://doi.org/10.1007/978-3-030-83647-4_23

erase complete areas (Fig. 1). Because of this, emergency measures and re-construction approaches can be based on what is left—e.g. partially destroyed constructions, ruins and rubble—and used as part of recovering strategies. This was the case with Lolol, a heritage village affected by the 2010 earthquake, occurring on 27 February in Chile's central-southern area, which had a magnitude of 8.8 M$_w$.

Fig. 1. A damaged house in Lolol after the 2010 earthquake. Source: Author.

1.2 Lolol

Lolol is located in the Colchagua Province, VI region of Chile. Dwellings are built as continuous façades but are also characterised by having porticos, which generate a particular spatiality to the public space (Fig. 2). It was declared a *Typical Zone* in 2003. After the 2010 earthquake, Lolol experienced damage and destruction of structures, but no fatalities occurred in the heritage area.[1]

---

[1] Three fatalities were identified in the whole commune (Ministry of the Interior and Public Security 2010), which consists of a larger area than the village of Lolol.

Fig. 2. A damaged house with porticos in Lolol after the 2010 earthquake. Source: Author.

The urgency of addressing the issues and challenges for seismic-prone areas is key since earthquakes are a cyclical process rather than a one-time event, impacting the timing of responses and how re-construction approaches are designed. Another seismic event will certainly be hitting the same area within a period of time. This implies that any re-construction approach should offer sufficient resilience to prevent future damage to the same buildings, something that was embedded in vernacular constructions but has been progressively lost as contemporary techniques replace them.

The Chilean state does not have a specific institution to assist with reconstruction, neither was one created after the most recent earthquakes. Instead, each existing Ministry was in charge of its own area. For example, housing reconstruction was dependent on the Ministry of Housing and Urban Development (MINVU)[2]—in which heritage areas were included—while churches were in the charge of the Ministry of Public Works (MOP) (see Footnote 2) (Fig. 3). This institutional arrangement meant that vernacular settlements were not treated as a group or heritage set, but each building was treated separately, generating coordination issues and impacting the heritage area as a whole unit.

---

[2] Their acronyms in Spanish.

Fig. 3. Lolol church after the 2010 earthquake. Source: Author.

Reconstruction of built heritage has occurred progressively over the years, and it is likely to continue to occur after future seismic events because mitigation strategies have not been implemented. This lack of prevention produces a built heritage that is continuously at risk. After large earthquakes, improvements are made to building codes, raising the standard for new constructions but not introducing consolidation measures for existing ones. This aspect leaves built heritage with an underlying vulnerability until such time as it is convenient for it to be replaced.

In Chile, there are many historical settlements located in various climatic conditions, which embody different ways of living and building, with dwellings characterised by a connection with their landscape, where the vernacular building techniques, such as adobe,[3] represent a construction culture that mixes indigenous and Spanish traditions, dating from the nineteenth and twentieth centuries. Reconstruction approaches after earthquakes in Chile have failed to preserve these values, mainly because the replacement of dwellings is preferred over repairs, in which the replication 'as it was before' is the most common strategy, generating authenticity issues [1].

After the 2010 earthquake, the Heritage Reconstruction Programme was created at the Regional Ministry Secretariat (SEREMI)[4] of the MINVU VI Region of Chile, and then replicated in other affected regions [2]. One of the main advances of this programme was to organise the post-earthquake work to allow repairs and retrofits using the total funding available for a new house, resulting in larger dwellings and the conservation of more built heritage dwellings (Fig. 4).

Fig. 4. A dwelling under repair in Lolol in 2013, showing the use of metallic meshes to stabilise damaged adobe walls. Source: Author.

However, that scheme was not fast in developing solutions. One of the reasons for this was the need to carry out damage assessments that require technical and professional expertise, and to gather information on the condition of each dwelling—as left

---

[3] Their acronyms in Spanish.

[4] Acronym from Spanish: 'Secretaría Regional Ministerial'.

by the earthquake—in order to start assessing any intervention. Extra funding and collaboration with professionals, students and universities were used to speed processes, yet they were not enough. For example, in Zúñiga, repairs from that programme did not start until three years after the 2010 earthquake.

Lolol was defined as a national priority by the aforementioned programme, as a way of showing the results of a repair strategy over complete replacement. After the same three years, from a total of 41 houses to have interventions in Lolol, 8 were finished and 11 were in progress. However, the process was much slower in other areas and a large number of affected dwellings never had interventions. This is because the housing subsidies—the governmental financing mechanism for housing reconstruction —are not designed for a post-earthquake situation. Overall, the main reason for the slowness of repairs has to do with documenting the situation post-earthquake in a fast and accurate way for the architectural designs. Thus, this paper will look at this stage of the process in order to see if the introduction of 3D-laser-scanning as an alternative method of analysis and architectural intervention post-earthquake could improve it.

2   3D-Laser-Scanning

3D-laser scanning—also known as LiDAR—is a recording technology that captures the built environment using laser measurements and a photo camera to capture colour information. The result is a coloured three-dimensional point-cloud with a precision of millimetres.

The amount and accuracy of data collected with this technique are of particular relevance to buildings due to the high level of accuracy, representing a step beyond other recording techniques. For example, whereas photogrammetry—specifically stereo-photogrammetry—is based on multiple photos to generate a 3D point-cloud, the result is usually less accurate [3], which impacts the architectural and damage assessment, and post-processing times tend to be longer. While photogrammetry is particularly useful for capturing detailed surfaces, e.g. painted murals, and it is potentially a more accessible tool than 3D-laser-scanning, its use in large areas with detailed results is yet to be studied.

Digital technologies have been used before to document the built heritage [4, 5], for conservation [6], for post-earthquake assessment [7] and for digital preservation [8]. They have also been used in conjunction with other technologies, such as photogrammetry and thermography [9] and remote sensing techniques for automatic damage assessments [10, 11, 12, 13]. However, there is a knowledge gap in addressing the larger scale of a whole heritage area with the same level of detail as a single building. This is significant in post-earthquake areas since damaged buildings can number in the hundreds, where a rapid and scalable approach from the existing context is key.

2.1   On-Site Data Capture in Lolol

The starting hypothesis is that terrestrial 3D-laser-scanning can be used as a powerful survey tool because of the amount of data that can be obtained in the limited period available in a post-earthquake situation before further changes or demolitions take place. To test this, three days were defined as a timeframe in the case study of Lolol. During this set period, a two-person team 3D-laser-scanned as much as possible.[5]

The method of collecting data was to set the terrestrial 3D-laser-scanner[6] in different locations separated by a range of 15 to 40 m while spherical, and paper targets were placed as reference points that remained still. The exterior spaces were captured from the streets and pavements, and the interior spaces by accessing the buildings. Each scan took almost five minutes, including the photographs that provided the colour information (Fig. 5).

Fig. 5. Example of the 3D point-cloud of Lolol in 2013 using three scans. Source: Author.

Currently, 3D-laser-scans can be geo-referenced and located automatically using post-processing software, but reference targets—chequerboards and spheres—were needed for the on-site capture, carried out in January 2013. These targets remained still in between scans, allowing them to be used as reference points to align the 3D scans more precisely later (Fig. 6).

After capturing the data on-site, the scans were aligned with one another to form the complete 3D model, a process that took at least three weeks' work.[7] The scans were grouped in specific clusters to facilitate the process. The scans were aligned within a

---

[5] Only scanned during daylight, since this is needed for capturing the colour information. The fieldwork was done in 2013 as part of the author's PhD research (see acknowledgements) that included two more heritage areas: San Lorenzo de Tarapacá and Zúñiga in Chile. Although the on-site data capture was in 2013, the PhD was finished in 2018. In addition, the author has had personal circumstances that delayed the publication of this paper.

[6] Faro Focus 3D s120 used.

[7] Using Scene software and counting full-time days of work.

cluster first, and then all the clusters together to form the whole heritage area. Post-processing times included cleaning and editing after alignment and depended on the outcome required—e.g. architectural drawings, such as plans, sections and elevations, or images and videos, needing several additional days to create and render.

Fig. 6. Example of the targets used in the 3D data capture of Lolol in 2013. Source: Author.

Because 3D-laser-scanning only captures visible surfaces, the particular portico configuration of Lolol was harder to record as, in order to get the full information of each building, scans were needed both from inside the porticos and from the pavements. This made data collection on-site slower than expected. Since the idea was to cover as much data of the whole historic area as possible, there was not enough time to record more interior spaces. Only the church and one dwelling were scanned completely from inside, plus a couple of spaces that were interiorly scanned when agreed and accessible directly from the porticos and pavements. Top surfaces were not acquired since drones were not accessible at that time, which means that the top views show roofs, ceilings and trees obtained from below. Despite all this, the result is a three-dimensional point-cloud composed of 195 scans, and almost six billion points,[8] covering almost the entire public area designated as *Typical Zone* (Fig. 7). The boundary between interior and exterior spaces is blurred and rich in gradual transition because of the porticos and interior spaces scanned.

---

[8] 5,981,474,370 points exactly.

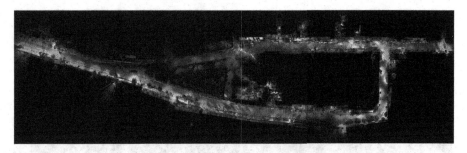

Fig. 7. Plan of Lolol, rendered from all the 2013 3D-laser-scans. Source: Author

The result has an accuracy of millimetres[9] and the data obtained can be measured, virtually cut and used as a basis for technical drawings, images, videos (Fig. 8), 3D printed models and virtual reality environments, among other applications (Fig. 9). In consequence, this technology can be considered a robust method for documenting buildings and faster to obtain more relevant data—such as distortions and cracks—than traditional post-earthquake documentation techniques.

Fig. 8. QR code and screenshots linking to a video of Lolol, exploring the data sectioned in plan view, exploring the interior spaces captured in 2013. Available here: https://vimeo.com/226779127 Source: Author.

---

[9] When using the model and procedure specified.

Fig. 9. View of Lolol, rendered from all the 3D-laser-scans taken in 2013. Source: Author.

All methods of representation have aesthetic characteristics, but 3D-laser-scanning offers the possibility of its specific quality. Visualisations and videos have an aesthetic of immateriality since the 3D data is composed of millions of points that give the perception of transparency. The attempt is to show the 3D data obtained in the best possible way, conveying fundamental viewpoints and selecting the most representative images, most of which it is not possible to obtain in reality—such as a section of a building—but it is possible by dissecting the 3D data. This new aesthetic represents a subject for further studies (Fig. 10).

Fig. 10. Section of Lolol, Chile, rendered from the 2013 3D-laser-scanning. Source: Author.

2.2   Limitations Encountered When Using Terrestrial 3D-Laser-Scanning

Because 3D-laser-scanning only captures surfaces, terrestrial laser scanners lack aerial information most of the time unless placed in a location higher than the target—e.g. the roof terrace of a nearby building, which was not possible in the case of Lolol.

Therefore, for future scanning processes, it must be complemented by other techniques depending on the target and aims of the survey. There is a whole range of methods—such as air drones—to capture what has not been caught by the terrestrial 3D-laser-scanner, but these were not applied since they were not accessible at the time of the fieldwork (2013) and the focus was only on the terrestrial 3D-laser-scanning experimentation. Currently, a multi-resolution and multi-sensor documentation approach can obtain more comprehensive results by taking advantage of combining data—e.g. based on photogrammetry—on top of the same geo-referenced 3D-laser-scan base [14]. As a post-disaster method, 3D-laser-scanning needs to be complemented with archival and historical analysis, and with the inclusion of social data from the inhabitants.[10]

The most significant problem encountered when applying 3D-laser-scanning to the case study was the noise produced by moving elements on the scene, given that most of the data was captured in public spaces. People, cars, trees, pillars, vegetation or other objects that interfered with the data collection of buildings, cast shadows on the desired target. This was avoided by increasing the number of scans and by placing the scanner in different positions, which made data collection slower. However, that noise was edited and cleaned when necessary using post-processing software. For future—institutional—surveys, the traffic of people and cars can be controlled when the record is taken to diminish their effect on the 3D-laser-data.[11]

Improvements have already been made to the technology. The new environmental scanners can capture a better data range in less time, with new models that range up to 330 m—instead of the 120 m of the model used. Resistance to rain, dust and extreme temperatures are also features of the latest model of Faro scanners available, along with an improved embedded photo camera—with better resolution and quality.

Tasks that were done manually, such as aligning the scans, can now be done automatically. The latest software has reduced alignment times by providing automatic alignment algorithms based on the building's features.[12] In addition, new scanners have also improved functions for locating the scans in real-time using a tablet computer. This allows for a better understanding of the data captured so actions can be taken on-site if areas are occluded.[13] This real-time feature is especially relevant since it allows the data to be manipulated right after its collection, extremely useful in post-disaster areas that require immediate action.

---

[10] Obtained in Lolol before and during the scanning process through questionnaires to the inhabitants. This data has been excluded from this paper to focus only on the LiDAR record.

[11] In addition, the newest version of the post-processing software—Scene—features filters to reduce noise on detailed parts of buildings, such as decorative railings, not available in 2013.

[12] The latest software—unavailable in 2013—can perform cloud-to-cloud and top-view alignments, where what is captured serve for referencing the position of each scan. This means that it is currently possible to 3D-laser-scan without the need for reference targets. Targetless registration is not useful in monotonous contexts, e.g., a desert, and it is less accurate. When spherical references are used, as in the case study, accuracy ranges from 0.1 to 1 mm. If cloud-to-cloud alignment is used, accuracy can decrease by up to 10 mm.

[13] A locator device from Faro can provide that feature even in older models. The result would be all the scans aligned together at the end of the on-site data capture, significantly reducing post-processing times.

Therefore, it will be assumed that terrestrial 3D-laser-scanning represents a precise recording method of the physical features of the built environment to argue for its crucial role in heritage re-construction.

3 Using the Record

This paper focuses only on the immediate post-earthquake response, using the data for creating physical emergency supports and for the repair and strengthening of existing structures. However, its application is relevant as a more comprehensive methodology for a wider long-term conservation strategy of housing in heritage areas that includes risk mitigation, planning and post-earthquake response, named as *re-construction.* This is to make a distinction between reconstruction—understood as current strategies of replication 'as before'—and *re-construction,* understood as to build again, as a step forward, respectful towards the past but adaptable to ever-changing social, cultural and physical contexts.

3.1 Post-earthquake Damage Assessment and Planning

The potential has been shown of 3D-laser-scanning as a quick survey tool, facilitating the required post-earthquake damage assessment. Here will be addressed its importance as a basis for design beyond the scale of one building to consider entire heritage areas without compromising the level of detail (Fig. 11).

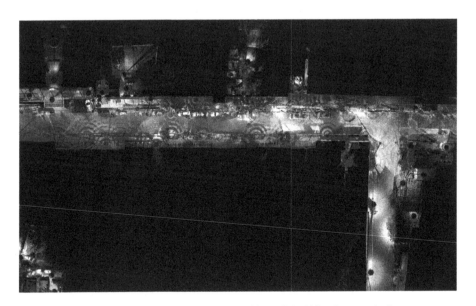

Fig. 11. Plan of the dwellings scanned in Lolol, Chile. Source: Author.

With that information, a wider re-construction approach can be planned, involving a series of intervention strategies according to the level of damage of each house, from emergency to the long-term, such as tailored supports, re-use and repair. Having established that, the focus of this paper is on the emergency actions and the repair of existing structures as one possibility.

These post-earthquake proposals are not definitive and do not claim to cover all possible aspects of re-construction. They stand as a series of strategies that may inform future designs, either separately or combined with other measures. The 3D-laser-scanning of Lolol was used to test these strategies, providing snapshots of the ideas. However, these are not as detailed as they could be and are presented just as a reference.

These alternative proposals are thought to match current governmental funding for emergency housing and reconstruction, in the hope they can be implemented—or at least not discarded because of insufficient funding. This is, of course, speculative since the cost of interventions depends on the specific conditions of each place, in terms of the availability and procurement of materials, workforce, market values and so on, but it helps to maintain interventions within certain limits.

Currently, there is no differentiation between short- and long-term re-construction. The short-term strategies proposed here acknowledge processes that occur in reality and that are not part of current reconstruction policies, to be implemented between the emergency and permanent housing. These are based on the housing subsidies for heritage areas after earthquakes, establishing a thoughtful approach to that long-term re-construction that allows for careful consideration in terms of re-using and retro-fitting, a key element for historical constructions.

3.2   Tailored Emergency and Repair Strategies

The main aspects proposed are the intervention within the same site, assuming that inhabitants will be living there, with a progressive design and construction separated into two different phases. First, securing safe habitation through emergency shelters and supports. As heritage areas are less populated than urban areas and plots have larger dimensions, temporary shelters are usually installed towards the back of each site. Even if temporary camps are provided locally, inhabitants come back to their properties sooner rather than later, inhabiting those spaces that are perceived as safe, even when they are not.

Second, addressing re-construction to improve that period between the emergency and the final result. This is mainly understood as re-use and retrofit of the affected dwelling, using the post-earthquake 3D record. The aim is to fit in that timeframe, recognising that current reconstruction approaches are slow and that there is a gap in how to improve living conditions in between the emergency and the permanent housing solution (Fig. 12).

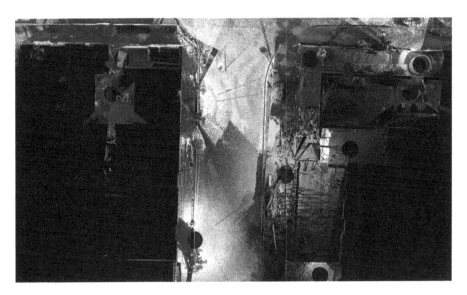

Fig. 12. Partial plan of a dwelling abandoned (left) and a dwelling under repair (right) as scanned during 2013 in Lolol, Chile. Source: Author.

For this, the guiding principles proposed are economy of resources, prefabrication and planning, aiming for a final progressive dwelling that will not have disrupted the affected family as much as if they had been displaced for the whole construction period. This process can also serve as an involvement strategy with the residents, who will benefit from the first-hand experience of repairing, reinforcing and rebuilding their dwellings.

The specific conditions of each household and site will be provided by the 3D-laser-scanning record and organised into complementary approaches. The idea is to use the record with the inhabitants to understand how they occupy their spaces, and then create a strategy of use during this period composed of emergency shelter at the back, and emergency supports to ensure safe passage and use of installations within the affected dwelling—such as a toilet and the kitchen. This also includes assessing damage to identify priorities for repair, re-use and re-construction of affected spaces, with actions such as the dismantling of walls to create reusable material and the construction of new spaces when required. This includes imagining the different stages of the dwellings in the near future (Figs. 13 and 14).

Fig. 13. Scheme of interventions within the site of an affected dwelling in Lolol, Chile, conforming to the interior courtyard based on the 3D-laser-scan data. Source: Author.

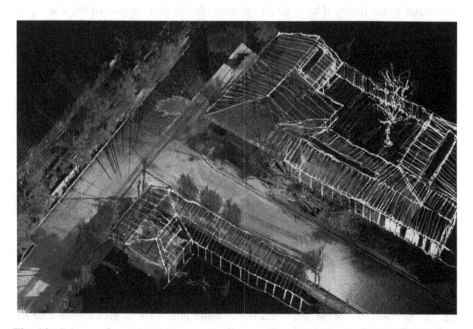

Fig. 14. Scheme of completed interventions for an affected dwelling in Lolol, Chile. Source: Author.

A proposed emergency shelter (Fig. 15) based on prefabricated panels—1.22 m by 2.44 m—is suitable for implementing fast and efficient temporary habitations, that can be adapted to different situations and negotiate transportation through difficult routes of existing dwellings. The novelty is using the contextual information provided by the 3D-laser-scanning to analyse its design and location in relation to the damaged house, remains and paths of use, as part of a strategy of occupation of the site that will be complemented by temporary supports and repairs, also based on that information.

Fig. 15. Flexible emergency shelter with panels with a central pivot, which could rotate to provide ventilation and shade during summer, conforming to a portico. Source: Author.

These features create a flexible space, which may be maintained and used by the inhabitants in the future, if located and installed after careful analysis of the site, e.g. to conform to an interior courtyard or patio (Fig. 16).

Fig. 16. Proposed view of the flexible emergency shelter installed in the back garden of the site conforming to an interior courtyard. Source: Author.

In addition, by using the 3D-laser-scan information, post-earthquake distortions can be identified to design specific supporting objects, depending on the level of damage, which can even be designed as permanent to increase seismic resistance. For example, wall supports that follow exactly the shape of the distorted surface according to the 3D-laser-scan (Fig. 17). This building's prosthetic has the potential to become an integral part of the building or to be used as a basis to expand the dwelling in the future, once removed from its initial location, becoming a trace of previous earthquake damage.[14]

Fig. 17. Emergency supports designed to fit the contours of the distorted wall after the 2010 earthquake in Lolol. Source: Author.

---

[14] If they cannot be created as unique pieces or if displacements are produced due to aftershocks, some reinforcements will still work if adaptable elements that can absorb differences between the 3D data and the reality are added. For example, standard supports to be used on both sides of a damaged adobe wall, with adjustable tensors connecting them.

Fig. 18. Exterior emergency supports proposed as temporary corridors. Source: Author.

Their use—exteriorly or interiorly—can reduce the need for complete rebuilding if applied on time, a view shared with Jigyasu [15]. Exterior supports can take the shape of porticos to hold damaged façades together and avoid their collapse over the public space (Fig. 18) while allowing a safer pedestrian passage.

Interiorly, these supports would help to address the risk of inhabitants passing under potentially vulnerable parts of the house, which may be dangerous in the event of a new seismic event, reducing demolitions. These would allow damaged dwellings to be used during certain hours of the day, in the form of access passages to toilets and kitchens connected to exterior spaces for evacuation in case of an earthquake. These elements can stay in place permanently if needed, or be re-used in the definitive dwelling. They can be prefabricated with millimetre detail informed by the 3D data, and their installation can follow paths of use according to the location of the spaces.

All these emergency strategies are complementary and depend on the specific condition of each house. Understanding that inhabitants usually continue to live on their sites even while works are in progress, the supports can create safe passages from the entrances of the houses to their back gardens, where the emergency shelter would be installed, ensuring a safer habitation within the same site. Following that, it is proposed that residents could act as potential supervision on-site 24/7, able to contact governmental technical professionals if issues arise. Besides, mobile technology and specialised apps, which could use the 3D-laser-scan data as a basis, would potentially allow the works to be tracked more efficiently than the sporadic technical visits during Lolol's reconstruction.

Fig. 19. View of an affected dwelling in Lolol from the 3D-laser-scanning. Source: Author.

All these strategies must be carefully thought through because spaces are partially used, which can be challenging considering the configuration of continuous façades in

Lolol. This requires planning from dismantling to building, which would need to be worked out in connection to storage spaces and passing routes. This is especially relevant if the materials from the dismantling are to be recycled and used in the final dwelling (Fig. 19).

To clear the areas that would be re-constructed, one proposal is to dismantle the affected part of the construction while building supports and storing the materials. It is proposed installing a metal structure at the back of the site, next to the shelter, that can serve for storing material temporarily or as walls for future extensions if located strategically from the beginning. This metal structure of thick and hollow walls would be filled with material from the dismantled part, clearing the area for re-construction, and taking advantage of that effort as an initial process of building. For example, if filled with old adobe bricks, the structure would ensure stability while the adobe would serve only as insulation material. It could be taken out again or these could just become the first walls of a future extension of the house (Fig. 20). All of this could be planned using the 3D data.

Fig. 20. View of the same affected dwelling in Lolol from the 3D-laser-scanning with proposed storage-walls for materials to be re-used. Source: Author.

4   Integrating Technology in Chilean Institutions

At a practical level, it is recommended to integrate accurate recording technologies, including 3D-laser-scanning for the conservation of Chilean built heritage—pre- and post-earthquakes. The starting point would be to include the risk management approach by creating a new institution that could provide guidance and coordination to current Chilean institutions.

This institution would implement public policies beyond governments and continue throughout disasters, embedding expertise and experience within current structures, at a national and local level. The idea is for this proposed institution to govern above other Ministries so that interventions can be comprehensive, integrated and geographically coordinated; not separated by funding or individual programmes. The challenge would be to maintain stable coordination and participation with other Ministries, local authorities and inhabitants, in order to create collaborations between existing funded programmes. Within this institution, a Heritage Department would be vital for implementing specific heritage policies, continuous recording and anticipating overall plans for Chilean heritage areas. Monuments, dwellings, and even public spaces would be incorporated in future intervention plans. This should consider constant coordination —or even integration—with the Undersecretariat of Cultural Heritage and the National Service of Cultural Heritage, part of the Ministry of Cultures, Arts and Heritage, created in 2017.

The equipment and expertise of 3D-laser-scanning—complemented by other techniques—should be embedded at the state level, to carry out constant documentation of built heritage and develop mitigation strategies. If connected with academia, the process and results can enhance debates and create collaborations, e.g. higher education students assisting in damage assessments, which would increase their practical knowledge and prepare them for future participation in the protection and appropriate intervention of built heritage. Preliminary studies could be carried out based on the records to set mitigation measures and management plans in the case of future earthquakes, aimed at avoiding the unnecessary destruction that can be identified and prevented. All of this would increase the coordination needed, and involve related professionals and local communities in the decision-making processes and in the development of public policy.

5 Conclusions

As a post-earthquake documenting tool, 3D-laser-scanning provides accurate information accessible at any time. Its usefulness for post-earthquake recording has been demonstrated in Lolol as a response to the need for a rapid, user-safe, accurate and potentially complete survey of damaged built heritage, but more than three days should be considered in order to include more interior spaces. If embedded at the institutional level—as suggested in the previous section—it can be considered as an affordable documenting tool, in comparison to traditional recording methods currently used, such as hand-measured drawing and photography. This is especially true if combined with other recording techniques—such as photogrammetry—that can complement the aspects not captured by the laser, such as aerial information and occluded areas. This offers huge potential, especially considering affordability and integration of inhabitants in a constant recording process, yet its application on a large scale is still a subject for further studies.

3D-laser-scanning, if integrated as an analytical method, in combination with archival, social and architectural analysis, can increase the number of preserved heritage buildings since it can help to tackle current emergency and reconstruction actions. This is because it constitutes a measurable survey that can be carried out immediately after the earthquake, providing relevant data for informed decision making during the emergency period. Furthermore, the information can—at the same time—serve for repair and design purposes, which is a key omission in current post-disaster surveys in Chile. 3D-laser-scanning data provides the contextual metric information required to make that process applicable to a high number of houses using similar resources. In addition, if previous records are available, comparative analysis can provide valuable information on how the structures and damage have evolved during that period.

For design purposes, it has been shown how a 3D-laser-scan provides an accurate basis on which to develop proposals in a short period of time, entirely changing the way post-earthquake interventions are carried out. A three-day 3D-laser-scan survey replaces more days of professionals on-site taking the required measurements for repair designs. Also, additional applications are obtainable from the same 3D data—such as tailored supports and digital evaluation.

3D-laser-scanning is a fast-moving technology. The specific procedure used to 3D-laser-scan in the case study is, in part, already obsolete by the time of submission of this paper. As seen, most of those limitations could be overcome by taking actions when scanning on-site, by using the latest technological advances and by complementing it with other methods, such as aerial mapping, photogrammetry, and social surveying. In this context, the real limitations of 3D-laser-scanning as a post-earthquake surveying tool if undertaken by the authorities might include budget (non) availability for acquiring and servicing the equipment; a failure for it to be involved at pace in public policies; and suboptimal administrative management of the data.

Mitigating the effects of earthquakes is not a task that can be done by only one institution of government. It is a multisectoral approach where every stakeholder plays a part in the challenge. Introducing technology to solve the aspects that make the processes of re-construction slower, such as documenting the as-built situation of the houses pre- and post-earthquakes, allows for this process to happen smoothly and for engagement to be maintained throughout.

Finally, if there is insufficient funding to provide the buildings with mitigation measures, the 3D-laser-scan of them can offer a range of possibilities for interventions if they are affected by an earthquake. Ultimately, it can provide a three-dimensional virtual model of the buildings that can survive in the digital realm for the future—if appropriately archived—which can be seen as another way of conservation.

Acknowledgements. Special thanks to Diego Ramírez, from GETARQ, who facilitated the 3D-laser-scanning equipment and to Felipe Lanuza, who assisted the author in the on-site scanning of Lolol. This was part of the fieldwork of the author's PhD research at the Bartlett School of Architecture, University College London (UCL), supervised by Professors Stephen Gage and Camillo Boano, which served as a basis for this paper. That doctoral research was funded by the National Agency for Research and Development (ANID), Scholarship Program Doctorado Becas Chile 2009-72100578. There was no connection with Faro Technologies at that time. In addition, this paper is one of the outcomes of the current research project: 'A sustainable re-construction method for seismic-prone heritage areas of India based on advanced recording technologies', led by the author at the Centre for Architecture, Urbanism and Global Heritage in NTU, funded by AHRC and DCMS (AH/V00638X/1), which is developing a methodology for India based on the previous research in Chile, with the support of Faro Technologies. For further information please visit: https://3d4heritageindia.com/.

References

1. Devilat, B.: Beyond the appearance of heritage: reconstruction of historic areas affected by earthquakes in Chile. Int. J. Architect. Res. **7**(3), 24–39 (2013). Special Issue on Post-Disaster Reconstruction. Archnet-IJAR, Archnet, MIT. Accessed 03 Mar 2021
2. MINVU: Reconstruction Plan. United Reconstructing a Better Chile. Housing, Neighbourhood, City. MINVU, Santiago (2011)
3. Ulvi, A.: Documentation, three-dimensional (3D) modelling and visualization of cultural heritage by using unmanned aerial vehicle (UAV) photogrammetry and terrestrial laser scanners. Int. J. Remote Sens. **42**(6), 1994–2021 (2021). https://doi.org/10.1080/01431161.2020.1834164
4. Historic England: 3D laser scanning for heritage. Advice and guidance on the use of laser scanning in archaeology and architecture (2018). https://historicengland.org.uk/images-books/publications/3d-laser-scanning-heritage/. Accessed 03 Mar 2021
5. Mateus, L.: Contributos para o projecto de Conservaçao, restauro e reabilitaçao. Uma metodologia documental basada na fotogrametria digital e no varrimento laser 3D terrestres. Thesis, Ph.D. Universidade Técnica de Lisboa (2012). http://home.fa.utl.pt/~lmmateus/investigacao.html. Accessed 03 Mar 2021
6. Russell, J.: Digital technologies by Scotland's national heritage body. In: Digital Cultural Heritage: Future Visions Symposium, 14 November 2017. UCL (2017)
7. Olsen, M.J., Kayen, R.: Post-earthquake and tsunami 3D-laser-scanning forensic investigations. In: ASCE Forensics Conference 2012, San Francisco, pp. 1–10 (2012)
8. Guidi, G., Russo, M., Angheleddu, D.: 3D survey and virtual reconstruction of archaeological sites. Digit. Appl. Archaeol. Cult. Herit. **1**, 55–69 (2014)
9. Cabrelles, M., Galcerá, S., Navarro, S., Lerma, J.L., Akashe, T., Haddad, N.: Integration of 3D-laser-scanning, photogrammetry and thermography to record architectural Monuments. In: 22nd CIPA Symposium, Kyoto, Japan, 15 October 2009 (2009)
10. Tarchi, D., Rudolf, H., Pieraccini, M., Atzeni, C.: Remote monitoring of buildings using a ground-based SAR: application to cultural heritage survey. Int. J. Remote Sens. **21**, 3545–3551 (2000). https://doi.org/10.1080/014311600750037561. Accessed 03 Mar 2021
11. Rastiveis, H., Eslamizade, F., Hosseini-zirdoo, E.: Building damage assessment after earthquake using post-event LiDAR data. In: The International Archives of the Photogrammetry, Remote Sensing and Spatial Information Sciences, vol. XL-1/W5 (2015). https://www.int-arch-photogramm-remote-sens-spatial-inf-sci.net/XL-1-W5/595/2015/isprsarchives-XL-1-W5-595-2015.pdf. Accessed 03 Mar 2021
12. Rovithis, E., et al.: Assessment of seismic loading on structures based on airborne LiDAR data from the Kalochori urban area (N. Greece). In: RSCy 2016: Fourth International Conference on Remote Sensing and Geoinformation of Environment, Paphos, Cyprus, vol. 9688, pp. 96880M-1–96880M-10 (2016). https://doi.org/10.1117/12.2241746. Accessed 18 Oct 2020
13. Sharma, R.C., Tateishi, R., Hara, K., Nguyen, H.T., Gharechelou, S., Nguyen, L.V.: Earthquake damage visualization (EDV) technique for the rapid detection of earthquake-induced damages using SAR data. Sensors **17** (2017). https://doi.org/10.3390/s17020235. Accessed 03 Mar 2021
14. Abate, D., Sturdy-Colls, C.: A multi-resolution and multi-sensor approach to the documentation of Treblinka extermination and labour camps in Poland. In: Digital Cultural Heritage: Future Visions Symposium, 14 November 2017. University College London (2017)
15. Jigyasu, R.: First aid to Nepalese cultural heritage for recovery and risk reduction. Presented at the 7th i-Rec Conference, Reconstruction and Recovery in Urban Contexts, 6–8 July 2015. UCL (2015)

Author Index